THE MODERNIST
SHAKESPEARE

Wyndham Lewis. Illustration to *Timon of Athens*. Folger Art Collection.

The Modernist Shakespeare

CRITICAL TEXTS IN A MATERIAL WORLD

HUGH GRADY

CLARENDON PRESS · OXFORD
1991

Oxford University Press, Walton Street, Oxford OX2 6DP

Oxford New York Toronto
Delhi Bombay Calcutta Madras Karachi
Petaling Jaya Singapore Hong Kong Tokyo
Nairobi Dar es Salaam Cape Town
Melbourne Auckland

and associated companies in
Beriini Ibadan

Oxford is a trade mark of Oxford University Press

British Library Cataloguing in Publication Data
Grady, Hugh.
The modernist Shakespeare: critical texts in a material world.
1. Drama in English. Shakespeare, William, 1564–1616.
Criticism
I. Title   822.33
ISBN 0-19-812222-5

Library of Congress Cataloging in Publication Data
Grady, Hugh.
The modernist Shakespeare: critical texts in a material world/Hugh Grady.
Includes bibliographical references and index.
1. Shakespeare, William, 1564–1616—Criticism and interpretation—
History—20th century. 2. Modernism (Literature) I. Title.
PR2969.G7 1991
822.3'3—dc20   90-38173
ISBN 0-19-812222-5

Typeset by Wyvern Typesetting Ltd, Bristol
Printed and bound in
Great Britain by Bookcraft Ltd,
Midsomer Norton, Bath

To my Father and Mother

Hugh Grady, Sr. (1903–1988)
Laura Duggan Grady (1907–)

Acknowledgements

WHAT turned out to be the research groundwork for this book I undertook as a senior assistant editor at Gale Research Co. of Detroit for Volume I of *Shakespearean Criticism* (Detroit: Gale, 1984).

The major sounding-board and adviser for this project over several years and in two cities has been Susan Wells, whose support and encouragement I gratefully acknowledge. And I want to thank colleagues at Temple University and Beaver College for reading and commenting on individual chapter drafts at various stages: Susan Stewart, Dan O'Hara, Larry Venuti, and Kevin Moore at Temple; Janice Haney-Peritz and Dick Wertime at Beaver.

The comments of an anonymous reviewer at the annual *Assays* helped the Tillyard chapter a great deal, and Walter Cohen gave me extremely helpful reactions and advice on three chapter drafts midway in the project. Lynda Boose was generous in sharing her expertise in comments on the last chapter. The final version responds to two astute readings performed by Terence Hawkes and Howard Felperin. In addition informal discussions about the ideas of the book with Jean Howard, Wayne Rebhorn, Barbara Bono, Jim Bono, Alan Singer, Larry Scanlon, Dick Kennedy, Michael Scrivener, Judith Newton, Deborah Rosenfelt, and Margreta de Grazia all contributed to the writing process.

My thanks, too, to Margreta de Grazia, Michael Bristol, and Gary Taylor for allowing me access to pre-publication versions of their own books in the late stages of work on this one.

Contents

Introduction

Contexts and Themes

Shakespearian criticism has long been in search of the authentic Shakespearian meaning, and almost every critic, including this one, writes as if s/he had come to be in possession of it. In fact, as had been recognized as early as the eighteenth century, the book-world of Shakespeare commentary is a scandal, a paper battlefield where armies of both ignorant and learned tilt and joust at each other in an ineffectual but never-ending contest of interpretations. Long ago, well before the mass of critical writings on Shakespeare reached the voluminous proportions of today's professional and international libraries of commentary, Hazlitt had sardonically observed that if we wished to perceive the splendours of human achievement, we should read Shakespeare; but if we wish to view the follies of human ingenuity, we may look to his commentators.

In undertaking this study of the history of Shakespeare criticism in the modern era, I have been more than once reminded of that acerbic observation from one of the great figures in Shakespeare commentary. But my aim here is not to despair at the unmanageable bulk and contention, the folly and arrogance, of so much critical discourse. It is rather to make use of the unique qualities of Shakespeare criticism in order to investigate and clarify the institutions and cultural forms which produce it—and produce as well the vast outpourings of the entire professionalized literary-critical enterprise in the modern world.

In what follows I will say very little of those curious abstractions of the critical imagination, 'Shakespeare himself', and 'the plays themselves'. It is not that I object to critical writing aimed at attempting to define the meaning of a work, its qualities as art and discourse, its relation to history and society. As long as we keep reading Shakespeare (and I take it as nonsense to suppose that we should or will ever stop reading him, if our culture survives), such writing—and the talking and teaching that accompanies it—is inevitable and needed. Here, however, I want to suspend momentarily *that* conversation and instead undertake a reflective discourse on the underlying assumptions which make such necessary and sometimes admirable talk and writing poss-

ible and which shape and limit it in ways which we are only now
beginning to appreciate fully. My book could be said to have been
written as a long meditation on an idea of Walter Benjamin's:

A historical materialist cannot do without the notion of a present which is not a
transition, but in which time stands still and has come to a stop. For this notion
defines the present in which he himself is writing history. Historicism gives the
'eternal' image of the past; historical materialism supplies the unique experience with the past.[1]

All interpretation bears within it the imprint of the moment of history
in which it was undertaken; but equally, the past only takes on meaning
through the inescapable present. There is nothing absolutely startling
in this idea. That avatar of conservative Modernist cultural orthodoxy,
T. S. Eliot, observed years ago that 'Shakespeare criticism cannot be
appreciated without some understanding of the time and of the place
in which it is written. . . . The views of Shakespeare taken by different
men at different times in different places form an integral part of the
development and changes of European civilisation during the last 300
years.'[2] I hope here to deepen and extend an insight which Eliot had
begun to have and did not develop—but to deepen and extend it in
ways that Walter Benjamin rather than T. S. Eliot would find most
amenable. Everything depends on how thoroughly one attempts to
apply the notion.

    The major line of interpretation of Shakespeare in the twentieth
century, we will see, is resolutely 'Modernist', that is, shaped and
structured by the new movements in literature and art that came into
prominence in the period after World War I. 'Our' Shakespeare, until
quite recently, has been very much a Modernist Shakespeare.

    However, far from being some return to Romantic notions of a
Zeitgeist dominating all cultural production in an age, this recognition
of the crucial role of changing aesthetic perceptions is in fact an
essential component of the kind of 'cultural materialism' which recent
Shakespearian criticism has attempted to develop. Modernism, which
has helped to define and organize how we have read Shakespeare for
most of our century, is one crucial strand of the complex differenti-

---

[1] Walter Benjamin, 'Theses on the Philosophy of History', in *Illuminations*, ed.
Hannah Arendt, trans. Harry Zohn (New York: Shocken, 1969), 262.

[2] T. S. Eliot, 'Shakespearean Criticism: I. From Dryden to Coleridge', in *A Companion to Shakespeare Studies*, ed. Harley Granville-Barker and G. B. Harrison (1934;
repr. Cambridge: Cambridge University Press, 1949), 289.

ations of modernized societies; literary-critical discourse is the over-determined product of a number of competing and contradictory aspects of that differentiation, including but not limited to the aesthetic. My goal here is to define the terms, through the concrete analysis of texts, of those complex interactions making up modern literary criticism.

Shakespeare's status as the most revered and celebrated—and most discussed—author in English and, indeed, in world literature, makes his works ideally suited to a study which aims to reveal the underpinnings and supports normally kept hidden beneath the surface of critical discourse. We have made Shakespeare so large that he is able to contain everything critical ingenuity could devise to say of any author. Shakespeare has been praised as the very summit of aesthetic achievement and the very embodiment of high culture; and he has been equally celebrated as a practitioner of vital popular culture against an effete court aristocracy. He has been seen as containing in its fullness the forms and rules of his age, as the very spokesman of Tudor orthodoxy; and he has been celebrated as constantly subverting and undermining that orthodoxy. He has been praised as the voice of Christian Europe in its greatest eloquence; and as the pen of a corrosive scepticism that announces the beginnings of post-Christian modernity. So great is the diversity of opinion, so disparate the interpretations, that it becomes possible simply to bracket the (finally unanswerable) question of what meanings the Shakespearian texts produced in their own social context and look to discourse on Shakespeare as a privileged entryway into how meanings are produced and disseminated in our own society. This is not to despair of our ability to produce useful discourse on what Shakespeare has meant either in the past or the present—as I said above, we can and must produce such discourse if we are to receive and make our own the remarkable artistry of the texts. It *is* to underline that no discourse on Shakespearian meanings can escape the enabling conditions of its own time and place, its own language and institutional matrix. It *is* to object to the naïve antiquarianism of so much contemporary Shakespeare scholarship—even sophisticated and radical criticism—that finds its professional justification in a misguided attempt to recover past meanings as if they existed without a relation to the present moment of the critic's own social and historical situation. It *is* to object to any understanding of literary or discourse criticism—especially of historical criticism—that attempts to locate itself anywhere else but in the give and take of the *Jetztzeit*, the here-and-now which is never completely homogenous with the past.

Least of all, however, am I suggesting that if recent generations of scholars and critics have been reading Shakespeare with professional and Modernist 'lenses', it would be a simple and liberating matter to take them off and recover the 'real' Shakespeare. We *can* take off those older lenses; we are manifestly now in the process of doing so, as the last chapter of this work will show. But there is no 'authentic' Shakespeare there for the picking. After the Modernist Shakespeare comes—the Postmodernist Shakespeare. There is, simply, no other alternative—unless it is to revive an older Shakespeare.

Such a study as this, of course, could only be undertaken in the context of a set of notions about literature, culture, and criticism that is itself a part of contemporary criticism or some segment of it—the current paradigm, as I refer to it below. It is clearly, too, written within the professionalist discourses that, as will be seen, have proved the quicksand of so many socially critical literary studies. Of the various choices of style and format open to me, 'professional' discourse seemed the only viable vehicle for this work, though I wish other options existed, as they perhaps will in the future.

This introduction concludes with a discussion of the theoretical framework employed here and its relation to similar attempts at cultural theory in contemporary literary studies. After that necessary exposition I begin to trace the formation of the 'modern' Shakespeare constituted in the enormous bulk of twentieth-century commentary on his works, with its roots in the late nineteenth century. 'Our' Shakespeare is formed through the interplay of two dynamically opposed aspects of modernity which can be designated, for reasons to be explained below, the forces of modern*ization* (economic, scientific, and technical in large measure) and the forces of modern*ism* (cultural and aesthetic and reactive to the former). The theory of modernization will be described in Chapter 1 along with the impact of modernization on the reading of Shakespeare in its earliest phases. Chapter 2 will shift the focus on to Modernism—theoretically first, in a discussion of some of the contributing factors involved in aesthetic paradigm shifts in modernized societies; then more concretely, in a case-study of the construction of a specifically Modernist Shakespearean criticism in the early work of G. Wilson Knight. Chapters 3 and 4 will focus on the two critical paradigms that dominated Shakespeare studies from the Forties through the Sixties, New Criticism and historical criticism—

both seen as enacting in their different ways a compromise between Modernist aesthetics and the modernizing ideology of professionalism. Chapter 5 documents the end of the period of the Modernist Shakespeare and the emergence in recent years of a Postmodern Shakespeare (or is it Shakespeare*s*?) in a dynamic still displaying a strong tension between professionalism and the aesthetic.

Modernism is an example of what I call here an 'aesthetic paradigm', and modernization a more global social and economic dynamic inherent in late capitalist society. The complex interaction of these two aspects of modernity is basic to the story of Shakespeare in the twentieth century as it is narrated here, a tale if not of 'carnal, bloody, and unnatural acts, | Of accidental judgments, casual slaughters, | Of deaths put on by cunning and forc'd cause, | And in this upshot, purposes mistook | Fall'n on th'inventors' heads', then at least a sobering story of interest disguised as disinterest, of critical ingenuity passed off as an objective property of iconic texts, of the presumptuous arrogance of professional literary critics, and of desperate symbolic attempts to save meaning, truth, and beauty in the increasingly hostile modern age. Some of the antinomies of this study will be familiar ones: culture and society, generalist and specialist, humanist and professional. In making use of these familiar concepts, my attempt has been to put them in a global context that will make clear the stakes and the interests involved in conflicts now so familiar that they require fresh surroundings to be seen again.

The Necessity of Theory

No one writes literary criticism in a vacuum: in writing, we bring along with us all the baggage of our basic social being—our beliefs and prejudices, our unconscious, our socialization, our education and formal training. Much of this has been more or less understood for centuries, but only in recent years has the insight been systematically applied in the world of literary studies. Not surprisingly, Marxist-influenced criticism, with its lengthy tradition of disclosing political and economic interests at work in texts which pass themselves off as 'value-free', 'objective', or 'disinterested', has been a major influence in the new interpretations, especially in Shakespeare studies—and the present work is no exception to that generalization, owing as it does a great deal to the Marxist tradition of ideology critique.

But to speak of 'Marxism' in the singular has become misleading and almost indefensible. The legacy of Marx has been divided, developed, recast, combined with other modes of thought and has produced a panoply of Marxisms making up an archive of competing discourses which include some of the major intellectual projects of the twentieth century—and some of the most appallingly self-deceptive and tyranny-abetting documents of human history. It is therefore not possible to rely on a few bland labels to communicate positions. Because the issues involved are often complex and because the stances I take are often at odds with what some critics, in an act of sexist hubris, insist on calling 'hard Maxism' (that peculiar economistic and dogmatic ideology which apparently produces a satisfying sense of phallic potency)—and most of all, because a study which emphasizes the profound influence of institutions and ideologies on critical discourse would seem to be self-contradictory without an attempt to define its own context—it has seemed to me indispensable to make explicit the theoretical scaffolding on which this study depends.

As I stated above, the influence of non-discursive, political, economic, and social factors—in short, of ideology and its sources—on literary criticism has long been known in practice and demonstrated for the case of Shakespeare criticism very well in recent years,[3] and in what follows ideology will play a crucial role as well. But one of the

---

[3] An incisive, path-breaking extended attempt to locate Shakespearian criticism in its social, political, and aesthetic setting is Terence Hawkes, *That Shakespeherian Rag: Essays on a Critical Process* (New York: Methuen, 1986). Three works still in press as I write also contextualize contemporary Shakespeare studies in ways complementary to the present work: Michael Bristol, *Shakespeare's America, America's Shakespeare* (London: Routledge, 1989); Gary Taylor, *Reinventing Shakespeare: A Cultural History 1642–1986* (New York: Weidenfeld & Nicolson, 1989); and Margreta de Grazia, *Shakespeare Verbatim: The Reproduction of Authenticity and the 1790 Apparatus* (Oxford: Oxford University Press, forthcoming). I refer to each of these works below at relevant sections of the argument. Several critics have discussed these issues at briefer length. See Jonathan Dollimore, *Radical Tragedy: Religion, Ideology and Power in the Drama of Shakespeare and His Contemporaries* (Sussex: Harvester, 1984), especially pp. 5–8; *Political Shakespeare: New Essays in Cultural Materialism*, ed. Jonathan Dollimore and Alan Sinfield (Ithaca, NY: Cornell University Press, 1985), particularly the essays in 'Part II: Reproductions, Interventions'; *Alternative Shakespeares*, ed. John Drakakis (New York: Methuen, 1985), especially James Kavanaugh, 'Shakespeare in Ideology', 144–65 and Jonathan Dollimore and Alan Sinfield, 'History and Ideology: The Instance of *Henry V*,' 206–27; Graham Holderness, *Shakespeare's History* (New York: St. Martin's, 1985), 164–200; and three essays in *Shakespeare Reproduced: The Text in History and Ideology*, ed. Jean E. Howard and Marion F. O'Connor (New York: Methuen, 1987): Jean Howard and Marion F. O'Connor, 'Introduction', 1–17; Walter Cohen, 'Political Criticism of Shakespeare', 18–46; and Don Wayne, 'Power, Politics, and the Shakespearean Text: Recent Criticism in England and the United States', 47–67. With the exception of *Shakespeare Reproduced* and Kavanaugh's article, these are all products of contemporary

initial surprises in my study of Shakespeare criticism was the obvious influence of what I have subsequently termed the aesthetic paradigm: a set of notions and practices including, but not limited to, assumptions of what constitutes an authentic literary art-work and of what is of value in such art; notions of unity, time, and space and of other aspects of form and structure; ideas of what subject-matter was inherently 'poetic' and what was not; assumptions of the value or lack of it of literature's mimesis of 'reality'—these and allied concepts to be discussed below—more often implied than stated and when stated more often asserted than justified—often proved more basic to how a critic read and interpreted Shakespeare than the ideologies and critical methodologies claimed by these critics when they assigned themselves to competing schools like Marxism, psychoanalysis, historical criticism, New Criticism, and so on; or when the labels proved meaningful, their usefulness usually depended on the labels' identification of specific aesthetic categories as privileged in the interpretations. It is to ground and account for that perception, without losing the political insights of the Marxist tradition, that the following sketch of a theory is offered, necessarily drawing on the conceptual framework of the contemporary critical paradigms.

The discussion will begin with the case of two Marxists of the Thirties whose shared politics could not prevent violently vituperative polemics, which arose in part from their positions as representatives of separate aesthetic paradigms. Foucault's notions of discursive formations, operating independently of the author's consciousness, can help us understand this debate and situate us within the critical framework that underlies the present study—provisionally.

An attempt to define a more adequate theoretical position, that takes into account among other things Foucault's last, anti-structuralist period and his affinities with the Frankfurt School, makes up the

British Marxist-influenced criticism, to which I will return in Chapter 5. The American 'new historicism', which I also briefly discuss in Chapter 5, could be said to have indirectly criticized the political interests of previous Shakespearian criticism, but it has tended to avoid direct discussion of the significance of the present on our readings of the past, as I will argue below. Much more forthright in this regard has been American feminist Shakespeare criticism, which has from the beginning focused on the political and sexist biases of much previous critical discourse. Further comments on this body of work will also be found in Chapter 5. For something approaching a full bibliography of 'Political studies of Shakespeare in the 1980s', almost all of which would have some relevance or affinity to my work, and including all three trends I have just mentioned, see the impressive list supplied by Walter Cohen, 'Political Criticism of Shakespeare', in Howard and O'Connor, *Shakespeare Reproduced*, 39–46.

burden of the rest of the Introduction. Particularly important for the period of Modernism is the Frankfurt notion of art's autonomy within the overall capitalist system (to which it is of course also linked). But I propose replacing the static concept of an 'aesthetic sphere', the usual term of the classical Frankfurt texts, with a coinage adapted from Kuhn's philosophy of science and to speak of an 'aesthetic paradigm' whose shifts explain the phenomenon and complexity of literary periods. The term also offers several advantages over Frank Lentricchia's proposal to use for similar purposes Foucault's notions of epistemes and discursive formations, and also over the related Althusserian concepts of ideology and interpellation which some critics have proposed to account for the relation between literary criticism and society. This in turn will lay the ground for a discussion in Chapter 2 of some of the mechanisms of paradigm shifts in the aesthetic sphere and of the special case of Modernism as an aesthetic paradigm with particularly fluid boundaries with its adjacents, Romanticism and Postmodernism.

In defining the special status of the aesthetic, however, I want to imply no lessening of the importance of ideology in also influencing critical texts. Because I think it has been underplayed in contemporary critical theory, I am here emphasizing the role of autonomous aesthetics in the twentieth century—that is, of Modernism. But Modernism in turn is incomprehensible without a consideration of its more global context, which I term here modernization. For reasons of expository convenience, I treat modernization separately, in Chapter 1, which therefore completes the theoretical framework of this study. It is in that chapter's examination of a new professional stratum, with its ideologies of positivism and professionalism, that the importance of ideology critique to this work will be most apparent. But let me begin with some initial categorical distinctions.

Ideology and Aesthetics in Criticism

The very term *ideology* begs some basic theoretical questions since it is a word that has come to have a multiplicity of meanings in a process that began well before Marx, accelerated in the Marxian texts themselves, and continued to produce new meanings in the subsequent Marxist tradition—not to mention in mainstream social science. The confusion has only been compounded since Louis Althusser redefined the term to mean something like culture in general, or its politicized, class-divided fragments. Althusser widened 'ideology' to include the whole set of epistemological lenses by which reality is constituted by or in individual subjects, in a conflation with Lacanian categories that has proved irresistible to numerous subsequent radical critics. But among other problems,[4] ideology is, for Althusser, 'without history'. The impact of Enlightenment on the form of belief-systems is much better captured by the Frankfurt theorists. In this view, which I adopt here, ideologies came into existence in part to replace the older mythic and symbolic belief-systems of religion and—what is important here—of art. Thus there is an opposition (and a possible complicity) between art and ideology which we can often observe at work in literary criticism—which is as well a rationalized discourse produced by Enlightenment.

As a striking illustration of this opposition at work—in this case, in the form of aesthetics undermining a commonly held ideology—consider two contributions made to the literary journal of the Communist International in the Thirties, *International Literature*. This example can serve as an initial introduction to the problems which the following theoretical apparatus will attempt to illuminate. The Russian M. Nechkina, claiming to be following Marx's usage, characterized Falstaff in the following way:

---

[4] It is true that Althusser's original formulation, which contrasted the relative truth of 'science' (pointedly and symptomatically including 'correct' Marxism) over and against everything else, which becomes 'ideology', is no longer much in vogue. Nowadays one finds more often post-structuralist-influenced versions of (post-) Althusserianism, which reject the original Althusserian concept of science to 'textualize' the theory so that everything becomes 'ideology'. But even here too much of the scientism implied in the older binary opposition between true 'science' and false 'ideology' survives, particularly the covert domination of the original scientism, with the result that the life-world becomes reductively politicized and ideologized: in trying to define the politicized dimensions of domination in the life-world, this concept of ideology covertly transforms the social totality and all social relations into one-dimensional instances of domination; liberation necessarily becomes counter-domination, in a precise replication of the dynamics of the disastrous Chinese Cultural Revolution, which supplied so much of the background to the original Althusserian theory. For the classic formulation of Althusser's notion of ideology, see his *For Marx*, trans. Ben Brewster (London: New Left Books, 1977), 233–4 and his essay 'Ideology and Ideological State Apparatuses (Notes towards an Investigation)', in *Lenin and Philosophy and Other Essays* (New York: Monthly Review Press, 1971), 127–86. For the Frankfurt School usage I employ here, see the collectively written article 'Ideology' in Frankfurt Institute for Social Research, *Aspects of Sociology*, trans. John Viertel (Boston, Mass.: Beacon, 1973), 182–205. The element of domination within science which Althusser ignores is prominently defined by the classic Frankfurt texts.

Falstaff for Marx was a kind of 'personified capital' of the epoch of the dawn of capitalism, which gave birth to the ... epoch of primitive accumulation. ... The fragments of feudal ideas are merely the building material for his new .bourgeois morality.[5]

A year later, *International Literature* carried a detailed and polemical reply by the British Marxist critic T. A. Jackson. Jackson shared Nechkina's methodological assumptions that the character Falstaff was a social type who 'represented' in some sense the broad historical categories of Marxist analysis ('the feudal epoch', 'the bourgeois', etc.). But his interpretation of Falstaff revealed him to be inhabiting a different perceptual world from Nechkina's:

... we deny, categorically, that Falstaff's morality was 'bourgeois' or that he typified in any sense of the word the 'coming bourgeois world.' Consequently, we draw from the character of Falstaff, and Shakespeare's handling thereof, deductions exactly opposite to those of Nechkina.[6]

Nechkina's Falstaff is that of the eighteenth century: a paradoxical rogue of unquestioned vices and depravity but great allure and attraction—a version that had been disseminated into Russia as late as 1836 by Pushkin.[7] In that ambiguous Englightenment mixture of the liberating and the enchaining, the good and the bad, Nechkina found the very simulacrum of Marx's ambivalent attitude toward early capitalism—a comparison given more point if we realize that Stalin's murderous appropriation of the Russian peasantry was discussed in the Soviet Union as a socialist version of pre-capitalist primitive accumulation necessary for Soviet industrialization.[8] That is Falstaff, in some sense, 'stands for' Stalin through a process of repressed substitutions.

Jackson's reply is notable for the sharpness of its polemics, surprising sharpness given the ideological and political bonds uniting the two critics. But he invests 'Falstaff' with an entirely different content:

Nechkina's assertion ... is outrageously false at every point. It is as we have seen, false as to the epoch indicated. It is grotesquely, and even cruelly false as

[5] 'Shakespeare in Karl Marx's "Capital"', *International Literature*, 3 (March 1935), 75–81; excerpted and repr. in *Shakespearean Criticism*, ed. Laurie Harris (Detroit, Mich.: Gale, 1984), i. 358.

[6] T. A. Jackson, 'Letters and Documents: Marx and Shakespeare', *International Literature*, 2 (Feb. 1936), 75–97; excerpted and repr. in Harris, *Shakespearean Criticism*, i. 361–5.

[7] A. S. Pushkin, 'Notes on Shylock, Angelo, and Falstaff', trans. Albert Siegel, *The Shakespeare Association Bulletin*, 16 (Jan. 1941), 120–1; excerpted and repr. in *Shakespearean Criticism*, i. 313–14.

[8] E. H. Carr, *Socialism in One Country (1924–26)*, Vol. i (1958; repr. Harmondsworth: Penguin, 1970), 219–26.

to Falstaff as Shakespeare presents him. . . . [Falstaff's] cowardice is not the mere cowardice of the flesh, of which in fact, when he is put to it, he is not really guilty. His is the cowardice of the innermost spirit—the canker consumption of a soul which has lost its bearings in a state of social transition, and has in consequence nothing but his own naked egoism to serve as his moral criterion and his object in life. . . . And, thus, Falstaff's degenerate egoism comes to be prophetic of the new degeneracy of today.[9]

In Jackson's reading, Falstaff is not bourgeois, but feudal, and hence in his proudfully unsentimental eyes, it was right for Shakespeare to have Hal banish him at the end. This overdetermined symbolic act around which so much critical controversy has swirled (seen in Freudian criticism as the very image of the ego's tragic but necessary repression of the id) is praised by Jackson as the depiction of a tragedy, but one that was richly deserved: 'His is, in fact the typical tragedy of a cynical degenerate egoism. He clings on to life; but has no use for his life when he has saved it at the cost of reputation, and everything else which would make it worth the saving'.[10]

Lurking in Jackson's depiction of Falstaff, we surmise, is a cultural figure of whom Nechkina was evidently without knowledge: A. C. Bradley's Falstaff, the 'bliss of freedom gained in humour . . . the enemy of everything respectable and moral' who annihilates all 'limits and obligations' with a consciousness as deep in its way as Hamlet's.[11] Jackson is immersed in a different aesthetic-symbolic universe, underneath the apparent ideological unity. This symbol of all that might well up in him to question his commitment as a Communist intellectual, we might surmise, must be banished by Jackson as unequivocally as by the newly crowned Henry V in Shakespeare's play and for similar reasons.

Of course, as we shall see, politics and aesthetics can be properly separated only by positing their connectedness at a different level. The exchange can be in part accounted for in terms of political shadow-boxing of which each writer seems unaware and which is based on differing silent allegorizations of *Henry IV*, allegorizations which speak through an apparent commitment to a shared theory of literature as representing the class struggle. In my reading of their readings, each has turned Falstaff into a figure of a semi-private mythology, rooted in

[9] Harris, *Shakespearan Criticism*, i. 364.
[10] Ibid.
[11] A. C. Bradley, 'The Rejection of Falstaff', *Oxford Lectures on Poetry* (London: Macmillan, 1959), 261–3.

disparate aesthetic paradigms, which attempts to make sense out of the pain and stresses of committed Communist intellectuals in the Thirties.

But there is more to Jackson's reply than this thinly disguised socio-psycho drama. In order to support the highly cathexed figure of Falstaff in his account, Jackson undertakes a survey of specifically *literary* sources of Falstaff (and thereby displays the critical paradigm he is working in): as a clown, as a Devil in morality mysteries, and as a Vice in medieval morality plays.[12] It is this dramatic ancestry which buttresses the argument that Shakespeare intended the audience to approve of Falstaff's banishment. Uncannily, this is in essence the thesis of a highly influential work by J. Dover Wilson, *The Fortunes of Falstaff*, which appeared in 1943, some seven years after Jackson's article.[13] Similarly Jackson makes use of studies of Elizabethan stage conventions and of modern social history—a panoply of techniques evidently unheard of by Nechkina—in the course of his overkill reply. Put in the context of what we might call, following Foucault, the archive of writings on literary analysis, Jackson's piece takes its place in a slowly unfolding generational reaction against the formerly hegemonic interpretation of Falstaff by A. C. Bradley, and its function as a political allegory becomes less prominent. In this context the supposed Marxism of the methodology dissolves into other affiliations. Jackson's emphasis on the play as an artefact constructed from an older dramatic tradition through a series of artificial stage-conventions links him with a group of literary positivists in Shakespeare criticism I will discuss below in connection with the 'modernization' of Shakespeare studies (most notably E. E. Stoll); more specifically, his use of Elizabethan history obviously links him with the new group of historical critics the most prominent of whom was E. M. W. Tillyard, whom I will discuss in Chapter 4. Looked at this way, Jackson's criticism is part of a larger archive of writings, some of which did not even exist at the time of the composition of his piece on Falstaff, and of which, of course, he could not have been aware.

Depending on the relative weight we wish to assign the individual peculiarities of the critic and of the more general (social and ideological) context which he reproduces and works in, then, it is possible to

---

[12] Harris, *Shakespearean Criticism*, i. 362.

[13] J. Dover Wilson, *The Fortunes of Falstaff* (Cambridge: Cambridge University Press, 1943).

posit two different but related interpretations of Jackson's Shakespeare criticism (and, by extension, other similar documents): (1) the interpretation of the play as part of an individual psychic, dream-like economy, accessible through methods like the Freudian hermeneutics of *The Interpretation of Dreams*—but only in cases where we possess the necessary associations and meanings which the drama took on in the dream-like act of private reading; and (2) the interpretation as constituted by the play of discourse and techniques which, put in the context of similar texts, can be understood to make up dispersed parts of separate 'discourses' as described by Foucault.[14] Any critical text can be assumed to arise from some interplay of such psychological and discursive forces—in complex and interpenetrating combinations; but while I separate them here to bring out a meaningful contrast, it is impossible finally to maintain anything like a rigorous categorical dichotomy.

The following study will provide occasional examples of the role of individual psychic fantasy, interacting with more public discourse, in forming critical writing; the chapter on G. Wilson Knight is a particularly interesting example, though the analysis there is nowhere near the bravura performance in this vein provided by Terence Hawkes in his analysis of J. Dover Wilson on *Hamlet* in *That Shakespeherian Rag*—and Hawkes is of course interested in the second level of analysis as well. But the major focus of this work is primarily on the second of the two kinds of interpretation defined above: the critical act as a part of a larger social construction by which it is determined and to which it makes specific contributions.

In getting at this level of discourse, I have made use of the terminology of Michel Foucault's *The Archaeology of Knowledge*, a work which, along with the other parts of Foucault's unfinished *œuvre*, opened up the issues I discuss here with a new clarity and precision. As will be apparent, I have not found it possible simply to incorporate Foucault's theories of discourse into the present studies, and in fact, I find aspects of them to be in need of considerable criticism and modification. In the following section, therefore, I will turn to issues of the current critical paradigm in the United States with a particular focus on aspects of Foucault's work that form part

[14] See Michel Foucault, *The Archaeology of Knowledge*, trans. A. M. Sheridan Smith (New York: Pantheon, 1972).

of a remarkable theoretical convergence in contemporary critical theory.

Beyond Subjectivism and Objectivism: The Contemporary Critical Convergence

In the present era, as Frank Lentricchia suggested in another context,[15] we seem to be witnessing the overcoming of a long period of sibling rivalry that followed in the wake of the deaths of long-lived, multiple father-figures like the New Criticism and logical positivism. This conjunction follows a period (since about 1970) that has been the most tumultuous and contentious in the short history of modern language study in the United States, with a series of surprisingly short-lived critical fads merging finally into a post-structuralist plurality of critical discourses: structuralism, phenomenology, hermeneutics, Marxism (in its several varieties), psychoanalysis, feminism, deconstruction, and the new historicism—as well as more traditional historical and formalist methodologies.[16]

Increasingly, however, many of us have detected the beginnings of a theoretical convergence among these competing schools, the working through of the sibling rivalry. Given the theoretical valorizing of difference, break, heterogeneity, and disparateness involved in many of these trends, it would be overstating the case to speak of a 'synthesis'. Nevertheless a broad dialogue is beginning to take place that is producing what I would term a Postmodernist theoretical convergence, a version of which provides the theoretical scaffolding for the present study.

A few years ago post-positivist cultural theory seemed to divide into two competing and incompatible approaches that have been described in several different ways. Perhaps the starkest version of the conflict was a confrontation between a phenomenology that privileged consciousness, temporality, and subjectivity (represented, let us say, by Poulet, of course, but also Sartre) and a structuralism that questioned

---

[15] Frank Lentricchia, *After the New Criticism* (Chicago, Ill.: University of Chicago Press, 1980), 326.

[16] For good accounts of this dynamic, see two recent works by Terry Eagleton, *Literary Theory: An Introduction* (Minneapolis: University of Minnesota Press, 1983), and *The Function of Criticism: From 'The Spectator' to Post-Structuralism* (London: Verso, 1984); the latter work especially stresses the kind of convergence in contemporary theory I am stressing here (pp. 85–124). For much greater detail, see Lentricchia, cited above. Lentricchia's account, however, is heavily influenced by his own preferences for a Foucault-based criticism.

these very categories with its emphasis on language as epistemological pre-structuring, synchronicity rather than history, and objectivity in its approach to cultural artefacts (Lévi-Strauss being the obvious representative of this trend).[17] As the influence of structuralism percolated through the Western academy, this split replicated itself in many forms and in many disciplines, at times with surprisingly violent rhetoric. The dispute was particularly in evidence within Marxist circles. In France Althusser heatedly attacked the 'humanist Marxism' in vogue in the late Fifties and early Sixties through his structuralist reconstruction of orthodox Leninism. This was perhaps the opening shot in a split that developed numerous ramifications.[18] In Britain there was a similar confrontation in the Seventies between proponents of the 'Cultural' Marxism associated wth E. P. Thompson, Ralph Miliband, and Raymond Williams and those influenced by Althusser's 'structuralist' Marxism.[19] In America followers of the German Frankfurt School around the journal *Telos* (and to a lesser extent around *New German Critique*) pushed for a synthesis of phenomenology and Marxism that understood structuralism—and specifically Althusser—as an

[17] See, for example, Lévi-Strauss's polemic answering Sartre in *The Savage Mind* (Chicago: University of Chicago Press, 1966), 245–69. An example of an Althusserian Marxist heavily invested in this distinction is Michael Sprinker, 'Sartre and Althusser', *Modern Language Notes*, 100 (Dec. 1985), 989–1011.

[18] Althusser's seminal essays, collected in *For Marx*, need to be situated in the political polemics which were their immediate context. While he has retrospectively been interpreted as bringing Marxism into the structuralist and then post-structuralist ages and while his impact on the doctrinaire world of French Communist Party theory was ultimately anti-dogmatic in its effect, he was also in his own way a perfectly orthodox Marxist–Leninist interested in the Sixties in discrediting the young Marx who had been championed by Eastern European democratic socialists and in the late Seventies in defending the 'scientificity' of the concept of 'the dictatorship of the proletariat' at the point when the French Party was mercifully jettisoning this notorious shifting signifier, which had long since become a scandalous ideological justification for tyranny. For accounts of these currents, see Arthur Hirsh, *The French New Left: An Intellectual History from Sartre to Gorz* (Boston, Mass.: South End, 1981) and Michael Kelly, *Modern French Marxism* (Baltimore, Md.: Johns Hopkins University Press, 1982).

[19] The (relatively) pro-Althusserian viewpoint has been championed by the journal *New Left Review* and particularly in two books by one of *NLR*'s editors, Perry Anderson, *Considerations on Western Marxism* (London: New Left Books, 1976) and *Arguments among British Marxists* (London: Verso, 1980). Anderson does not consider himself an Althusserian, but his positions have certainly been influenced by Althusserian themes. On the other side the most prominent figures have been the former editors of *New Left Review*, now associated with *Socialist Register*. The best known polemic from this wing is E. P. Thompson, *The Poverty of Theory and Other Essays* (New York: Monthly Review, 1978). An interesting attempt to conceptualize the debate is Stuart Hall, 'Cultural Studies: Two Paradigms', in *Culture, Ideology, and Social Process: A Reader*, ed. Tony Bennett *et al.* (London: Batsford, 1981), 1–38.

outright theoretical enemy. There seemed to be, as the title of the late Jay Gouldner's interesting book put it, two Marxisms—one 'critical', one 'scientific'.[20]

The complex turn from structuralism to post-structuralism seemed at first to exacerbate the split as symbolized by the frequently encountered pairing of Foucault and Habermas as two polar avatars of culture theory in post-1980 intellectual circles: Foucault, the Nietzschean champion of 'language' against reason; Habermas, the 'humanist' theorist of communication against power and domination.[21] In some sense this still seemed a bifurcation that betrayed its origins in the structuralist affinities of the early Foucault's thought and the hermeneuticist-phenomenological strain within Habermas. But this polarization of Foucault and Habermas was much less stable than it appeared at first. Since the appearance of *Michel Foucault: Beyond Structuralism and Hermeneutics* by Hubert Dreyfus and Paul Rabinow, a different picture of Foucault has emerged. Dreyfus and Rabinow, with Foucault's support, reveal the extent to which Foucault underwent an anti-structuralist turn after the appearance of *The Archaeology of Knowledge* and specifically revised his earlier notions of the autonomy of discourse. The newer genealogies instead focus on the networks of institutions and their technologies of power which underlie the discourses (pp. 104–17). And structuralism (which Foucault never identified with in any case but which certainly influenced *The Order of Things* and *The Archaeology of Knowledge*) was itself called into question, in the insights of his new theories of 'subjection', as being part of the process of creating disciplinary technologies (pp. xxvi–xxvii). The end result causes us to rethink Foucault's place among major twentieth-century schools. With his critique of bio-power and his Nietzschean diagnosis of Western subjects enthralled by rationalized technologies, including, to an extent structuralist disciplines, he can hardly remain what he has been in so many articles and books of the Seventies and early Eighties, the 'structuralist historian of discontinuities'; in light of his last works, Foucault seems instead to be in that line of thinkers concerned to delineate the underside of Enlightment reason at the same time as they

---

[20] Alvin W. Gouldner, *The Two Marxisms: Contradictions and Anomalies in the Development of Theory* (New York: Seabury, 1980).

[21] For example, reference to such an opposition between Habermas and Foucault survives in a work that, as we shall see, goes far towards undoing that opposition— Hubert Dreyfus and Paul Rabinow, *Michel Foucault: Beyond Structuralism and Hermeneutics*, 2nd edn. (Chicago, Ill.: University of Chicago Press, 1983), 130.

make use of it to criticize itself.[22] The major work that now seems to be linked with Foucault's thought is Horkheimer and Adorno's *Dialectic of Enlightenment*, with its sources in Marx, Freud, Nietzsche, and Weber and which in turn became a major source for Habermas. The connection was obscure at first precisely because Habermas had in his 'linguistic turn' abandoned the Nietzschean aspects of Horkheimer and Adorno's *Dialectic of Enlightenment* that most resonated with Foucault's favourite themes; more recently, however, Habermas has presented in a series of published lectures the results of a study of French poststructuralism, with Foucault the figure he finds most amenable to his own thinking on several matters.[23] And in a late interview, Foucault himself acknowledged his affinity to the older Frankfurt School theorists.[24]

Similarly, Derrida's widely disseminated version of Saussurean linguistics produced, instead of the closed, 'objective' structure that

---

[22] See Dreyfus and Rabinow, *Michel Foucault*, p. xxvi; Paul Rabinow, Introduction, *The Foucault Reader* (New York: Pantheon, 1984), 13–14; Mark Poster, *Foucault, Marxism, and History: Mode of Production versus Mode of Information* (Cambridge: Polity, 1984), 13–16 (the passage is more critical of the Frankfurt School than is my own argument); Peter Dews, 'Adorno, Post-Structuralism and the Critique of Identity', *New Left Review*, 157 (May/June 1986), 29; and a major work on the relation of the Frankfurt School and post-structuralism, also by Peter Dews, *Logics of Disintegration: Post-Structuralist Thought and the Claims of Critical Theory* (London: Verso, 1987).

[23] The growing distance between Habermas and the earlier Frankfurt School views culminated in a critique of the Nietzschean element of *Dialectic of Enlightenment* by Habermas in 'The Entwinement of Myth and Enlightenment', *New German Critique*, 26 (Summer 1982), 13–30. For a detailed discussion of Habermas's partial turn away from Horkheimer and Adorno in this regard, see Peter U. Hohendahl, 'The Dialectic of Enlightenment Revisited: Habermas' Critique of the Frankfurt School', *New German Critique*, 35 (Spring/Summer 1985), 3–26. Hohendahl touches less satisfactorily on the issue of relations between Habermas and Foucault in that article, but he made good on that defect in his informative 'Habermas' Philosophical Discourse of Modernity', *Telos*, 69 (Fall 1986), 49–65. The hostility suggested by Habermas's notorious classification of Foucault as a 'young conservative' (in 'Modernity—an Incomplete Project', in *The Anti-Aesthetic: Essays on Postmodern Culture*, ed. Hal Foster (Port Townsend, Wash.: Bay, 1983), 14) was eventually replaced by more amicable relations between the two theorists, culminating in the graceful tribute paid to Foucault after his death by Habermas, in which Habermas discovered affinities within their differences on the nature of reason. See Jürgen Habermas, 'Taking Aim at the Heart of the Present', *University Publishing*, 13 (Summer 1984), 5–6. A work of major importance, also just appearing in English as I revise, is the record of Habermas's historic intellectual encounter with Foucault and French post-structuralism, Jürgen Habermas, *The Philosophical Discourse of Modernity: Twelve Lectures*, trans. Frederick Lawrence (Cambridge, Mass.: MIT Press, 1987). Hohendahl discusses these lectures in the second of the two articles cited above.

[24] Foucault stated: 'Now, obviously if I had been familiar with the Frankfurt School, if I had been aware of it at the time, I would not have said a number of stupid things that I did say and I would have avoided many of the detours which I made while trying to

subjectivist theorists found so inimical, the open-ended play of difference. The older subjectivist–objectivist split between French and German theory then became much less polarized, and theorists discovered considerable affinities between Derrida and Adorno's notions of negative dialectics.[25] Many Althusserians, as I indicated earlier, influenced by post-structuralist trends, have quietly abandoned the scientism of Althusser's early founding distinction between 'science' and 'ideology' with the result that 'everything is ideology', and the world is textual in something very close to Derrida's sense.[26]

There of course remain many differences and contentions around such problems as the nature of subjectivity, reason, and knowledge; there is no danger of running out of arguments. But in the new theoretical space opened up by the post-structuralist revolution, the unlikeliest connections are now possible. Analytic philosophy, for example, long the most notorious instance of Anglo-American stodgy isolationism, is now through Rorty engaged in synthesis and a dialogue with post-structuralism in which real affinities have emerged. The history of science and literary theory are now on speaking terms after decades of mutual ignoring. Theology and Marxism, in a number of locations, find common ground. Only through such a sense of hidden affinities and convergence is the following work possible.

This study, then, is situated theoretically in Frankfurt-derived Critical Theory, construed loosely enough to include borrowings from Foucault, Derrida, Raymond Williams, and the American theorist of science Thomas Kuhn. It is broadly, but not uncritically, 'post-structuralist' through the theoretical convergences indicated above.

With the contribution of the richly nuanced and highly developed

pursue my own humble path. . . . It is a strange case of non-penetration by two very similar types of thinking which is explained, perhaps, by that very similarity.' ('Structuralism and Post-Structuralism: An Interview with Michel Foucault' by Gerard Raulet, trans. Jeremy Harding, *Telos*, 55 (Spring 1983), 195–211.)

[25] See especially Michael Ryan, *Marxism and Deconstruction: A Critical Articulation* (Baltimore, Md.: Johns Hopkins University Press, 1982), 73–80 and both works by Peter Dews, cited above. Habermas discusses parallels between Adorno and Derrida (in a context quite critical of the latter) in *The Philosophical Discourse of Modernity*, 185–90.

[26] For an interesting account of British attempts to forge a new critical paradigm based on Althusserian Marxism and elements of several French structuralists and post-structuralists (Saussure, Lacan, Foucault, Derrida) see Alex Callinicos, *Is There a Future for Marxism?* (London: Macmillan, 1982). The second half of the book, which argues for the superiority of a reconstituted Trotskyist Leninism as an alternative to a post-structuralist Marxism seen as having theoretically 'failed', is less interesting. A number of contemporary Marxist critics—Jonathan Dollimore, Catherine Belsey, Lawrence Venuti, and James Kavanaugh, for example, are now working the terrain rejected by Callinicos.

aesthetic theories of the Frankfurt School theorists—not only Horkheimer and Adorno, but also Walter Benjamin and Herbert Marcuse—it is possible, I believe, to achieve the social history of literature which contemporary writers like Frank Lentricchia have correctly seen as implied by Foucault. We can, I believe, affirm contemporary critical theory's goal of overcomig the complete separation of art and literature from the rest of social life and the goal of a double hermeneutic that would (non-objectively) grasp the historical situation of the literary art-work through a methodological consciousness of the reader's situation in the historical present.[27] The major contribution of Frankfurt School theory in this process, quite clearly, would be a partial reversal of much current thinking about the status of the aesthetic—and of that pejorative, aestheticism—in contemporary society.

For the Frankfurt theorists, aestheticism emerges, not as the opposite of the kind of historical and social understanding of literature now rightly stressed by so many contemporary theorists; but instead, the autonomy of art is itself historically situated as one of the most characteristic outcomes of the development of fully capitalist social relations.

Ideologies like the several forms of aestheticism which have developed from the social situation of autonomous art in the modern era—notably including several versions of Modernism—can serve positive critical functions, maintaining trans-capitalist visions and values—at the same time that they distort and conceal art's connections to social life. But as Adorno in particular argued, a certain historically aware aestheticism is a desirable approach to art in an era of colonizing and levelling ideologies and practices which threaten to absorb everything resistant to a life of pure commodity-exchange.[28] Frankfurt theory in its turn can benefit from the increased concreteness and materiality of Foucault's focus on institutions and discourses.

Among the most important corollaries of these notions to emphasize here are the following: clearly any attempts to include art and literature

---

[27] I am thinking particularly of Lentricchia's influential *After the New Criticism*, which calls for each of the theoretical criteria just mentioned and hopes to accomplish them through a Foucault-influenced approach to literary history. Particularly valuable, I believe, is Lentricchia's critique of the American Derrideans, 'History or the Abyss: Poststructuralism', which points out that the Yale Critics fail to understand textuality as full of concrete historical determinations—see especially pp. 189–210. The great weakness of Lentricchia's work, from my point of view, is its too easy excoriation of 'aestheticism' as the enemy of an emerging post-structuralist criticism.

[28] The seminal Frankfurt work in this context is probably Max Horkheimer and Theodor Adorno, *Dialectic of Englightenment*, trans. John Cummings (New York:

within some unified episteme including the sciences is fundamentally misguided (that is not to *preclude* mutual influence, but to avoid an a priori assumption of such influence); similarly any attempt to assimilate art to the dialectic of power/knowledge runs the risk of illegitimately failing to recognize art's differentiation from instrumental reason and slighting art's subversive powerlessness and non-utility, its status as a carrier of anti-instrumental values and practices. Similarly an assimilation of art to 'ideology' would lose sight of art's critical and Utopian dimension, and a recognition of the differentiation of art from both instrumental reason and from ideology is assumed throughout the present work.

Many of these complexities can be conceptualized, in fact, with the help of a borrowing from T. S. Kuhn's celebrated concept of the 'paradigm'.

Paradigms: Scientific, Critical, and Aesthetic

As is well known, Thomas S. Kuhn proposed in 1962 the concept of 'paradigms' as an alternative to the then prevailing notion in the history of science that change in scientific theory proceeded on the basis of a steady accretion of evidence which slowly confirmed or modified existing theory and produced gradual 'progress'. Kuhn took exception to this view for two reasons. First, he believed it was inadequate in understanding those fundamental wholesale theoretical renovations — the Newtonian, the Einsteinian — which he called scientific revolutions, in which old theories were not simply modified but discarded and replaced by something entirely diffferent.[29] Second, and more

---

Seabury, 197). Standard secondary works are Martin Jay, *The Dialectical Imagination: A History of the Frankfurt School and the Institute of Social Research, 1923–1950* (Boston, Mass: Little, 1973) and David Held, *Introduction to Critical Theory: Horkheimer to Habermas* (Berkeley: University of California Press, 1980). In addition to Fredric Jameson's well-known *Marxism and Form: Twentieth-Century Dialectical Theories of Literature* (Princeton, NJ: Princeton University Press, 1971), John Fekete and John Brenkman in a number of works have both been early contributors to the enterprise of a systematic application of Frankfurt themes to the literary criticism of English studies. A recent and bracing work in the same vein is Susan Wells, *Dialectics of Representation* (Baltimore, Md.: Johns Hopkins University Press, 1985), and several essays in the recent *Postmodernism and Politics*, ed. Jonathan Arac (Minneapolis: University of Minnesota Press, 1986) also discuss the relevance of Frankfurt theory to contemporary literary critical theory.

[29] Thomas S. Kuhn, *The Structure of Scientific Revolutions* (Chicago, Ill.: University of Chicago Press, 1962), 1–22. Convergences between Kuhn and Foucault were pointed out by Dreyfus and Rabinow, *Michel Foucault*, 197–200.

subtly, he believed the notion of steady progress in the positivistic notion of science was untenable and even hubristic, and in the last section of *The Structure of Scientific Revolution* he made a brief argument for a non-teleological trajectory for the overall scientific project that would be analogous to Darwin's notion of natural selection:

The *Origin of Species* recognized no goal set either by God or nature. Instead, natural selection, operating in the given environment and with the actual organisms presently at hand, was responsible for the gradual but steady emergence of more elaborate, further articulated, and vastly more specialized organisms. Even such marvelously adapted organs as the eye and hand of man—organs whose design had previously provided powerful arguments for the existence of a supreme artificer and an advance plan—were products of a process that moved steadily *from* primitive beginnings but *toward* no goal. (p. 171)

Similarly, Kuhn projected a succession of paradigms which were adaptive to the changes of instruments and observations at given moments in scientific development, but which could not be understood as 'positive' knowledge of nature moving to greater and greater approximations to the truth.

Kuhn's theory has had a remarkably protean career over the three decades since it first appeared. Assimilated and critiqued—for the moment—in the history of science, it has now penetrated into discussions of sociology, philosophy, political science, theology, and art and literary history.[30]

Kuhn is on record as believing that any transference of the notion of paradigm shift to art and literary history would have to work out the profound differences between science and the arts, differences which he believes the obvious parallels between scientific revolutions and changes of literary periods tend to obscure.[31] This need to differentiate the two enterprises is of course in line with the supposition I have outlined above on the post-Enlightenment differentiation of reason.[32] But the anti-positivist thrust of Kuhn's concept of paradigms as necessary mediations between us and our knowledge of nature—the paradigm as an epistemological category—points to a fruitful direction

[30] See the anthology on applications of Kuhn in a number of fields, *Paradigms and Revolutions: Appraisals and Applications of Thomas Kuhn's Philosophy of Science*, ed. Gary Gutting (Notre Dame, Ind.: University of Notre Dame Press, 1980).

[31] T. S. Kuhn 'Comment', *Comparative Studies in Society and History*, II (October 1969), 404.

[32] The lack of such differentiation is one of the weaknesses of one of the first applictions of Kuhn to literary theory, Steven Ryan's interesting exploration of the

for the application of Kuhn to literary theory. Kuhn devoted a good deal of his energy to demonstrating that evidence was much less decisive in accounting for what was accepted and not accepted in scientific debates than had been assumed in older positivistic models of the history of science, since, as he demonstrates, what counts as evidence is highly dependent on the paradigm through which the evidence is interpreted (pp. 77–90); there can be no 'direct', unmediated access to nature as such. Kuhn's theory is anti-positivist and anti-empiricist, and this quality accounts for the widespread interest in Kuhn in our era of anti-positivist consensus. At the same time, however, referentiality is not abandoned by Kuhn. The 'crisis' that always precedes a scientific revolution (paradigm shift) always results from an accretion of discrepancies between theory and observation: in that sense, nature, as it were, 'speaks through' the paradigm, but by displacing and disturbing rather than by direct manifestation of itself. The existence of a non-cultural, non-artefactual object of study in the natural sciences remains a fundamental mark of difference between them and the 'human sciences', and helps explain the prevalence of a notion of a unitary 'state of the art' in the sciences as opposed to the more divided and pluralistic human sciences. But many features of Kuhn's theory are applicable to the different circumstances and epistemological status of the humanities because Kuhn's theory is so well grounded in a kind of sociology of research communities, some of the characteristics of which transcend the differences between objects of knowledge.

I will be applying aspects of Kuhn's 'paradigm' to two separate but related spheres. The first, and I suspect less controversial application, will be to refer to 'critical paradigms'. These operate within the discourse sphere of commentary and interpretation of literary texts with institutional roots that have shifted in the course of post-Enlightenment culture from coffee-houses and journalism to academia, and in the process have undergone the various kinds of modernization alluded to already and to be further discussed in the next chapter,

relevance of Kuhn to literary history, 'The Importance of Thomas S. Kuhn's Scientific Paradigm Theory to Literary Criticism', *The Midwest Quarterly*, 19 (Winter 1978), 151–9. Ryan believes there is one scientific paradigm which dominates everyone's world-view and which therefore profoundly conditions art—a view which fails to take differentiation into account. But the article goes on to speak of artistic paradigms separate from scientific ones, a distinction which I believe is the more fruitful application of Kuhn.

including a conscious modelling after the procedures of the natural sciences.

In Kuhn's model, the 'hard' sciences show permeability to interests and ideologies that may be surprising to believers in 'scientific objectivity'. While Kuhn credited observational anomalies between theory and experiment as playing a definite role in scientific revolutions, he also defined a very large role for, to use a term Kuhn did not, political factors of several sorts. Career self-interest accounts for an observed tendency for new paradigms to be championed by the young and opposed by the old. National pride and rivalries play a part, as do ingrained prejudice and habit, religious belief or its lack, and larger cultural, political, and social currents (pp. 149–58). Given that literary study lacks the experimental practices of hard science, the influence of such political and non-discursive factors as ideology, self-interest, and prejudice can be expected to play an even larger role in the on-going critical debates in this sector, and this opening to non-paradigmatic factors in explaining paradigm shift is a crucial one in my use of Kuhn's concept, and I should note that it is a relatively undeveloped portion of his theory.[33] Nevertheless Kuhn is not as naïve about the role of power in knowledge as he is sometimes assumed to be, and my attempt to adapt his notion to a project of a historically and socially conscious literary theory hinges on this 'opening' to the outside within the theory of paradigm shifts.

Other applications of Kuhn's theories to the literary sphere will emerge in the concrete cases below. Again, it should be clear that the relatively close parallel occurs because of the close sociological resemblance between the two communities, particularly if we think of both in their academic environments, the dominant institutional setting of both groups in recent decades. What Kuhn was getting at was a kind of general dynamics of a specialized and institutionalized community engaged in a common knowledge programme in the post-Enlightenment West, the shared situation of academic critics and scientists in the twentieth century. In addition, the academic literary profession

---

[33] This 'opening' to non-scientific factors is indicated by Kuhn in the following passage: 'I have said nothing about the role of technological advance or of external social, economic, and intellectual conditions in the development of the sciences. . . . Explicit consideration of effects like these would not, I think, modify the main theses developed in this essay. . . .' (Kuhn, *Structure of Scientific Revolutions*, p. xii). Certainly Kuhn is here defending his lack of enquiry into the effects on science of societal factors and mistakenly attempting to minimize them, but he is also leaving a space for such factors, and it is that space I am seeking to open up.

modelled its journals and research methods to some extent on the natural sciences, and this modelling accounts for some of the parallel as well. For these reasons there should be little problem in recognizing the existence of 'critical paradigms' in the literary field, less universally accepted than those of hard science and not tied to scientific experimentation, but otherwise recognizably analogous.

There is a further extension possible of the concept of paradigm in the literary field, however, with fewer direct parallels but with important and persuasive ones nevertheless. As an approach to the problem of literary periods discussed above, we can and should, I think, speak of 'aesthetic paradigms' the 'shift' of which is constitutive of the periodic revolutions in aesthetic forms and values which cause the succession of literary 'periods'.[34] Such a rethinking of the idea of periods need not cause a revolution in the duration and boundaries, or even the convenient labels widely disseminated and institutionalized in the 'fields' and specializations of academic literary criticism, (although such changes are not precluded either). One immediate advantage of the notion of paradigm is that it allows us to think of competing or symbiotic paradigms (the coexistence of late Romanticism and realism in the Victorian period is the best example of symbiosis) co-existing in the same chronological period. But the major advantages of thinking of the succession of periods as a series of paradigm shifts have to do with the way the notion of paradigm allows us to think of literary activity as a social and historically changing practice autonomous from, but related to, the social totality of which it is a part and to conceive of literary artworks as existing in an intersubjective sphere which is the product of the labour of a large community to which individuals can make distinctive contributions. 'Men make their own history', Marx wrote in a much-quoted passage, 'but they do not make it just as they please; they do not make it under circumstances chosen by themselves, but under circumstances directly encountered, given and transmitted from the past. The tradition of all the dead generations weighs like a nightmare on the brain of the living'.[35] A similar dynamic of individual

---

[34] This application of Kuhn to literary history seems to have been first discussed in print by James S. Ackerman, 'The Demise of the Avant-Garde: Notes on the Sociology of Recent American Art', *Comparative Studies in Society and History*, 11 (October 1969), 371–84. Kuhn himself noted a parallel to art and literary history in the 'Postscript— 1969' to the 2nd edn. of *Structure of Scientific Revolutions* (Chicago, Ill.: University of Chicago Press, 1970), 208.

[35] Karl Marx, *The Eighteenth Brumaire of Louis Bonaparte* (New York: International, 1963), 15.

agency operating within and against a given aesthetic paradigm is precisely the model of the anxiety of influence and tradition I advocate here.

Against the kind of pantheon of giants assumed by Harold Bloom in *The Anxiety of Influence*, twelve or so 'strong poets' forming a trans-historical community, the idea of an aesthetic paradigm would situate the major poet or author in a given literary situation created by the social interaction of audience, institutions, and fellow literary practitioners: Shakespeare at a given stage of English versification and drama, in the wake of his ('major' and 'minor') predecessors, writing for a socially concrete audience, in that peculiar balance of liberty and subordination of the Globe theatre, at a certain pivotal stage in the larger culture. None of this 'explains' why Shakespeare is Shakespeare and Greene is Greene, but it does underline how much of Shakespeare's writing was 'given', paradigmatic, rather than chosen, and suggests explanations for that anomaly to any theory of 'innate' genius—or 'strong poets'—why 'geniuses' tend to come in clusters and to populate certain societies and historical junctures rather than others. The 'strong poet effect'—the case of the apparently isolated individual who grasps and transforms some particular sphere of culture—is in reality the effect of a social process, in which one figure reaps benefits the ground for which had been laid by many others.

On the other hand, the notion of an aesthetic paradigm suggests an important modification of one of the most provocative, but ultimately, I believe, problematically neo-positivist aspects of post-structuralist theory: the tendency to reduce individual consciousness (the self, the author) to the nugatory status of 'illusion' caused by the play of determinant social and psychological forces. One is reminded of the observation of Hegel's which Marx was so fond of, to the effect that our notion of the essence of a thing must include its appearance. Many post-structuralist theorists, it seems to me, have been notably unsuccessful in retaining 'the appearance' in theories of subjectivity and agency, that is in preserving a notion of the self while showing its de-centred nature. In particular, there are problems with Althusser's theory of ideology and interpellation in this regard,[36] and while I

---

[36] To put it briefly, Althusser attempted to 'socialize' Lacan by understanding subjectivity as an effect of the assimilation (*by* what he never attempts to explain) of a totalized Ideology such that an essentially external social identity is interiorized and falsely valorized as the self. For Althusser, however, the Lacanian play of desire among various signifiers, with its possibility of change and of creativity, has no clear equivalent. For Lacan, the subject is always split in itself, and only in part located in the symbolic

recognize the affinities between those notions and the theory of this work, I offer the concept of an aesthetic paradigm in part as an attempt to take account of those problems while preserving what is valuable in the Althusserian notions. My aim is to open up a much needed space for agency in the theory of the interaction between the subject and the social. For as Fredric Jameson in particular has persuasively argued, even if we grant a clear sense in which the 'self' is an 'illusion', then we are left to explain the workings of a 'subjectivity effect' which has its own kind of reality.[37]

The notion of the paradigm allows these interactions to be thought in terms of individuals interacting with a collective, social construct in the intersubjective sphere without the problematic notion that humans are doomed to be wholly determined from without through the domination of ideology. The paradigm can, in certain obsessive personality types, 'take over' an individual consciousness in something of

discourses that Althusser renames ideology; for Althusser, the subject seems entirely a function of these discourses, and it is strangely unitary, becoming a kind of biological video display terminal for the wholly determining signals of Ideology. The result is a de-psychologized Lacan and a totalizing Marxism which threatens to reduce agency out of existence. Similar problems result when this train of thought is further extended so that a literary art-work is simply the sum total of the productive transformations of ideology effected by the interplay of social and psychic forces operating across the otherwise empty space of the author. The best-known application of Althusser in this regard is Pierre Macherey, *A Theory of Literary Production*, trans. Geoffrey Wall (London: Routledge, 1978). Terry Eagleton's first major theoretical statement, *Criticism and Ideology: A Study in Marxist Literary Theory* (London: Verso, 1978) was also written in this vein and indebted to Macherey. Eagleton has since moved beyond Althusser to positions embracing Walter Benjamin, Habermas, Raymond Williams, and Derrida (see below, Chapter 5). It is not that such theories lack attractive features: they rightly situate the literary work in a social and psychological context and rightly undermine the basis of both the older biographical criticism that dominated French academic criticism until the Sixties and of the antiquarian and formalistic critics of the Anglo-Saxon world of the same period. But if there can now be little question that older notions of a transcendental Self and a timeless art-work can no longer be sustained under rigorous inquiry in today's most advanced critical paradigms, it is equally true that attempts to reduce subjectivity to a play of Ideology must themselves be placed under suspicion, and their complicity with the scientistic and positivistic tendencies of instrumental reason taken into account. In addition to the texts cited in n. 4, see for Althusser's self-understanding of his relation to Lacan, in the appendix to his *Lenin and Philosophy and Other Essays*, 'Freud and Lacan', 189–219. I am indebted to Susan Wells for the interpretation of Lacan here. See Ellie Ragland-Sullivan, *Jacques Lacan and the Philosophy of Psychoanalysis* (Urbana: University of Illinois Press, 1987) for a useful summary of Lacan's often hermetic writings. I should add that a number of post-Althusserians believe that the basic Althusserian concepts can be modified by post-structuralism to overcome the kinds of difficulties I am raising here, but such an enabling revision remains to be systematically performed.

[37] Fredric Jameson, 'Postmodernism, or The Cultural Logic of Late Capitalism', *New Left Review*, 146 (July–Aug. 1984), 63.

the manner of Althusserian ideology, but the paradigm is much less global and totalistic a concept: aesthetic and scientific paradigms, for example, operate in separate spheres as bodies of knowledge and techniques which one consciously learns; there is a distinct distance between the self who learns and the subject-matter assimilated. The paradigm is a given on which one works without necessarily identifying with it or accepting it as one's own. It is true that, like Althusserian ideology, it entails more than appears at first: Kuhn emphasizes that the paradigm is a practice that is imitated through modelling and that many of its suppositions are never brought fully to consciousness. Nevertheless it is finally separate from the decentred self who works in, with, and against it. The notion of the paradigm, then, allows us to think through the intricate dialectic of the interpenetration of the social and the individual without effacing either of this mutually inter-penetrating pair.

The Parameters of This Study

Finally let me note that it has occurred to me, as I am sure it will to many readers, that my claims concerning the influence of Modernism on how we read Shakespeare would receive strong corroboration if this study were extended to include performance history. Certainly there, in the theatre, in such celebrated productions as Peter Brook's *Lear* and *Titus Andronicus*, the intersection of Shakespeare and Modernism is palpable.

On consideration, however, it seemed to me injurious to the unity of this work to undertake such an extension. The theatre involves a different community of interpreters, a different social and economic matrix, and different problems of interpretation from those with which I am dealing in this account of critical texts. I hope readers with a knowledge of twentieth-century Shakespearian performance can themselves make the connections which my work suggests.

In this work above others, there is no claim for some individual, isolated originality. My hope rather is to have grasped and contributed to aspects of the new critical paradigms and to show how they cause us to rethink radically the recent past of Shakespeare studies. The acknowledgements and footnotes record the numerous specific indeb-tednesses, but I want here to make explicit a general debt to the writings of Raymond Williams, who sadly passed away during the late stages of my work on this volume.

I

Modernizing Shakespeare: The Rise of Professionalism

Modernism and Modernization

Literary critical discourse has never been an unmediated expression of a prevailing aesthetic paradigm. It came into existence in something like a recognizably modern form in the Enlightenment, but in the Romantic period split off sharply from what was coming to be thought of as literature proper. Critical discourse was rational and purposive in its mode of expression while Romantic poetic language in particular was cultivating the inexpressible and the elusive as its proper domain. But Romantic criticism shared with that of the previous century a locus in a generalized, public sphere of coffee-house, magazine, and lecture-hall. It was a significant part of a new bourgeois social formation coming into existence with its new and revolutionary forms of critical rationality, destined to help transform Europe out of its anachronistic political monarchism. 'Modern European criticism', Terry Eagleton has rightly noted, 'was born of a struggle against the absolutist state.'[1]

With the consolidation of the new order in the nineteenth century, however, literary criticism became significantly transformed; it passed out of the sphere of public discourse properly speaking, becoming instead a knowledge/power of new bureaucratic institutions. The modern, academic form of literary criticism developed in the late Victorian period as part of the transformation of the capitalist system from its entrepreneurial to its current corporate form and became something far from its earlier and heroic incarnation. The sea-change that Shakespeare criticism underwent from the nineteenth to the twentieth century is overwhelmingly the result of the transference of discourse on Shakespeare to a new bureaucratic setting (the modern University) and to a new class of authors (academic professionals).

---

[1] Terry Eagleton, *The Function of Criticism: From 'The Spectator' to Post-Structuralism* (London: Verso, 1984), 9.

This entailed fundamental changes in the audience addressed, the social purpose, and the forms of writing on Shakespeare—changes that have been partially obscured because of many academic critics' attempt to claim the older culture of Shakespeare studies (I am thinking of such magic names as those of Dryden, Samuel Johnson, and S. T. Coleridge) as their own and partially because the new profession characteristically considered any questions concerning the social matrix underlying its own discourse to be illegitimate, outside its professional field of knowledge. Even much of contemporary radical theory has followed this path: as we will see below, early post-structuralism has targeted the Arnoldian 'cultural' tradition in its critique of English studies while largely ignoring professionalism, the cultural tradition's 'mighty opposite' in twentieth-century literary studies.

In this chapter I will attempt to redress this balance and define some of the crucial determinants of modern critical discourse. Literary criticism contains influences from the dominant aesthetic paradigm, to be sure, but also from the institutions and ideologies in which it is produced. In a word, modern critical discourse has become professionalized, and professionalism in its turn is best understood as a key aspect of the global process we can conveniently call modernization.

Modernism is the particular aesthetic paradigm that has until very recently dominated twentieth-century art and literature, and it has inherited and transformed the social functions of post-Enlightenment art as a carrier of those values inimical to the increasingly dominating institutions and practices of instrumental reason. But this modern function of art is only intelligible situated within its more global context of modernization.

In what follows I will turn to recent theories of modernization, with a particular concern with the apparently innocent category of professionalization and its relation to these larger processes. The rise of professionalism in the late nineteenth century should be understood as an integral part of the process of bureaucratization that transformed capitalism and produced the modern social forms with which Weber, and following him, Habermas, have grappled.

With this theoretical context in place, I turn to the case of Shakespeare studies in the nineteenth century and trace the changes in scholarly methodology which resulted when modernization, in the form of positivist ideology, impacted on what was already a culturally central activity of Shakespeare commentary, producing a new and symptomatic critical phenomenon, the 'disintegration' of the Shakespearean text.

While disintegration was ultimately erased from the received traditions of Shakespeare studies, other, less virulent forms of professionalism emerged, this time housed in the new research universities, where the young discipline of English studies was in formation and turning its attention necessarily to the case of Shakespeare. But new positivist tendencies had to contend with the slightly older 'cultural' tradition, producing the generalist–specialist debate that continues, in various forms and modes, to the present. The victorious methodology that emerged from the give-and-take was positivist literary history, well exemplified by that perfect specimen of the new professionalism in the American academy, E. E. Stoll, whose career will be briefly discussed as representing the end point of the transformations which this chapter is seeking to define: at the beginning of the Modernist period, Shakespeare has been converted from the icon of Romantic traditionalists like Coleridge to the object of a panoply of new scholarly technologies, developed first in civil society proper, then in the academies, that seemed to threaten to disintegrate the Bard of the Romantic Age out of existence. It was in the response to this perceived threat, in the generalist and cultural reactions to late, scientistic nineteenth-century scholarship, that the Modernist Shakespeare began to take form. The traditionalist response to the forces of modernization was failing, until it transformed itself—into the new guise of Modernism.

The Dynamics of Modernization

The term 'modernization' has become well known in the literature of contemporary sociology and economics, from whence it has migrated to a number of theories of literary modernism. Modernization denotes the process of economic development, with all its attendant social and cultural eruptions, entailed by industrial capitalism, a process of constant innovation and dislocation. Marx was perhaps the first to define the peculiar institutionalization of accelerating social change that the triumph of capital entailed, and among those portions of his legacy still relevant to the present are certainly those cadenced phrasings defining the dynamics of the new order: 'The bourgeoisie cannot exist without constantly revolutionizing the instruments of production, and with them the relations of production, and with them all the relations of society. . . . Constant revolutionizing of production, uninterrupted disturbance of all social relations, everlasting uncertainty and agitation, distinguish the bourgeois epoch from all earlier ones.'[2] And again, in a more flamboyant language, Marx intoned: 'All fixed, fast-frozen relations, with their train of ancient and venerable prejudices and opinions, are swept away, all new-formed ones become antiquated before they can ossify. All that is solid melts into air, all that is holy is profaned, and men at last are forced to face ... the real conditions of their lives and their relations with their fellow men'.[3]

The dry pages of *Capital* worked out the analysis that underlay Marx's double-edged description, emphasizing what no contemporary economist would question, that capitalist economics is a system whose internal dynamics result, in fits and starts to be sure, in constant expansion and growth. Twentieth-century theorists—Lukács, Adorno, Marcuse, Habermas—highlighted a crucial cultural corollary of this characteristic: a tendency, in capitalist society, for more and more areas of human life to become 'colonized' through a process of 'commodification'—that is, a constant expansion of products and services offered in the market-place to fulfil needs once met outside the market—or to meet needs that have been created by modern advertising and consumer culture.

From a larger-scale perspective, modernization is a process that empties the countryside, fills the cities, and sprawls into suburbs; that harnesses science and technology to the service of product development, creating and destroying whole industries and regions in a matter of a generation or two; that destroys traditional livelihoods and small entrepreneurs and creates huge private economic enterprises, which in turn produce entire nations of employees; that subordinates the great 'underdeveloped' regions of the planet—their populations and their ecosystems—to the demands of an expansionary and self-serving productive apparatus. Of course, as Marx, and even his increasingly pessimistic disciples argued, modernization also creates the conditions for the possible emancipation of the human race—through the abolition of poverty, the conquest of disease, the liberation of women, the sustain-

---

[2] Karl Marx and Frederick Engels, *The Manifesto of the Communist Party*, in Karl Marx, *Political Writings*, vol. i, *The Revolutions of 1848*, ed. David Fernbach (New York: Vintage, 1974), 70.

[3] Ibid., pp. 70–1. The application of these passages from the *Manifesto* is suggested in Marshall Berman, *All That Is Solid Melts into Air: The Experience of Modernity* (New York: Schuster, 1982), 87–129. I draw from Berman's valuable account, among others noted, throughout the discussion of modernization. The title of his work is, of course, taken from the passage from Marx just given.

ing of the earth's ecology, and a rational, steady-state economy controlled by human values, rather than the reverse.[4]

In recent years Jürgen Habermas has developed and modified the
notion of instrumental reason into a theory of modernity that is one of
the major intellectual projects of the last two decades of Western
thought,[5] and it is to Habermas that I turn to supply the theory of those
aspects of modernity that underlie the professionalization of literary
criticism which we so take for granted.

For Habermas, modernization resulted in the 'differentiation' of a
formerly unitary culture into three autonomous spheres of rationality:
the technical-administrative, the practical (in the sense of ethical), and
the aesthetic. Increasingly the leading role in modern societies is taken
by technical-administrative reason integrated into the dynamics of
capitalist expansion. As Habermas put it:

... traditional structures are increasingly subordinated to conditions of
instrumental or strategic rationality: the organization of labor and of trade, the
network of transportation, information and communication, the institutions of
private law, and, starting with financial administration, the state bureaucracy.
Thus arises the substructure of a society under the compulsion of modernization. The latter eventually widens to take in all areas of life: the army, the
school system, health services, and even the family.[6]

In other words, the colonization of 'traditional', aesthetic, and practical
spheres of life is an aspect of the dynamic of modern capitalist society,
a process, as Weber understood, of erecting iron bars of deformed
rationality around every human subject.

---

[4] The opening chapter of Berman is a particularly effective attempt to capture something of the double-edged potential of modernity as it has been expressed in the words of
a surprising number of artists and intellectuals of the last century—Marx, Nietzsche,
Kierkegaard, Whitman, Ibsen, Baudelaire, Melville, Carlyle, Stirner, Rimbaud, Strind-
berg, Dostoevsky, and many more—see especially pp.15–36.

[5] Habermas is of course building on older Frankfurt School attempts to confront the
Marxian legacy in the twentieth century with its apparent predictive failure—that is, to
deal with the unexpected longevity of capitalism in the West and the unforeseen
developments of Fascism and Stalinism. The older Frankfurt School theorists and then
Habermas increasingly turned to the classic sociology of Max Weber to supplement
Marx's basic account of modernization. Weber had emphasized in his work the importance of tendencies to rationalization and to bureaucratization that Marx had not treated.
These Weberian themes, deepened and radicalized in Adorno and Horkheimer's *Dialectic of Enlightenment*, constituted the Frankfurt critique of instrumental reason discussed
in the Introduction in connection with the genesis of autonomous art in the
Enlightenment.

[6] Jürgen Habermas, *Towards a Rational Society: Student Protest, Science, and Politics*,
trans. Jeremy Shapiro (Boston, Mass.: Beacon, 1970), 98.

Professionalism

An important insight into the concrete processes of modernization is gained if we insert into Habermas's description of modernization recent studies of the rise of professionalism in the late nineteenth century. Although the three oldest professions—medicine, the law, the religious ministry—have roots in the medieval and ancient worlds, professionalism and most modern professions came into existence within a relatively compact era in the nineteenth century. Empirically speaking, one good measure of the age of professionalism is the 'wave of associations'—the formation of the major national professional associations like the American Medical Association or the Modern Languages Association—within forty-seven years in the United States (1840–87) and within a fifty-five-year time span in Britain (1825–80). Professionalism is an essential component of the second phase of modernization, the age of corporate consolidations, of the growth of bureaucracy, and of the harnessing of science to technology.[7]

Magali Larson's original and useful analysis, *The Rise of Professionalism*, is particularly apposite for my purposes here because she deftly works out the paradoxical situation whereby the material roots of profession-forming in the economic market-place require changes in the ideologies and belief-systems of society. A profession, to speak in economic terms, is an organized body of practitioners of some discipline or skill in social demand. In its most characteristic form, the profession achieves a monopoly on its skill or technology, which it enforces through a system of credentialing—licensing, examinations, required education, etc. (pp. 15, 31–9). The profession becomes economically viable when its practitioners, bound together by their credentialed command of some socially recognized knowledge, are able to create a sufficient demand for their services to sustain their (usually high) salaries.

There are fascinating and detailed histories of each of the professions, but the general pattern is similar in each. At the heart of each profession lies what Larson called the 'cognitive conditions of professional monopoly' (p. 31), and we recognize what Foucault has called a 'knowledge/power'. A profession, Larson argues, requires a body of knowledge or a discipline that must meet certain objective

[7] Magali Scarfatti Larson, *The Rise of Professionalism: A Sociological Analysis* (Berkeley: University of California Press, 1977), 4.

requirements if it is to command social demand and legitimacy. The body of knowledge in question must, for example, be developed and theoretical, outside the boundaries of 'general knowledge' and complex enough to require more than casual study to master. At the same time it must be capable of being standardized and, to some extent, quantified, in order to fit into the system of licensing, examination, and the other components of the credentialed society. Larson defines those conditions thus: 'It must be specific enough to impart distinctiveness to the professional "commodity"; it must be formalized or codified enough to allow standardization of the "product"—which means, ultimately, standardization of the producers. And yet it must not be so clearly codified that it does not allow a principle of exclusion to operate: where everyone can claim to be an expert, there is no expertise' (p. 31).

In what follows I want to sketch out the way in which modernization, mediated through the specific process of professionalization, intervened in and transformed the nature of literary studies,[8] including those of Shakespeare, in the late nineteenth and early twentieth centuries. At the end of the process, we will arrive at the modern academic literary professional housed in the vastly expanded bureaucracies of higher education in the twentieth-century West. However, the first steps of literary professionalization, perhaps surprisingly, took place largely outside of academia, within the remarkable sphere of bourgeois civil society of Victorian England and America. As Larson points out, most professions begin in the market-place and only later migrate to the more protected and institutionalized homes in the bureaucracies of the state or private sectors (p. 9). So was it with the professional literary specialist. Consequently I will first sketch out a picture of the status of Shakespeare in Victorian bourgeois society at the moment of the beginning of professionalization and then examine in some detail one of the first attempts at constituting a literary knowledge/power in Shakespeare studies: the case of disintegration—a case which reveals oppositional forces, hostile to professionalism, at work. Finally I will turn to the rise of the modern university as the institution which

[8] The work of GRIP (Group for Research into the Institutionalization and Professionalization of Literary Studies) was an early effort in this direction which encouraged my own work here. See also Eagleton's *Function of Criticism* and Gerald Graff, *Professing Literature: An Institutional History* (Chicago, Ill.: University of Chicago Press, 1987). David Shumway of the GRIP project is presently at work on a book which also uses Larson, Foucault, and Marx in a discussion of professionalism and the rise of American literature.

inherited (and still contains) the unresolved conflict between the professional and generalist missions of literary study in modernized societies.

Now to grasp fully the import of Habermas's theory of modernization with which I am working here, it is imperative not to 'moralize' prematurely the terms of the analysis. Contained within the categories of analysis is certainly an ethically-tinged critique of commodification and a suspicion of the general processes of modernization, as in the classic works of the first generation Frankfurt School theorists. But by the same token there is no necessary endorsement of the traditions and institutions which modernization devastates. Everything depends on the specific political and social responses we can make to the challenges and crises to which we are condemned. Thus there can be no automatic condemnation—or celebration—of specific modernizations, even if we agree in general terms with Horkheimer and Adorno in *Dialectic of Englightenment* that '. . . the fully enlightened earth radiates disaster triumphant' (p. 3).

Shakespeare and the High Bourgeois Culture of the Nineteenth Century

At the beginning of the nineteenth century occurred that stage of modernization in England and America in which the industrial system had become established and was producing its sweeping series of changes, without yet having entered its bureaucratic, corporate phase. Shakespeare criticism was written for the 'cultivated' public and disseminated in editions of the works, public lectures, books, and—above all—in magazines and newspapers.[9] Shakespeare's plays were prominent in the repertory of both English and American theatres and were assumed to be the intellectual property of men (and increasingly of women) of any cultural pretensions—and of many without any such pretensions, as the recent study of Lawrence W. Levine

---

[9] The crucial importance of the late Enlightenment in inventing many of the scholarly techniques and procedures which later professionals would systematize is the subject of the elegantly demonstrated argument by Margreta de Grazia, *Shakespeare Verbatim: The Reproduction of Authenticity and the 1790 Apparatus* (Oxford: Oxford University Press, 1991). De Grazia singles out in particular the unpublished 1790 edition of Shakespeare's works by Edmund Malone as strategically crucial in enacting a series of assumptions that have defined Shakespeare studies ever since—or at least until very recently: the notion of an authentic text and of determinate interpretations of the texts, as well as the need for historical background and of accounts of Shakespeare as a unitary author of the works.

demonstrates.[10] But Shakespeare was not a staple of the higher education curriculum, which was still dominated by classical studies.[11] The highly bureaucratized systems of modern education with which we are familiar did not yet exist. Discourse on Shakespeare took place instead in that 'public sphere' which Terry Eagleton, developing Habermas, has recently described as the originating point of English literary criticism.[12] Shakespeare was of course prominent in the paradigm shift between neo-classicism and Romanticism that was still being discussed in England and the Continent, and there was nothing 'antiquarian' about the passionate championing of Shakespeare as the prototype of a literary genius and the great exemplar of organic form that was so prominent in the writing of Romantics like (to take the most influential example) Samuel Taylor Coleridge. Even before the Age of Romanticism Shakespeare had become what he was so often called in both England and America, a secular Bible, a revered body of thought, values, characters, words, and forms held to be the common property of a culture.[13] The need for 'authentic' texts that this status created would be an unexamined given for all sides in the often tumultuous debates that would take place later in the century.

The Romantic moment was also an age, as Raymond Williams has shown on several occasions,[14] when Art was invented; and Shakespeare, in the Romantic deconstruction of the older classical duality between Art and Nature, became perhaps the major example of a poet whose organic forms demonstrated the idealistic and monistic unity of art and nature over and against a debased industrialized

---

[10] *Highbrow/Lowbrow: The Emergence of Cultural Hierarchy in America* (Cambridge: Harvard University Press, 1988). Levine shows that early nineteenth-century productions of Shakespeare's plays in America were given on the same bill as jugglers, acrobats, and other 'sideshow fare' to audiences of broad social composition.

[11] Graff, *Professing Literature*, 19–35.

[12] Eagleton, *Function of Criticism*, 9–67.

[13] Thanks to Gary Taylor's remarkably concise, witty, but thorough narrative of Shakespeare's reproduction in British and later American culture over several centuries, *Reinventing Shakespeare* (New York: Weidenfeld & Nicolson, 1989), it is now possible to get a concrete sense of this centrality. Equally insightful in a more explicitly theoretical mode, Michael Bristol's *Shakespeare's America* (London: Routledge, 1989) has undertaken the difficult task of defining the elusive centrality of Shakespeare in anti-traditional American culture, seeing that centrality as 'a kind of anomaly in that it entails respect and admiration for an archaic world-consciousness deep inside the American project of *renovatio*' (p. 2). See de Grazia for the historical development of the need for an 'authentic' Shakespeare, a topic to be further discussed below.

[14] See, for example, *Key Words: A Vocabulary of Culture and Society*, rev. edn. (New York: Oxford University Press, 1983), 40–2.

Society which had never contaminated him. As Coleridge wrote, 'Nature, the prime genial artist, inexhaustible in diverse powers, is inexhaustible in forms. Each exterior is the physiognomy of the being within, its true image reflected and thrown out from the concave mirror. And even such is the appropriate excellence of her chosen poet, of our own Shakespeare, himself a nature humanized, a genial understanding directing self-consciously a power and an implicit wisdom deeper than consciousness.'[15]

This Romantic moment of Shakespeare ciriticism, now understood to have its sources in the eighteenth-century Enlightenment and to have been given a peculiar German twist which Coleridge channelled back into England, has in the twentieth century been canonized as a classic moment of critical giants on whose shoulders we miniature moderns, disillusioned of the worst Romantic excesses, it is true, now stand. After Coleridge and Hazlitt, so the traditional story goes, were some minor curiosities—and A. C. Bradley. After Bradley comes Eliot and the Academy.[16]

Of course the situation is much less unitary and more complex than this simplified received account's description. Co-existing in the late nineteenth century were competing—often passionately so—critics and critical discourses from which came about the beginnings of professionalization in Shakespeare studies. Out of the remarkable voluntary activities of a group of energetic, largely non-academic scholars came the methodology and much of the initial work establishing 'modern' notions of Shakespeare's life and texts. The individuals most involved in these initiatives—F. J. Furnivall, F. G. Fleay, J. M. Robertson, and E. E. Stoll, to name those I will discuss—were men who went against the grain of the larger 'cultural' tradition and attempted to 'modernize' Shakespeare studies in now forgotten ways. From the point of view of these modernizers, Bradley was an anachronism—a Romantic who had not learned the lessons of professional literary criticism, an enemy from the 'other side' to be attacked and marginalized. Let us listen, for example, to the new accents of the American E. E. Stoll as he takes on Bradley on Falstaff:

---

[15] *Shakespearean Criticism*, extracted in *English Romantic Writers*, ed. David Perkins (New York: Harcourt, 1967), 500.

[16] See for example Arthur M. Eastman, *A Short History of Shakespearean Criticism* (New York: Random, 1968). For the period in question, Eastman treats Gervinus, Lowell, Dowden, Swinburne, Pater, Shaw, Tolstoy, Bradley (the only one to receive a chapter to himself), Bridges, Stoll, and Schücking.

In Shakespeare criticism, as in most things Anglo-Saxon but sport, there has been little professionalism. The best as well as the worst of our scientists and artists have done their work without learning how to do it, and our critics, like our soldiers, have won their Waterloos on cricket fields. For two hundred and fifty years Englishmen and Americans have been writing about the character of Falstaff, and hardly three or four of these have been students of the stage. Since 1777 they have followed in the steps of Maurice Morgann, a country gentleman of philosophic bent and literary taste who seems to have known little of the acted drama and to have loved it less.[17]

Ironically, however, the techniques that the new literary academic professionals like Stoll used arose in large part from non-academic origins. The beginnings of the application of instrumental reason to literature—which I take as the hallmark of the kind of scientistic professionalism I am trying to isolate here—certainly can be traced back to the earliest attempts to edit Shakespeare in the eighteenth century, an activity intimately connected with the rise of the entrepreneurial 'man of letters' of whom Samuel Johnson can be seen as the most successful prototype. This eighteenth-century amateur incipient professionalism climaxed, as Margreta de Grazia has shown, in Edmund Malone's late Enlightenment scholarship. Malone was a lawyer who only was able to devote himself to his Shakespearean vocation after coming into sufficient money to abandon his legal practice.[18]

This pattern of private scholarship continued into the nineteenth century. Following in Malone's footsteps in the next generation in America were a group of Philadelphia lawyers who organized the Philadelphia Shakespeare Society in 1852 and inspired H. H.

---

[17] E. E. Stoll, 'Falstaff', *Modern Philology*, 12 (October 1914), 65. An interesting and revealing ideological slippage, by the way, is at work in Stoll's characterization of Morgann—who is in any case a stalking-horse for Bradley (who had in turn rescued Morgann from obscurity). In fact Morgann was not a leisured gentleman, but a professional and highly active civil servant in eighteenth-century colonial affairs; he advocated a conciliatory approach to the American colonies and the abolition of slavery in the West Indies—see Daniel A. Fineman, Biographical Introduction to *Shakespearean Criticism* by Maurice Morgann, ed. Daniel A. Fineman (Oxford: Clarendon, 1972), 3–36. But Stoll wants to invoke the stereotype of the dilettante gentleman-farmer as a foil to his own status as a professional of the new science of English studies now ensconced in the universities.

[18] See de Grazia, *Shakespeare Verbatim*, for a thorough study of Malone's pivotal contributions to what eventually became the modernization and professionalization of Shakespeare.

Furness's celebrated Variorum Shakespeares.[19] Well-known names like Malone and Furness, however, only constitute the tip of the iceberg of private Shakespeare scholarship in both Britain and the United States throughout the nineteenth century. We can get some idea of the strength and passion of Shakespeare studies in high bourgeois nineteenth-century culture from a fascinating 1889 book written by one L. M. Griffiths, identified on the volume's title-page as 'Honorary Secretary of the Clifton Shakspere[20] Society'. Griffiths displays a virtual missionary zeal in promulgating the study of Shakespeare as one of the highest activities conceivable for the middle and leisured classes:

It is most desirable that persons busy with a daily occupation should have some outside intellectual diversion in which they can engage in a methodical manner. For this purpose nothing can be better than a Shakspere-Society with its endless ramifications of beauty, enjoyment, and interest. To people of leisure such a society offers boundless facilities for a zest and satisfaction in life which it would be difficult to obtain in any other way. . . . The literary criticism of which a society of ordinarily well-informed men and women is capable may not add anything to the knowledge of experts, but, at least, it will be a delight and an illumination to many to whom the wealth of Elizabethan drama has not yet afforded much beyond the riches of Shakspere himself, or to whom, perhaps, his work is known only by a superficial acquaintance with the more frequently acted plays or, possibly, by a perfect familiarity with most of the well-quoted passages.[21]

[19] Alfred Van Rensselaer Westfall, *American Shakespearean Criticism: 1607–1865* (New York: Wilson, 1939), 4. More recently Michael Bristol has focused on Furness and the Philadelphia society in his *Shakespeare's America*, 64–70.

[20] This spelling was insisted upon by F. J. Furnivall's prestigious New Shakspere Society (see below), which has obviously influenced the practice of the Clifton group. The spelling was in fact widespread in the last two decades of the nineteenth century on the grounds that it was that used by Shakespeare in his will and Stratford mortgages — or at least, it was an ideal type of the variant spellings found on those documents — see Frederick J. Furnivall, 'The New Shakspere Society (The Founder's Prospectus Revised)', in the supplement to *Transactions of the New Shakspere Society*, 1st ser. 1 (1874), 6 n. 1. The new orthography also conveyed the interest in spelling-reform shared by many English philologists and social reformers in the period, and it signalled the distrust with which Furnivall and his disintegrating followers approached the received texts of the First Folio and quartos: they couldn't even be trusted to spell his name correctly, the reformed orthography tells us succinctly. At the same time the insistence on standardization, so foreign to the orthographical practices of the 'authentic' Renaissance, is a silent reminder of the Enlightenment imprint in the search for histori-cal accuracy.

[21] L. M. Griffiths, *Evenings with Shakspere: A Handbook to the Study of His Works* (Bristol: Arrowsmith, 1889), 2–3.

Griffiths supplies detailed instructions for the organization of such groups of ladies and gentlemen and offers the curious the benefits of the long experience of the Clifton group. A membership of twenty-five—eighteen 'gentlemen' and seven 'ladies'—is said to be ideal, since on alternate meetings the society reads the plays aloud with assigned parts. A system of substitute or 'associate' members is advocated as a solution to occasional inevitable absenteeism from the regulars, and the amount of dues—a guinea for the regulars, half that for the associates—is suggested. On weeks following the readings, meetings are devoted to criticism of the play just read, with reports from the members on a set of topics to be researched for each play.[22]

In a chapter somewhat misleadingly titled 'Some Minor Matters', Griffiths sounds that note of moral earnestness that is the unmistakable signifier of the high bourgeois culture of the period:

In some societies entertainments of a nature lighter than that of the ordinary meetings are sometimes held. Even a society so serious as the New Shakspere Society had, as long as it could afford it, an annual musical entertainment. These diversions, probably, in all cases contain an element of danger. Introduced often, they would doubtless tend to the demoralisation of the more regular work. (p. 53)

On the other hand meetings which are 'cold, formal, and dry' are to be avoided (p. 54); tea is normally served first (p. 26). And some concession to levity may safely be made on occasion:

An annual dinner might be permitted. Possibly a reading in winter, to which the public would be admitted, or one or two private open-air readings in the summer, might be desirable introductions. But trivialities, such as regular musical evenings, members citing their favourite passages or setting and working out Shakspere-puzzles, and the like, should be all sternly discountenanced. (p. 54)

---

[22] Listed in alphabetical order: aesthetic criticism; anachronisms; animals; arts and sciences; biblical and religious allusions; classical and mythical allusions; coins, weights, and measures; demonology and witchcraft; dress and social customs; early dramatic representations; fine art; geography; grammar; historical references; law and heraldry; meat and drinks; medicine and surgery; metre and authorship; music and ballads; oaths and exclamations; personal histories; plants; play-craft; puns and jests; rare words and phrases; satire and irony; similes and metaphors; sources and history; sports and pastimes; trade and commerce; tradition and folklore; and 'various readings' (37–8). The author does note of his topics that 'this plan has, I think unfortunately, fallen much into disuse', but he recommends that 'half-a-dozen short, departmental reports' grace every critical session, particularly to encourage participation from 'the most busy, the most nervous, or the most recent critics' (p. 38).

It is impossible to avoid being amused at the tone and the nearly parodic quality of this undertaking, but we should also make an effort to appreciate the rather extraordinary qualities of the enterprise described in Griffiths's book. This serious and systematic study of Shakespeare's texts is being undertaken independently of any academic institution and entirely within civil society on a voluntary basis as a means of self-cultivation and of contributing to a high-minded sense of cultural mission. It is participatory and—discounting for the moment the 'pre-selection' which the British class-system imposed in advance on who the members would be—egalitarian in its basic mode of operation. For example Griffiths emphasizes the need for each member to come to his or her own judgement and to avoid reliance on the opinions of supposed authorities (pp. vii, 38–9). By contemporary standards, of course, the critical suppositions that guided the members were naïve. Griffiths believed that Shakespeare's characters were 'flesh-and-blood beings whose analogues may be met with in every-day life. They are to be paralleled amongst our own friends and acquaintances . . .'. But of course such a supposition meant that the social skills of everyday life were excellent hermeneutic training and that every reader was therefore equipped with the wherewithal to contribute to the discussion.

Societies like the Clifton one described by Griffiths were widespread in the late nineteenth century in England and in America.[23] The most prestigious was undoubtedly the New Shakspere Society,

---

[23] The United States, Westfall reports, boasted 'hundreds' of Shakespeare societies, led by branches in Philadelphia (founded in 1852) and New York. On this and related topics, see Westfall, *American Shakespearian Criticism*, 4 *et passim*, Bristol, *Shakespeare's America*, 64–70, and Frances N. Teague, 'A Nineteenth-Century Shakespeare Reading Club', *Shakespeare Newsletter* (May 1977), 20. More information on the American societies is available in the letters of the American Shakespearean Joseph Crosby (1821–91), a selection of which has been published in *One Touch of Shakespeare: Letters of Joseph Crosby to Joseph Parker Norris, 1875–1878*, ed. John Velz and Frances Teague (Washington, DC: Folger, 1986).

Britain seems to have lagged behind America somewhat in forming societies, since Griffiths alludes to the need of the 'old country' to emulate the new in this regard. Griffiths's own ambition was that 'there should be a Shakspere-Society, not only in every town, but in every set of people that can get together at least a dozen men and women with any literary desires' (p. 2), but it is uncertain to what extent his ambition succeeded. The New Shakspere Society claimed nine affiliated branches after one year of existence and a total of 450 members after two years—see *New Shakspere Society: First Report, July, 1875* (*Transactions of the New Shakspere Society*, 1st ser. 2 (1874), suppl.), 5–6. But Griffiths complained of the overly 'specialist' bias of the New Shakspere Society and advocated separate but co-operating organizations such as his own, with a 'more popular basis' than the New Shakspere (pp. 355–7).

alluded to by Griffiths, which had been founded in London in 1873 through the efforts of Frederick James Furnivall, a remarkably diverse and energetic Victorian, in many ways with the same relationship to nineteenth-century literary scholarship as Josiah Wedgwood and Arkwright earlier had had to commercial manufacture. Like them, he was a systemizer and organizer who worked with already existing technology but reorganized (and 'modernized' it) by dividing it into simple procedures to be performed along a proto-assembly line, step by step.[24]

Furnivall specialized, not like modern scholars with concentrations in literary 'periods', but in devising research programmes for other specialists to pursue. During the course of his career, for example, he organized, among other things, the London Working Men's College (1852), the Early English Text Society (1864), the Chaucer Society (1868), the New Shakspere Society (1873), the Wiclif [*sic*] Society (1881), the Browning Society (also 1881), and the Shelley Society (1886), all of which performed still valued scholarly, often textual work through following a systematic plan for scholarship suggested by Furnivall. He also was instrumental in beginning the Oxford English Dictionary project. Remarkably enough, Furnivall accomplished all this on his own time without remuneration.[25] He was, in a word, a modernizer who, like a nineteenth-century industrialist, applied administrative-technical reason to create a new field of endeavour: an important segment of modern literary scholarship. But Furnivall performed his accomplishments in the context of a now vanished social milieu in which specialization and professionalization were novel and not yet fully established, and his work in the Christian Socialist movement belies any one-dimensional notion of him as a literary industrialist, a role which I stress here for obvious reasons. It is certainly striking

---

[24] The influence of contemporary industrialization on nineteenth-century Shakespeare scholarship is a theme of Aron Y. Stavisky, *Shakespeare and the Victorians: Roots of Modern Criticism* (Norman: University of Oklahoma Press, 1969), 23–49. Stavisky is particularly interested in demonstrating a continuity from eighteenth-century Enlightenment criticism to Victorian scientistic scholars like Furnivall and Fleay and then to certain strains of twentieth-century criticism, as against what he sees as the mistaken conflation of the Victorians with Romanticism. More recently Gary Taylor has taken up the theme of the influence of nineteenth-century scientism — and political gradualism — on the Shakespeare scholarship of the era — see *Reinventing Shakespeare*, 153–60.

[25] 'Furnivall, F. J.', *The Dictionary of National Biography*, Supplement (Jan. 1901–Dec. 1911), ed. Sidney Lee (London: Oxford University Press, 1912). He had inherited a considerable sum from his father who, Sidney Lee tells us, had made a fortune keeping a private 'lunatic asylum' in his house, but the younger Furnivall lost much of the inheritance when a bank holding substantial parts of his fortune failed.

to a modern reader to notice the vigorous productivity of voluntary institutions of civil society in bringing about modernization—a process, which, of course, was to doom such institutions.

The New Shakspere Society

The programme which Furnivall gave the New Shakspere Society upon its founding in 1873 was a complexly over-determined one which united several strands of Victorian culture and was in many ways similar to Griffiths's largely recreative, more provincial society. Furnivall summed up the aims of the new society thus: 'To do honour to SHAKSPERE, to make out the succession of his plays, and thereby the growth of his mind and art; to promote the intelligent study of him, and to print Texts illustrating his works and his times, this *New Shakspere Society* is founded.'[26] Furnivall's research programme put great emphasis on the use of 'versification tests'—the statistical study of the metrics of Shakespeare's plays—in order to settle remaining questions on the chronology and authorship of several 'problems' in the canon of Shakespeare's works, and it is because of the controversies engendered by its championing of a statistical, 'scientific' method that the New Shakspere Society is remembered today—if it is at all. Before examining versification and its polemics, however, it is probably well to point out that in Furnivall's original research-scheme, the tests were purely one means of attaining the end of settling questions of chronology as a preparation for the really serious work of understanding the growth of Shakespeare's mind—'the only sound method' of literary study as far as Furnivall is concerned. In some ways Furnivall simply wanted to do for Britain what had already been accomplished for Shakespeare studies in Germany. He writes:

It is a disgrace to England that while Germany can boast of a Shakspere Society which has gathered into itself all its country's choicest scholars, England is now without such a Society. It is a disgrace, again, to England that even now 258 years after SHAKSPERE's death, the study of him has been so narrow, and the criticism, however good, so devoted to the mere text and its illustrations, and to studies of single plays, that no book by an Englishman exists which deals in any worthy manner with SHAKSPERE as a whole. ... The profound and generous 'Commentaries' of Gervinus—an honour to a German to have written, a pleasure to an Englishman to read—is still the only book known to me that comes near the true treatment and the dignity of its subject,

[26] Furnivall, 'The New Shakspere Society (Founder's Prospectus Revised)', 6.

or can be put into the hands of the student who wants to know the mind of SHAKSPERE. (p. 6)

Most readers will need reminding that Gervinus's now little-read monumental study of Shakespeare's complete works was widely praised in the late Victorian period in England, not only by Furnivall, but by most of his generation.[27] Gervinus was a German professor and therefore was himself a product of the professionalization of literary studies in the German university system of the nineteenth century, his systematizing criticism made possible both by the German state-created educational bureaucracy and by the Hegelian synthesis in German cultural studies. His work was a chronologically ordered discussion of Shakespeare's plays with a view to discovering Hegelian patterns of growth and development into a logically complete philosophical system in the complete works. Gervinus had incidentally made use of versification tests to aid him in arriving at the chronology of the works that he needed to carry out his study, but the tests were decidedly subordinated to the 'higher' philosophical and aesthetic criticism. In fact Gervinus's work is a perfect example of criticism informed by what Ricardo J. Quinones has called the 'historical values' that dominated the late nineteenth-century realist aesthetic paradigm—and a good deal of its philosophy and science; as Quinones argued in two connected works to which I will recur in Chapter 2, the historical values included the privileging of chronologically ordered narrative with an emphasis on historical continuity and growth and a concomitant valorization of logic, character, and responsibility.[28]

Furnivall, like most of his generation of Shakespearians (notably including Dowden[29] and Bradley) was equally steeped in the historical values which were destined to be overthrown in the Modernist revolu-

---

[27] G. C. Gervinus, *Shakespeare Commentaries*, trans. F. E. Bunnett, rev. edn. (London: Smith, Elder, 1877). Furnivall wrote the introduction to a lower-priced reprint, which he hoped to popularize further in England. The vast influence of Gervinus on English and American Shakespeare scholarship was forcibly obscured by the anti-German revisions of the World War I period.

[28] Ricardo J. Quinones, *The Renaissance Discovery of Time* (Cambridge: Harvard University Press, 1972) and *Mapping Literary Modernism: Time and Development* (Princeton, NJ: Princeton University Press, 1985).

[29] It is in fact possible in this regard to see Dowden's still quite readable biography of Shakespeare, with its division of the life and works into unitary but organically connected periods (the apprenticeship of the early plays, a worldly phase connected to the *Henry IV* plays, a dark phase connected to the tragedies, and a serene last period of the late romances) as the culmination of the Society's programme—see Taylor, *Reinventing Shakespeare*, 160–8.

tion of the next century. Furnivall was quite explicit in his desire to follow Gervinus's example of subordinating 'lower' (technical) criticism to 'higher' (aesthetic) criticism in promoting the Society's own versification tests, but he could not import German social relations and traditions to England along with German cultural productions. In the event, he succeeded in demonstrating once more that technique can take on a life of its own, independent of the structures that would contain and subordinate it.

At the first meeting of the New Shakspere Society (Friday, 13 March 1874), Furnivall introduced two papers to be read which he believed represented two of the main directions Shakespeare research should take. The first paper was F. G. Fleay's study of Shakespeare's versification and its relation to questions of authorship and chronology—a subject, as we have seen, central to Furnivall's research programme. The second was a presentation by Richard Simpson, 'The Politics of Shakespeare's Historical Plays'.[30] The second subject—the 'political background' of Shakespeare's plays—was in the long run to play a central role in the professionalization of Shakespeare studies, as we shall see shortly and in Chapter 4. But in the late Victorian period it caused less notice than the now almost forgotten programme of versification analysis of which Fleay—the 'industrious flea' to his colleagues—soon made himself a chief expert.

Frederick Gard Fleay (1831–1909) came from a less privileged social position than Furnivall; Fleay's father's occupation is described by Sidney Lee in the *DNB* as 'linen-draper',[31] and Fleay had to struggle to get a Cambridge education (his parents moved to Cambridge to help support him). After a distinguished academic career that included mathematical and classical training, Fleay became a deacon and Anglican priest and began to work in secondary education as a teacher and headmaster, publishing several works on education and spelling reform. In 1884 he left the Church of England, having grown sceptical of many of its doctrines and having come under the influence of—what else?—the positivism of Comte.

Encouraged by Furnivall to join the New Shakspere Society at its founding in 1873, Fleay devoted the next twenty years of his life to Shakespeare studies, with metrical or versification tests his specialty.

---

[30] Richard Simpson, 'The Politics of Shakespeare's Historical Plays', *Transactions of the New Shakspere Society*, 1st ser. 2 (1874), 396–441.
[31] 'Fleay, Frederick Gard', *The Dictionary of National Biography*, Supplement (Jan. 1901–Dec. 1911), ed. Sidney Lee (London: Oxford University Press, 1912).

It is significant that both Furnivall and Fleay had mathematical training as undergraduates. Furnivall repeatedly claimed that his literary scholarship was an application of the scientific method: 'The study of Shakspere's work must be made natural and scientific', he wrote, '... and I claim that the method I have pursued is that of a man of science.'[32] On another occasion Furnivall wrote that Shakespeare's text must be approached 'as the geologist treats the earth's crust, as the comparative anatomist treats the world'.[33] His method also required the work in scansion associated with the classical training of nineteenth-century higher education, and it is doubtful for that reason that 'metrical tests' will ever be revived as a scholarly activity, even though they are still cited in textual and chronological discussions.

The heart of the method involves producing tables of statistics recording the percentages of the verse lines of each play employing certain metrical characteristics.[34] The most frequently used categories were end-stopped vs. runover lines, ten-syllable lines vs. lines with a 'feminine' (extra syllable) ending, and rhymed vs. unrhymed lines. Fleay concentrated on counting syllables and rhymes, while Furnivall studied the changing proportions of end-stopped and unstopped lines.[35] This labour-intensive method of analysis was peculiarly suited to the scientistic and positivistic tenor of the times in its mathematical procedures at the same time that it promised to provide a key to the growth and development of Shakespeare's mind and art—that analogue to Hegelian philosophy and to evolutionary theory which, as we have seen, Furnivall believed the 'only sound method' of literary study. Furnivall put it this way: 'Fortunately for us, SHAKSPERE has himself left us the most satisfactory—because undesigned—evidence of the growth in the mechanism of this art, in the gradual changes in his

[32] Quoted in 'Furnivall, Frederick James', *The Reader's Encyclopedia of Shakespeare*, ed. O. J. Campbell and E. G. Quinn (New York: Crowell, 1966).

[33] Furnivall, *The Literary World*, 9 July, 1887; quoted in Louis Marder, *His Exits and His Entrances* (Philadelphia, Pa.: Lippincott, 1963), 133.

[34] An early but uninfluential instance of verse-testing was by Richard Roderick in 1758, but the method was reinvented and entered Shakespeare studies through the work of Edmund Malone, who used versification analysis in 1778 to help establish the chronology of Shakespeare's works for which he is well known. A more elaborate set of tests was used in 1833 by William Spalding. The New Shakspere Society credited James Spedding, in his article 'Who Wrote Henry VIII?' (*Gentleman's Magazine*, August 1850) as the founder of the method. On all this, see J. Isaacs, 'Shakespearean Scholarship', in *A Companion to Shakespeare Studies*, eds. Harley Granville-Barker and G. B. Harrison (1934; repr. Cambridge: Cambridge University Press, 1949), 316.

[35] Griffiths, *Evenings with Shakspere*, 350–1.

versification during his life, changes that must strike every intelligent reader, and which I cannot at all understand the past neglect of'.[36]

In such a critical paradigm 'Shakspere' is still a part of Nature, as he was for the Romantics. The difference lies in the shift from Romantic empathetic and hermeneutical relations with Nature to the instrumental techniques of positivistic science. And with such a shift in methodology, as Habermas has emphasized, comes a shift in the epistemological 'interest' or motivation underlying the knowledge. Behind the apparently 'neutral' and 'disinterested' rhetoric of science lies a power relationship and an interest of control and manipulation. The same shift is apparent in the professionalization of Shakespeare criticism undertaken by the New Shakspere Society. 'Shakspere', the 'chosen poet' of Nature for Coleridge, becomes a natural object, subject to the rules of classification and enumeration of instrumental reason.

As I have emphasized, Furnivall, like Gervinus before him, sought to keep the instrumentalist methods clearly subordinated to hermeneutic criticism. But the verse tests proved more corrosive and contentious than he had imagined. The supposition, made by Furnivall, that the verse-tester knows something that the author did not—in this case, the gradual change over time of verse techniques—effects a subtle but decisive shift in authority, from 'author' to 'critic'. For the scientist, after all, Nature is dumb and must speak through her interpreters. If Shakspere is Nature, then he too must be 'supplemented'. It was not long before the use of metrical tests to provide solutions for the correct chronologization of Shakespeare's plays passed over into authorship questions. The era of 'disintegration' in Shakespeare studies had begun, and Shakespeare, who would survive the contemporaneous assaults of the Baconians, nearly succumbed to the polemics of a group of literary 'men of science'—with uncanny parallels to late twentieth-century literary professionals.

The Strange Case of Disintegration

With the statistical methods of versification at his disposal, Fleay and like-minded literary 'scientists' began to turn their attention to the authorship problem in the Shakespeare canon. There was already precedent for doubting the canonicity of several plays—*Titus Andronicus* and the *Henry VI* plays in particular (and in fact none of the

[36] Furnivall, 'The New Shakspere Society', 7.

disintegrators ever questioned the notion of canonicity or authenticity; they simply classified the Folio texts, or many of them, as inauthentic). Fleay signalled his readiness to use the metrical tests to settle questions of the canon at his very first presentation before the New Shakspere on 13 March 1874:

There are two ends to be served by [metrical tests]. If an author has distinctly progressed in the manipulation of his art, if he has different manners of work in different periods of his life, such tables are very valuable for determining the chronological order of his productions. This is the main use which the Director of our New Shakspere Society [Furnivall] anticipated from the application of metrical tests, and the table I have formed for Shakespeare's [*sic*] plays will, I have no doubt, be useful for this purpose. But the far more important end from my point of view will be the determination of the genuineness of the works traditionally assigned to a writer. These metrical tests made me suspect the genuineness of the *Taming of the Shrew*, parts of *Timon*, *Pericles*, and *Henry VIII*, when I was not aware that they had ever been suspected. . . .[37]

The application to questions of authorship was not really so big a leap. If quantitative measurements could detect stylistic changes over the career of a single author, why could they not be relied on to detect as well the disparate verse-styles of different authors, particularly in the context of unquestioned Enlightenment notions of a unitary and transcendant individual author? Fleay was the most insistent that the tests used should eliminate all question of subjective judgement as far as possible, and consequently he favoured such relatively 'objective' methods as counting the number of rhymes, syllables, and stresses—as against attempts to tabulate pauses in the line or other procedures 'which partly depend on the aesthetic sense of the critic and are consequently indefinite as to quantity'.[38] Of course, as practice soon showed, even the methods advocated by Fleay involved such far from definite matters as Elizabethan pronunciation, particularly of proper names. In addition, Fleay himself apparently changed his mind about certain classifications when, years after his first analysis, he issued revised tables.[39] But Fleay was convinced that scientific training could

[37] F. G. Fleay, *Shakespeare Manual* (1876; repr. New York: AMS Press, 1970), 126.
[38] Ibid., p. 108.
[39] See J. M. Robertson, *The Shakespeare Canon* (London: Routledge, 1922), 7. Robertson, who was certainly sympathetic to Fleay's cause, wrote, 'All counting of double-endings is somewhat insecure, inasmuch as there are a number of doubtful words, capable of being read either as monosyllables or as dissyllables; a number more which may be read as either dissyllables or trisyllables; and a number of lines of which the scansion may be varied, so as to make them either irregular or regular' (p. 7).

overcome such problems: 'The great need for any critic who attempts to use these tests is to have had a thorough training in the Natural Sciences, especially in Minerology, classificatory Botany, and above all, in Chemical Analysis. The methods of all these sciences are applicable to this kind of criticism, which, indeed, can scarcely be understood without them.'[40]

To illustrate the procedures of disintegration, let me take one case—and one to which I will recur in the last chapter—that of *Timon of Athens*. Fleay divides the play—by what means the divisions were first arrived at is significantly *not* explained—into two sections, with certain acts and scenes assigned to Shakespeare, the remaining (scattered) acts and scenes to an unknown hand. The analysis of the metre produces the following argument:

> The rhythm of the two portions of the play differs in every respect. The Shakespeare parts are in his third style (like *Lear*), with great freedom in the rhythm, some 4 and 6 syllable lines, some Alexandrines with proper caesuras, and rhymes where the emphasis is great, at the end of scenes, and occasionally of speeches in other places. The other parts have irregularities, both in defect and excess, of every possible kind. There are lines of 8 and 9 syllables, Alexandrines without caesura, imperfect lines in rhyming couplets, broken lines preceding rhymes, and other peculiarities, not one of all which is admitted in Shakespeare's rhythmical system.[41]

The problem is, of course, that the same evidence can be and has been interpreted in any number of ways: that Shakespeare left a play unfinished, parts in rough draft; that he was revising another playwright or a second playwright was revising him;[42] that he was revising an older play of his own; that the 'roughness' and irregularities are part of the over-all aesthetic effect of the play and were designed by Shakespeare as such. It has been the failure of textual criticism to have devised procedures to settle such disputes that is partially responsible for the demise of 'disintegration'. The other reason, if I may anticipate

---

[40] Fleay, *Shakespeare Manual*, 108.

[41] Ibid., p. 205.

[42] Candidates for the 'second playwright' of *Timon* have included Thomas Heywood, George Chapman, Thomas Middleton, Cyril Tourneur, and John Day. Modernist twentieth-century scholarship, with its assumptions of the organic unity of texts, largely abandoned the two-author theory. More recently, however, a version of it was revived in 1975 by David J. Lake, *The Canon of Thomas Middleton's Plays: Internal Evidence for the Major Problems of Authorship* (Cambridge: Cambridge University Press, 1975), 279–86, and several contemporary scholars have followed suit in supporting the two-author hypothesis and Middleton as the second playwright, as Postmodernist attitudes toward textuality come to the fore.

myself, is its replacement by critical paradigms for which such questions are simply beside the point.

Before he was finished with his analysis of the Shakespeare canon, Fleay had pronounced three plays as 'works which he probably never wrote a line of'—*Titus Andronicus, 2 Henry VI*, and *3 Henry VI*; two plays with only 'isolated scenes' by Shakespeare—*1 Henry VI* and *Edward III*; three plays begun by Shakespeare and finished by others—*Timon of Athens, Pericles*, and *Troilus and Cressida*; two plays jointly written with Fletcher—*Henry VIII* and *The Two Noble Kinsmen*; and several other anomalies it were useless to record here.[43]

Fleay, however, was to be done one better by his disciple J. M. Robertson (1856–1933), a younger man who lived well into the twentieth century but who certainly should be counted as another of the extraordinary lay literary scientists of the Victorian era. Robertson, born on the Isle of Arran, left school at the age of thirteen and became a widely read, self-educated man. After working for a newspaper as a young man, he was drawn to the journalistic organ of a group of radical free-thinkers, hostile to orthodox religion and conservative politics. Robertson eventually became editor of the *National Reformer*, the voice of the free-thinkers, and then a Member of Parliament as a Liberal 1906–18. As well as works in the history of free-thought and in political theory, Robertson wrote several books in Shakespearian studies and was taken seriously indeed as a scholar—perhaps his most eminent endorser was the young T. S. Eliot in the opening of the famous essay '"Hamlet" and His Problems'. In his late years he concentrated on Shakespeare studies and produced the last volumes of the disintegrators' case to a world that had shifted paradigms decisively away from his methods and suppositions.

In his 1930 'conspectus', *The Genuine in Shakespeare*, Robertson summed up a lifetime of study and analysis in the tones of one who knew his battle had been lost. But he persisted, railing against 'the orthodox' and 'Foliolaters' for their pig-headedness in not recognizing that, of all the works of the Shakespeare canon, perhaps only *A Midsummer Night's Dream* was completely and entirely Shakespeare's own creation. This was a kind of *reductio ad absurdum* for the concept of the authentic unitary author, but Robertson never developed that poss-

---

[43] A summary is provided in his *Shakespeare Manual*, 58–61, and the authorship of each play briefly discussed (along with other questions) in separate short sections on the individual plays, pp. 22–57.

ibility. Instead he pursued his own strict logic—it all depends on what one makes of the 'sources' Shakespeare used, and Robertson simply took a particularly strict, post-Enlightenment view of authorial originality.[44]

Clearly disintegration for Robertson was of a piece with the political and religious demystifications to which he had devoted his life. What is striking in reading Robertson in the present context is how far he has been forced to retreat from Fleay's ideal of applying the scientific method to settle questions of chronology and authorship. Writing in the wake of numerous polemics and wrangles, Robertson has given up on the idea that the kind of consensus that Kuhn saw as the essence of a genuine science could ever be achieved among the various disintegrators. For Robertson, only an ear for verse and the taste to distinguish between great and lesser poetry can allow us to distinguish the 'genuine' Shakespeare from his (numerous) collaborators. Robertson had attempted and failed to reconcile Fleay's metrical statistics with those of his rival König's (pp. 6–8); he has few hopes that agreement can ever be achieved on such matters. He retreats, then, into his own version of the traditionalist Matthew Arnold's touchstone method of criticism.

The Traditionalists Strike Back

'Traditionalists' like Arnold, of course, had not been silent during the age of disintegration. One of the most memorable moments of Victorian scholarly wrangling, in fact, was the set-to between Furnivall and the poet and critic A. C. Swinburne. It was a dispute which, because of the violence of its rhetoric, has attracted the attention of several writers.[45] And in many ways it is one of the first explicit debates between those two now familiar antagonistic sides of literary studies, the generalist and the specialist, the subjectivist and the objectivist. In addition to polemics in *The Athenaeum*, Swinburne devoted an entire book to his case against Fleay and Furnivall's 'versification tests'. *A Study of Shakespeare* is a discussion of Shakespeare's style across the entire canon with emphasis on verse technique as perceived by 'the ear' rather than 'the fingers'. Drawing on his reputation as a master of

---

[44] I am indebted to Margreta de Grazia for this observation.

[45] See for example Oscar Maurer, 'Swinburne vs. Furnivall', *University of Texas Studies in English* (1952), 86–96; Stavisky, *Shakespeare and the Victorians*, 77–107; and Marder, *His Exits and His Entrances*, 131–7.

verse sound-effects, Swinburne presented his own, 'traditional'
credentials of expertise:

Properly understood, this that they call the metrical test is doubtless, as they
say, the surest or the sole sure key to one side of the secret of Shakespeare; but
they will never understand it properly who propose to secure it by the
ingenious device of numbering the syllables and tabulating the results of a
computation which shall attest in exact sequence the quantity, order, and
proportion of single and double endings, of rhyme and blank verse, of regular
lines and irregular, to be traced in each play by the horny eye and the callous
finger of a pedant. 'I am ill at these numbers'; those in which I have sought to
become an expert are numbers of another sort; but having, from well nigh the
first years I can remember, made of the study of Shakespeare the chief
intellectual business and found in it the chief spiritual delight of my whole life,
I can hardly think myself less qualified than another to offer an opinion on the
metrical points at issue.[46]

   Granting the new Victorian interest in verse techniques, we should
have no difficulty seeing that Swinburne is working from within a late
version of the Romantic critical paradigm. For him, as for Coleridge,
Shakespeare is nature herself, imaged this time in a borrowed
metaphor from Victor Hugo on Shakespeare: 'The greatest poet of our
age has drawn a parallel of elaborate eloquence between Shakespeare
and the sea; and the likeness holds good in many points of less significance than those which have been set down by the master-hand' (p. 1).
The image enables him to go on to distinguish two opposed attitudes
to take in seeking to understand the sea/Shakespeare: in effect, the
instrumental and the hermeneutic, the objective and the subjective.
Swinburne, whose letters show evidence of a lively interest in, and
respect for, scientific learning,[47] is anxious not to deny the necessity of
instrumental reason. But like so many other figures of counter-
Enlightenment, he wants to define its boundaries securely:

The material ocean has been so far mastered by the wisdom and the heroism
of man that we may look for a time to come when the mystery shall be manifest
of its furthest north and south, and men resolve the secret of the uttermost
parts of the sea: the posers also may find their Columbus. But the limits of that
other ocean, the laws of its tides, the motive of its forces, the mystery of its

   [46] Algernon Charles Swinburne, *A Study of Shakespeare* (1909; repr. New York: AMS,
1965), 6–7.
   [47] Stavisky, *Shakespeare and the Victorians*, 87.

unity and the secret of its change, no seafarer of us all may ever think thoroughly to know. No wind-gauge will help us to the science of its storms, no lead-line sound for us the depth of its divine and terrible serenity. (p. 2)

Here we find even Nature a concession to the other side, so long as poetry and Shakespeare are divided off from the domains of scientism. This is certainly an instance of what Matthew Arnold described in his own way as the substitution of art and poetry for a no longer adequate religion as the chief means of giving life its meaning, very much an instance of *fin-de-siècle* aestheticism. Properly 'modernized', as we will see in the next chapter, it will be the chief strategy of twentieth-century Modernists in their own successful assault against scientism in literary studies. Here, for Swinburne, God is, in effect, in the unquantifiable *je ne sais quoi* of Shakespeare's blank verse.

Ultimately, the demise of disintegration was to come about from the convergence of two powerful objections: one was developed from the kind of arguments promoted by Swinburne and like-minded humanists; the second came, in the name of science, from within the ranks of textual critics themselves. Taken together, these two developments laid the basis for the subsequent triumph of Modernism in Shakespeare studies which the remainder of this volume will examine.

In the short run, the polemics had their own consequences. The contentious Furnivall was unable to take Swinburne's attempt to delegitimate his own expertise without a fight, and a series of polemics resulted. Furnivall called Swinburne, punningly, 'Pig's Brook'; Swinburne retorted in kind by calling Furnivall 'Brothels-dyke' (from the Latin *fornix* and *vallum*). Swinburne wrote a funny and malicious parody of a New Shakspere meeting,[48] and Furnivall widened his attack by including Halliwell-Phillipps as the object of his contumely in the pamphlet *The 'Co.' of Pigsbrook and Co.* As a result, the New Shakspere Society lost members and influence. Fleay had his own set of separate grievances with Furnivall, and he too left the Society.

Is it mere coincidence that the attempt to found a 'science' of 'Shaksperology'[49] was made by men of such fierce contentious spirit and was marked by a rhetoric of railing and vituperation at every point?

[48] 'Report of the Proceedings on the First Anniversary Session of the Newest Shakespeare Society', Appendix, *A Study of Shakespeare*, 276–309.

[49] This term was coined by a member of the New Shakspere as one which, though admittedly barbaric, denoted a 'just and true idea' of the scientific approach needed in the field to establish facts and causes of facts. See Thomas Tyler, 'Shakspere Idolatry', *Transactions of the New Shakspere Society*, 1st ser. 12, Part 2 (1887–92), 191–212. The paper was read at a society meeting in October 1888.

I think not: the professionalization of literary studies implies changes which almost guarantee polemics, whether in our own era or the Victorian age.

One important reason for disputation was the new importance of the expert himself as a source of knowledge. Disintegration brought out the significance of this shift in dramatic and extreme fashion by under-mining the authority of the author and canon as supreme sources of signification. The disintegrators' 'Shakspere' could no longer be the secular Bible of the English-speaking world[50] because it had been de-centred, no longer the great example of organic unity that Coleridge and Swinburne assumed it to be. It was an effect to be accounted for, a bit of inert nature to be spread out and classified. In the long run, as Swinburne saw, this would mean that Shakespeare would no longer be a living part of contemporary culture; he would become instead the property of experts. Instead of guaranteeing the authenticity of the secularly sacred texts of the national poet, the disintegrators were undermining them, displaying a subversive tendency within pro-fessionalism that would lie dormant after them until our own era.

Even though they were amateurs, their positivist ideology was highly professionalist in its implications. For example the set of suppositions that led the 'public' to make Shakespeare its contemporary were false-hoods to be unsentimentally rectified, starting with the premise that the texts of the plays were easily accessible to the common reader. Only an expert was now qualified to know, in Robertson's phrase, 'the genuine in Shakespeare'. Hence, the authority of the (scientific) critic is everything, the old authority of the text and author nothing. From the Victorians to the present, criticism has tended both to oscillate and to seek an accommodation between this reductive objectivism of pro-fessionalism and an uncritical hermeneutics of subservience to tradi-tion—bad subjectivity following from bad objectivity, as a Hegelian might put it.

In this situation are contained the seeds of two separate sorts of polemics, both kinds of which may be observed in the Victorian age— and in our own.

There are first of all the seeds of polemics among the disintegrators.

---

[50] Shakespeare was not the only central Western author to be put in question in this period: both the Homeric poems and the various texts that make up the Bible were analysed in this period, and the 'disintegrating' conclusions, casting grave doubt on the received traditions of a single Homer and of Moses' authorship of the first books of the Bible, have now themselves become received wisdom in subsequent scholarship.

In the absence of a shared, authoritative paradigm, everything hinges on the authority of individual critics. In the case of disintegration, no single paradigm was ever established; proto-paradigms were offered by specific individuals who vied for authority and hegemony. Inevitably a personalization of pre-paradigm debate occurred. Furnivall had polemics, not only with Swinburne, but with Fleay. In the last act of the drama of disintegration, Robertson took on the world. The failure to constitute a shared paradigm created a *bellum omnium contra omnes*.

Second are the seeds of a larger debate, one which continues, in different form, in our own time. The death of the author and his replacement by the professional critic is bound to lead to objections from humanists whose reactions to modernity have led them to see art and literature as Utopias resistant to the commodification and colonization of the life-world brought about by capitalist modernization. For such critics the Modernizers at best simply miss the main point about literature, and at worst—and disintegration was, until recent years, the worst case actualized—they undermine the ramparts of Utopia. Swinburne is a perfect example: he is willing to concede Nature itself to the enemy, so long as the god of unquantifiable versification in Shakespeare is unmolested. But pressed on this point, his response will be tenacious and fierce. This anger is surely symptomatic and displaced in a complex set of exchanges in which 'life' has been replaced by 'literature', and the result is a faintly ridiculous overloading of the literary as the last repository of value in the wake of modernization (Swinburne is hardly the last to undertake this stance— it becomes in fact the major thrust of much of mainstream Modernist criticism in the twentieth century, as we shall see). At the same time, however, as an intimation of the sterilizing and dehumanizing effects of modernization on daily life under bureaucratic capitalism, it is surely raising a much needed, if ambiguous protest against something now coming into sharper focus only in our own era, in both capitalist and 'socialist' societies: the impersonal workings of instrumentalized power.

In the midst of his overkill reply, Swinburne manages to sound both populist and élitist notes in succession, invoking both tradition and indignation at what amounts to a robbing of the general public of what had until the new professionalization been its common property:

Once admitted as a principle of general application, there are no lengths to which [disintegration] may not carry, there are none to which it has not carried, the audacious fatuity and the arrogant incompetence of tamperers with the authentic text. Recent editors who have taken on themselves the high office of guiding English youth in its first study of Shakespeare have proposed to excise or to obelise whole passages which the delight and wonder of youth and age alike, of the rawest as of the ripest among students, have agreed to consecrate as examples of [Shakespeare's] genius at his highest.... words that for centuries have touched with fire the hearts of thousands in each age since they were first inspired—words with the whole sound in them of battle or a breaking sea, with the whole soul of pity and terror mingled and melted into each other in the fierce last speech [Macbeth's] of a spirit grown 'aweary of the sun,' have been calmly transferred from the account of Shakespeare to the score of Middleton. And this, forsooth, the student of the future is to accept on the authority of men who bring to the support of their decision the unanswerable plea of years spent in the collation and examination of texts never hitherto explored and compared with such energy of learned labour . If this be the issue of learning and industry, the most indolent and ignorant of readers who retains his natural capacity to be moved and mastered by the natural delight of contact with heavenly things is better off by far than the most studious and strenuous of all scholiasts who ever claimed acquiescence or challenged dissent on the strength of his lifelong labours and hard-earned knowledge of the letter of the text. Such an one is indeed 'in a parlous state'; and any boy whose heart first begins to burn within him, who feels his blood kindle and his spirit dilate, his pulse leap and his eyes lighten, over a first study of Shakespeare, may say to such a teacher with better reason than Touchstone said to Corin, 'Truly, thou art damned; like an ill-roasted egg, all on one side.' (pp. 19–20)

While few will be tempted to emulate the harumphing and haranguing of Swinburne, contemporary literary theory might well follow the lead of recent radical theorists of professionalization and support him, at least in general terms, in his objections to the disempowering effects of professionalism on public life. A general de-skilling of the working class has been observed as the outcome of the modernization of the workplace, and the process has extended into education and family relations.[51] From our vantage point in the late twentieth century, we can see clearly that while Swinburne's side won the battle of disintegration, it lost the war of professionalization. For better and for worse, there are no more Clifton Shakspere Societies, and even contemporary radical criticism arises from within the ideology of professionalism, in many ways blind to its own enabling assumptions.

[51] A central and important statement of this position was provided by the late Harry Braverman, *Labor and Monopoly Capital: The Degradation of Work in the Twentieth Century* (New York: Monthly Review Press, 1974). See also the collection *Between Capital and Labor*, ed. Pat Walker (Boston, Mass.: South End, 1979), particularly the opening essay in the collection, John and Barbara Ehrenreich, 'The Professional-Managerial Class', pp. 5–45.

The Rise of 'Scientific' Bibliography

In the event within Shakespeare studies, however, an accommodation between the humanists and textual criticism was worked out that produced a stable division of labour and a consensus that has, for the area of textual studies at any rate, continued up to the present period. There was never a decisive repudiation of 'verse tests' of the sort that Swinburne desired. As late as the Sixties, some college textbooks of Shakespeare's works included such tables as part of the normal apparatus with which the modern student should be acquainted. But the basic integrity of the traditional Shakespeare canon was affirmed in a series of studies by the proponents of what came to be known as 'scientific bibliography', which had the effect of establishing the authority of the Folio text at a higher level than had existed since the first attempts at Shakespeare editing in the eighteenth century. The potential symbiosis between a traditional humanist criticism reverentially interpreting received texts and a scientific criticism that would guarantee the desired cultural authenticity is not hard to see. And the new bibliographers managed to achieve what eluded the disintegrators: a shared methodology and consensus on certain results that constituted a kind of paradigm which has survived, though of course changing and evolving, to the present day. Of interest in the present context is the way in which the new paradigm largely sidestepped, rather than disproved, the arguments of the disintegrators;[52] a conjuncture of interests, which I will attempt to define shortly, served to impel the new textual hegemony of A. W. Pollard, R. B. McKerrow, W. W. Greg, and J. Dover Wilson.

The decisive event in the history of Shakespearian textual criticism that led to the downfall of disintegration was A. W. Pollard's division of the known quarto texts of Shakespeare's plays into the two still widely used categories of 'good' and 'bad' quartos. Pollard (1859–1944) was another non-academic scholar, at the time of his first Shakespearian publications a librarian at the British Museum with expertise in rare books. He was a member of another of the remarkable private literary societies begun in the Victorian Age, the Bibliographical Society. The latter was founded, not by the ubiquitous Furnivall, but by J. Y. W.

---

[52] The disintegrators were pilloried, however, by E. K. Chambers and the acerbic Greg, who disparaged their amateurism and pointed out numerous inconsistencies and even arithmetical errors—see Taylor, *Reinventing Shakespeare*, 285. But while this cast doubt, it could hardly be said to disprove the disintegrating thesis.

MacAlister in 1892; three years earlier, MacAlister had begun the journal *The Library*, which published many of the decisive arguments of the 'new' or 'scientific' bibliography and became the official organ of the Society in the 1920s. Pollard became an editor of *The Library* in 1904.[53]

Pollard's work, sustained and elaborated by the younger McKerrow and Greg, was of the sort that is paradigm-overthrowing, upsetting the scholarly orthodoxy of several earlier generations.[54] This orthodoxy had been established by Samuel Johnson[55] and elaborated by Malone and the Victorians who followed him.

Malone and the Victorians had been puzzled by the claim of the two Folio editors (Shakespeare's fellow players John Heminge and Henry Condell) to have 'cur'd' and presented 'perfect in their limbs' texts which, they said, had before been circulated through 'diverse stolne, and surreptitious copies, maimed, and deformed by the frauds and stelthes of iniurious imposters . . .'.[56] Their textual analyses proved that many of the Folio texts had themselves been set up from earlier quarto editions, and the natural reaction of nineteenth-century scholarship was to doubt the integrity of the player-editors. This widely shared scepticism about the probity of the Folio editors greatly contributed to the disintegrators' case: if the Folio editors had misled

---

[53] W. W. Greg, 'Pollard, Alfred William', *The Dictionary of National Biography*, 1941–1950.

[54] Pollard, of course, had forerunners, notably Furnivall's enemy Halliwell-Phillipps. For a nuanced and detailed account of the origins of the 'new bibliography', on which I draw, see Frank P. Wilson, *Shakespeare and the New Bibliography*, ed. Helen Gardner (Oxford: Clarendon, 1970), 11–13. A much more theoretically sophisticated account, which stresses the arbitrary and contingent in the new bibliography, is Margreta de Grazia, 'The Essential Shakespeare and the Material Book', *Textual Practice*, 2, no. 1 (Spring 1988), 69–87. And see Taylor, *Reinventing Shakespeare*, 234–8, for a differently inflected account of the new bibliography focused around Greg and linked to photography and academic scientism.

[55] Johnson's view of the Folio text is expressed in the following: 'Copied for the actors, and multiplied by transcript after transcript, vitiated by the blunders of the penman, or changed by the affectation of the player; perhaps enlarged to introduce a jest, or mutilated to shorten the representation; and printed at last without the concurrence of the author, without the consent of the proprietor, from compilations made by chance or by stealth out of the separate parts written for the theatre: and thus thrust into the world surreptitiously and hastily, they suffered another depravation from the ignorance and negligence of the printers . . . It is not easy for invention to bring together so many causes concurring to vitiate a text' (*Proposals*, 1756), 3; quoted in Wilson, *Shakespeare and the New Bibliography*, 11.

[56] 'To the great Variety of Readers', repr. in *The Riverside Shakespeare*, eds. G. Blakemore Evans *et al.* (Boston, Mass.: Houghton Mifflin, 1974), 63.

their readers concerning the textual basis of the Folio plays, then there was no reason to trust their judgement concerning what was and was not a canonical Shakespearian work.

What Pollard's division accomplished was a vindication of the Folio editors. Their reference to 'stolne' copies could be interpreted as referring to the 'bad', pirated quartos; whereas the quartos that had been used as the basis for various of the Folio texts were invariably 'good' quartos, presumably countenanced by the author or his company, and not to be included in the condemnations of Heminge and Condell. Their advertisement in the opening of the Folio was, Pollard argued, essentially correct. The 'bibliographical pessimism' of Sidney Lee's representatively Victorian approach to the text could be replaced by a 'healthy and hardy optimism'.[57] Guided by such a spirit and by his access to surviving Elizabethan and Jacobean dramatic manuscripts, Pollard was able, persuasively, if conjecturally, to suggest that many of the texts behind the Folio versions were Shakespearian autographs used as prompt-copies by the players: '. . . if what happened with other plays by other playwrights is any guide to what happened to Shakespeare's some of these prompt copies were probably in his autograph. Some of them, also, were probably *not*; but it may be claimed that at every stage in the passage of a play from Shakespeare's study the balance of probabilities is in favour of optimism.'[58] Writing thirty years after Pollard, Greg demolished the latter's argument. The three manuscript prompt-books adduced by Pollard, Greg says, are hardly typical of the period, and in any case only one of the three is an autograph—and that a 'fair' rather than a 'foul' (original draft) copy.[59] Remarkably, however, while demolishing his argument, he retains his 'optimism':

In 1923 Pollard hoped that 'Ten years hence . . . we may know more than we do now as to what these manuscripts were' that lay behind the printed editions, and his own optimistic approach has borne fruit. If not within ten years, yet now, thirty years later, we may claim to know a good deal more about Shakespeare's manuscripts than we did. And if what we have learnt has shaken some of Pollard's arguments, it has at the same time vindicated his optimism, for the position as we now see it is in a way more favourable to his underlaying thesis than that which he himself envisaged. In place of texts printed from

[57] Quoted in Wilson, *Shakespeare and the New Bibliography*, 13.

[58] A. W. Pollard, *The Foundations of Shakespeare's Text*, (London: Oxford University Press, 1923), 7.

[59] W. W. Greg, *The Shakespeare First Folio: Its Bibliographical and Textual History* (Oxford: Clarendon, 1955), 93–6.

autograph prompt-books more or less sophisticated by the book-keeper, present-day criticism is inclined to see texts printed from Shakespeare's unadulterated drafts.[60]

The evolution of position from Pollard to Greg illustrated by the above two quotations is, I believe, typical of much of the work of the 'scientific bibliography' developed in the Bibliographical Society: radical changes in 'proof', continuity in 'underlaying thesis'. Consider, to take a more recent example, the footnote affixed by Helen Gardner to her 1970 reprint of a classic description of the history of the new bibliography:

It is ironic that it is precisely in this section [on typographical evidence], where the author turned to 'the comparative security of formal bibliography', that most correction and supplementation of his article is required. His own judicious comment ... that in bibliography the 'fact may be rock-like, but the interpretation a castle of sand built on the rock' needs to be supplemented by the observation that some 'facts' have proved to be less rock-like than supposed.[61]

There is no doubt that Pollard, McKerrow, and Greg rightfully supplanted the disintegrators'—and their more modest mainstream colleagues'—version of the production of the Shakespearian quarto and Folio texts. Their approach was more concrete and less speculative than that of the disintegrators, based as it was on extensive research into the mechanics and procedures of Elizabethan playhouse and printhouse practices. Just as clearly the post-war work of Charles Hinman and Fredson Bowers[62] would appear to have rightfully extended and to a certain extent replaced that of Greg and his colleagues. And, more recently yet, under the influence of Postmodernist trends to be discussed in Chapter 5, we have taken another turn in this story, with a new textual criticism more open to 'undecidableness' and equally valid variations than was the previous work.[63]

---

[60] Ibid., p. 96.

[61] Wilson, *Shakespeare and the New Bibliography*, 34.

[62] For a recent critical account of Fredson Bowers, see Bristol, *Shakespeare's America*, 102–9.

[63] The pioneer of this new direction was E. A. J. Honigmann, *The Stability of Shakespeare's Text* (London: Edward Arnold, 1965), but it could be said to have come of age—and critical hegemony—with the recent widespread acceptance of the notion that *King Lear* exists in two separate textual versions—a position first argued by Michael J. Warren, 'Quarto and Folio *King Lear* and the Interpretation of Albany and Edgar', in *Shakespeare: Pattern of Excelling Nature*, eds. David Bevington and Jay L. Halio (Newark: University of Delaware Press, 1978) and then by Steven Urkowitz, *Shakespeare's Revision of 'King Lear'* (Princeton, NJ: Princeton University Press, 1980). See Bristol,

But as with all paradigm shifts—and I am choosing not to consider at the moment the interesting but complex question of the 'scientificity' of their procedures—that from bibliographical pessimism to optimism takes place from a complex of influences, including many that have nothing to do with the 'facts'. Clearly no 'smoking gun' was ever produced to justify the confidence in the authority of the Folio that the new bibliography promulgated. Instead, a plausible scenario for the production of the Folio was developed that was at least not falsified by known 'facts'—but, as I indicated above, the various 'proofs' were not stable and shifted over time in a Derridean process of supplementation, deferral, and transference. Looking back from 1964, Fredson Bowers commented, 'From our present point of experience ... it is genuinely sad to look back to the high confidence of a John Dover Wilson juggling the bolts of the New Bibliography like the hero of a Strauss tone poem.'[64] After an additional twenty years of anti-positivism, sadness has to be replaced with a methodologized hermeneutic of suspicion. There is, for instance, the suspicious convenience with which the new bibliographers fulfilled the desire for authority and certainty concerning the texts of a culture's secular Bible. Writing in 1949 the humanist F. E. Halliday was by no means convinced that the disintegrators had been disproved;[65] but he has grave doubts about the direction that acceptance of their arguments would take us:

With such instruments the disintegration of the canon and the theoretical reconstruction of the way in which the plays were composed is fascinating work—and a fascinating pastime—but not without danger, for once we abandon the authority of the Folio 'we have lost our only safe anchorage, and are afloat upon a wild and violent sea, subject to every wind of doctrine'.[66]

The nearly universal acceptance of the new bibliography in the light of the far from certain and stable nature of its proofs argues strongly that it fulfilled ideological functions and was welcomed as a legitimator of a desired authoritative Shakespeare. The split between science and humanism that so preoccupied the Victorians was, thanks to Greg and company, overcome, or at least rendered moot for the case of the

---

Shakespeare's America, 109–19 for an account of this shift (on which I draw here) and an argument for a complex and contingent relation between the newer bibliography and post-structuralism.

[64] Fredson Bowers, *Bibliography and Textual Criticism* (Oxford: Clarendon Press, 1964), 3; quoted in Stavisky, *Shakespeare and the Victorians*, 104.

[65] F. E. Halliday, *Shakespeare and His Critics* (London: Duckworth, 1949), 211–18.

[66] Ibid., p. 214.

Shakespeare canon. Humanism was triumphant—under the sign of
science.

Politically, the New Bibliographers were a more conservative, less
contentious group than the disintegrators. Unlike the 'free-thinking'
Robertson, the antisabbatarian Christian Socialist Furnivall, or the
resigned clergyman Fleay, Pollard, we are told, was a 'sincere church-
man' and 'deeply religious in a mode peculiarly his own'.[67] Greg, who
could be sharply critical in his reviews, had no specific religious affiliation, but he was, as F. P. Wilson put it, 'fortunate in being able to
follow his bent without the distraction of earning a living. From his
Wimbledon home he was a constant visitor to the British Museum and
in almost daily touch with Pollard and McKerrow'.[68] But he seems to
have had no other prominent public interventions than bibliographic
ones. Such characteristics complement that conserving thrust of the
group's supposedly 'scientific' work. The strong social ties among the
founding triumvirate of Pollard, McKerrow, and Greg (John Dover
Wilson, who went through an early phase that was mildly disintegrationist, but who also had important ties with the three named here,
forms a separate case) are a complicating factor, obscuring the sense in
which the three could have been said to have formed a viable
paradigm. Since, however, their work has been accepted subsequently
as of founding importance and has been widely adopted in numerous
editions and textbooks, we are probably justified in seeing the 'new
bibliography' as constituting a critical paradigm as previously described—even if, as I have suggested, its wide acceptance was based on
factors independent of its claimed (and problematic) scientificity.

Apparently, then, for more traditionally humanist critics of the late
nineteenth and early twentieth centuries, there were two different
types of 'scientific' criticism—both using the rhetoric and claiming the
rigour of the sciences of administrative-technical reason, but one successful, the other dead. The 'dead' science of disintegration proved
corrosive to the text and authority of a poet whose lack of authority
could not be countenanced. The 'live' one provided a reasoned, if
hardly iron-clad basis for raising the authority of extant Shakespeare
texts to levels unprecedented in the history of Shakespeare textual
criticism. As late as 1949, F. E. Halliday thought that the contention
between the two approaches was unsettled and that '. . . we are all

[67] Greg, *DNB*, 1941–50, 682.
[68] F. P. Wilson, 'Greg, Sir Walter Wilson', *The Dictionary of National Biography*,
1951–60.

disintegrators up to a point'.[69] In another few years, the disintegrators were all but forgotten.

Without this change, the triumphant versions of Modernist interpretation of Shakespeare to be discussed below would have required major revisions, founded as they were in an unshakeable faith in the organic unity of the texts which they analysed.

In our own day, under the influence of contemporary themes of decentring and fragmenting, disintegration begins to take on new facets. Its peculiar methodology of metrical analyses will undoubtedly be left to rest in peace, laden as it is with the residues of a vanished classical pedagogy and the internal logical contradictions between the objective and the subjective to which I have alluded previously.

But in its corrosive questioning of the organic unity of the individual plays and in its undermining of the authority of the cultural icon known as Shakespeare, disintegration seems like a strange, empiricist deconstruction *avant la lettre*. Certainly the hostility which disintegration provoked has been matched in our time by some of the initial denunciations of deconstruction by our own Modernist 'traditionalists', who saw, like their Victorian counterparts, a dangerous and philistine challenge to the one sphere of modern society that contained the values and forms now assaulted on all sides by modernization.

Unlike the disintegrators, however, contemporary deconstruction has been founded on a critique of positivism and empiricism that gives it an ultimately quite different relationship to modernization, but it is much more implicated than were the amateur disintegrators in the institutions of professionalization. But I will return to these topics in my final chapter.

The Rise of Professional Academic Critics

The conflict between traditional humanists like Swinburne and proto-professional specialists like Furnivall and Fleay might have been satisfactorily resolved in textual criticism for several generations, but it proved irrepressible elsewhere, most notably in the academic institutions which were being transformed into modern research universities during the heyday of disintegration in the late nineteenth and early twentieth centuries. The same conflict in approaches to literature that animated the polemics on disintegration was present from the beginnings of English as a subject of study in the curricula of American and

[69] Halliday, *Shakespeare and His Critics*, 214.

British higher education. Disintegration itself made no great headway in academia: American professors were too preoccupied with the study of Shakespeare's 'dramatic systems', so the commonplace went, while the Germans saw him as a philosopher, and the British as a poet. Textual studies, quite anachronistically, were dominated by non-academics until well into the twentieth century in socially conservative Britain. Other phases of literary criticism, however, rapidly migrated to the new institution of the modern university, where the generalist–specialist dispute took on new forms and meanings. Like all the other professions, that of the literary scholar-critic (the hyphenated ambiguity is, of course, very much the point of much early academic contention) sought a bureaucratic shelter after an early entrepreneurial phase that, as we have seen, depended on the independently wealthy for much of its early energy. The university was a 'natural' home for professional literary men and, indeed, multiplied their number far beyond any that Victorians could have dreamed of. In its new bureaucratic phase, many of the same tendencies that helped create disintegration and its successor, 'modern textual criticism', can be observed at work. No profession can exist without its knowledge/power, and an appropriate disciplinary practice for English studies, with Shakespeare a prominent figure to be dealt with, had to be invented.

Just a few years ago it was all but impossible to speak within the profession of literary studies of its own history. Today, thanks to the pioneering work of Richard Ohmann, the GRIP project, and now Gerald Graff, it is more possible to try to define the enormous but elusive impact of professionalization on how we read and understand such seminal cultural artefacts as the works of William Shakespeare. Let me begin with a look at Gerald Graff's recent *Professing Literature*, rich in source materials and judicious in its narrative assumptions, and offering a critique of recent radical discussions of the role of English in education. Graff has made a valuable contribution in pointing out that many contemporary radical critics[70] give too much credit to the ideological pretensions of education heroes like Arnold, I. A. Richards, or

---

[70] This is the primary emphasis of such path-breaking works as Peter Widdowson (ed.), *Re-Reading English* (London: Methuen, 1982); William Spanos, 'The Apollonian Investment of Modern Humanist Education: The Examples of Matthew Arnold, Irving Babbitt, and I. A. Richards', *Cultural Critique*, 1 and 2 (Fall and Winter 1985–6), 7–72, 105–34; Paul Bové, *Intellectuals in Power: A Genealogy of Critical Humanism* (New York: Columbia University Press, 1986); and Janet Batsleer, *et al.* (eds.), *Rewriting English: Cultural Politics of Gender and Class* (London: Methuen, 1985). I will recur to this topic in Chapter 4 in relation to recent British critiques of E. M. W. Tillyard.

T. S. Eliot by taking at face value their claims for the centrality of 'culture' in modern society (pp. 1–15). In reality professional English studies have often been a much more mundane, more tedious business, often, as the traditionalists feared in their own exaggerated way, corrosive to the pretensions of traditional culture to embody the 'lost centre' of a Western civilization ensnared in the unprecedented complexities of modern capitalism. Thus our estimates of the Arnoldian mission of English studies need to be tempered with the realization that that mission was undermined from the start by the very forms of professionalism which made it possible. It is in the dialectic between Modernist culture and modernizing professionalism that what happens to Shakespeare studies in the twentieth century can best be comprehended. Let me then briefly review the terrain covered in the discussion of Victorian scientism with a view this time of its relevance to the immense transformations of higher education that began in the late Victorian period.

By the early nineteenth century, as I noted above, a triumphant Romantic criticism had produced a Shakespeare who stood with Art and Nature defiantly in opposition to the mechanized reality of nascent industrial society. But the older Coleridge—and a host of Victorian disciples, most notably Matthew Arnold—understood the difficulty of finding a social agent for the vision that Shakespeare symbolized. Cultural traditionalists like Coleridge and Arnold despaired at the wreckage of the surviving amenities and values of traditional society in the wake of modernization. Coleridge wanted a 'clerisy', a secular caste whose occupation it would be to preserve and expand the insights of art, literature, and culture in an increasingly commercial civilization.[71] Matthew Arnold, as is well documented, saw that the recently instituted national public educational apparatus could in fact, with the right curriculum, undertake many of the tasks that Coleridge thought required the existence of a clerisy. To simplify a story which has by now been told many times,[72] English literature and Shakespeare entered the educational system in the nineteenth century as part of the effort to preserve a sense of cultural unity in the face of the fragmentation and differentiations brought on by modernization.

Paradoxically, as I have indicated, English was constituted as an Arnoldian 'centre' in an institution formed by the very fragmenting and

---

[71] On this point and in much of the general argument I am indebted to Raymond Williams, *Culture and Society, 1780–1950* (1958, repr. New York: Harper, 1966).

[72] See below, Chapter 4, for a discussion of recent literature on this topic.

corrosive forces that Arnold thought English should conjure away. At the same time that English was being introduced into the curriculum, the nature of the educational institutions of the West became transformed. The old college was giving way to the modern university; English was being professionalized.

The seminal development in the process was undoubtedly the revolution in higher education in the late nineteenth century that created the modern research-oriented University. In America the key date in this history is 1876, when the Johns Hopkins University was established in Baltimore on the model of German higher education—a development soon imitated by Harvard, Yale, and the University of Chicago.[73] The story in Britain had different rhythms but a similar outcome. From the point of view of the history of Shakespeare studies, the key change was in the nature of the college English teacher.

Before the transformation, the core of 'humanistic' education was the classics, with an emphasis on grammar and a slow march through set texts—the detail work was held to be the kind of 'strenuous mental exercise' that built character and developed the intellectual faculties, much as physical exercise developed the body.[74] The study of English literature took place largely around the edges of the main curriculum—in extra-curricular literary societies, in courses in rhetoric. English literature as such was part of the curriculum in high schools, 'practical' (non-collegiate) schools, and finishing schools before it entered the sacred groves of 'higher' learning proper. English literature and modern languages were thought to be particularly appropriate for girls and women as subjects that were less mentally 'strenuous' than Latin, Greek, and mathematics and hence suitable for ladies-in-training.[75] Many of those who taught English in the early colleges were in fact clergymen without any particular literary training. Such a teacher, wrote an early observer of American education, 'was a doctor of divinity who spoke and wrote the mother tongue grammatically, had a general "society knowledge" of the literature, and had not specialized in this or any other academic subject'.[76]

The rise of the modern university was to change all that. In a word, from the point of view of the new university, what early teachers of college English lacked was 'professionalism', and the formation of

[73] Graff, *Professing Literature*, 57.
[74] Ibid., pp. 19–35.
[75] Arthur N. Applebee, *Tradition and Reform in the Teaching of English: A History* (Urbana, Ill.: National Council of Teachers of English, 1974), 13.
[76] Quoted in Graff, *Professing Literature*, 24.

modern academic criticism is intimately entwined with the rise of a new social phenomenon and a new ideology in the late nineteenth century: the modern professional and professionalism, respectively.

In one way the professors at the new research universities were more fortunate than many of their fellow professionals in the late nineteenth century, with much less of a burden of legitimizing their services than, say, the various competing sects of the medical profession. The institutions which provided their salaries and without which the profession would have been non-existent, the colleges and universities, could point to a centuries-old history and set of traditions which, of course, lent an aura of prestige and status to what was in many ways a new social role—particularly in the case of English and the modern languages. And in addition to the prestige of its past history, the new universities benefited from the general wave of professionalization. The university was itself a key link in the overall social strategy of the entire professional movement. We have seen how credentialing was a key component in the social viability of any profession. After some experiments with licensing and examination by professional associations, more and more of the professions adopted a system of professional schools linked to liberal arts colleges and universities as the solution to the problem of standardization and legitimation in training new practitioners. The trend of requiring the professional trainees to have completed a regular liberal arts programme before beginning their professional training proper, with roots in eighteenth-century notions of gentility, also began in the nineteenth century, though it was hardly universal.[77] Thus the universities could count on a good deal of outside support in their expansion, and the result in America was a significant increase in enrolments in the 1890s, with steady expansion thereafter up until the 1960s.

Within the expanding universities, the newly constituted or re-defined English curricula also benefited from 'outside' social trends, particularly the erosion of support for classics as the centre of the undergraduate curriculum. Graff argues that the collapse of classics in the fourth quarter of the nineteenth century resulted from the increasingly revealed gap between the educational ideals of the old colleges and the changing society which they served. The classics were associated with the training of an old republican élite of patrician ambitions, which, however, became more and more removed from the power centres of American society as industrialization progressed throughout

[77] Larson, *Rise of Professionalism*, 151–5.

the nineteenth century.[78] The new universities forged links with broader social strata and undertook, in addition to training future élites (now often of different social and cultural backgrounds from the older 'bluebloods'), a mission of upward social mobility for élites of the middle classes. Out of these trends a consensus developed against the classics, but much of the educational ideology of 'general culture' and the liberal arts which had been associated with classics migrated to the new English departments.

Thus university English programmes were presented, virtually simultaneously with their births, an educational role of considerable importance, including a heavy dose of 'liberal arts' ideology. But other institutional conditions led to other ideological influences. With the hegemony in American higher education of the (Americanized) 'German model' through Johns Hopkins and its imitators, a new and powerful determinant of the new English programmes become clear: that there would have to be expanded course-work in the vernacular language supplying something of the disciplinary 'strenuous training' of the old classics courses had become clear; that English literature would come to new prominence in promoting the 'culture' of the upwardly mobile student populations also seemed certain. But the new research model of Hopkins and its followers brought about one more highly significant characteristic for the future of all literary criticism: the discipline would have to 'professionalize' and meet those requirements of disciplinary coherence and standardization already discussed. How was a professional discipline to be constituted out of the motley assortment of classical rhetoric, Enlightenment and Romantic theorizing, 'general knowledge', and literary gossip and history that had formed the English curriculum, such as it was, in the older colleges and schools? In the atmosphere of positivism and the scientific method prevailing in the new-model universities, this inevitably meant the injection of a certain scientism into the new discipline, although, as we have seen, there were from the beginning objections to this trend.

One early solution was that German import, philology.[79] Harvard's Francis James Childs, the celebrated ballad collector, was an early champion of American philological studies, and he helped Harvard develop a programme of rigorous study of modern languages with

[78] Graff, *Professing Literature*, 22.
[79] See Applebee, *Tradition and Reform*, pp. 25–9, and Graff, *Professing Literature*, 65–97, for accounts of philology in late nineteenth-century American colleges and universities.

emphasis on mastery of the medieval versions—Anglo-Saxon and Middle English, Old French, and Old High German.[80] Through the philological model, the 'strenuous' quality of the classics was imported wholesale to English. As Graff put it, 'The philologists had solved the problem that had perennially thwarted the claim of English literature to be a classroom subject: that you could not examine in it'.[81] In an MLA session in 1892, one Frederick A. Marsh noted (with a touch of sarcasm) that 'the early professors had no recondite learning applicable to English, and did not know what to do with classes in it, they can now make English as hard as Greek'.[82]

As noted, generalist opponents to the philological approach existed from the first, and their objections were eventually to help bring about the eclipse of philology as a mainstay of university English curricula. The most common objection was that the specialized and austere nature of the philological study made it unsuitable for general education. Much more appropriate for the '95%' of students who could not be counted on to display much of an interest in their professor's specialized pursuits were readings in English (and later American) literature.[83] But the great weakness of the late nineteenth-century generalists, argues Graff, was their lack of a suitable methodology, an organized knowledge/power, which could take the place of philology in the curriculum.[84] By the Nineties, disillusionment with philology was widespread. But what took its place was not the 'aesthetic' criticism dreamed of by the generalists; instead, literature programmes turned to that method that accompanied verse tests in the first meetings of the New Shakspere in 1874: historical criticism. And there is no better representative of how these trends in American higher education impacted on Shakespeare studies than the writings of E. E. Stoll (1874–1959).

E. E. Stoll: American Professional

I have already quoted Stoll's characteristically scornful prose as a symptom of the new professional consciousness in literary studies at the turn of the century. Although his specific contributions to Shakespeare criticism have long since been superseded, Stoll is still

---

[80] Applebee, pp. 26–7.
[81] Graff, *Professing Literature*, 73.
[82] Quoted in Graff, p. 74.
[83] Ibid., pp. 77–80.
[84] Ibid., p. 96.

fondly remembered for his contributions to an evolving professional methodology in literary academics,[85] and Stoll is rightly accorded a strategic place in any attempt to trace the genealogy of contemporary historical criticism in Shakespeare studies. A native of Ohio, Stoll took his Ph.D. from Harvard in 1895 and then studied in Germany. After a six-year teaching appointment at Case Western University (1906–12), Stoll settled at the University of Minnesota, where he taught until 1942 as a Shakespeare specialist. He was a prolific—and increasingly testy—author of books, mostly on Shakespeare. He had a wide following in American Shakespeare studies, although, like J. M. Robertson, he lived to see himself go out of style. He died in 1959 at the age of 85.

Stoll's solution to the problem of founding a knowledge/power for Shakespeare studies was deceptively simple; he thought that an immersion in the history and techniques of drama, with particular attention to the differences between the Elizabethan and the modern stages, was the key to understanding Shakespeare—and to teaching him. His enemy, at least in the earliest periods of his writing, was always the same: 'Romantic' criticism, particularly that of Bradley. And the great mistake of that approach, against which Stoll wrote repeatedly, was the confusion of life with art.

In this stance we can see that basic movement in the professionalization of criticism—the de-legitimation of the competence of lay readers. We have seen earlier how the Victorian Clifton Shakspere Society based its discussions on the premiss that the analogues of

[85] René Wellek, for example, says, 'Stoll has done much to put Shakespeare firmly back on the stage and to refute the pseudoproblems of modern Shakespearean scholarship, such as Iago's "motiveless malignity" or Falstaff's "courage". He has shown that there is much archaic technique in Shakespeare, who must not be judged with the standards of Ibsen or Shaw', *A History of Modern Criticism, 1750–1950*, 6 vols. (New Haven, Conn.: Yale University Press, 1955–86), vi. 69. Eastman in *A Short History of Shakespearean Criticism* remembered Stoll with one-third of a chapter and a mixed but appreciatory thumbnail evaluation: 'The most exuberant of the no-nonsense school of Shakespeare criticism in America, E. E. Stoll combines a firm historical approach, an exciting theatrical awareness, and a simplistic way of thinking, feeling, and judging' (p. 209). In *The Reader's Encyclopedia of Shakespeare*, Stoll gets a small notice, and he is praised in John Holloway's article on 'Criticism—20th Century': 'Bradley's scanty attention to the theatrical side of the plays found more sophisticated compensation in the work of E. E. Stoll ... Stoll's keen sense of dramatic stylization, of the essential difference between real world and play-world, was a valuable insight, and it is perhaps a pity that his work has not been more influential.' And most recently, Harry Levin praised Stoll as the 'scholar from whom I learned most', contrasting him favourably with Harvard's celebrated but imperious George Lyman Kitteridge. Levin saw Stoll's iconoclasm as a salubrious break with received wisdom in Shakespeare studies—see *Shakespeare and the Revolution of the Times: Perspectives and Commentaries* (New York: Oxford University Press, 1976), 17–20.

Shakespeare's characters could be found in the ordinary life of ordinary people. Stoll's stance is one of a constant denunciation of that supposition and an emphasis on the artifice and illusory qualities of art that at times seems quite contemporary, at times dogmatic and old-fashioned.

There is, in fact, a notable continuity of cantankerousness between the British disintegrators and the American Stoll, rooted in the professional arrogance each assumed in order to establish for themselves the authority that the supposed need for their expertise leeched from the text and author. The problem with Stoll, George Lyman Kitteridge told Harry Levin, was that 'he thinks he's superior to Shakespeare'.[86] The positivism of the late nineteenth century, ensconced now in the new research universities with their new disciplines of knowledge/power, speaks clearly enough in *ex cathedra* pronouncements like the following assertions from Stoll:

> The time is past for speaking of Shakespeare as utterly impartial or inscrutable: the study of his work and that of his fellows as an expression of Elizabethan ideas and techniques is teaching us better ... We know that the poet is not with Shylock, for on that point, in this play as in every other, the impartial, inscrutable poet leaves little or nothing to suggestion or surmise. As is his custom elsewhere, by the comments of the good characters, by the methods pursued in the disposition of scenes, and by the downright avowals of soliloquy, he constantly sets us right.[87]

Stoll's attempt to throw a net of one-pointed logic around Shakespeare's plays, along with his insistence that only a professional knowledge—and the testicularity to insist on it—can lead to a proper understanding and interpretation of the plays, is much cruder than the work of the generation of historical critics who would follow him, like Lily Campbell and E. M. W. Tillyard. Nevertheless, the critical methodology—the production of a single correct interpretation of the play through the guidance of an external body of knowledge—will be the dominant critical paradigm in American university English departments until the New Critical revolution of the Forties. Its positivism is not as directly scientistic, perhaps, as the mathematical procedures of the disintegrators, but its faith in the mastering power of the procedures of instrumental reason and in the transparency and univocality of meaning mark it clearly as part of the same positivist upsurge of the

[86] Levin, p. 17.
[87] E. E. Stoll, *Shakespeare Studies: Historical and Comparative in Method* (New York: Stechert, 1942) 262–3.

age of professionalism. In that methodological sense there is a clear line of transmission through the ideology of professionalism from Stoll's era to later American historical critics and to E. M. W. Tillyard (see below, Chapter 4).

Ironically Stoll himself was unable to recognize the continuity between his own positivist practice and that of the following generation of more properly historicist critics like Lily Campbell and O. J. Campbell. They were following in his footsteps with their quest for a body of lore which could be counted on to provide *the* single correct reading of the text and solve the problem of founding an adequate knowledge/power for English studies. Stoll, apparently, was not flexible enough to see in their turn away from dramatic history towards cultural and intellectual history a continuity with his own work. To him such an approach put 'art' too directly in contact with 'life'. And his notion of Shakespeare's art as essentially simple and emotional could not countenance the complexities of 'humour' psychology as elucidated by Lily Campbell and O. J. Campbell. Such professional learning, Stoll tells us scornfully, is 'antiquarianism', and violates the fundamental rule that in drama, things *must* be what they seem.[88]

Not surprisingly Stoll proved equally hostile to Modernism in literature[89] and to one of the first Modernist critical methodologies, the close reading techniques of William Empson.[90]

In the narrative I am constituting here, Stoll's *specific* disciplinary solution represents a point of equilibrium that proved short-lived. His work can be seen as expressing what gets carried over into academic criticism from the defeated Modernizers of disintegration, but in an accommodation with 'subjectivist' or hermeneutic reading techniques, rather than the scientistic mathematical analyses of the disintegrators.

In that way, at a very general level, Stoll represented the wave of the future for the study of literature in the expanding research universities

---

[88] E. E. Stoll, *From Shakespeare to Joyce: Authors and Critics; Literature and Life* (New York: Ungar, 1944), 138–45.

[89] Ibid., pp. 359–60.

[90] With his firm belief in the existence of but a single, authorized interpretation of a literary work, it is no surprise to find Stoll taking a dim view of Empson's pioneering work: ' "As if it were not enough that living poets should be unintelligible", says Mr F. L. Lucas, "our critics father the same quality in retrospect upon the dead. In a recent work with the Apocalyptic title, *Seven Types of Ambiguity*, it has been revealed to an admiring public that the more ways a poem can be misunderstood, the better it is." One couplet of Herbert's is made to mean four different things; but as Mr. Lucas thinks, so far from meaning all four at once, the passage does not mean any of them'—*Shakespeare and Other Masters* (1940; repr. New York: Russell, 1962), 6.

of the first half of the twentieth century. He found a method, through the study of the work's historical context and background, to incorporate positivism in literary studies without incurring the hostility of humanist traditionalists as the disintegrators had. He continued the project of modernizing professionalism that the disintegrators epitomized, but he jettisoned any attempt at 'Shaksperology', a hard science of Shakespeare studies. There are no tables, no statistics; at the heart of his work is a dogmatic but hermeneutic approach to reading the text, based on his expertise in a body of knowledge— which, as we have seen, meant for Stoll a knowledge of Elizabethan dramatic techniques. This solution promised to solve two of the profession's needs: it gave the teacher–critic something to teach (to the students and to the public, he became an authoritative guide to allowed and disallowed readings of Shakespeare); and it also constituted a research programme, an elementary paradigm, for other professional researchers: the body of knowledge was not closed or final; its content and contours were open to argumentation and dispute, and Stoll welcomed all to join in the fun.

Stoll's paradigm, however, proved no match against the new reading techniques being developed by G. Wilson Knight and others that would, in effect, reconstitute Shakespeare as a Modernist text; and he refused to countenance those versions of historical criticism that, as I will argue in Chapter 4, formed a secret alliance with other aspects of the Modernist programme. Positivism outlasted Stoll's long and prolific academic career, but, in the Modernist era, positivism had to find a guise less hostile to the new paradigms which swept all before them.

2

Constructing the Modernist
Paradigm and G. Wilson Knight's
Spatial Hermeneutics

From Modernizers to Modernists

The defeat of the disintegrators by the new bibliographers was a major step leading up to a paradigm shift in Shakespeare studies, but the construction of a new paradigm came slowly. It is instructive to see just how much T. S. Eliot, for example, was willing to grant to the modernizers in his brief forays into Shakespeare studies in the Twenties. Everyone remembers, in Eliot's 'Hamlet and His Problems', the famous definition of 'objective correlative' and the diagnosis that *Hamlet* 'is the "Mona Lisa" of literature'.[1] But how many remember Eliot's praise of J. M. Robertson and E. E. Stoll for moving against the 'misleading' Hamlet criticism of Coleridge and Goethe (pp. 95–6)? In fact the case Eliot sketches for his view that the play is 'an artistic failure' is the case of the disintegrators:

Mr. Robertson points out, very pertinently, how critics have failed in their 'interpretation' of *Hamlet* by ignoring what ought to be very obvious: that *Hamlet* is a stratification, that it represents the efforts of a series of men, each making what he could out of the work of his predecessors. The *Hamlet* of Shakespeare will appear to us very differently if, instead of treating the whole action of the play as due to Shakespeare's design, we perceive his *Hamlet* to be superposed upon much cruder material which persists even in the final form. (pp. 96–7)

And Eliot goes on to endorse Robertson's discussion of the supposed survival within the text of a lost version by Kyd—and even Robertson's hobby-horse thesis that the hand of Chapman must somehow be present, perhaps as an intermediary between Kyd and Shakespeare (p. 98).

That these passages in Eliot's famous essay now seem shards from some previous forgotten episode of Shakespeare criticism is powerful evidence of the sea-change that transformed Shakespeare studies over

---

[1] T. S. Eliot, 'Hamlet and His Problems', in *The Sacred Wood* (1920; repr. New York: Barnes, 1964), 95–103.

the course of the first few decades of the twentieth century. The would-be modernizers of Shakespeare gave way to a new critical paradigm: that of Modern*ism*. This process was, of course, complex and many-sided and involved continuities as well as breaks.[2] To some extent Modernism was a return to the Romantic criticism which was the target of the modernizers, but it was a return with some decisive differences, differences which will appear clearly as we shift our attention to one of the seminal figures in the construction of a Modernist Shakespeare: G. Wilson Knight.

Knight's criticism is, I believe, one of the key places where the construction of the Modernist Shakespeare can be observed at close hand. My first task, however, will be to clarify the nature of the aesthetic paradigm shift, constitutive of a change in literary periods, which I am positing as fundamental to changes in twentieth-century Shakespeare criticism beginning with Knight. Once those theoretical clarifications are established, I will turn to the concrete complexities of Knight's criticism.

Literary Periods and Paradigm Shifts

The notion of paradigm shifts can help to overcome one of the most notable gaps within the classical Frankfurt aesthetic theory I am working with: the lack of concrete literary history and periodizations in the theory. Adorno and Habermas in particular tend to speak only of one long, post-Enlightenment period of modernity, a practice clearly inadequate to account for concrete cultural history in the West.

The idea of an aesthetic paradigm increases the flexibility and dynamism of this theory by positing that, far from being constituted once and for all, the aesthetic sphere, in a complex relationship of distance and interpenetration with the rest of social life, developed its own autonomous history, manifesting a series of changes that characteristically culminate in the aesthetic revolutions we think of as the ill-understood boundaries of literary periods. It is useful to think of the aesthetic sphere as a paradigm in order to grasp it as a dynamic system of practices in an intersubjective sphere undergoing constant development, change, and revolution over time. 'Paradigm' helps us break down the false unity of the idea of a sphere and allows us to picture a

---

[2] See Gary Taylor, *Reinventing Shakespeare: A Cultural History 1642–1986* (New York: Weidenfeld & Nicolson, 1989), Chapter 5, for an amusing, suggestive, and differently inflected account of the shift to Modernism in Shakespeare studies.

complex of artistic practices the totality of which no one individual can grasp but which are constituted as separate paradigms pragmatically and heuristically—as needed, even by hazard—by artists and writers learning techniques, methods, and forms. The heuristic flexibility of Kuhn's original term, adaptable to macro- and micro-levels,[3] makes it particularly useful for getting at the concrete complexities of aesthetic development. Similarly it should be clear that what constitutes a paradigm in any given case is an intersubjective decision. That is a particular constellation of available aesthetic forms and practices must eventually be accepted by the larger interpretive community, or it is perceived as being irrelevant, outside the (usually intuitively grasped) paradigm.

The '*Weltanschauung* effect'—that often noted sense that the cultural products of an era tend to share formal characteristics as if they were all manifestations of a unitary Spirit of the Age or *Zeitgeist*, productive of a single world-view—would in this context be the outcome of the acceptance of a single aesthetic paradigm by large numbers of artists and writers. Periods of relatively unitary paradigms— where the impression of unity is not to be accounted for by the order-imposing selections of literary historians—would suggest Gramscian concepts of 'dominant' paradigms with their corollaries of 'oppositional', 'emergent', 'archaic', and so on.

In Kuhn's model of paradigm shifts in science, a period of crisis was seen to precede the scientific revolution which resolved it, a period when a number of anomalies between a theory's predicted results and experimental observation accumulated. Kuhn took some pain to demonstrate that in practice the anomalies were never as clear-cut as retrospective accounts of them might lead us to believe, and that numerous other factors entered into shifts in scientific opinions.

In the aesthetic sphere, clearly such a mechanism of change is untenable. For periods of representational art, we might posit a slowly forming gap emerging between the changing everyday life and the artistic forms seeking to represent it—clearly *one* of the factors involved in the Modernist revolution—but artistic forms can never be reduced to their relation to the social. Adorno, better than any theorist I know, grasped this point. In the first place the aesthetic paradigm is

---

[3] In later reflections, Kuhn emphasized the importance of 'small scale' paradigm shifts, not just the major ones constitutive of scientific revolutions. See 'Postscript—1969', in his *The Structure of Scientific Revolutions*, 2nd edn. (Chicago, Ill.: University of Chicago Press, 1970).

best conceived of as an archive of available forms or of representational contents understood as formal elements. Such aesthetic forms possess an inner dynamic, a self-constituted vector of change of a formal and technical sort. Adorno rightly insisted on this point over and over—art cannot be conceived as an unmediated self-expression;[4] it involves the material world and material techniques which have their own kinds of resistances and logics. The art-object is not the passive receptacle of artistic vision—or of ideology or culture, for that matter; it has its own kinds of assertiveness over its 'creator'—whether conceived as an individual or a collective. The history of art-forms has a definite autonomy. Literature is no exception to these qualities; although the materiality of language is paradoxical and elusive, it is now widely recognized.

But the changing history of art-forms is not *hermetically* autonomous. Adorno liked to say that each art-object was a unique monad, always carrying traces of the social totality in which it was embedded. In its relative autonomy, the aesthetic paradigm's changes are linked to those of social history, but neither directly nor simply. Characteristically, social history is *mediated* into the aesthetic paradigm by the displacements and transformations it works on *form*. One of Adorno's favourite examples was the degeneration of Schoenberg's twelve-tone music system, caused, Adorno thought, by a cluster of factors, including a growing technologism, a flight from freedom by composers, and a tendency toward disintegration within the dynamics of the system itself.[5] Similarly, in the discussion of G. Wilson Knight below, I will explain how a growing 'spatialization' in the techniques of Modernist literature and criticism can be understood as resulting from complex mediations from social history.

In what follows then, 'Modernism' will be treated as an aesthetic paradigm developed through artistic practice and critical reception in a dynamic that has been chronicled on numerous occasions.[6] Lentricchia with his *After the New Criticism* in particular offers in a few paragraphs a pointed description of what I call an aesthetic paradigm

[4] Theodor Adorno, *Aesthetic Theory*, ed. Gretel Adorno and Rold Tiedmann, trans. C. Lenhardt (Boston, Mass: Routledge, 1984), 11–18 *et passim*.

[5] See Allbrecht Wellmer, 'Truth, Semblance, Reconciliation: Adorno's Aesthetic Redemption of Modernity', trans. Maeve Cooke, *Telos*, 62 (Winter 1984–5), 96.

[6] Similar theories of Modernism compatible with the approach taken here, and on which I draw, are Marshall Berman, *All That Is Solid Melts into Air: The Experience of Modernity* (New York: Simon and Schuster, 1982) and Ricardo J. Quinones, *Mapping Literary Modernism: Time and Development* (Princeton, NJ: University of Princeton Press, 1985).

shift to Modernism in process (he sees it as an illustration of the workings of the Foucaultian discursive formation):

In order to write within the dominant sense of the poetic in the United States in the last decade of the nineteenth century and in the first decade of the twentieth, one had to employ a diction, syntax, and prosody heavily favoring Shelley and Tennyson. One also had to assume a certain stance, a certain world-weary idealism which one was wearing. . . . The dramatic rise of both Robinson and Frost after 1913 was not the result of a collective coming to good sense on the part of the magazine editors, critics, contemporary poets, and other instruments of a repressive poetic discipline that had confined Robinson and Frost to speaking in a void [in their early poetic careers]. (p. 199)

Lentricchia, however, is forced (uncomfortably, I believe) into the position of grouping unpublished poets in the same category as Foucault's marginalized populations of the insane, criminals, ethnic minorities, the destitute and other victims of the technology of the body (pp. 195–9); whereas it seems clear to me that precisely by virtue of the non-bodily oppression of the unpublished (an estate whose suffering is real on its own level and which I do not by any means suggest should be trivialized), they come under the operations of a different social mechanism from that of *surveillance*. Instead they are unfortunate enough to be working in a paradigm unacceptable to the hegemonic cultural institutions of their day acting as an interpretive community. In some instances such repression could clearly take on the more global and social dimensions with which Lentricchia wished to invest the paradigm's censoring and repressing processes in general—say eighteenth-century attempts to ban Voltaire. But would Lentricchia's verdict be the same, I wonder, in the case of Modernist organs turning down Georgian odes to blithe spirits? There is a kind of autonomous vector at work in the aesthetic sphere, with a certain moral dimension or latency, to be sure, but which cannot without loss be unmediatedly moralized. The idea of a paradigm shift avoids such unintentional moralism while the attempt to import Foucaultian notions of discipline into the workings of the aesthetic sphere is in this way misleading.[7]

Similarly the Foucaultian discursive formation is hermetically autonomous, while on the contrary the necessity to mediate between the

[7] Jameson advocates a similar non-moralistic approach to the paradigm shift constitutive of Postmodernism. See his 'Postmodernism, or The Cultural Logic of Late Capitalism', *New Left Review*, 146 (July–Aug. 1984), 85–6.

aesthetic and society at large is decisively important. If we posit with Adorno that the aesthetic as such came into existence as a critical and Utopian alternative to instrumental reason and capitalist discipline, we do more justice to the concrete nature of aesthetic practice and to Foucault's originality by understanding the aesthetic sphere as having other modes than the disciplinary. A hopefully more adequate notion of the differentiation and separation of art from society—that art is nevertheless founded in and conditioned by the very social relations it critically reflects on—is the guiding thread of the following account of Shakespeare in the twentieth century.

The works of interpretive criticism of Shakespeare I will examine have arisen from their separate institutional frameworks with complex interconnections to the overall social system. No one interpretative code could possibly exhaust their manifold of interpenetrations and plurality of meanings. But because they map so well with the basic instituting differentiations of the aesthetic from the social, the themes of Modernism and modernization will draw out a particularly instructive story regarding the role of literary art in twentieth-century American and British societies.

Given the complex interplay of forces involved in changes in the aesthetic paradigms, the explanation for the periodic paradigm shifts constitutive of literary periods must involve several levels and sets of complex interactions. Without pretending that they are definitive or exhaustive, I believe we can isolate four different sets of dynamics involved in the production of a (therefore overdetermined) paradigm shift constitutive of a new aesthetic period: the formal, the economic, the psychological, and the semiological or meaning-giving effect.

The first, or formal level, I have just discussed. Paradigms are dynamic, changing systems with their own logic but with limited capabilities for development—limited, at least, at a practical experiential level. At a certain point, artists experience them as being played out, completed, no longer open to innovation. At this level the crisis preceding the paradigm change is essentially a crisis of depletion, which can only be solved by a new paradigm.[8]

Of course this sense of depletion is itself a historically constituted quality, the forms of ancient Egyptian art being the notorious but far from unique example of an unchanging aesthetic paradigm whose

---

[8] Ackerman saw this level of change as one of the major applications of Kuhn's theory to literary history ('The Demise of the Avant-Garde: Notes on the Sociology of Recent American Art', *Comparative Studies in Society and History*, 11 (Oct. 1969), 371–84).

stasis was evidently valued. The unending quest for artistic novelty is essentially a feature of art in the capitalist West, and several Marxist critics, particularly Frankfurt School figures, have pointed out the relevance of Marx's analysis of capitalist production as an autonomous process generative of ceaseless revolutions in the means of production, a process in the meantime greatly magnified by the development of consumer culture and mass media and advertising, and catching up the work of art in its aspect as a commodity within this overall dynamic. The high valuation of novelty within the commodity sphere is transferred into the aesthetic sphere, as Baudelaire for one recognized, and Benjamin following him. And as Benjamin saw, the loss of artistic aura entailed in commodification (the art-work as equivalent to so much exchange value) and mechanical reproduction requires ever new, ever different forms, just like detergents. The inner dynamic of change within the paradigm is thus given a powerful 'push' by the surrounding capitalist dynamics.

A third level of dynamics is that isolated and mapped by Harold Bloom in his ground-breaking, provocative, but flawed work on literary influence already referred to more than once.[9] Bloom described how the Oedipal complex entailed the compulsive desire of one artist to slay and castrate the literary master(s) through a series of intricate strategies and ploys constitutive of literary history. The problem here, as Lentricchia saw, is that Bloom ends up completely ignoring the complex historical matrix in which this drama takes place. The revolt is not only the revolt of the son against the father, but also of the present, that strait gate which Benjamin recognized as one that the Messiah must be assumed to be ready to enter, against the past, that dead hand of the generations upon the living. But a psychological or Freudian compulsion to change must certainly be taken into account as a strong element in literary revolutions.

The fourth or semiological level refers to the process by which autonomous aesthetic forms become signifiers in the course of being read and interpreted by large numbers of individuals over many years within a culture; I am getting at the *ageing* of the art-work. It is an effect of the *audience's reception* of the work—the collective impact of numerous private and public interpretations—and can be described as a process through which an autonomous style becomes a historical icon, charged with the countless meanings interpreted into the

---

[9] Harold Bloom, *The Anxiety of Influence: A Theory of Poetry* (New York: Oxford University Press, 1973).

work(s). This process of iconization becomes complete when an art-work—Shakespeare's canon is perhaps the supreme example—absorbs so much that it becomes transcendent of any particular histori-cal epoch, one of the celebrated timeless masterpieces of traditional literary history. And indeed, only some art-works are rich and multi-valent enough to achieve this status; I imply no depreciation of these masterworks but rather wish to call attention to the social processes which produce them.

Most art-works, of course, do not become classics, but instead are experienced over time as becoming 'dated', irrelevant, or exhausted by interpretation to that date. This kind of icon *manqué* then becomes a *period piece* in a certain dynamic I am trying to isolate and which is thus central to periodization. If a work survives as a period piece rather than slipping into oblivion, then all its particularities of content and of form and technique will be experienced as bathed in the nostalgia for the past epoch it is the virtue of the object to evoke, with a retrospective re-coding of the work's formal elements which will now seem quaint, evocative of the vanished, and/or alien. The work will become a signi-fier of its absent cause, the historical moment of its genesis. Style, that signifier desiring only to be itself, to escape signification, cannot escape its reinterpretation as a marker of its day. The historical dimension transparent because shared by those for whom the work was con-temporary, only now, retrospectively and through a creative act of interpretation, will appear. And we know that a new act of this drama has begun—that we ourselves have entered a new 'period'—when yesterday's 'modern art' begins to appear as period pieces. Periods are never 'objective'; they are always functions of an interpreting present acting intersubjectively. History is always for and of the present, and our conceptions of periods—and of masterpieces like Shakespeare's works—will tell us as much about ourselves and our 'moment' as they do of the historical object(s) that they attempt to capture.

The Fluid Boundaries of Modernism

In the present context, only one period—Modernism—is to be fore-grounded, but it is a period with boundaries with two others—Roman-ticism and Postmodernism—and it will be clarifying to end this exposition of a theoretical framework with a discussion of how I con-ceive the succession of major paradigms constitutive of literary periods since the formation of autonomous art in the Enlightenment—a discussion necessary, too, to ground the treatment of Postmodernism in Chapter 5. Of course this is only a working and provisional model, necessarily abstract and schematic, but it can serve as an initial illustration of the idea of aesthetic paradigms at work, with a more detailed development of the formation of a Modernist paradigm to come in the subsequent chapters.

Kuhn's scientific revolutions were brought about by sharp breaks between successive paradigms. The new paradigm resulted from a new theoretical foundation with very little continuity with the overthrown paradigm.[10] Congruent as this model is with our contemporary preference for disparateness and *coupures*, it cannot, I believe, be transferred wholesale to a theory of aesthetic paradigms, which on the whole display marked features of continuity. This is particularly true in the case of Modernism, with its fluid boundaries with the contiguous periods on both ends.

At the first end—that of Romanticism—the argument made years ago by Frank Kermode, Harold Bloom, and others,[11] to the effect that Modernism should be understood as a continuation of Romanticism, indeed in Bloom's version, simply late Romanticism, has much to offer. The continuity had been effaced by the anti-Romantic rhetoric of many of the most influential Modernist theorists, like Irving Babbitt, T. S. Eliot, Ezra Pound, and their numerous and influential followers, which served to obscure the very real links between Modernist and Romantic aesthetics. Both aesthetic systems shared, for example, an ideal of 'unified sensibility', a fusion of reason and emotion: Blake and Wordsworth are particularly clear and repetitive on the need to reconstitute a (redeemed) faculty of reason in union with the feelings and the imagination, in terms extremely similar to (but of course not identical with) those immensely influential formulas enunciated in anti-Romantic terms by T. S. Eliot.[12] Both Romanticism and Modernism tend to give preference to the intuitive and the emotional over the ratiocinative nevertheless. And—what Bloom argued most convincingly—the poetry of each is constituted primarily through the figure of the *symbol* (de Man would later prefer to say *allegory*) in a Copernican

[10] Kuhn, *Structure of Scientific Revolutions*, 91.

[11] Frank Kermode, *Romantic Image* (London: Routledge, 1957) and Harold Bloom, in several works, for example 'The Central Man: Emerson, Whitman, Wallace Stevens', *Massachusetts Review*, 7 (Winter 1966), 23–42.

[12] Eliot's celebrated formulation, that a 'unification of sensibility' gave way to a 'dissociation of sensibility' in English poetry after the seventeenth century, is found in his 'The Metaphysical Poets', *Selected Essays* (New York: Harcourt, 1964), 241–50.

revolution of poetic techniques initiated by Wordsworth in which the source of meaning was transformed from Nature to Man.[13]

The transitional Symbolist aesthetics of Baudelaire, Mallarmé, and Rimbaud inherited much of this but instituted some decisive shifts, which, culminating in Modernism proper, seem to me sufficiently disparate to justify the notion that they amount to a different paradigm—but one, unlike Kuhn's, with considerable continuity with its predecessor. Their turn from Romantic themes of nature to a focus on the urban and artificial is a very great change, with some basic implications that fundamentally alter what is experienced as 'poetic' or 'aesthetic'. There is a noticeable occultation of Man as Subject in all their poetry, resulting in a characteristically Modernist effect of subjectivity without a subject. And the panoply of new 'shock effects' pioneered by Baudelaire and Rimbaud (but rarer in their poetry than is sometimes assumed) and multiplied by their twentieth-century successors is a further dramatic shift from Romantic practice.

Several critics have proposed various terms to capture this relation of continuity and break between Modernism and Romanticism: Hugo Friedrich speaks of Modernism as anti-Romantic Romanticism, Quinones seeing within Modernism a 'counter-Romanticism'.[14] Here I will speak of separate but historically related paradigms to capture a similar notion of the relation of Romanticism and Modernism.

A complicating factor is the status of 'realism', sometimes assigned its own period (the late nineteenth century) in literary histories, sometimes treated as a separate tradition or aesthetic. The notion of paradigms can easily accommodate these ambiguities. I would be inclined to trace the formation of a 'realist' paradigm in non-neoclassical Enlightenment practices clearly influenced by the new prestige of Enlightenment rationality. In the nineteenth century an updated realism reached a stable accommodation with late Romanticism/Symbolism through a division of labour (the novel vs. the lyric, with drama divided) which replicated within the aesthetic sphere the larger mutually complicit split between reason and the irrational of

[13] Harold Bloom, 'The Internalization of Quest-Romance', in *Romanticism and Consciousness: Essays in Criticism*, ed. Harold Bloom (New York: Norton, 1970), 3–24.
[14] Hugo Friedrich, *The Structure of Modern Poetry from the Mid-Nineteenth to the Mid-Twentieth Century*, trans. Joachim Neugroschel (Evanston, Ill.: Northwestern University Press, 1974); Ricardo J. Quinones, *Mapping Literary Modernism: Time and Development* (Princeton, NJ: Princeton University Press, 1985), 120–8.

Victorian culture.[15] As is widely recognized, elements from both realism and Romanticism entered into the new Modernist paradigm as practised by, say, Joyce and Proust.

At the other chronological limit of Modernism is the problem of Postmodernism, now greatly in dispute. Again there is a clear element of continuity involved in virtually all the formulations of the concept of Postmodernism but enough evidence of differences to suggest strongly the notion that the present moment is seeing the emergence of a new paradigm, with an important impact on criticism. I would emphasize two novel features that seem crucial to a case for seeing a separate Postmodernist paradigm in formation: (1) a breakdown of certain of the key constituting hierarchical oppositions of High Modernism, notably the Modernist separation of the art-work from popular culture, and (2) a decisive shift from older, Romantic and Modernist ideas of organic unity in the direction of problematizing unity as an aesthetic principle. But the discussion of these issues is properly deferred to the last chapter on contemporary trends in Shakespeare criticism.

In the analysis of the various forces—formal, economic, psychological, and semiological—imparting a dynamic of change to post-Romantic literary history, it could be noticed that the three extra-aesthetic factors all involved an element of forgetting and repression—manifestly in the Oedipal dynamics of influence and through a cognate level of what Russell Jacoby has called 'social amnesia' in the socio-psychological dimension of economic reproduction,[16] a repression of history inherent in a culture like ours whose economy is so implicated in a recycling of spurious newness. Finally at the level I have called semiological, an element that could be called a will to be different, apparent, as Fredric Jameson suggests, in the mechanical 'retro' periodization of recent decades in current American cinema, is in evidence. It is as if the prestige of the new in our culture leads to a sense of separate periods based on the slimmest of differences. The continuities persisting at both ends of the Modernist paradigm may bear traces of a 'forced', violent, and repressive set of transformations.

It seems at times that the two earlier paradigm shifts of the modern era—the constitution of the Age of Reason and the Romantic Revolt

---

[15] Raymond Williams's discussion of John Stuart Mill is the classic description of the complicitly divided mind of bourgeois Victorians in England. See his *Culture and Society, 1780–1950* (1958; repr. New York: Harper, 1966), 49–70.

[16] Russell Jacoby, *Social Amnesia: A Critique of Conformist Psychology from Adler to Laing* (Boston, Mass.: Beacon, 1975).

against it—were more fundamental and far-reaching than either of the paradigm shifts involving Modernism. Perhaps from some later perspective it will appear that one enormously stable aesthetic paradigm peculiarly suited to the social formation of the capitalist West in which it is embedded underwent a slow mutation over centuries before giving way to something else that we cannot imagine. The classic Frankfurt texts seem to treat it in that way, giving us a Modernism synonymous with the era of autonomous art and consequently founded in the Enlightenment differentiation. In the same vein, Habermas prefers to conceptualize Postmodernism as simply a new stage in a still incompletely unfolded modernity.[17] Certainly a long-term continuity is the continuity of the capitalist social arrangements and the hegemony of instrumental reason which form the context for autonomous art.

Granting all this, however, these Frankfurt themes seem to give us a literary history more monolithic and unified than does justice to the concrete complexities of the case, and they fail to develop the implication that an autonomous aesthetic sphere mediating socio-historic development should manifest an autonomous history of its own, a history that a concept like the aesthetic paradigm gets us much closer to, without requiring that all paradigm shifts—which, after all, are finally the conceptualizations of an historical present—should be seen as of the same order.

Perhaps a model for dealing with these necessary distinctions is provided by the suggestion of Claudio Guillén that we adapt from the *Annales* historians notions of three different levels of duration in historical periods: long durations, usually measured in centuries, involving basic demographic and geographic factors; middle or *moyennes durées* of from ten to fifty years involving economic and social developments; and the brief durations of political events.[18] Within the model of paradigms I am working with here, the long duration would refer to the long modern era beginning in or shortly after the Renaissance and which constituted the very form of the autonomous aesthetic paradigm. The middle level would refer to the dominance of the paradigms of literary periods properly speaking, of which Modernism

---

[17] Jürgen Habermas, 'Modernity—An Incomplete Project', in *The Anti-Aesthetic: Essays on Postmodern Culture*, ed. Hal Foster (Port Townsend, Wash.: Bay, 1983), 3–15.

[18] Claudio Guillén, 'On the Forms of Literary Change', *Proceedings of the 8th Congress of the International Comparative Literature Association*, Vol. I: *Three Epoch-Making Literary Changes: Renaissance—Enlightenment—Early Twentieth Century*, eds. Béla Köpeczi and György Vajda (Stuttgart: Bieber, 1980), 50–1.

is the basic example here. And short periods would refer to the micro-literary history equivalent to Kuhn's periods of 'normal science' in which variations within paradigms are accumulated.

As I argued at the beginning of the previous chapter, it seems apparent that critical paradigms, while they are certainly influenced by the prevailing aesthetic paradigm at any given moment, are also open to other influences, in particular to political ideologies and to the micro-politics of the institutions in which they are embedded. In the complex systems of differentiation that have emerged since the Enlightenment, it is clear that literary criticism has been much more unqualifiedly rationalist and unilinear in its discourse than the works of literature on which it reflects and, as we have already seen, much more open to the effects of instrumentalization and institutionaliza-tion inherent in modern capitalist society. Twentieth-century Shakespeare criticism in particular has been a site of contention in which discourses deriving from the autonomous aesthetic paradigm—predominantly the paradigm of Modernism—have competed against discourses deriving from the larger socio-economic dynamic of twentieth-century life—discourses of modernization. In the early texts of G. Wilson Knight, to whom I now turn, such a confrontation is palpable. In light of Knight's current, underrated reputation, however, my first task will be to re-present his critical innovations so that their significance for twentieth-century Shakespeare studies can be more justly appreciated. I will then establish the links between Knight's critical methods and contemporaneous Modernist literature and art and show how both Knight and Modernism are reactions against the processes of modernization described in Chapter 1, with Knight and his fellow Modernists emerging as re-functioners of 'art' and 'culture' in the hostile terrain of modernized, twentieth-century society.

Knight in Critical History

Knight's current reputation is decidedly mixed. In René Wellek's influential history of criticism, for example, Knight emerges as a naïve and self-contradictory theorist given to frequent schematism, impressionism, and intellectual fuzziness.[19] In the 1971 Preface to a

---

[19] René Wellek, *A History of Criticism, 1750–1950*, 6 vols. (New Haven, Conn.: Yale University Press, 1955–86), Vol. 5: *English Criticism, 1900–1950* (1986), 128–38.

collection of essays he then thought might be his last,[20] Knight complained bitterly of not receiving his due in several contemporary accounts of Shakespeare studies in the twentieth century, arguing that his name belonged with those of Eliot, Richards, Leavis, Empson, and L. C. Knights.[21] Trying to mediate between these two polar approaches to Knight's significance, Gordon Jones suggested that Knight was a giant, but one from a different era and therefore decidedly 'out of critical favor'. Knight, Jones suggested, was the 'last giant of Romantic Shakespeare interpretation'.[22]

With certain qualifications, I will argue that Knight's claim for his own historical importance is entirely justified and that it is as a Modernist rather than a Romantic that he should be remembered. The qualifications, and they are qualifications that would call into question much of Knight's writings since the three seminal books on Shakespeare (*The Wheel of Fire*, *The Imperial Theme*, and *The Crown of Life*) all have to do with a growing eccentricity in Knight's later work, an eccentricity linked with Knight's growing interest in Spiritualism. In his later work, Knight has claimed to have communicated with his dead brother, constructed a theory of acting linked to Spiritualism through the nineteenth-century figure François Delsarte, argued for the presence in Shakespeare of various Spiritualist and even Buddhist ideas, and discussed the connection between mysticism and masturbation.[23]

While Knight (in *Shakespearean Dimensions*) wrote that his interest in Spiritualism dated from an unpublished work written in 1951-2, well after the composition of his most influential works in Shakespeare criticism, he claimed that his 'other-dimensional intuition' was present in his works 'from the first' (p. xi). And there is just enough continuity between the early, highly original but disciplined Shakespeare 'interpreter' endorsed by T. S. Eliot and the crotchety, whimsically unfashionable older Knight to cast a retrospective pall over the earlier works. Wellek's unkind listing of the qualities of the Knight of *Christ and Nietzsche* (1948), representative, says Wellek, of all Knight's later work,

[20] In fact Knight lived until 20 March 1985, dying at the age of 87, and he brought out an additional volume of literary criticism in 1984, *Shakespearean Dimensions*.

[21] G. Wilson Knight, *Neglected Powers: Essays on Nineteenth and Twentieth Century Literature* (New York: Barnes and Noble, 1971), 18.

[22] G. P. Jones, 'Visions and Revisions: Recent Shakespeare Publications', *University of Toronto Quarterly*, 52 (Fall 1982), 107.

[23] G. Wilson Knight, *Shakespearean Dimensions* (Towata, NJ: Barnes and Noble, 1984), pp. xi– xxi, *et passim*. Similar themes are sounded in his *Neglected Powers*.

will strike many readers as applicable to aspects of the earlier writings
as well:

> ... the flattening out of any distinctions, the reconciliation of everything with
> everything, the monotonous conclusion that the world is pervaded by dualisms
> —tempest and music, disorder and order, evil and good, darkness and light,
> tragic and comic, which are reconciled or rather abolished in immortality,
> infinity, mystery, the other world of ghosts (p. 132).

Wellek goes on to assign Knight some positive virtues and a certain
importance in twentieth-century Shakespeare criticism, but his overall
place in Wellek's ambitious critical history is clearly coloured by Wellek's distaste for the later Knight. Knight is a minor figure, one of the
'New Romantics' whose chief importance is their (partial) influence on
T. S. Eliot, 'by far the most important critic of the twentieth century in
the English-speaking world'.[24]

I will not attempt to argue with Wellek's overall assessment of the
historical importance of the two critics, which, from some general
enough perspective, seems more or less accurate. But if one's field of
vision is restricted to the area of Shakespeare criticism considered as
an ample enough domain in its own right, then we must certainly
reverse Wellek's rankings. In twentieth-century Shakespeare criticism,
it is Eliot who seems the eccentric and dated interloper (with a few
exceptional passages of extreme brilliance), Knight the major figure of
watershed importance. For at least four of Shakespeare's plays—
Measure for Measure, Troilus and Cressida, Timon of Athens, and
Pericles—and perhaps as well for the entire group of late plays other
than *The Tempest*—it is no exaggeration to say that adequate understanding and appreciation of each, from our current vantage-point, can
be said to date only from Knight's essays on these plays.[25] By refusing
to label the plays 'failures' and by finding a thematic unity in each
where earlier critics found only confusion or artistic carelessness,
Knight discovered artistic merits in these plays that permanently
changed readers' expectations towards them, even when they might
disagree with the specifics of this or that 'interpretation'.

Knight's historically central role in modern Shakespeare criticism

[24] Wellek, *History of Criticism*, v. 176.
[25] The history of criticism on *Timon of Athens* can be followed through the excerpts
and notes which I prepared in *Shakespearean Criticism*, ed. Laurie Harris (Detroit, Mich.:
Gale, 1984), i. 451–536 and in Francelia Butler, *The Strange Critical Fortunes of
Shakespeare's 'Timon of Athens'* (Ames: Iowa State University Press, 1966); on *Pericles*, see
Shakespearean Criticism, Vol. 2; and on *Measure for Measure* and *Troilus and Cressida*, see

has certainly had its recent defenders, as in the short remarks of Gordon Jones cited above and, at much greater detail, in S. Viswanathan's *The Shakespeare Play as Poem*, which contains a scholarly survey and general assessment of Knight's criticism as a whole. Here I will undertake a more focused approach to Knight's work, seeing him primarily as the earliest significant critic attempting to reinterpret Shakespeare's plays as Modernist art-works. For this purpose the 'early' Knight's *The Wheel of Fire* and *The Imperial Theme* are the key texts, and many of the personal idiosyncrasies, which had no influence on the evolving paradigm of Modernist Shakespeare criticism of which Knight was such a central architect, are simply irrelevant. I note in passing, however, that the occult was a conspicuous object of interest for such giant Modernist figures as Pound, Eliot, and, of course, W. B. Yeats—undoubtedly because of its status as an anti-positivistic mode of thought and because of its connections to such Modernist preoccupations as myth, symbol, and mystery.

In asserting the central importance of Knight's criticism in the formation of the Modernist Shakespeare, however, I am of course not arguing that Knight's critical practice, even in the early works, can simply be appropriated for the present, Postmodern period. Even at their best, Knight's actual analyses of Shakespeare's plays will inevitably strike many contemporary readers as idiosyncratic and marred by his pervasive straining after now dated literary effects (what Wellek called the old attempt at evocation) as he constantly attempts to describe the qualities of Shakespeare's poetry through his own 'poetic' style, a style that will strike many readers as anachronistic. At his Spiritualist worst, we wonder, like Robert Sale in 1968, how a writer so bizarre could have attained so high a reputation in some circles.[26] In what follows, without denying any of Knight's often considerable strangeness, which has its own attraction to the catholic and anti-élitist tastes of Postmodernism, I hope to answer precisely Sale's rhetorical question. The answer lies essentially in grasping that Knight's criticism—or aspects of it—was a central and defining moment of the complex story of how we in the twentieth century have come to read Shakespeare. In this process Knight was both a creative agent and a passive receptacle of a new kind of critical discourse, responding to the

S. Viswanathan, *The Shakespeare Play as Poem: A Critical Tradition in Perspective* (Cambridge: Cambridge University Press, 1980), 73–80.

[26] Robert Sale, 'G. Wilson Knight', *Modern Language Quarterly*, 29 (Mar. 1968), 77–83.

new Modernist paradigm. Among other things, developing paradigms
are great intellectual 'filters' or repressors: the end result of the processes of adaptation, trial-and-error, and the other market-like forces
described in Kuhn's theory of scientific paradigms is to winnow out
much (valuable or not) intellectual 'chaff'. In any influential critic,
some ideas, we say, 'strike a responsive chord', while others may
puzzle us or be ignored in the excitement of the chord-striking. In
discussing Knight, I want to concentrate on those resonant chords,
seeing them as revelatory of a developing new critical paradigm of
which he is largely unconscious.

It was Knight's development of techniques of reading what he called
the 'spatial' aspects of the work that constitute his peculiar importance
in the history of Shakespeare criticism. These techniques in turn
became widely adopted, permeating critical practice in the heyday of
the New Criticism from the Forties through the Sixties.[27] And beyond
the era of New Criticism, Knight's influence continued through
Northrop Frye, a former student of Knight's at Toronto and one
whose use of myth and of abstracted character-types clearly owes
much to his former teacher's writings on Shakespeare. Knight has also
been seen as an analogue of continental phenomenological critics like
Georges Poulet,[28] thus preparing the ground for their reception in the
Anglo-American world. In the post-structuralist turn of recent years,
however, Knight has seemed considerably less contemporary, so
dependent is his method, as will be soon apparent, on a now suspect
concept of organic unity.

Knight was not alone in developing the techniques of 'spatial
analysis' in Shakespeare studies in the Twenties and Thirties. As
Kuhn discussed at length, it is a characteristic of paradigm shifts that
they occur through several rather than a single step, and consequently
the production of a new paradigm is seldom the work of a single
individual.[29] In this case there were two kinds of co-creators at work
with Knight. First, he was undoubtedly influenced by Eliot's poetry
and other Modernist art-works, and, second, other Shakespeare critics

---

[27] Viswanathan has the fullest account of Knight's subsequent influence. A partial list
of critics whose work on individual plays was clearly influenced by Knight includes such
diverse figures as F. R. Leavis, Terence Hawkes, Roy Walker, Francis Fergusson, S. L.
Bethell, Paul Siegel, Roy Battenhouse, L. C. Knights, D. A. Traversi, and Robert
Heilman (Viswanathan, *Shakespeare Play as Poem*, 73–95).

[28] René Wellek wrote in 1963: 'I suspect that Georges Poulet ... has read Wilson
Knight' (*Concepts of Criticism*, 216; quoted in Viswanathan, p. 67, n. 10).

[29] Kuhn, *Structure of Scientific Revolutions*, 54–6.

clearly can be seen as having independently developed a similar reading technique through the study of Shakespeare's image-patterns. In Germany, Wolfgang Clemen developed something analogous to Knight's method in a work published in 1936,[30] but his work never had a wide following among Anglophone Shakespearians. In the present context, the lectures and essays of Caroline Spurgeon,[31] culminating in her 1935 book *Shakespeare's Imagery*, merit more attention as an independent and also influential working-out of widely disseminated 'spatial' techniques.

Even more unfashionable at present than Knight, Spurgeon undoubtedly was a co-pioneer with Knight in constructing the Modernist paradigm.[32] But Spurgeon, as is well known, vitiated her interesting and cogent work by reverting to the nineteenth-century paradigm of biographical criticism in the belief that the imagery of the plays was a privileged means of access to Shakespeare-the-man's personality. And for reasons she never satisfactorily explained, but which were probably part of the misguided attempt to get behind the fictions of the plays to the 'real' Shakespeare, she defined 'imagery' very narrowly, restricting her search for patterns only to metaphors and similes and within those figures only to one of the two terms of comparison, the vehicle. Hence she criticized Knight's claim that 'gold' was a central image in *Timon of Athens*, because, she argued, only once is gold, 'however much it may be [otherwise] emphasized', used as the vehicle of a comparison.[33] Instead, Spurgeon draws attention to a line of images involving fawning dogs, a pattern obviously related to the play's theme of ingratitude and false friends (p. 345).

As a number of critics have observed, it is difficult to see from this or other examples what is to be gained by restricting the scope of inquiry into the patterns formed by Shakespeare's images as Spurgeon had done. Surely Knight's patterns built around gold as a verbal motif, a

[30] Wolgang Clemen, *The Development of Shakespeare's Imagery* (London: Methuen, 1951) is the English version.

[31] Although Spurgeon's major book did not appear until 1935, articles and public lectures on her studies in the image patterns came earlier, in time, for example, to have possibly influenced Knight. See Viswanathan, *Shakespeare Play as Poem*, 71.

[32] Gary Taylor focuses attention on Spurgeon as one of a new generation of (non-feminist) female scholars after World War I (*Reinventing Shakespeare*, 239–41) and as one of many Modernists exploring the influence of the unconscious in Shakespeare (pp. 245–7).

[33] Caroline Spurgeon, *Shakespeare's Imagery: And What It Tells Us* (Cambridge: Cambridge University Press, 1935), 344–5.

rhetorical subject of set speeches, and a stage prop in the play's dramatic action strike most readers as more central to their experience of
reading *Timon* than Spurgeon's fawning dogs.

Because, then, of Spurgeon's biographical intention and her narrow
definition of the image and because of Knight's broader subsequent
influence, Spurgeon's contribution to the developing Modernist
paradigm was less central than Knight's, and I will accordingly focus
on his work as more representative of the intersubjective paradigm-
construction in process, although by its very nature it involves many
individuals.

Knight's criticism, I believe, provides a privileged vantage-point for
viewing the process of mediation between an aesthetic and a properly
critical paradigm. Knight is clearly a conduit for something of which he
is only partly aware: the larger aesthetic paradigm of Modernism. But
his *intentions* are clearly of an altogether different order, and his intentions provide a distinct coloration to the project of his criticism. Knight
presents an unusually interesting case of the interworkings of a specific
and highly individualistic subjectivity working with and against the
larger culture. The next step in this investigation will be an examination of Knight's self-understanding.

Knight Presents the Centred Spatial Text

Knight's best known and most influential manifesto is Chapter One
of *The Wheel of Fire*, titled 'On the Principles of Shakespeare Interpretation'. This essay, devoid of the kind of impressionistic purple passages that now date so many of the specific readings of the plays, reads
well today, and is an excellent introduction to Knight's self-
presentation.

Early in the essay Knight introduces the then decidedly unfashionable term 'interpretation', which T. S. Eliot later admitted initially
blocked his sympathy for Knight. Knight uses the term, however, as an
alternative to 'criticism', with its connotations of judgement. He says
that he wants to avoid the critical procedures of fault-finding that in
past Shakespeare criticism interfered with a proper appreciation of the
text. Instead he urges a procedure of a willing suspension of *judgement*,
a deferral of evaluation in favour of attempting to *understand*. If we are
reminded of Madame de Staël's dictum, *Tout comprendre, c'est tout
pardonner*, we are rewarded by Knight's comment that 'Now it will
generally be found that when a play is understood in its totality, these

faults will automatically vanish'.[34] Unsympathetic critics (for example Wellek) have pointed out that Knight himself hardly sticks to his own distinction, since several of his 'interpretations' amount to wholesale reevaluations of the plays' aesthetic merits.[35] Such objections seem to me accurate.

But if we recall the shift in the source of authority in reading that the modernizers had effected, a shift from author to critic as the insurer of correct understanding, we can see in Knight's gesture the first of many reversals in critical practice. The claim to be (merely) 'interpreting' Shakespeare is a strategy for apparently re-establishing the authority of Shakespeare as author for the new critical theory Knight became famous for: the 'spatial' interpretation of a play. It was a gesture against the elevation of the authority of the critic brought by modernization, as well as a way of forestalling those familiar empiricist objections against his new method, that the innovation amounted to a 'reading into' the text of foreign modes of thinking. And it was, of course, a consummate piece of self-deception, for Knight's methods of reading were very much a part of the twentieth century.

As Knight presents it, however, his triumph in his new reading is modestly displaced, as a new instance of the Bard's triumph against petty-minded detractors (the modernizers). But Knight does not disguise his sympathy for the Romantic criticism that the modernizers had attacked. As his explanations develop, the signifier 'interpretation' begins a *glissage* towards more technical and delimited (but Romantic) meanings:

In reading, watching, or acting Shakespeare for pure enjoyment we accept everything. But when we think 'critically' we see faults which are not implicit in the play nor our enjoyment of it, but merely figments of our minds. We should not, in fact, think critically at all: we should interpret our original imaginative experience into the slower consciousness of logic and intellect, preserving something of that child-like faith which we possess, or should possess in the theater. It is exactly this translation from one order of consciousness to another that interpretation claims to perform. Uncritically, and passively, it receives the whole of the poet's vision; it then proceeds to re-express this experience in its own terms.

But to receive the whole Shakespearean vision into the intellectual consciousness demands a certain and very definite act of mind. One must be prepared to see the whole play in space as well as time (pp. 2–3).

[34] G. Wilson Knight, *The Wheel of Fire: Interpretation of Shakespeare's Tragedy* (1930; repr. Cleveland, Ohio: Meridian, 1964), 2.
[35] Wellek, *History of Criticism*, v. 131.

In this description of the act of interpretation there is more than a hint of Romanticism and of that 'dissociation of sensibility', the separation of feeling from reason, that was anathema to Eliot and his Modernist followers—and of course, a host of waving red flags for the contemporary critical theorist. Nevertheless, Eliot was willing to overcome his misgivings about 'interpretation' ('It has taken me a long time to recognize the justification of what Mr. Wilson Knight calls "interpretation" ', Eliot wrote, in order to 'enlarge [his] understanding of the Shakespeare pattern' and to affirm that Knight has found 'the right way to interpret poetic drama').[36] Clearly what counted for Eliot and for generations of Knight's readers was the 'spatial' method of interpretation which Knight developed and which constitutes the concrete signification of 'interpretation' as his chapter develops. For later critics Knight is almost always the theorist of the 'spatial' text, almost never of 'interpretation'. Such practice reflects what Knight contributed to the changing critical paradigm: a new technique of reading Shakespeare, a technique, if I may anticipate for the moment, which refunctions the Shakespearian play as a Modernist text. But what did Knight mean by his key statement, 'A Shakespearean tragedy is set spatially as well as temporally in the mind' (p. 3)? Primarily 'spatial' is the opposite of 'temporal' and designates a mental rather than natural volume; it is a category Knight constitutes by searching for intelligible patterns formed by those aspects of the play not connected with time-flow, plot, or its associated cause-and-effect structure (pp. 3–5). Repetition and recurrence of some single element (say, an image, word, or theme) 'spread out' over the 'space' of the play was the usual pattern Knight sought as a first step. The general technique has become a staple of literary analysis since, but it is worthwhile to look at the peculiarities of Knight's influential version of the method, and the best way to do so is to examine in detail an example of Knight at work. Probably the single most fully developed example is the essay 'The Transcendental Humanism of *Antony and Cleopatra*', the first of two chapters in *The Imperial Theme* devoted to a play whose erotic mingling of life and death and whose exotic imagery made it peculiarly appealing to Knight, with his Spiritualist interests.

Knight begins by looking for repetitions of an identifiable 'image'— this basic unit of analysis being defined broadly enough to include, as was mentioned above, rhetorical figures, 'literal' descriptions, verbal motifs, stage props, and dramatic special effects like storms. For ex-

---

[36] T. S. Eliot, Introduction to Knight, *Wheel of Fire*, pp. xv, xx, and xxi.

ample the serpent and snake imagery which Knight traces out for *Antony and Cleopatra* begins with descriptive details in the dialogue (the comparison of Cleopatra to the 'Serpent of the Old Nile') and ends with the actual stage-prop serpent at Cleopatra's breast in the climactic suicide scene.[37]

The next step in Knight's analysis is the attempt to discover the interrelation among the various strands of imagery thus identified and thereby to unify the play's 'space'. The serpent and snake imagery, then, is related to a more inclusive pattern: because of its association with the Nile, the serpent is connected to a larger number of references to aquatic animals, and these in turn are seen as forming a contrast to aerial animals, so that all together we have a pattern of the 'continued suggestion of immaterial life-modes, beautiful and volatile, swimming free in ocean and air. . . . In this play nature is ever at work, blending, mingling, dissolving element in element, to produce new strangeness, new beauty. The natural imagery thus reflects our life-theme: the blending of elements reflects the blending of sexes in love' (p. 229).

With this reference to 'theme' we arrive at the intermediate level of analysis. As Gary Taylor has pointed out, Knight's use of the term includes a fruitful ambiguity between two earlier separate meanings: 'theme' in music and 'theme' in rhetoric, the subject on which one writes (p. 221). This *glissage* evokes Symbolist dreams of a musical poetry to which Knight was obviously attuned. In addition, the image-pattern is expected to be revelatory of a larger 'theme' or dramatic concept reflected as well in the play's 'temporal' aspects. The individual image, then, is meaningful only to the extent that it partici-pates in a larger spatial pattern; it is a part in a part–whole dialectic. Clearly, Knight *expects* the 'patterns' to organize themselves into those larger units of meaning in the play, its 'themes'. Thus, in the example just cited, the serpent imagery is related to more and more inclusive patternings of the play until it fits into a 'spatial' pattern large enough to make some kind of satisfying sense: the serpent imagery is, ultimately, 'related to our erotic theme'. And that theme, as the analysis proceeds, will in turn be related to Knight's overall interpreta-tion of the play.

From our present vantage-point, such assumptions of unity perhaps seem arbitrary and gratuitous, overly 'centred' and even wildly logo-

---

[37] G. Wilson Knight, *The Imperial Theme: Further Interpretations of Shakespeare's Tragedies* (New York: Barnes and Noble, 1931), 227–8.

centric in Derrida's terms. But such assumptions of unity were part of the paradigm, part of Modernism's inheritance from Romanticism, and a pointed if silent rejoinder to the corrosive pretensions of the disintegrators. Even so ideologically an anti-Romantic as T. S. Eliot could slip effortlessly into an essentially Romantic doctrine of unity (and feel himself 'modern' in doing so): 'The genuine poetic drama must, at its best, observe all the regulations of the plain drama, but will weave them *organically* (to mix a metaphor and to borrow for the occasion a modern word) into a much richer design . . .'.[38] Knight's assumptions of the work's unity, while they place much less emphasis on tension and dissonance than became orthodox through American New Criticism, are certainly well within the Modernist paradigm. And one should admire his dexterity in deploying his notion of unity. The method is particularly gratifying because of its seeming power to 'explain' details that would otherwise be simply gratuitous bits of 'realism': 'Hence our earth is here fruitful', writes Knight, 'and many references to life-processes occur, throwing the sex-talk of Cleopatra's girls into a new light' (p. 229). The essential assumption remains even today a pedagogical stand-by.

Knight's achievement in his extended analysis of *Antony and Cleopatra* is to have organized a prodigious number of the play's images and themes into the unified vision he presents at the essay's end. His analysis includes comments on vowel assonance (pp. 201–4), the identification of verbal motifs around geographical names (pp. 206–8) and the idea of 'world' (pp. 208–9), a series of horse images (pp. 212–14), a recurrent motif of kingship (pp. 215–16) and of gold and riches (pp. 217–18) — all these he then unifies as aspects of 'the impregnating atmosphere of wealth, power, military strength, and material magnificence' (p. 218). But the definition of space is only half over at this point. There follows a similarly complex inventory of images and motifs concerning the erotic, which he classifies in an 'ascending scale' from the material to the spiritual. This list includes images and dramatic instances of feasting (pp. 219–20), music (pp. 220–2), a recurrent motif of love as lust (pp. 222–6), a strand of 'personal and physical, especially facial, details' (pp. 226–7), an inventory of animal images, finally resolved, as I noted above into two groups of 'aquatic' and 'aerial' animals (pp. 227–9), and images of harvest and fertility (pp. 229–32).

---

[38] Preface to *Wheel of Fire*, p. xxi.

Then comes the attempt to unify this immense material through the identification of certain mediating images and finally a set of master 'symbols' that absorb and represent all the other image-patterns, motifs, and themes. In the present instance, the mediation is provided by his organization of the animal images into opposed classes of 'air' and 'sea' animals and then paralleling this opposition to a separate set of recurrent oppositions between 'land' and 'sea' (pp. 227–9 and pp. 233–6). Having established these dualisms (and many more will be identified before the essay concludes), Knight goes on to identify the play's master image—repeated, he says, throughout: it is the image of 'melting', 'mingling', and 'dissolving' mentioned above. He finds instances of it in the references to the Nile's flooding, in gold melting, in the repetition of the word 'mingle' (p. 236), and in several other places, notably Antony and Cleopatra's sexual union.

Knight had been explicit in defining just how centred—that is, dominated by some single idea—he assumed the Shakespeare play to be in the theoretical chapter of *The Wheel of Fire* (p. 14). Nowhere is this assumption more fully exemplified than in his reading of *Antony and Cleopatra*, which finally identifies two unifying mega-symbols at the play's 'core':

I have now shown that our whole vision is condensed, crystallized in these single delineations of our two protagonists, both strongly idealized, ablaze with impossible beauty or infinite in majesty and power. The finite and infinite are blended in these descriptions. So, too, in the story, is element everywhere blended, mated, with element, sun with earth or water with air, giving birth to the 'strange serpent' of Nile, or the strange forms of 'hail', 'snow', or evanescent and multiform cloud. It is throughout a life-vision, a mating of essence with essence. (p. 261)

Ultimately, Knight argues, the vision merges life with death 'in a high metaphysics of love'; we have arrived at the Knightian Spiritualism and the doctrine of the soul's immortality and into a region where few have chosen to follow Knight. But if other Shakespearians shunned or ignored his Spiritualism, his techniques of reading, Knight's spatial hermeneutics, permeated the subsequent era of Shakespeare interpretation. There was something in Knight's hermeneutics that made his considerable strangeness simply beside the point.

Modernism and the Spatial Text

In retrospect, Knight's hermeneutics of space can be seen, even though he never acknowledged such a connection, as linked with several strands and currents of Modernism in the art and literature of his day. The theory of 'spatial' reading, as I have explained it above, can best be understood as a brilliantly devised strategy to accomplish two goals of Modernist aesthetics leading to the transformation of that monument of nineteenth-century culture, 'Shakespeare', to a Modernist icon: (1) the recoding of the central epistemological categories of time and space so that 'time' is perceived as nineteenth-century, mechanical, and old-hat; space as twentieth-century, revolutionary, and modern; and (2) the goal of establishing the autonomy of art as a value in itself on several levels and in several senses (to be discussed in the next section). These two goals, as we shall see, are closely connected.

Of course the formulation by which 'time' is nineteenth-century, 'space' twentieth-century is a reduction of a much more complex phenomenon. Knight, in 1930, never attempted to relate his theory of the spatial to anything outside of Shakespearian studies, but to a 1930 reader of *The Wheel of Fire*, the idea must have seemed vaguely familiar and vaguely Modern. The ground for making the connection was not clearly established until the classic 1945 essay by Joseph Frank, 'Spatial Form in Modern Literature'[39] and a specific connection to Knight's work came later when Frank attempted to define the qualities that united such Modernist novels as *Ulysses*, *A la recherche du temps perdu*, and (his central text) *Nightwood* by Djuna Barnes. In a brilliant piece of *bricolage*, he argued that all three novels worked in different ways to undercut the kind of sequential chronology we associate with nineteenth-century realist novels and were structured so that readers had to suspend their sense of chronology and link together as a unified pattern images and ideas dispersed into disparate, widely separated points in the novel's chronology. We had, he said, to perceive these disparate elements 'reflexively, in an instant of time'—they were no longer separated by chronology, but spread out in an abstract mental 'space'. Hence, the modern novel had a 'spatial form'—just like the Shakespearian play as defined by Knight in 1930.

Frank began his meditation on time and space in the arts with a

---

[39] All citations to this essay are to the revised and condensed version in *Criticism: The Foundations of Modern Literary Judgment*, rev. edn., ed. Mark Schorer, Josephine Miles,

rereading of Lessing's Enlightenment classic *Laokoon* (1766), a pioneering work of aesthetic theory. Lessing divided the arts into two categories according to their material media: the arts of time (music, poetry) and the arts of space (painting, sculpture), and Lessing went on to criticize attempts to overcome this basic distinction, based as he thought on irreducible facts of material existence, in such forms as allegorical paintings and descriptive poetry. Now Frank was less interested in Lessing's strictures (he sees nothing wrong with Modernist attempts to 'spatialize' literature) than he was in this classic precedent for thinking of aesthetic form in terms of these basic epistemological categories. As his argument progresses, he in effect redefines time and space not as the 'essences' implied in Lessing's prescriptive usage of them in *Laokoon*, but as 'two extremes defining the limits of literature and the plastic arts in their relation to sensuous perception' (p. 381). It then becomes possible 'to trace the evolution of art forms by their oscillations between these two poles' (p. 381). And Frank sees a tendency to 'spatialization' throughout the art-forms of High Modernism, in the rise of abstraction in the plastic arts (painting's abandonment of representation means cutting one last link to time) and, as he explains in detail, in both Modern poetry and fiction.

Time manifests itself in literature, he argues, mainly as narrative, and so subverting the temporal nature of language necessarily meant subverting 'normal' narrative sequence, producing structures that might be seen as fragmentary or unstructured. In Eliot's *The Waste Land* and in Pound's *Cantos* Frank found such a 'radical transformation . . . in esthetic structure' (p. 382) in which 'syntactical sequence is given up for a structure depending on the perception of relationships between disconnected word-groups. To be properly understood, these word-groups must be juxtaposed with one another and perceived simultaneously' (p. 383). In the novel, such techniques were applied on 'a gigantic scale' to produce Joyce's *Ulysses*, and in a subtler way with allied but different techniques in Proust (pp. 384–8).

With Frank's definitions in mind, consider Knight's initial description of spatial structure in Shakespeare: 'By this I mean that there are throughout the play a set of correspondences which relate to each other independently of the time-sequence within the story: such are

and Gordon McKenzie (New York: Harcourt, 1958), 379–92. The original essay appeared in *The Sewanee Review*, 53 (Spring, Summer, and Autumn 1945), 221–40, 433–56, 643–53. A revised and somewhat expanded version can be found in Joseph Frank, *The Widening Gyre: Crisis and Mastery in Modern Literature* (New Brunswick, NJ:

the intuition–intelligence opposition active within and across *Troilus and Cressida*, the death-theme in *Hamlet*, the nightmare evil of *Macbeth* ... Now if we are prepared to see the whole play laid out, so to speak, as an area, being simultaneously aware of these thickly-scattered correspondences in a single view of the whole, we possess the unique quality of the play in a new sense.'[40]

No wonder Frank, reflecting thirty years after the initial publication of his 'Spatial Form in Modern Literature', wrote, giving an example of a source which never found its way into the original essay, 'I distinctly recall, for example, writing down the famous passage from G. Wilson Knight's *The Wheel of Fire* (which several commentators have quite rightly spotted as related to my own point of view) where he asserts that "a Shakespearian tragedy is set spatially as well as temporally in the mind", and that there are in the plays "a set of correspondences which are related to each other independently of the time-sequence of the story".'[41]

Clearly, then, Knight's hermeneutics of the spatial text is not only the innovation in Shakespeare interpretation that he claims it is; it is also a method closely paralleling and unconsciously modelled on the aesthetic innovations of the poetry and fiction of the Anglo-American avant-garde of the Twenties.[42] Knight is doing for the *reception* of Shakespeare what Joyce had done for the *production* of the novel: both writers re-function a received aesthetic form to downplay its temporality and emphasize a different kind of aesthetic structure that can conveniently be called 'spatial'. Knight's criticism is clearly part of one of those revolutionary moments when an older paradigm gives way to a new. His immediate impact, even in the face of idiosyncratic differences from influential figures like Eliot (who, as we saw, endorsed *The Wheel of Fire*), and his widespread and long-term influence, sketched briefly above, all attest to the paradigmatic quality of Knight's work.

The idea of a shift in the perceived value and meaning of time and space in aesthetic form as we move from the Victorian to the Modern is

Rutgers University Press, 1963). There have been several other reprints, and translations into Spanish and French.

[40] Knight, *Wheel of Fire*, 3.

[41] Joseph Frank, Foreword to *Spatial Form in Narrative*, ed. Jeffrey R. Smitten and Ann Daghistany (Ithaca, NY: Cornell University Press, 1981), 8.

[42] Viswanathan, too, notes the connection between Knight's methods and several forms of Modernist literature and criticism (*Shakespeare Play as Poem*, 42–7), as does Gary Taylor, *Reinventing Shakespeare*, 221–2.

a startling concept which would seem to historicize categories which, if
any can, would seem to make a claim for an eternal, ahistorical status.
In the wake of greater familiarity with Saussure, we would now tend to
qualify the boldest assertions of this thesis somewhat and borrow
the terms 'diachronous' and 'synchronous' to help us rethink the
issues.[43] But such rethinking cuts both ways, and Saussure's linguistics
and the structuralist movement he inspired lose some of their claim to
scientific autonomy in the process and come to be seen as part of the
Modernist aesthetic paradigm shift as well.

A recent comparatist study of the Modernist movement, Ricardo J.
Quinones's *Mapping Literary Modernism: Time and Development*, is a
very helpful attempt to synthesize and conceptualize the history of
these larger issues. Quinones thinks through the paradigm shift
(without using that term) resulting in Modernism in terms of a changing experience of time. In his earlier *The Renaissance Discovery of Time*,
Quinones had described the genesis in the Renaissance of what he
calls the 'historical values', epitomized for him by the transformation of
Shakespeare's Prince Hal into Henry V: history itself is made into a
kind of myth, historical continuity becomes uniquely valued, and ideas
of causality, logic, individual character, and responsibility are given
new significance by the invention of history, that is, of time as a process
of development in the world. After completing this book, Quinones
wrote in its sequel, he happened to reread *The Magic Mountain*, and he
'was intrigued by the realization that what Mann had in his novel (and
more particularly in the character of Settembrini) described the end of,
I had, in my study, described the beginning of'.[44] It was the genesis of
a new study, based on the notion that Modernism involved a
fundamental reworking of such basic categories of experience and of
art as time and space, and Quinones's survey of major Modernist
works, which show a fundamental preoccupation with time as a theme,
independent of the kind of shift in form Frank and Knight were
involved in, has its own persuasive force.[45] Essentially, argued

---

[43] See the essays collected in Smitten and Daghistany, *Spatial Form in Narrative*,
especially Frank's own retrospective, 'Spatial Form: Thirty Years After', 202–43, which
sees Genette's structuralist narrative theory as in the direction he would now develop his
own theory.

[44] Quinones, *Mapping Literary Modernism*, 33–4.

[45] Besides *The Magic Mountain*, there are several of Mann's other works—*Budden-brooks*, *Death in Venice*, and *Dr. Faustus*; Lawrence's *The Rainbow* (centrally) and several
other works in part; Proust's great cycle; Eliot's *The Waste Land* and *Four Quartets*;
Joyce's *Ulysses* and *Finnegans Wake*; Virginia Woolf's *To the Lighthouse* and *Mrs. Dalloway*;

Quinones, 'Modernists began to regard experience as multi-leveled and time not as a regularly flowing, sequential phenomenon' (p. 91). Or, as an earlier critic put it in a passage Quinones quotes approvingly:

> ... one feature that links the movements at this center of sensibility we are discerning is that they tend to see history of human life not as a sequence or history not as an evolving logic; art and the urgent now strike obliquely across. Modernist works frequently tend to be ordered, then, not on the sequence of historical time or the evolving sequence of character, from history or story, as in realism and naturalism; they tend to work spatially or through layers of ⸗consciousness, working towards a logic or metaphor of form.[46]

The same themes can also be found from an entirely different direction. A similar notion of a shift in the perceptions of time and/or space at the beginning of the Modernist period is another of the shared ideas of Foucault and Habermas. 'Aesthetic modernity is characterized by attitudes which find a common focus in a changed consciousness of time', writes Habermas. For Foucault, the modern period began with a shift from the Classical Age's spatial preoccupations to the nineteenth century's fixations on time and history. But the literary Modernism I am discussing has its equivalent in Foucault's thought in the coming to consciousness of linguistics in the twentieth century, a kind of spatializing that leads to the end of the Age of History.[47]

In short, the Modernist revolution involved a shift in the uses of time and space in art-works—a shift which in turn is linked to another of the themes discussed in the Introduction: a growing autonomy of art in the Modern period. This is a theme developed explicitly in Knight, in terms that also constitute a virtual manifesto against the positivist critical procedures that were the subject of the previous chapter. This in turn will bring us back, at a much greater level of specificity, into the question of how we are to understand the causes of such shifts in the aesthetic paradigm.

and important essays by Nietzsche, Ortega y Gasset, T. E. Hulme, Wyndham Lewis, and, of course, Bergson.

[46] Malcolm Bradbury, *Modernism*, ed. Malcolm Bradbury and James McFarlane (New York: Penguin, 1976), 50; quoted in Quinones, *Mapping Literary Modernism*, 5.

[47] Jürgen Habermas, 'Modernity—An Incomplete Project', in Foster, *The Anti-Aesthetic*, 5, and Michel Foucault, *The Order of Things: An Archaeology of the Human Sciences* (New York: Vintage, 1973), 217–343. Admittedly, Foucault's chronology differs from the others discussed, but still shows significant parallels.

Knight's Anti-Positivism

Knight himself nowhere concedes that his criticism represents anything more than a discovery or development in how best to read
Shakespeare, but what *can* be discerned in Knight's text is an acute
consciousness of the critical concepts he is working *against*, and this
familiar consciousness of revolt against the previous generation allows
us to situate Knight's consciously anti-historical criticism clearly
within cultural and institutional history: for Knight the Modernist
Shakespeare arises in a reaction against the positivist modernizers.

Once more the theoretical chapter of *The Wheel of Fire* can serve as a
convenient text. We have already noted Knight's opening gambit of
distinguishing his own supposedly non-judgemental method of 'interpretation' from criticism properly speaking and how that claim soon
gave way to a definition of the analysis of the 'spatial structure' of the
Shakespeare play. With that move, Knight's enemy begins to be
defined too:

One must be prepared to see the whole play in space as well as in time. It is
natural in analysis to pursue the steps of the tale in sequence, noticing the logic
that connects them, regarding those essentials that Aristotle noted: the beginning, middle, and end. But by giving supreme attention to this temporal nature
of drama we omit what, in Shakespeare, is at least of equivalent importance. A
Shakespearean tragedy is set spatially as well as temporally in the mind. (p. 3)

'Spatial' is, above all, the negation of 'temporal', and time emerges
as the obstacle to a proper understanding of Shakespeare—time, that
is, of a certain kind: sequential time, time structured, as Aristotle
described the perfect plot, in a strictly logical cause-and-effect chain.
This notion of the temporal element of drama as an Aristotelian cause-
and-effect plot is reinforced at the end of a digression on the 'natural'
proclivity of the mind to assimilate drama as a purely temporal art:

Since in Shakespeare there is this close fusion of *the temporal, that is, the plot-
chain of event following event*, with the spatial, that is, the omnipresent and
mysterious reality brooding motionless over and within the play's movement, it
is evident that my two principles thus firmly divided in analysis are no more
than provisional abstractions from the poetic unity. But since to make the first
abstraction with especial crudity, *that is, to analyse the sequence of events, the
'causes' linking dramatic motive to action and action to result in time*, is a blunder
instinctive to the human intellect, I make no apology for restoring balance by
insistence on the other. (p. 5, emphasis mine)

Hence closely connected to the critique of Aristotelian plot as an adequate critical category comes Knight's quickly sketched rejection of source studies, condemned because of their reliance on false ideas of rational causality (pp. 7–8) or of intentionality, a topic by which several practices of the modernizers—Stoll's emphasis on stage conventions, several biographers' on economic factors, for example—are quickly disposed of as missing the point.

Finally, when Knight arrives at that central nineteenth-century pre-occupation in Shakespeare criticism, character, we see that his target has been widened to include not only the modernizers but also central aspects of Romantic criticism. At this point his break with Romanticism in favour of more properly Modernist categories becomes clear:

So often we hear that 'in *Timon of Athens* it was Shakespeare's intention to show how a generous but weak character may come to ruin through an unwise use of his wealth'; that 'Shakespeare wished in *Macbeth* to show how crime inevitably brings retribution'; that, 'in *Antony and Cleopatra* Shakespeare has given us a lesson concerning the dangers of an uncontrolled passion'. These are purely imaginary examples, coloured for my purpose, to indicate the type of ethical criticism to which I refer. It continually brings in the intention-concept, which our moral-philosophy, rightly or wrongly, involves. Hence, too, the constant and fruitless search for 'motives' sufficient to account for Macbeth's and Iago's actions: since the moral critic feels he cannot blame a 'character' until he understands his 'intentions', and without the opportunity of praising or blaming he is dumb. . . . Ethics are essentially critical when applied to life; but if they hold any place at all in art, they need to be modified into a new artistic ethic which obeys the peculiar nature of art. . . . By noting 'faults' in Timon's 'character' we are in effect saying that he would not be a success in real life: which is beside the point, since he, and Macbeth, and Lear, are evidently dramatic successes. (pp. 9–11)

The play, then, is not life, but art. This essentially Symbolist notion, adopted and transformed in numerous ways by Modernism and Post-modernism, is at the heart of Knight's critique of nineteenth-century character studies. He stresses that the Shakespearian play should not be conceived of as a mirror of life in the mode of the realist novel. As Knight tries to define what offends him about moralizing Shakespearian criticism, he begins to pair 'art' and 'life' as antitheses, as separate domains with separate laws, the confusion of which can only lead to improper art criticism: 'Ethics are essentially critical when applied to life; but if they hold any place at all in art, they need to be modified into a new artistic ethic which obeys the peculiar nature of art

...' (p. 11). Against early historical critics who suggest it is necessary to recreate a lost Elizabethan value-structure in order to understand Shakespeare properly, Knight is equally dismissive:

In ages hence, when perhaps tempests are controlled by science and communism has replaced wealth, then the point of Shakespeare's symbolism may need explanation; and then it may, from a new ethical view-point, be necessary to analyze at length the moral values implicit in the Cordelia and Edmund conceptions. But in these matters Shakespeare speaks almost the same language as we, and ethical terms, though they must frequently occur in interpretation, must only be allowed in so far as they are used in absolute obedience to the dramatic and aesthetic significance: in which case, they cease to be ethical in the usual sense. (p. 10)

Now Knight has been criticized often enough for a naïve underestimation of historical difference, and the passage above is testimony to this characteristic critical lacuna. What is now more useful to point out, however, is how the lack of historical consciousness fits in with the whole project of a spatial hermeneutics, as a part of the Modernist revolt against nineteenth-century time and preoccupation with history. The removal of the literary work from historical flux is a decisive step toward separating art from its social context. The 'spatialization' process reinforces this increased autonomy. Knight's practice is here again at one with Modernism's in general. And Knight's insistence on erecting a clear line of demarcation between art and life is therefore fully in line with the hermeneutics of spatialization and clearly in the mainstream of Modernist aesthetics and its associated formalist critical paradigm.[48]

As was the case with the French Symbolists and with their Modernist descendants, the autonomous sphere of art was constituted most urgently over and against nineteenth-century positivism and scientism. This tendency is apparent in Knight in several ways.

There is in the first place an explicit hostility to a wide variety of the modernizing criticisms of the late nineteenth century, all, as was noted above, seen to be tainted with the essentially scientistic, positivistic vice of mechanical causality. That is the problem with source studies, with analyses of dramatic structure, with biographical efforts to recreate

[48] One might plausibly argue that Knight threatens the autonomy of art from an altogether different direction, not from 'life' but from 'metaphysics', that is, his peculiar quasi-religious Spiritualism, into which, as has been noted, he tends to 'translate' Shakespeare. However it is precisely at the point when Knight succumbs to this temptation that he leaves the Modernist paradigm.

Shakespeare's 'intentions' (pp. 6–12), and with studies of 'the stage and the especial theatrical technique of Shakespeare's work' (p. 13) like Stoll's. Over and over in his critique of these methods Knight speaks of their common employment of an alien logic or of methods unsuited to the nature of art (pp. 7–14). This alien sensibility is never precisely defined, but Knight seems clearly to be thinking of Romantic distinctions between analytic reason and the powers of imagination, for example, in his critique of the notion of a discoverable poetic intentionality:

'Intentions' belong to the plane of intellect and memory: the swifter conscious-ness that awakens in poetic composition touches subtleties and heights and depths unknowable by intellect and intractable to memory. That consciousness we can enjoy when we submit ourselves with utmost passivity to the poet's work; but when the intellectual mode returns it often brings with it a troop of concepts irrelevant to the nature of the work it thinks to analyze, and, with its army of 'intentions', 'causes', 'sources', and 'characters', and its essentially ethical outlook works havoc with our minds, since it is trying to impose on the vivid reality of art a logic totally alien to its nature. In interpretation we must remember not the facts but the quality of the original poetic experience. . . . (p. 7)

Not only is causality suspect because of its association with the nineteenth-century values of history and temporality that I emphasized above; it is also suspect because it is a notion derived from scientific study of mechanical forces in the non-organic world and therefore alien to the organic and imaginative logic of the autonomous art-object. Art for Knight, as it had been for Swinburne, is clearly a domain to be kept free from the colonizing attempts of modernizers to import science—more precisely, nineteenth-century positivistic science—into the aesthetic sphere.

On this point there is clear continuity between Knight and mainstream Romanticism, and the tendency is central enough in Knight (along with a lack of specificity in his condemnations of an undifferentiated 'reason') to justify (at least partially) the classification of Knight as a Romantic by critics like Wellek and Gordon Jones mentioned above. There is no harm in such a label, and it captures something about Knight, provided, however, the term Romantic is not meant as a substitute for 'Modernist'. Earlier in this chapter, I sketched a theory of periodization that accounts for this ambiguous designation because the relation of the Romantic paradigm to the Modernist paradigm is one of both continuity and break, depending on what theoretical areas one focuses on. His relation to his Romantic predecessors could be defined through either of two 'figures' for the relations of influence defined by Harold Bloom:[49] *clinamen*, or a limited agreement up to a certain point, after which the reading 'swerves' to a new direction, as when Knight credits Bradley with originating spatial analysis through Bradley's idea of atmosphere;[50] or *tessera*, the figure of 'completion and antithesis', as when he credits Coleridge, Hazlitt, and Bradley with the first beginnings of his general method of interpretation (p. 2) which, however, he can only complete by adding 'spatial' analysis to their temporal-based methods.

Knight's complex relation to Romanticism in many ways mirrors that of Modernism as a whole, which continued Romanticism's hostility toward instrumental reason, but transformed it in an act of counter-modernization against 'modernization' properly speaking. Many of these techniques were already present in Baudelaire and Rimbaud (I am thinking of such features as a radical shift in poetic imagery from nature to the city, from ideality to evil, and from vision to hallucination). A central portion of the Modernist impulse involves re-inscribing the technical accomplishments of Western culture for use within art, in modes of celebration and in modes of protest.[51] This is one of the real breaks between Modernism and Romanticism, one of the most important justifications for assigning to the Modern its own period.

Knight himself took some steps of counter-modernization in the 1947 Prefatory Note to *The Wheel of Fire*, where, like Ortega y Gasset before him, he invokes Einstein as a fellow Modernist against nineteenth-century science and, by analogy, against nineteenth-century character studies in Shakespearian criticism (p. ix). He quotes from a contemporary popular account of modern physics, which contrasted post-relativity and post-quantum mechanics notions of 'form, pattern, and symmetry' against older notions of static particles, the particle theories being said to have had their heyday from about 1870 to 1910. Knight sees an exact analogy between his more dynamic concepts of characterization and post-Einstein physics, not least because the older Newtonian physics was not in his view overthrown,

[49] Harold Bloom, *The Anxiety of Influence: A Theory of Poetry* (New York: Oxford University Press, 1973). Definitions of the figures of influence are given on pp. 14–15 and discussed in sequence *passim*.

[50] *Wheel of Fire*, Preface to 1947 edn., p. vii.

[51] Quinones provides an excellent discussion of this in *Mapping Literary Modernism*, 40–86.

so much as shown to have a much more limited application than had previously been thought. 'Even the dates [1870–1910]', he says, 'roughly, fit' (p. vii).

Earlier in the same Prefatory Note, Knight had been at pains to distance himself from any implications that his critique of nineteenth-century criticism should be seen as directed primarily against A. C. Bradley, the greatest of the character-analysts (p. vii). He does this mainly by associating Bradley with his Romantic predecessors ('I write of Shakespeare—as indeed did Coleridge, Hazlitt, and Bradley—as a philosophic poet . . .') and by claiming that Bradley's notion of the play's 'atmosphere' was an early version of his own notion of the 'spatial'. With the analogy to post-relativity physics, Knight overcomes apparent contradictions and situates his own theories vis-à-vis the past in three agreeable ways. First, a continuity with the Romantic tradition is maintained. Second, a paradigm shift is described which is a genuine breakthrough even while continuity is maintained. And third, most subtly, the critics of the period 1870–1910 are singled out as particularly 'wrong'. With Bradley already excluded, it is clear that Knight is contrasting his Romantic Modernism against a (now suddenly outdated) nineteenth-century scientistic modernization. It must have been a very satisfying Preface to write. With one move he has inscribed himself simultaneously within the 'central . . . imaginative and metaphysical' (p. viii) tradition of Coleridge, Hazlitt, and Bradley and squarely within the twentieth-century Modernist paradigm. And he was essentially correct in so doing.

Knight, Professionalism, and Culture

Knight, then, had a fairly good grasp of what in his criticism was innovative, and what could be traced back to nineteenth-century sources. Of his indebtedness to contemporary Modernism, he was almost completely unaware. His spatial hermeneutics, which now appears as inescapably Modernist, seems to have appeared to Knight himself as a good idea which he had one day in the late Twenties.[52]

Such limited self-awareness, far from some peculiar weakness of

[52] The connection which Knight himself notes as a possible 'source' of his criticism was sexual in nature. In a passage which offers fascinating material for a psychoanalytic reading of Knight which cannot be attempted here, Knight wrote: 'In my own life I recall first a period of sexual frustration . . . followed by a more successful release through indulgence in thoroughly abnormal fantasies; and it was about then, according to my recollection, that the literary patterns of my Shakespearean interpretations began to

Knight's, is in fact pervasive in the circulation of cultural ideas and values, the very soil on which, as Adorno insisted, the social whole is mediated into art-works (and into the constitution of art-works through reading) despite the consciousness of the supposedly sovereign creator. The case of Knight is also an excellent example of Adorno's dictum that such mediation characteristically occurs, not as content (as in the misguided aesthetics of socialist realism) but as form. And I will end this discussion of Knight's relation to the Modernist paradigm by attempting to work out the relation of his hermeneutics of spatialization with the more global historical forces operating on the sphere of aesthetics at the beginning of the Modernist period.

At the level of institutional history, the phenomenon of Knight's criticism is clearly linked to the establishment after World War I of English as a University subject with all the requirements of professionalization, disciplinary bodies of knowledge, and professional-pedagogical techniques of reading literary texts that were discussed in Chapter 1. Knight studied English at Oxford in the Twenties, taking his BA in 1923 and his MA in 1931. He taught at the University of Toronto from 1931 to 1940 and at the University of Leeds from 1956 until his retirement in 1962. Institutionally speaking, he was very much an academic critic, and the techniques he pioneered were of course widely adopted in teaching and in academic literary criticism. The very industriousness implied by his method—hunting, keeping track of, classifying, and unifying hundreds of details within a given play—implied a professional commitment inimical to the journalistic and lecture-hall styles of much of nineteenth-century British criticism. In that sense, Knight's criticism is very much a continuation of the modernization of Shakespeare undertaken by the generation of turn-of-the-century scholars to whom he was otherwise so opposed, temperamentally and methodologically.

Knight's professionalism, however, paradoxically contained a strong element of anti-professionalism. The eccentric Spiritualism along with the other crotchets of his later works is of course one clear sign of such a tendency—indulged in after his career was well established, his professional reputation assured. But there is a more subtle element of anti-professionalism, evident in the early works as well: by reaching

suddenly unfurl' (*Neglected Powers*, p. 30). Elsewhere Knight wrote of his discovery of Eliot's poetry (and that of other Modernists) in the late Twenties. Not surprisingly, Knight also had an early strong taste for the Romantics (Preface to *Gold-dust: With Other Poetry* (London: Routledge, 1968), pp. xii–xviii).

back, over, as it were, the generation of modernizers to claim an affiliation with Coleridge, Hazlitt, and Bradley, Knight sought to forge a connection (Bradley is obviously a transitional figure in this regard) with the organic intellectuals of high bourgeois nineteenth-century culture, with the 'cultural class' that Coleridge thought ought to exist as a 'clerisy', and which, as we have seen, Matthew Arnold attempted to transfer into the British national educational apparatus. Knight's attack on the scientist techniques of the modernizers should be read as part of an attempt to resituate the forces of culture within the University and its associated educational infrastructure. In that sense Knight, and a whole generation of academic Modernists—notably including the American New Critics, to whom I will turn shortly—are direct followers of Matthew Arnold, that pioneer of 'culture' within modern education.

Now to use a language of intentionality that is only a retrospective reconstruction and a figure of exposition, we could speak of the 'task' that confronted the proponents of 'culture' within the academy in the early twentieth century. The older, Romantic and realist paradigms would no longer do in the midst of the widespread sense of cultural collapse and crisis that World War I concentrated and focused. The aesthetic paradigm of Modernism offered a new form for 'culture' (along with the potentiality for the end of culture advocated by surrealism). The Anglo-American Modernists, led by Eliot and Pound, rose to the occasion and inscribed within Modernism a place for a (somewhat reformulated) Tradition. But the Tradition had itself to be modernized, to be rethought according to the new codes of the new aesthetic paradigm. Eliot's chief contribution to this task was of course his reinscription of Donne and the English Metaphysical poets as proto-Modernists. On Shakespeare he deferred—to G. Wilson Knight.

Knight's Shakespearian criticism, then, is a privileged case in which the impingement of the larger aesthetic paradigm on the more rationalized and institutionalized critical paradigms can be rather clearly discerned. Knight's synchronous reading of the Shakespearian text responded to the same complex of influences that led to what Frank described as the 'spatialization' of the novel, that subversion of traditional realism's peculiar conventions of chronology and representation undermined by Joyce, Kafka, and Proust. Frank linked the shift with the Modernist revolution in the plastic arts, the replacement of representation by abstract expressionism:

[Spatial form] is the exact complement in literature, on the plane of esthetic form, to the developments that have taken place in the plastic arts. . . . [T]he reason for this identity is that both are rooted in the same spiritual and emotional climate—a climate which, as it affects the sensibility of all artists, must also affect the forms they create in every medium.[53]

Frank, ever the *bricoleur*, then wove his theory into the ready-to-hand speculations of the German aesthetic theorist Wilhelm Worringer, whose work *Abstraction and Empathy* had already entered Modernist discourse through the dissemination of certain of its concepts by T. E. Hulme. Worringer had posited two polar approaches to style in the history of painting and sculpture. There was a naturalistic impulse, found in the classic phase of ancient Greece and in Europe from the Renaissance through the nineteenth century, based on empathy with nature. At the other pole Worringer put styles based on abstractions, which he found in varied forms in primitive societies, Byzantine and medieval culture—and in the Modern period. Such styles, he theorized, were a reflex of societies for whom nature was problematic, either because of its threatening and chaotic presence on technologically primitive cultures or, in the modern era, because the complexities of mechanized and urbanized life constituted a new kind of crisis of the natural.[54] Frank was particularly struck by Worringer's view that abstraction, by removing the object from its naturalistic setting, also removed it from the time-flux of the phenomenal world and thus de-emphasized temporality in the art-object.

From the present vantage-point, Worringer's theory seems something of a pastiche of the favourite topoi of late nineteenth-century German cultural studies, its assumptions of cultural unity too global, its schema of styles too reductive to command assent. But in the element that Frank seized on—the notion that the modern era was seeing a fundamental shift in aesthetic forms and that behind the shift in forms was a more global and general cultural crisis—there is, I believe, a valuable insight, seconded, as we have seen, by numerous other writers.

The revolt against time in the arts was a deeply felt revolt against history—the Hegelianized sense of history that had become the West's mythology and self-justification: history as progress, the present as the desired outcome of all that had come before. When history revealed itself instead to have given birth to Yeats's slouching beast, to Joyce's

[53] Frank, 'Spatial Forms in Modern Literature', 391–2.
[54] Ibid., pp. 390–1.

nightmare, to Eliot's hollow men, then history, as it had been understood, history with a *telos*, had lost its *raison d'être* and in that sense no
longer existed. Time was replaced by space, history by myth.[55]

Progress, Benjamin wrote sardonically in his famous thesis on
Klee's painting 'Angelus Novus', is the storm driving the angel of
history uncontrollably ahead, his back to the future, his eyes able to see
only the past's 'catastrophe which keeps piling wreckage upon wreckage and hurls it in front of his feet'.[56]

Modernism, as Benjamin recognized, was the art-paradigm of an
era which could no longer pretend that the Angel of History knew
where she was going. G. Wilson Knight's hermeneutics of space, like
that of his fellow Modernists, then, should be understood as part of the
effort to come in out of the storm.

[55] Cf. Quinones, *Mapping Literary Modernism*, 21–39, and Kuhn on Darwin's similar
function, *Structure of Scientific Revolutions*, 170–2.

[56] Walter Benjamin, 'Theses on the Philosophy of History', in *Illuminations*, ed.
Hannah Arendt, trans. Harry Zohn (New York: Schocken, 1969), 257–8.

3

The New Critical Shakespeare:
The Tensions of Unity

The Specificity of the New Critics

The American New Criticism, which was destined to restructure
English studies decisively in the newly expanded universities of the
early years of the post-World War II era in the United States, and
which then became the dominant methodology in American
Shakespeare studies in the first twenty-five years of that period, was
born among a group of young poets in the American South as an
alternative to the modernizing, positivist disciplines that controlled the
study of literature in the prestigious graduate centres of the first half of
the century. In its origins it was another cry of protest against the
draining-out of meaning from modern life; in its moment of greatest
influence, as the ruling critical methodology of a vast American
higher-education empire in the Sixties, it had become a disciplinary
technique of pedagogy and publication, its old critical edge dulled by
the processes of professionalization which it had undergone.

Like G. Wilson Knight's spatial approach to Shakespeare, New
Criticism was, from its beginnings, linked with the Modernist movement in poetry, and in its battles with the dominant modernizing
approaches to literature that reigned in the academies, it is not difficult
to recognize its affiliations with the same generalist and humanist
ideologies, deriving from the Matthew Arnold tradition, which Knight
had tried in his own way to 'modernize'. But the New Criticism
became something different from Knight's critical methodology,
developing out of the peculiar conjunctures and currents at Vanderbilt
University in the era of World War I and its aftermath; its contours
were shaped too through a series of complex interactions with British
sources and analogues and American institutions.

For reasons to be discussed below, Shakespeare and his age played a
privileged and important part in New Critical literary history and
critical practice, but of course the methodology and practice had wider
and more general parameters. I will accordingly begin with a general
account of New Criticism, with emphasis on its relations to Modern-

ism and modernization, showing how the early political phase of the
founding New Critics survived in displaced form in the criticism, and
then examining in this light the highly influential New Critical textbook *Understanding Drama*'s approach to *1 Henry IV* as a way into the
impact of New Criticism on Shakespeare studies. A section on British
analogues will briefly chart New Criticism's complex relations with its
British sources and counterparts, especially with *Scrutiny*. This will
lead into an assessment of the larger cultural affinities of New Criticism, including unexpected, if limited, links to the Frankfurt School,
suggestive of possibilities never actualized as New Criticism took its
place as the hegemonic professionalized critical discourse in the
expanding English departments of the Fifties and Sixties in a completely depoliticized form.

   Accounts of New Criticism that treat it primarily as a synthesis of
I. A. Richards and T. S. Eliot get at an important part of the complex
picture, but they underestimate the specificity and coherence of a
remarkable group that began meeting in Nashville, Tennessee around
1915 to discuss what they called 'philosophy' and to read and discuss
each other's poetry. The core of this group—John Crowe Ransom,
Allen Tate, Robert Penn Warren, Cleanth Brooks (the last two came
to the group later than the others)—maintained an intellectual collaboration over several decades that was the essential impetus for the
development of American New Criticism, and their collaboration pre-
dated the reading of Richards and Eliot that helped energize and focus
the group's critical ideas in the Twenties.[1]

   In his insightful but neglected *The Critical Twilight*, John Fekete
divides the collaboration into three phases, the first two of which are
often ignored or treated so summarily that their significance is lost
sight of. But in the genealogy of New Criticism, traces of the less-
known first two phases survive in metamorphosed form in the last
and best-known phase, and it is therefore crucial that they be
excavated. The first phase began in Nashville as John Crowe Ransom,
who had been a Vanderbilt undergraduate, returned after three years

   [1] For this point, I am indebted primarily to two sources each of which emphasizes the
importance of the Vanderbilt connection in the genesis of New Criticism: Louise
Cowan, *The Fugitive Group: A Literary History* (Baton Route: Louisiana State University
Press, 1959) and John Fekete, *The Critical Twilight: Explorations in the Ideology of Anglo-
American Literary Theory from Eliot to McLuhan* (London: Routledge, 1977), 37–103.
There is now an extensive literature on the Fugitive-Agrarian roots of New Criticism. A
good bibliography is provided in the notes of William E. Cain, *The Crisis in Criticism:
Theory, Literature and Reform in English Studies* (Baltimore, Md.: Johns Hopkins Univer-
sity Press, 1984), 288–9 n. 23.

at Oxford to join the Vanderbilt faculty and slowly developed a circle of students interested in poetry and metaphysics. The group was Southern American and mostly middle-class, but, according to Cowan, there was little initial self-consciousness of the peculiar position of Southern intellectuals. That would come later. Instead, they were more likely to discuss French Symbolist poetry, the Elizabethans, or the classics.[2] After a period of interruption caused by World War I, and with the fructifying presence of Allen Tate, who was in his final undergraduate year when he began to take part in the group in 1921, a decision was made to found a poetry magazine as a vehicle for the burgeoning poetic production of the circle. The result was *The Fugitive*, the first issue of which appeared in the spring of 1922. Ransom described their effort in these terms:

The editors of THE FUGITIVE are amateurs of poetry living in Nashville, Tennessee, who for some time have been an intimate group holding very long and frequent meetings devoted both to practice and to criticism. The group is evidently neither radical nor reactionary, but quite catholic, and perhaps excessively earnest, in literary dogma. The writers sign their work with assumed names for the present, with special reference to the local public, on the theory that the literary issue must not be clouded with personalities.[3]

The group was soon caught up in discussions, stimulated by the outside contributions of Robert Graves, of how the tradition of English poetry (and prosody) related to the project of writing modern poetry. A fair sample of the discussion is provided by an editorial which Tate wrote for the journal sometime after his first reading of Eliot, who seemed to him the essence of modern poetry: 'Perhaps T. S. Eliot has already pointed the way for this and the next generation. But there are and will be many still faithful to an older, if not more authentic, tradition; for the old modes are not yet sapped. However, the Moderns have arrived, and their claim is by no means specious. *The Fugitive* doesn't attempt arbitration; it is humble; besides, it has other fish to fry. But which tradition can the American honestly accept? A fair, if stale question'.[4]

Tate could not at this point grasp that in this quest for a reconciliation of modernity and the tradition, he was already very much within the paradigm which Eliot, among others, was beginning to formulate for Anglo-American Modernism.

[2] Cowan, *Fugitive Group*, 34.
[3] Quoted ibid., p. 59.
[4] Quoted ibid., p. 83.

In this first phase of what would become New Criticism, the social roots and intellectual affiliations of this potent methodology are clearly present. The Fugitives are 'men of letters', generalists with primary interest in the production of poetry rather than literary scholarship. They were of the University, but in a provincial outpost of academia that had been imperfectly modernized and still required Latin and Greek for its BA students as late as 1909–10, the year Ransom graduated;[5] hence, they were without the passion for positivist scholarship that prevailed in the hegemonic Universities. In line with their anti-positivism, many of the group were religious men and saw the decline of religious belief as one of the tragedies of modernization. They were Southerners, but they had international connections and experience: Ransom and Brooks both studied at Oxford, for example, and Nat Hirsch, who was instrumental in the actual organization of the *Fugitive* magazine, had travelled in the Orient. And the group, especially in its central members, was Modernist in taste and poetic production, preoccupied with the problem of transforming and preserving culture in the new environment of modernity which was, belatedly, changing the face of the American South.

The importance of the Southern location did not become fully clarified until the group entered its second phase in the Depression Thirties, the Agrarian Movement.[6] As both Cowan and Fekete report, the Fugitives had felt torn between the Old and New South, unable to countenance the slavery of the Old,[7] but unwilling to endorse what seemed to them the philistine spirit of industrial capitalism. Hence, while paying lip-service to their Southern surroundings, they felt affinities with Baudelaire, Hart Crane, and T. S. Eliot rather than to any regional literary traditions. Ransom set the tone for the group in the

[5] Ibid., p. 33.

[6] The relation between the Fugitives and Agrarians, according to Cowan, could be described as follows. The Fugitives were 'a quite tangible body of sixteen poets who . . . met frequently from 1915 to 1928' (ibid., p. xvi). By 1930 the core of the Fugitives—Ransom, Tate, R. P. Warren, and Donald Davidson—the four will henceforth be referred to as the Fugitive-Agrarians—joined eight others to form a scholarly group known as the Agrarians with a right-wing political and economic focus. The Agrarians' first work was the publication of an anthology called *I'll Take My Stand*, and they contributed extensively to magazines throughout the Thirties, advocating the preservation of the traditional Southern way of life against the encroachments of industrial modernization.

[7] It would be a mistake, however, to assume that the Agrarians were exemplary anti-racists. Their defence of Southern civilization and Southern class and caste distinctions was deeply complicit with Southern racism. Fekete gives a fine, succinct analysis of racism in the Agrarian writings in *Critical Twilight*, 233–4 n. 28.

Fugitive days by characterizing the South as simply the most 'European' part of the United States,[8] that is, more in touch with its traditions and culture, more inclined to cultivate graciousness in daily life than the industrial North, but otherwise not some 'exceptional' region to become obsessed with. In the context of the Great Depression and the rise of the American Communist party, the South became a symbol of resistance to modernization—with Soviet communism understood as representing the last phase of industrialization rather than its opposite.[9] The South became the bulwark against modernization that Modernist poetry sometimes dreamed of being, and Ransom thought that the key question of the day was, 'How can the Southern communities, the chief instance of the stationary European principle of culture in America, be reinforced in their ancient integrity as centres of resistance to an all-but-devouring industrialism?'.[10] The backwardness of the South, in a fascinating inversion of Lenin's argument that uneven development in Russia transformed its very backwardness into a revolutionary force, became the South's strength, making its intellectuals more receptive to, and equipped for, the anti-modernizing strategies of twentieth-century aesthetic Modernism. Ransom had no need for a theory of an organic society as, say, Leavis in Britain would have; the American need only cultivate and reinflect some of the most cherished myths of Southern self-description and self-justification from the previous century in order to produce a native alternative to modernization. As Louise Cowan wrote (clearly sharing their mystique), they discovered that 'as Southerners they possessed decided advantages, both as poets and critics. They found that they still held, instinctively, without effort, the "world picture" that Shakespeare had held; they understood from within, as they discovered, those pieties which undergird the entire Western literary tradition and which William Faulkner later came to call the "old verities"'.[11]

Throughout the Thirties the Agrarians kept up the rhetorical assault, publishing dozens of articles in sympathetic conservative journals like *The American Review*.[12] Their solution to the problems of

---

[8] Cowan, *Fugitive Group*, 14.

[9] Fekete, *Critical Twilight*, 71.

[10] Quoted ibid., p. 69.

[11] Louise Cowan, *The Southern Critics: An Introduction to the Criticism of John Crowe Ransom, Allen Tate, Donald Davidson, Robert Penn Warren, Cleanth Brooks, and Andrew Lytle* (Dallas, Tex.: University of Dallas Press, 1972), 9.

[12] Ibid., p. 14.

industrial capitalism was a return to the land, a revival of non-market, subsistence farming that would solve immediate economic problems and, incidentally, preserve the traditional Southern way of life and its 'arts of living': 'social arts of dress, conversation, manners, the table, the hunt, politics, oratory, the pulpit'.[13]

Agrarianism, of course, found no substantial social base in Depression America and faded away, one more forgotten bit of social scheming from the Thirties. But the impulses which gave birth to it as an isolated, intellectual political movement continued to animate its progenitors as they moved North and into the last, most influential phase of their development, their rebirth as New Critics.

In their last phase of development, according to Fekete's useful narrative schema, the Fugitive-Agrarians ended their conservative anti-capitalist trajectory by finding an accommodation with the system in the Northern universities, where they gained more influence and social impact than they ever had in their overtly political days. The critical theory and methodology they developed as a home for the values and aspirations of their Fugitive and Agrarian past found a waiting audience for much the same reason as Knight's work: it was a method recognizably 'humanist' and 'generalist' in orientation, Modernist in sensibility and concepts, and complex enough to satisfy the disciplinary criteria of professionalism.

As usual, Ransom led the way. In 1937 he moved north to Ohio, becoming editor of *The Kenyon Review* in 1939, a post he held until his retirement in 1959. The move was both symbolic and efficacious, the outcome of a strategy announced in the final chapter of *The World's Body* (1938), 'Criticism, Inc.'. Backing away from the failed goals of agrarianism and evidencing a new willingness to find virtue in modern science, Random announced a change of allegiance to a new vehicle for cultural reform, the society's institutions of higher education. A number of wry pronouncements in *Kenyon Review* editorials over the next decade would explain Ransom's turnabout against agrarianism. In one rumination, he wrote:

... the Southern Agrarians did not go back to the farm, with the exceptions which I think were not thoroughgoing. And presently it seemed to them that they could not invite other moderns, their business friends, for example, to do what they were not doing themselves. Nor could they even try to bring it about that practising agrarians, such as there might still be in the Old South, should

13 Ransom, quoted in Fekete, *Critical Twilight*, 68–9.

be insulated from the division of labor and confined securely in their gardens of innocence. An educator or a writer cannot abandon the presuppositions behind his whole vocation. . . . I find an irony at my expense in remarking that the judgment just now delivered by the Declaration of Potsdam against the German people is that they shall return to an agrarian economy. Once I should have thought there could have been no greater happiness for a people, but now I have no difficulty in seeing it for what it is meant to be: a heavy punishment. Technically it might be said to be an unhuman punishment, in the case where the people in the natural course of things have left the garden far behind.[14]

Ransom had grasped that modern art, though it contains the memory of its archaic origins, was itself a product of differentiation and modernization. The whole Fugitive-Agrarian enterprise, he astutely observed, '*reviews* and contributions to *reviews*, fine poems and their exegesis' are 'triumphs of muscular intellect' impossible to imagine in a truly agrarian economy.[15] There could be no going back, and, for better or worse, it was to modern art in the University curriculum— New Criticism—that Ransom pinned his transfigured hopes. As both Cowan and Fekete agree, Ransom had in effect turned his attention away from the South toward redefining what Allen Tate would call in the title of one of his books the profession of the man of letters in the modern world. Henceforth literature, and the proper criticism of it, would have to carry the values and structures that modernization was crushing out of the South and the world. But to fulfill this mission, criticism would have to find a haven, and that haven, for want of a better, was in the universities. Allies would be needed, and Ransom found them in I. A. Richards, T. S. Eliot, and Yvor Winters—the main subjects of his book-length study, *The New Criticism*, which coined the term still in use to designate this complex Anglo-American collaboration. According to Ransom in his manifesto, 'Criticism, Inc.', such a New Criticism would have to be more 'professional' and 'more scientific, or precise, or systematic'[16] if it was to carry the day against the positivism of old-style literary history that was, as we have seen, hegemonic in the major centres of North American learning at the point that Ransom changed the focus of his energies.

[14] John Crowe Ransom, 'Art and the Human Economy', (1945), repr. in *Beating the Bushes: Selected Essays, 1941–1970* (Norfolk, Conn.: New Directions, 1972), 133–4. The essay first appeared in *Kenyon Review*, 7 (Autumn 1945) as a commentary on articles by W. P. Southard and Adorno. The surprising convergence between Adorno and Ransom will be discussed below.

[15] Ibid., p. 133.

[16] Ransom, *The World's Body* (1938; repr. New York: Scribner, 1964), 329.

Ransom's growing preoccupation with the problem of effecting a paradigm shift in literary studies is reflected in his pleas to the old guard in a 1940–1 issue of *Southern Review*: 'They [American literary scholars] have done so well, in fact, that the job is about finished, and they must look for another job, like the victims of technological unemployment; or to see them under a more dignified figure, as the entrepreneurs, they must look for another field for their capital investment.'[17] The older generation, he goes on, can bask in its glory, but the young know 'how ripe the times are for a revolutionary shift of strategy'.[18] He is like an insurgent political leader, plotting his moves. Ransom's basic strategy might be described this way. In order to move New Criticism into the universities and thereby find a home for a revitalized, Arnoldian and Modernist approach to literary studies, he was willing to make efforts to modernize and professionalize that approach. In the aftermath of the Agrarian failure, it seemed to Ransom that only professionals could be counted on to take up the necessary work: '. . . it must be developed by the collective and sustained effort of learned persons—which means that its proper seat is in the universities', he wrote.[19] In case the point was lost, he tried to bring it home in a metaphor that became the title of the chapter: '. . . the whole enterprise might be seriously taken in hand by professionals. Perhaps I use a distasteful figure, but I have the idea that what we need is Criticism, Inc., or Criticism, Ltd.'[20] True, Ransom went on to predict—quite correctly, as it turned out—that the greatest opponents of his scheme were the then current holders of the professorships in the major universities. But in the light of the vast production of New Critically influenced publication in the Fifties and Sixties, Ransom's figure takes on a more sinisterly predictive power than he foresaw: New Criticism, indeed, became a huge conglomerate of instrumentalized discourse, the mirror in many ways of the productive apparatus which, in its origins, it had so passionately denounced. Ironically, it seems clear that the first steps in this direction were taken by the leading New Critics themselves, under Ransom's leadership.

Allen Tate, however, was an important dissenter along this path. Tate demurred in what was reportedly an embittered isolation in the transitional period of the Forties. His contempt for orthodox academic

---

[17] Ransom, 'A Strategy for English Studies', *Southern Review*, 6 (1940–1), 226.
[18] Ibid., p. 227.
[19] Ransom, *World's Body*, 329.
[20] Ibid., p. 330.

scholarship, along with a pointed condemnation of the university's complicity in the business civilization, appears clearly, for example, in the following passage:

... the historical scholars, once the carriers of the humane tradition, have now merely the genteel tradition; the independence of judgment, the belief in intelligence, the confidence in literature, that informed the humane tradition, have disappeared; under the genteel tradition the scholars exhibit timidity of judgment, disbelief in intelligence, and suspicion of the value of literature. These attitudes of scholarship are the attitudes of the *haute bourgeoisie* that support it in the great universities; it is now commonplace to observe that the uncreative money-culture of modern times tolerates the historical routine of the scholars. The routine is 'safe', and it shares with the predatory social process at large a naturalistic basis. And this naturalism easily bridges the thin gap between the teachers' college and the graduate school ...[21]

Given these entrenched attitudes, Tate was not optimistic.

Nevertheless, *The Kenyon Review* was joined by *The Hudson Review*, *The Sewanee Review* (which Tate edited 1944–6), and *The Southern Review* (founded by Cleanth Brooks and Robert Penn Warren in 1935 as a successor to Blackmur's defunct *Hound and Horn*) as disseminators of the new methodology.[22] But perhaps most influential of all were the three New Critical textbooks brought out as an embodiment of the new critical doctrines and approaches: *Understanding Poetry* (1938) and *Understanding Fiction* (1943), each of which was edited by Brooks and Warren; and *Understanding Drama* (1945), edited by Brooks and Robert Heilman.

Once disseminated, New Criticism took on a new life and mission far beyond the control of its Southern progenitors and consequently must be seen in a broader context. Ransom had gambled that the Modernism inherent in New Critical methodology could overcome the instrumentalization inherent in academic professionalism, Tate's protests notwithstanding. The outcome of Ransom's strategic compromise, once the process was taken over by the larger profession as a whole, was I believe a fatal weakening of New Criticism's challenge to modernization in literary studies—although nothing was ever to be the same again after the New Criticism.

From the strength of the initial resistance, it appeared at first that the New Critical revolution might accomplish its transvaluation. René

---

[21] Allen Tate, 'The Present Function of Criticism', in *Collected Essays* (Denver, Colo.: Alan Swallow, 1959), 7.
[22] Fekete, *Critical Twilight*, 88.

Wellek recalled the battles of an earlier day occasioned by the appearance of this new phenomenon:

> ... in a way the younger generation may find it difficult to realize, [in the universities] a purely philological and historical scholarship dominated all instruction, publication, and promotion. I remember that when I first came to study English literature in the Princeton Graduate School in 1927, nearly sixty years ago, no course in American literature, none in modern literature, and none in criticism was offered. . . . Most of the New Critics were college teachers and had to make their way in an environment hostile to any and all criticism. . . . It took Blackmur, Tate, and Winters years to get academic recognition, often against stiff opposition, and even Ransom, R. P. Warren, and Cleanth Brooks, established in quieter places, had their troubles. . . . I still remember vividly the acrimony of the conflict between criticism and literary history at the University of Iowa, where I was a member of the English Department from 1939 to 1946.[23]

In Wellek's terms, New Criticism was clearly successful and revolutionary. But the picture is more complex than that. In fact, though the paradigm shift occurred with surprising rapidity, it appears from our present viewpoint that Ransom lost his wager.

Ransom himself expressed profound misgivings over the progress of the New Critical revolution in 1949, in a review of a poetry anthology edited by his old nemesis Max Eastman, one of the outspoken critics of the New Critical revolution. In his usual courtly way, Ransom paid tribute to Eastman's intelligence and commitment while politely taking exception to some details of his theory. And as if in concession to Eastman's misgivings, Ransom wrote:

> How confidently, twenty years or so past, were some of us offering a new 'understanding of poetry'! I will not say, How brashly; for the innovation was real, it was momentous; but it was not complete, and now it has bogged down at a most embarrassing point. In the academy the verbal analysis has pretty well secured its place and tenure, but its end-products are only half finished, and their ragged showing does not alleviate the original apprehensions of the opposition.[24]

New Criticism, Ransom says, is in danger of becoming 'the merest exercises with words'; the justified reaction to this narrowing of criticism, he fears, however, might be to overthrow the gains that have

---

[23] René Wellek, *A History of Criticism, 1750–1950*, 6 vols. (New Haven, Conn.: Yale University Press, 1955–86), vi. 146–7.

[24] John Crowe Ransom, 'Poets and Flatworms', *Kenyon Review*, 14 (Winter 1949), 159–60.

been made but remain 'half finished'. Critics, he writes, 'have tended to rest in the amorphous experience which they make of the poem without finding there, or seeking, anything to bind it all together or to engage with some notable human concern in the reader'.[25] One direction Ransom would encourage is aesthetic theory. And he would seem to be, by implication, open to situating the texts in a matrix of social, cultural, and political concerns such as Eastman often attempted.

But the matter was by now out of Ransom's hands. New Criticism was in the hands of the 'profession', for better or for worse, and from our present vantage-point, it seems clear that it suffered the fate of philology and historical scholarship, becoming instrument-alized, depleted, and irrelevant. The widespread 'forgetting' of its origins in social protest amounts to a striking instance of social amnesia, the collective repression of what 'doesn't fit' in cultural memory.

The rapid accommodation of New Criticism by the academy—a revolution completed, according to common consensus, by 1955—was due to currents larger than those created by the Fugitive rock thrown into the cultural pond in Nashville in the Twenties. The strain of generalist and humanist championing of 'literature' against the spe-cialization and modernization of literary studies was a protest that, as I noted in Chapter 1, was part of the English-studies scene from its very beginnings and had been drifting in search of a significant modern vehicle for its propagation. In that context, the New Critics were, as William Cain has written, the most articulate and convincing of a number of anti-modernizing discourses that might have provided a rallying point for generalist academic professionals—Babbitt's New Humanism and Marxism are the two Cain mentions as alternatives;[26] these were the very two Ransom had found failing in his call for a New Critical revolution in academia in *The World's Body* (pp. 332–4). The existence of British analogues like Leavis's *Scrutiny* group weighs in as additional evidence for this claim. In any case, the institutional success of New Criticism was, as is agreed by all parties today, at one level revolutionary in its impact, completely recasting and reordering the teaching of English in America and forming the basic assumptions

---

[25] Ibid., p. 159.
[26] William Cain, *The Crisis in Criticism: Theory, Literature and Reform in English Studies* (Baltimore, Md.: Johns Hopkins University Press, 1984), 95–103.

which, Cain goes on to argue, survive in disguised form even in the present, post-New Critical moment. At this point, therefore, it might be useful to review some ways in which New Criticism formed a new critical paradigm by crystallizing and then reorganizing several of the trends I have been tracing in this study, before looking at the specific impact on Shakespeare studies.

Like all the generalist Arnoldian methodologies, the New Criticism was anti-positivistic and value-laden, in pointed distinction to the instrumentalistic scholarly methods—literary history, source- and influence-hunting, philology, for example—that it supplanted. Its emphasis was on the experience of literature 'from the inside', as Cleanth Brooks once put it, and this meant an opening to emotion and hence to the values which underlie the emotions—an opening all the more potent because disguised, as was Knight's, as simply a submission to the text-object which was given primacy and authority. More indirect and subtle than the overt ethical discourse of the New Humanists, New Criticism nevertheless clearly fulfilled the functions which Arnold had assigned for culture in its battle against anarchy; it inculcated in its own way the habits of sweetness and light, through its training of readers' capacities to feel and understand emotional nuances, ethical dilemmas and ambiguities, and complex states of feeling and thought. It was thus suitable to fulfill the humanist and generalist demands for a literary discipline of broad educational relevance to provide 'culture' for the suddenly massified student bodies of the post-World War II period.

In fulfilling a task which had been defined in the Victorian period and which had a distinctly old-fashioned aura, however, New Criticism was aesthetically Modernist, opposed to the 'historical values' that had dominated the Victorian approach to the humanities. There was none of the positivist literary history or the focus on sources and influences or the other methods of Victorian scholarship that held sway in the universities well into the Forties. At the same time, New Criticism managed to avoid the overt moralizing, the sentimentality, and the impressionism that formed the unavoidable accompaniment to positivism in the dissociated Victorian sensibility. The new approach was precise and subtle and distinctly Modernist and spatial: first, the text was isolated from any evolutionary stream it might have previously been organized into, and second, it was subjected to a minute analysis of image and other structures conceived as unified in a single instant of time. It thus closely paralleled, as I mentioned previously, G. Wilson

Knight's spatial hermeneutics. But the New Critical notion of unity, much more open to tensions and fissures than was Knight's method, presents distinctive features to which I will return shortly.

Finally, in fulfilling the demands of humanists and Modernists, New Criticism succeeded in becoming sufficiently 'professional' to meet the disciplinary requirements of complexity and methodology defined in Chapter 1. Ransom's capitulation to the rhetoric of scientism in his *Kenyon Review* period had been designed precisely to meet such requirements, and the subsequent hegemony of New Criticism in the American academy is evidence enough that he succeeded—at least for a twenty-year period and, as some have argued, even up to the present.[27] But its success at one level brought about its failure at another.

In the process of achieving such widespread success and becoming institutionalized, New Criticism clearly underwent a process of instrumentalization. The element of social criticism, its specifically conservative anti-capitalism, became obscured as its reading techniques became appropriated and adapted to the 'industrial' requirements of a burgeoning academic establishment in the post-war era. Having rewritten the canon, reorganized the curriculum and the standards of professional literary study, and redefined what it meant to be a 'professional man [*sic*] of letters in the modern world', New Criticism quickly became a new orthodoxy as complacent in its assumptions and as oppressive in its disciplinary power as the older scholarship it had overthrown. The dynamics of professionalization, I would argue, overcame the (right-wing) insurgent intentions of its originators. In fact, as Cain astutely argued, having accomplished its work, New Criticism as such disappeared: it became simply 'criticism', the close reading of texts through New Critical heuristics (and a few others more lately admitted in the name of broadmindedness) having become *the* professional activity *par excellence* of members of English departments who continue to think in New Critical categories without the New Critical theory that generated them. But this is an old, old

---

[27] Cain argues that New Criticism suffered the fate of all successful revolutions: it became institutionalized with the double effect of (1) having its basic assumptions, most notably that of the primacy of 'close reading' in the discipline of English letters, become so widespread that they are no longer recognized as New Critical, although in fact through such assumptions New Criticism continues to set the terms of the debate; and (2) losing the critical edge of many of its original principles through a process of accommodation to its institutional settings. In this way the New Critical movement is long dead, but New Critical assumptions still dominate the standards and curricula of

story, surprising only to those unconsciously caught up in the powerful paradigmatic process.

Constructing the New Critical Shakespeare

With such sweeping currents in the air, it was inevitable that Shakespeare studies, by now well ensconced in the universities, would be affected. And in truth, the case of Shakespeare was one that the founding New Critics were anxious to confront for their own reasons. Shakespeare was a central figure in the New Critical theory of history and a challenge in the task of adapting reading techniques that had been primarily designed for the reading of lyric poetry to larger scale literary works.

My reference to a New Critical historical theory may surprise some readers—after all, the method was and is often criticized for its supposed slighting of 'historical background'. But René Wellek has argued convincingly that the historical scheme worked out by Cleanth Brooks in *Modern Poetry and the Tradition* and *The Well-Wrought Urn*, shared in its essentials by the other original Fugitive-Agrarians, and institutionalized in the shape and implicit hierarchies of the present literary canon, amounts in fact to a theory of history.[28] It is a theory partially based on the same fragmentary remarks of T. S. Eliot on the dissociation of sensibility that, as we shall see in Chapter 4, had so inflamed the Cambridge English programme of the Twenties.[29] And Eliot's sketch of a theory, we have seen, powerfully reinforced certain strands of Southern self-definition dear to the Agrarians after a parallel process of Modernist myth-making.

In the Eliot-influenced history, the age of Donne and Shakespeare was privileged as a historical moment that was beginning to be modern but not yet dissociated; it was a unique moment in which the most valued works of English literature were produced. If the New Critics' identification with the revival of Donne had misled any readers as to

most American Departments of English, more than twenty years after its supposed demise (pp. 104–21). It is hard to disagree with this analysis, which I adapt in what follows. This view is also consistent with Fekete's argument, written before the post-structuralist paradigm shift, seeing the third phase of New Criticism's trajectory as one of accommodation to the capitalist system which it had opposed from the right.

[28] Wellek, *History of Criticism*, vi. 148–9.

[29] Ransom, however, was politely but firmly sceptical of Eliot's schema in a detailed discussion of Eliot's essay 'The Metaphysical Poets' in Section 5 of the chapter on Eliot in *The New Criticism* (Norfolk, Conn.: New Directions, 1941). But Eliot's theory was crucial to Cleanth Brooks's seminal works in literary history (see above) and was certainly one of the components of the New Critical programme.

the place of Shakespeare in the New Critical pantheon, Cleanth Brooks was anxious to set the record straight: 'I began by suggesting that our reading of Donne might contribute something to our reading of Shakespeare, though I tried to make plain the fact that I had no design of trying to turn Shakespeare into Donne, or—what I regard as nonsense—of trying to exalt Donne above Shakespeare.'[30] Brooks goes on in a vein reminiscent of Spurgeon and Knight in England, studying the development and meaning of selected lines of imagery in *Macbeth*. The methodology of this pioneering essay, 'The Naked Babe and the Cloak of Manliness', in fact, advances beyond Knight's methods only in incidentals. Like so many others, Brooks mentions Spurgeon only in order to make use of her discoveries and to take issue with her pre-Modernist suppositions (pp. 32–4). On G. Wilson Knight, for whatever reason, he is silent. But like Knight he wants to put the discovery of image patterns in the service of notions of the organic unity of the work of art, rather than, like Spurgeon, to get at the historical Shakespeare. 'What is at stake', he writes, 'is the whole matter of the relation of Shakespeare's imagery to the total structures of the plays themselves' (p. 32). His solution is strikingly reminiscent of Knight's in the latter's analysis of *Antony and Cleopatra* (see Chapter 2): here Brooks relates the image patterns to central and apparently Coleridgean 'symbols', held to 'dominate the play' (p. 32) and to give us a kind of interpretive guide to the moral implications of Macbeth's tragedy:

The clothed daggers and the naked babe—mechanism and life—instrument and end—death and birth—that which should be left bare and clean and that which should be clothed and warmed—these are facets of two of the great symbols which run throughout the play . . . with a flexibility which must amaze the reader, the image of the garment and the image of the babe are so used as to encompass an astonishingly large area of the total situation. And between them—the naked babe, essential humanity, humanity stripped down to the naked thing itself, and yet as various as the future—and the various garbs which humanity assumes, the robes of horror, the hypocrites disguise, the inhuman 'manliness' with which Macbeth endeavors to cover up his essential

---

[30] Cleanth Brooks, *The Well-Wrought Urn* (New York: Harcourt, 1947), 28–9. Gary Taylor points out that this passage had not appeared in an earlier version of the chapter published as an essay, 'Shakespeare as a Symbolist Poet', *Yale Review*, 34 (1944–5), 21–46. Taylor thinks the earlier version presents Shakespeare as 'secondary to Donne' (Taylor, *Reinventing Shakespeare*, 265–7), but he does not explain why Brooks changed the emphasis in the later version.

humanity—between them, they furnish Shakespeare with his most subtle and ironically telling instruments. (p. 49)

As close as Brooks is in this essay to Knight's spatial hermeneutics, there are tell-tale differences of emphasis. Brooks is much more interested than Knight was in irony and in how the unity of the Shakespearian metaphors he studies is threatened by discord and heterogeneity. He calls our attention to a description of Macbeth's blooded sword as 'Unmannerly breech'd with gore' and glosses the unfamiliar participle as meaning 'covered as with breeches', producing an incongruous and, as he has it, shocking, effect still potent in the present day. He has uncovered, of course, precisely that baroque tension, that clash of affect and denotation, characteristic of Donne's Metaphysical style and, so it was thought, of Symbolist and Modernist poetry. Knight, as I mentioned, was characteristically much quicker to posit an overriding unity in the plays he analyses. Clearly Brooks is anxious to redefine spatial hermeneutics under the full influence of New Critical theory and practice and to go beyond the British critics working in similar directions. But to judge how well he succeeded, we should turn to a richer analysis, that of *1 Henry IV* in the New Critical textbook *Understanding Drama*.

Reading 1 Henry IV *with Brooks and Heilman*

Understanding Drama, edited by Cleanth Brooks and Robert Heilman (professors at Louisiana State University at the time of publication), was the last of a series of college literature anthologies which, as I mentioned previously, were among the most effective disseminators of New Critical methodology to the American academy.[31]

The anthology presents much material to justify the traditional idea of a 'formalist' bias in New Criticism. Much attention is paid to the notion that drama is a distinct literary genre with its own formal problematics which each playwright must resolve. But this material is among the least original in the text. Just beneath this formalist veneer can be discerned a compelling preoccupation with the theme of what the authors call 'the way of the world', a notion of human social life as morally 'relativistic', characteristic by complexities of motivations and actions, which require numerous 'compromises'—in general a world to be approached only through the complex mediations of layers of

---

[31] Cleanth Brooks and Robert B. Heilman, *Understanding Drama* (New York: Holt, 1945).

protective irony. Irony, I will argue, is the central, master concept of the anthology.

While *Understanding Drama* does, indeed, present an 'approach' to literature, a set of instructions for reading a number of canonical plays, it also, quite unabashedly, presents an approach to 'life', the life-world of common human experience, which the plays are held to represent and illuminate. And that approach is one plainly marked by the experiences of Fugitive-Agrarians who have decided to make their peace with the ways of the world and, through a strategy of wily compromise and accommodation, find a place within it. Moreover, I believe, it is this stance toward the social that gave New Criticism its enormous appeal in the immediate post-war period, and which led it into directions far beyond those foreseen by its originators. With its aura of a necessary trafficking with a corrupt world (but always through protective irony), it took its place as a kind of structure of feelings which helped 'make sense of' (justified) that era of McCarthyism and the Cold War, when a generation of intellectuals was learning to transform traditional 'American idealism' in foreign policy to institutionalized terrorism, whether through nuclear blackmail or CIA-directed coups and covert interventions.[32]

As might be expected in an introductory textbook written by critical innovators, the book's introduction mixes received commonplaces and the newer critical doctrines somewhat haphazardly. There are definitions of 'exposition', 'progression', and 'plausibility'—all already familiar concepts in 1945. But there are also unexpected forays into the topics of poetry's relation to drama and of the 'naturalness' of poetic drama that bespeak New Critical preoccupations. And if the question behind these ruminations can be imagined to have been, 'Can New Criticism discuss drama in other ways than tracing its image patterns and symbols?', the imagined answer, by the end of the discussion is: 'Yes. We can concentrate on dramatic action as interrelated with, but conceptually distinct from, verbal texture and pose the question of the play's unity.'[33] And by the time we have worked our way

---

[32] For an insightful demonstration and elaboration of these comments, see Mark Walhout, 'The New Criticism and the Crisis of American Liberalism: The Poetics of the Cold War', *College English*, 49 (December 1987), 861–71. Walhout, too, believes the traditional labelling of the New Critics as 'formalists' misses a good deal of their historic specificity.

[33] Note for example, the passage: 'Drama and poetry are both concerned with presenting situations which will be meaningful. Poetry uses imagery, rhythm, symbols, statements, as the words of the author or of some character, spoken to himself or to

through the discussions of all the plays, and most particularly after that of Shakespeare, we would have to add: 'Above all, we can treat the posited unity as problematic and conceptualize all the surpluses, deferrals, and disparatenesses that threaten or contradict that unity as ironies forming a complex structure whose unity can perhaps never be fully understood but is accepted as an act of faith.'

It is through the concept of irony and its peculiar relation to unity—and the ways in which these apparently formal questions impinge upon a relation to the social as well as the literary 'text'—that American New Criticism develops into something distinct from, and even more influential than, the spatial hermeneutics developed by G. Wilson Knight, even while retaining certain family resemblances to this and other British cousins.

Like the other New Critical textbooks, this one is marked by a deliberately provocative, strategic bypassing of 'literary history' as it was understood at the time. But there was no lack of guidance for the teacher. In fact, as compared with later anthologies, Brooks and Heilman's is rather lavish in apparatus and scant in choice of texts. There is an opening section of thirty-one pages which attempts to discuss the specificity of drama as a distinct literary form, and each of the plays has additional commentary in the form of an introduction, a discussion section with questions after each act, and a conclusion with more questions. The 515-page anthology contains only eight complete plays. The plays are pointedly presented out of chronological order, and in the following sequence: Oscar Wilde's *Lady Windermere's Fan*, *Everyman*, Plautus's *The Twin Menaechmi*, George Lillo's *The London Merchant*, Richard Sheridan's *The School for Scandal*, Ibsen's *Rosmersholm*, Shakespeare's *1 Henry IV*, and William Congreve's *The Way of the World*. They are arranged in three categories: Wilde's play stands alone to illustrate 'How the Problems Are Met'; *Everyman*, Plautus, and Lillo are 'Simpler Types'; and the last four are 'More Complex Types'.

While this arrangement is certainly not historical, it is doubtful that the label 'formalistic' is a very helpful one in getting at the controlling principles of selection and order. The problem with the term 'formalism' in this connection is that it obscures the New Criticism's social and political connections.

someone else. Drama depends almost entirely on what people do and say to each other: meanings, thought, feelings must in the main be externalized in conduct (though the conduct need not be violent or sensational)' (p. 23).

In the first place, we should note, the plays are categorized, not by genre or other purely formal criteria, but by the quite different judgement of whether the play is of a 'simpler' or a 'more complex' type. As we soon learn, a synonym for 'more complex' is 'mature'—that is, characteristic of age, experience, and wisdom (see, for example, pp. 385–6). This is of course a value judgement, partially aesthetic, partially ethical—something of which the New Critics were themselves well aware. The arrangement of the textbook, in its progression from the flippant and cynical Wilde (as they present him, criticizing his play as melodramatic) to the twin climaxes of *1 Henry IV* and Congreve's *The Way of the World* (a title which thematizes the book's secret preoccupation) suggests a process of *Bildung* through which the student is expected to advance in wisdom if not in age and learn to negotiate the ways of the world through mastering the ability to 'balance' the conflicting values and visions of complex literary works.

For a supposedly formalist text—to pursue the same point through a slightly different tack—the anthology is strangely deficient in representing the most studied and valued traditional dramatic form: tragedy. True, Lillo's play is generically tragic, but it is a throwaway, a 'simpler' type. Ibsen's *Rosmersholm* is no comedy, to be sure, but the authors explicitly maintain that it 'falls short of tragedy' (p. 314). Not to put too fine a point on the matter, what we would expect is what almost every present-day anthology virtually always includes, at least one Greek and one Shakespearian tragedy. But if we examine the scanty remarks the authors make on the tragic, we can realize that in this text, tragedy cannot be allowed to speak: it holds the place of absolute values, above the ways of the world and must, on this occasion of accommodation and institutionalization (New Criticism's truck with the ways of the world in the fleshpots of the academy), be held in reserve and kept in silence: 'In tragedy, we may say, there is no easy way out, because the characters are coming to grips with what is permanently true. In tragedy, therefore, we expect to find symbols of permanent values' (p. 79). Comedy, in contrast, or at least the type practised by Wilde, 'is not concerned with fundamental problems of good and evil'. It is instead focused on 'the realm of sociology, of people's attitudes and opinions, which change from time to time and hence need not be taken with ultimate seriousness. The problems are those of an external world, the world where matters can be managed and arranged, where compromises can be made, and agreeable solutions arrived at. In terms of [Wilde's] play this is the world of comedy—a world of moral relativism. Here we do not have a world of moral absolutes, of fundamental principles of conduct, of an underlying moral structure that cannot be tampered with' (p. 79).

In the discussion of *1 Henry IV*, as we shall see, the implied evaluation of a good and moral tragedy and a bad and cynical comedy is silently dropped, but the insistence that comedy is fundamentally concerned with the 'ways of the world' and 'moral relativism' is retained through some very fancy—and self-deconstructing—footwork. *Understanding Drama* could easily be retitled *Understanding Comedy*—or better yet perhaps, *Adapting to the Ways of the World*.

The reading of *1 Henry IV* presented by Brooks and Heilman in their anthology, then, is a personally disclosive one, displaying the preoccupations of the transition from Agrarianism to New Criticism—preoccupations that will resonate in the Cold War context in a myriad of ways. The critical techniques they develop and elaborate to carry their vision, however, will enter other social contexts and take on other meanings.

Put in their contexts in the history of criticism of the Henry IV plays, Brooks and Heilman's reading of the play is a revolutionary innovation that could be said to constitute a minor paradigm shift in its own right. Their powerful concept of irony allows them to outflank and reconceptualize one of the oldest critical cruxes in Shakespeare studies—whether we as readers are to be of Falstaff's or of Prince Hal's party. Their now inevitable-sounding answer was: both—and neither. 'The probability is', they write blandly, 'that we shall miss the play if we assume that Shakespeare is forcing upon us a choice of the *either-or* variety. Is it not possible that Shakespeare is not asking us to choose at all, but rather to contemplate, with understanding and some irony, a world very much like the world that we know, a world in which compromises have to be made, a world in which the virtues of Falstaff become, under changed conditions, necessary, and thus, in a sense, accommodated to virtue?' (p. 384). A critical scaffolding had finally been erected to encompass and support the tedious wrangling of generations of critics over 'the meaning' of the rejection of Falstaff. If it was not a Copernican revolution in criticism, it was certainly a Hegelian one, in the sense of a method of thought based in an overcoming of previously defined antinomies through breathtaking dialectical syntheses (and in the additional sense, if I may anticipate, of positing a kind of Absolute Knowledge in which the tensions are theoretically resolved).

Although, following textbook conventions, the commentary on the play lacks a scholarly apparatus of attributions and notes, it is easily apparent that the discussion is grounded from the first in the history of comment on the plays, and much of the writing is in the form of shifting dialogues with past, sometimes named, sometimes unnamed commentators. In their opening remarks, for example, the authors immediately name Falstaff as a centre of past critical interest and define two readings of the play, both of which are held to be problematic: that *1 Henry IV* is a 'rather stodgy history redeemed only by Falstaff and the tavern scenes'—a loose rendition of A. C. Bradley's well-known essay on Falstaff and a fair paraphrase of E. K. Chambers's brief remarks on the *Henry IV* plays;[34] and a second view that values the historical portion of the play and sees Falstaff as a unity-destroying intrusion (p. 317).[35] The question of the play's unity is thereby raised in the very first paragraph of commentary on the play; it will receive extended treatment in Brooks and Heilman's conclusion. It might be useful to examine at this point the argument the authors make urging students to at least entertain the possibility that the play is indeed unified:

Still, it will not do for us to begin by assuming that [the play lacks real unity]. There is abundant evidence that Shakespeare strove here as elsewhere for a total unity. The play will be more interesting—and, as a matter of fact, the character of Falstaff himself will seem the more brilliant—if we are able to see how he fits into the play as a whole than if we take him merely as a brilliant excrescence on the play . . . (p. 318)

---

[34] See A. C. Bradley, 'The Rejection of Falstaff' (1902), repr. in *Oxford Lectures on Poetry* (London: Macmillan, 1959), 247–78 and E. K. Chambers, *Shakespeare: A Survey* (London: Sidgewick & Jackson, 1925), 118–26. The relevant excerpts can be found in *Shakespearean Criticism*, i. 333–7.

[35] This last is a position I am unable to confirm was ever put in print, given the long, virtually uninterrupted praise of Falstaff as a dramatic creation enunciated even by those critics like Samuel Johnson and G. G. Gervinus who 'condemn' Falstaff as embodying the 'inferior' side of man within what they see as the value-structure of the play(s). Many critics, however—notably Bradley—believed Falstaff threatened the unity of the plays, but I have found none who wished therefore that Shakespeare had not invented him. One imagines this as something Eliot might have said in the revisionary spirit of 'Hamlet and His Problems', but, so far as I know, he did not. Brooks and Heilman possibly are thinking of remarks made by Lily B. Campbell, the historical critic, who noted in her *Shakespeare's 'Histories': Mirrors of Elizabethan Policy* (San Marino, Calif.: Huntington Library, 1947) that the Falstaff story obscures the historical movement of the plays (but without quite wishing away Falstaff). The date of this work, 1947, makes it postdate *Understanding Drama*, but it is possible the New Critics had heard of Campbell's views by other means.

The 'abundant evidence', however, will turn out to be the schema of unity erected through the reading of the critics in an (undefined) hermeneutic circle. Characteristically, the pivotal positing of unity is rightly highlighted but theoretically unjustified. At work here is of course the influence of the Modernist paradigm with its valorization of space and organic unity. As mediators between Modernism and the incipient mass audience constituted by the student readers of the textbook, Brooks and Heilman are essentially saying, 'Trust us'. This stance accounts in very large part for the characteristic bewilderment of generations of the students of New Critical professors who, as has often been noted, left their classes convinced that their mentors possessed secret knowledge of the meaning of texts that was inaccessible to them. The students were, in this sense, right.

The reading of *1 Henry IV* performed by Brooks and Heilman is, therefore, a spatialized reading, such as G. Wilson Knight had developed and Brooks had shown his talent for in his analysis of Macbeth discussed previously. Here, however, an effort is made to go beyond a dependency on the 'lyric' or 'poetic' characteristics of the text—its images and symbols. Instead, the authors attempt a spatial reading which organizes specifically *dramatic* qualities of the text, qualities they had defined in the opening section of the textbook as revolving around plot and action. In fact, their method also makes heavy use of that traditional category of Shakespeare analysis, the character. But, in pointed distinction to Bradley, the characters here are always subordinated to the overall 'system' of the play's (presupposed) organic unity; they are presented as centres of values and points of view mutually defined through a system of ironic interactions.[36] This leads to a dizzying series of compare-and-contrast paragraphs in which an effort is made to 'see' each point of view in its positivity, then as implicitly 'critiqued' by the other points of view.

First, the myriad characters are divided into three groupings— court, tavern, and rebel—each with its own value-system (pp. 329–30). Then, in a series of questions after Act II, the student is led into

[36] The 'source' for such a critical technique is undoubtedly the brief but highly influential narrative theory of Henry James's Prefaces, well known for its effect on New Critical approaches to the novel. But the method is also reminiscent of the 'philosophical criticism' of the nineteenth-century German Hegelian Shakespearians Ulrici and Gervinus (the latter briefly discussed in Chapter 1), who also subordinated their discussion of characters to an attempt to define the overall dramatic system of the plays. This apparently random analogy takes on significance below, when I argue that Brooks and Heilman have, apparently inadvertently, recreated certain procedures of Hegelian system-building in their reading of *1 Henry IV*.

beginning the work of charting the intricate parallels and contrasts of the three groups. For example, in Question 1, the student is asked, '. . . may it be said that Percy is careless and impetuous with regard to momentous events, preparing for them far less carefully than the prince and his friends prepare for the really well-planned Gadshill robbery? If so, how does this anticipate later events' (p. 344). No effete advocates of the open-ended question here, may it be said.

In the same section, we are also prepared to see Falstaff as complexly ironic: '. . . [Falstaff's] statement, "I am a rogue, if I drunk today," is primarily an emphatic way of asserting his thirst. But taken literally, it is a gross and obvious falsehood. Falstaff hardly intends to be taken literally, and when he is taken literally, he does not attempt to argue the point: "All's one for that," he says. But the literal meaning is perfectly true: Falstaff is a rogue—although a very pleasant rogue' (p. 345). The term 'literal' self-destructs under the torture given it here, perhaps, but the reading is shrewd and superior to anything that had come before in defining the disparate affects which the history of criticism had proved Falstaff capable of provoking—only here, the critical wrangling is (apparently) resolved, into a single if complex, moment of insight. It might be justly said of this, and similar passages, that we are a single step short of deconstruction—a topic to which I will return shortly.

Finally in this section the notes lead us to contemplate Hotspur in the light of the intricate parallels and contrasts. The short scene in Act II where Hotspur reads and angrily denounces a letter from a conspirator refusing to join his rebellion is probed in the light of the previous tavern-scenes. Hotspur's monologue is organized into the thematics of 'cowardice' and of 'true/false' that previous notes had defined in the tavern sequence. Hotspur's self-assurance, the authors suggest, has to be interrogated by an audience aware of the earlier complexities. And here Brooks and Heilman raise a question which they had touched on earlier in the text in their discussion of Wilde and which they will seek to answer below in terms of *1 Henry IV*: what might be the 'design' they ask, of the repeated uses of the terms 'true' and 'false' in so many different contexts in the play? Their qualified answer is well worth noting, for it will in turn raise questions to be resolved in the crucial concluding section of the commentary:

May it not be a reminder, perhaps, of the complexities one runs into when one sets out to define *true* and *false* (like the difficulties presented by the word *coward*)? What *is* truth? If Falstaff's fellow-hold-up men do not observe their commitments to him, they are in one sense not *true*; if Hotspur's party do not stick to him, they are not *true*. But if the associates are not *true* to Falstaff and Hotspur respectively, are they not, in another sense, the more *true* to the king? It may be just to suggest that here we have a relativistic view of what is true and false; if that is so, it immediately leads us to ask the question, 'Is Shakespeare, in presenting the complexities of truth, going to be content to say that it is relative, or, in the political world about which he writes here, will he present, finally, an *absolute truth*? Or will he be true in several ways at once? (pp. 348–9)

The bogy of relativism—in some studies, the very essence of Modernist ethics—haunts Brooks and Heilman here as it haunted their generation. We will see below the gymnastics they undertake—futilely, I will argue—to exorcize it. It is a case where a conservative ideology conflicts with a Modernist aesthetic sensibility.

In the notes after Act III, Brooks and Heilman present some unoriginal interpretations of Hotspur and King Henry, but these of course are necessary components of the dramatic 'system' they are defining for the play. Hotspur is seen to be ironized as unrealistic and impulsive (p. 359, Q. 3). The King is seen as having a 'bad conscience' (p. 360, Q. 5) and an obsession with a 'narrow formula of success' that hides his own political mistakes from him (p. 360, Q. 6). We are prepared for a double-edged evaluation of Hal as 'a better politician than his father, though his genuine delight in Falstaff may redeem him, for many readers, from the charge that he is . . . "a vile politician" ' (p. 360, Q. 7). And we are finally given a gloss to Falstaff's roguishness: he lacks political seriousness and a sense of responsibility (pp. 360–1, Q. 8). For the moment, students are allowed to 'balance' the irony in the figure of Hal, who seems to express the positivity through the lack of which the King, Hotspur, and Falstaff are judged wanting—a familiar enough move in previous criticism.

In the concluding 'Notes' on *1 Henry IV*, however, this essentially eighteenth-century structure of irony is superseded. Brooks and Heilman intend to have it as many ways as they can: Bradley will be shown to have been right in valuing Falstaff, but wrong in thinking he destroyed the unity of the play; Falstaff and Hotspur are 'foils' (p. 377) to Hal, but they are each 'above him' in different but equally valid ways. But in another sense they both fall short of Hal, who forms an Aristotelian 'golden mean' between their excesses (pp. 377–9);[37]

---

[37] Brooks and Heilman credit Robert Penn Warren for this idea (p. 377), which formed the thesis of a later article, William B. Hunter, Jr., 'Falstaff', *South Atlantic Quarterly*, 40 (Jan. 1951), 86–95.

Falstaff is a 'philosopher' whose vision is as acute as any in the play (pp. 379–80), but he is revealed 'in action' as lacking the commitment that the truly heroic require—the battle-scenes are said to 'subordinate Falstaff, for all his delightfulness, to something larger (somewhat to the resentment of readers to whom Falstaff is a kind of demigod); and this subordination itself is a unifying process' (p. 382). This last point is in turn so heavily qualified, however, that it constitutes one of the points at which Brooks and Heilman's argument virtually self-destructs—or deconstructs itself, as we shall see.

The attempt to hold in balance these disparate and conflicting readings of the plays leads into the denouement of the commentary with its final resting-point in an appeal to what is called 'Shakespeare's irony' and 'mature comedy'—two terms which amount to pretty much the same thing. We should look closely at the means by which this 'still point' at the heart of motion is reached.

The first point established is the one I reproduced earlier as the critical innovation which goes furthest in allowing for the kind of 'balance' Brooks and Heilman want to establish: the notion that the reader *should not* attempt to 'choose' between the conflicting worlds of Falstaff and Hal, but rather should 'contemplate, with understanding and some irony' the complex structure the play presents as a kind of simulacrum of the world of experience in modernity (p. 384).

But the authors are not content simply to leave matters at this point; by itself, this might smack too much of Croce's aestheticist view of Shakespeare's histories, which saw them as 'without passion for any sort of particular ideals, but . . . animated with sympathy for the varying lots of striving humanity',[38] or of Keats's Romantic notion of 'negative capability'. Brooks and Heilman must prove themselves to be requisitely 'tough-minded'. They therefore, for the first time, turn to the rejection of Falstaff at the end of Part 2, that crux which is so much more resistant to 'balance' than the more jovial ending of Part 1. They quickly define the two traditional readings of the rejection: the one arguing that by the end of Part 2 we have lost much of our sympathy for Falstaff and are ready for the rejection; the second that the rejection is simply the final epiphany of Hal's strain of cold-blooded Machiavellianism that we might have noticed from the first (p. 385). The New Critical solution, of course, is 'having the matter both ways':

Is not the real point this: that in Hal's rejection of Falstaff something is lost as well as gained—that a good king, one grants, must reject Falstaff, but that in

[38] In *Ariosto, Shakespeare, and Corneille*; quoted in *Shakespearean Criticism*, i. 445.

the process by which a man becomes a good king, something else—something spontaneous, something in itself good and attractive—must be sacrificed; that growing up is something which man must do and yet even in growing up he loses, necessarily, something that is valuable? (pp. 385–6)

Shakespeare, they continue, neither sentimentalizes nor moralizes the situation. Bradley, they implicitly charge, was a sentimentalist, regretting the practical necessity of the rejection; but J. Dover Wilson, explicitly cited in the discussion, is seen as a 'moralizer' who unnecessarily 'blackens' Falstaff, refuses to see his positivity, and thereby slights the 'fullness' and 'maturity' of Shakespeare's irony. Only by granting both Hal and Falstaff simultaneously their 'moments', only by constituting a 'unity' in which these apparently conflicting values can both be true, do we approach the greatness of Shakespearian 'mature comedy' (p. 386).

Finally Brooks and Heilman are ready to differentiate themselves from Croce and Keats and exorcize the demon of 'moral relativism': '. . . Shakespeare's final attitude toward his characters (and toward the human predicament, generally) is one of a very complex irony, though it is an irony which will be either missed altogether, or easily misinterpreted as an *indifferent relativism—that is a mere balancing of two realms of conduct and a refusal to make any judgment between them*' (p. 386, emphasis mine). There is instead, they argue, valorization in Shakespeare, apparently conflicting valorizations which, however, can be sorted out and understood by putting each at its proper 'level': Hal is right to reject Falstaff at 'his' (political?) level, Falstaff in turn right to feel crushed and right in general in his anti-political sallies and criticisms which are 'on certain levels', 'thoroughly valid' (pp. 386–7). It is at this point that the authors recur to the distinction between tragedy and comedy which had been elliptically made in the discussion of Oscar Wilde's *Lady Windermere's Fan*; once more comedy is said to eschew the world of absolute values and to restrict itself to a non-transcendent realm, 'a world of compromises'. Shakespeare's comedy, here, however, in contrast to Wilde's supposed callowness, is 'mature'—'fully aware of the seriousness of the issues' (p. 386). As always in a New Critical essay, it is the final paragraph, which must attempt to evoke and hold in wholeness the paradoxes, tensions, and ironies previously defined, that is crucial:

If the prince must choose between two courses of action—and, of course, he must choose—we as readers are not forced to choose; indeed, perhaps the core of Shakespeare's ironic insight comes to this: that man must choose and yet that the choice can never be a wholly satisfactory one. If the play is a comedy in this sense, then the 'comic' scenes of the play turn out to be only an aspect of, though an important aspect of, the larger comedy. To repeat, the reader must decide for himself whether he can accept the play as a fully unified organism. But the reader who can so accept it may well feel that it represents Shakespeare's most sophisticated level of comedy, a comedy, indeed, more fine-grained and 'serious' than the romantic comedies such as *As You Like It* and written with a surer touch than the 'bitter' comedies such as *All's Well That Ends Well*. (p. 387)

And we recall the earlier definition of the peculiar unity said to be characteristic of 'mature' Shakespearian comedy: '... here Shakespeare has given us one of the wisest and fullest commentaries on human action possible in the comic mode—a view which scants nothing, which covers up nothing, and which takes into account in making its affirmations the most searching criticism of that which is affirmed. For such a reader, Shakespeare has no easy moral to draw, no simple generalization to make' (p. 386).

Let us review some of the intricate footwork being undertaken here. With their endorsement of the theory of Hal as 'golden mean', Brooks and Heilman come very close to organizing the materials of the play so that Hal—as he is revealed in the battle-scenes—becomes the embodiment of the highest values of the play and a measure against which the other characters may be judged. This is a very old and traditional approach which had been revived in the Forties by E. M. W. Tillyard (whom they don't mention) and J. Dover Wilson in *The Fortunes of Falstaff*. It is an approach which allows the complex series of parallels and contrasts and the clash of ethical visions to be finally fixed and frozen in an ordered array that can be logically conceptualized and which gives the play an ethical import. Irony is crucial to such a reading—irony as a structure of values such that we are able to judge the behaviour of any character and find it either satisfactory and not subject to irony—the case of the ultimately heroic Hal in this reading; or we could find the action ethically deficient in some way and there- fore subject to irony, as in the cases of Hotspur and Falstaff. The schema demands, of course, a clear, fixed, and authoritative set of accepted norms somehow manifest in the overall structure of the play. It is a structure, as I mentioned, typical of neo-classical thought and perfected in the novels of Jane Austen.

The problem is of course Falstaff. If *1 Henry IV* is to be read as informed by a stable ethical system, Falstaff must be firmly contained, as he is, momentarily, in the 'golden mean' schema. But as Sigurd Burckhardt so insightfully pointed out, that kind of symmetry, represented in the play by Hal's twin valedictions over the vanquished bodies of Hotspur and Falstaff, is exploded when Falstaff rises up undead.[39] Exactly the same thing happens in Brooks and Heilman's commentary. Falstaff is repeatedly resurrected, not allowed to remain in a stable relation of subordination to Hal in the commentary's construing of the play's value structure. Each statement of 'balance' is supplemented by a qualification, which in fact destroys the previous balance. And, in an interminable Derridean process, Falstaff is continually buried again, just after being resurrected. The difference from a Derridean structure of deferment, of course, is that Brooks and Heilman assert that, in principle, the movement can be frozen: 'Here we come to the crucial problem of unity: what attitude, finally, are we to adopt toward Falstaff and the prince? Which is right? With which of the two are our sympathies finally to rest?' (pp. 383–4). It is at this point that the refusal to make an 'either-or' choice is put forward as the solution, an emphasis repeated in the crucial last paragraph. But this undermines the insistence that Shakespeare is no 'moral relativist', that, as a mature writer, he has a stable if complex value-system in the work. This consideration in turn leads them to a new formula:

... in Hal's rejection of Falstaff something is lost as well as gained—that a good king, one grants, must reject Falstaff, but that in the process by which a man becomes a good king, something else—something spontaneous, something in itself good and attractive—must be sacrificed; that growing up is something which man must do and yet that even in growing up he loses, necessarily, something that is valuable? (pp. 385–6)

But this formula resists the hierarchicization that could freeze it into stability. The metaphor of 'growing up' would seem to imply the superiority of Hal over. Falstaff, of maturity over childhood. But elsewhere in the essay, this hierarchy is shown to be capable of inversion as the writers ring the changes on 'childish' and 'child-like' (p. 379). Which, after all, is the 'higher' of these 'levels'? Not to answer this question would be to fall into the 'relativism' that they fear, to admit that even in the 'everyday' world of comedy—that is, for them, the social world—there may be conflicts which admit of no clear resolution. Such an admission would undo the firm separation that they posited between the tragic and the comic. It would reveal that 'compromise' is no easy matter, even in the degraded comic (social) world where we presumably live without touching the tragic absolutes, reserved 'elsewhere'. It might even confront these former Agrarian absolutists with the truth of the bargain they have made: that the urbane 'compromise' involved in the transformation from Agrarians to New Critics may have involved those 'absolute principles' that were supposedly reserved elsewhere sacrosanct, in some realm above the social.

The formula of 'something lost, something gained', it seems to me, comes as near as any in the essay in holding for a moment in a single conceptualization the conflicting discourses which the critics are attempting to fuse into a unity. Brooks and Heilman have spontaneously reproduced what the Lukács of *The Theory of the Novel* defined as 'the highest freedom that can be achieved in a world without God':[40] the novel's double-edged irony. They are immersed in that problem of modernity which Lukács described as follows:

> This negativity of the central characters requires a positive counterweight and, most unhappily for the modern humorous novel, this 'positive' counterweight can be nothing else but the objectivation of the bourgeois concept of decent behaviour. . . . This is the artistic reason why Dickens' novels, so marvellously rich in comic characters, seem in the end so flat and moralistic. He had to make his heroes come to terms, without conflict, with the bourgeois society of this time . . . (pp. 106–7)

Only by constantly deferring the question of positivity, by invoking the kind of cosmic and interminable ironic interplay which Lukács sees as accounting for the greatness of the Sancho Panza–Don Quixote relation in Cervantes's novel, is it possible to surmount the problem and achieve what Lukács calls the 'negative mysticism' of art. The price paid, of course, is a lack of clarity and stability, the acceptance of a constant deferral of full meaning, and this Brooks and Heilman are not fully prepared to do. They need to posit the moment when the deferral ends and freezes into a coherent, spatial structure that can be clearly conceptualized and hierarchized without losing any of the previous, apparently conflicting 'moments'. In short, they are involved, in their

---

[40] Georg Lukács, *The Theory of the Novel*, trans. Anna Bostock (Cambridge, Mass.: MIT Press, 1971), 93.

unsystematic but intellectually serious project, in the same kind of problem which Hegel had tried to solve with his notorious concept of Absolute Knowledge.[41]

Let me isolate one facet of the complex machinery of Hegel's discussion of the problem, which will highlight the similarities to Brooks and Heilman on the dramatic system of *1 Henry IV*: 'Consciousness, at the same time, must have taken up a relation to the object in all its aspects and phases and have grasped its meaning from the point of view of each of them.'[42] We recall the vertiginous attempt which the New Critics made to see each of the characters from the point of view of the others. And again: 'This [the resumption by consciousness of previously objectified knowledge] is the movement of consciousness, and in this process consciousness is the totality of its movements' (p. 790). Clearly, in their attempt to grasp 'Shakespeare's irony', his 'mature comedy', to 'have it both ways', Brooks and Heilman are engaged in a similar attempt to reconcile the unreconcilable in an ultimately mystical moment. But while Hegel is explicit that at the end of the journey, 'The chalice of this realm of spirits / Foams forth to God His own Infinitude' (p. 808), Brooks and Heilman are more reticent.

Surprisingly, the secular place-holder of Absolute Knowledge in the *Understanding Drama* reading is authorial intentionality. The essay was written years before Wimsatt defined 'the intentional fallacy', and Brooks and Heilman make full use of that 'heresy' here. What was Shakespeare's attitude? they ask (p. 383). What was 'Shakespeare's final attitude toward his characters (and toward the human predicament, generally)' (p. 386)? But of course, as has often been pointed out, since Renaissance literature in general lacks the kind of documentation that would give even the slightest possibility of understanding an author's 'empirical' intention, the terms here serve only a rhetorical, authority-conferring function, much as G. Wilson Knight's claim to be 'interpreting Shakespeare' without value-judgements did.

[41] Jameson's discussion of Hegel's Absolute Knowledge is relevant here, too: 'From this perspective, Hegel's notion of Absolute Spirit is seen as just such a[n] [ideological] strategy of containment, which allows what can be thought to seem internally coherent in its own terms, while repressing the unthinkable ...' (Fredric Jameson, *The Political Unconscious: Narrative as a Socially Symbolic Act* (Ithaca, NY: Cornell University Press, 1981) 53). Shortly after this comment, Jameson goes on to identify the Hegelian totalizing strategy with Modernist organic unity (p. 56), thus further corroborating the point I am making here about an analogy between New Critical unity and Hegel.

[42] G. W. F. Hegel, *The Phenomenology of Mind*, trans. J. B. Baillie (New York: Harper, 1967), 790.

'Shakespeare's attitude', the authorial intentionality, then, is simply a question-beggar, a plausible, but casual synonym for the structural unity which they themselves have posited. The question of unity, insisted upon by Brooks and Heilman from the very beginnings of their commentary as the key question of the play, has a hidden content. On unity rests the possibility of a kind of Absolute Knowledge, of a holding together of otherwise self-deconstructing versions of the play's structure. No wonder they speak of it as a 'choice' which not all readers will make. At one level simply a matter of critical presupposition, at another the choice for unity is a choice for faith in a kind of knowledge that can be approached but never grasped as presence. In *The Well-Wrought Urn* Brooks had hinted at the religious significance of this kind of unity in his thought as he defended Donne's use of paradox:

I submit that the only way by which the poet could say what 'The Canonization' says is by paradox. More direct means might be tempting, but all of them enfeeble and distort what is to be said. This statement may seem the less surprising when we reflect on how many of the important things which the poet has to say have to be said by means of paradox: most of the language of lovers is such ... so is most of the language of religion—'He who would save his life, must lose it'; 'the last shall be first'. Indeed, almost any insight important enough to warrant a great poem apparently has to be stated in such terms.[43]

This kind of complex irony is the manifestation of the absolute in the world of the contingent. God is, as Nabokov liked to say, in the details. But he should have added: in the unified *totality* of the details—at least, if he were speaking for Brooks and Heilman.

We can follow the slow discovery of this quintessential Cleanth Brooks move in the otherwise inexplicable logical muddle made by the authors' attempt to transfer the theory of comedy they sketched in the discussion of Oscar Wilde's 'simple' *Lady Windermere's Fan* to the 'complex' case of Shakespeare. The confusion begins when, at one point in the reading of *1 Henry IV*, students are explicitly asked to review the arguments concerning comedy as the realm of compromise and relativism that had been made in the discussion of *Lady Windermere's Fan* (p. 387, Q. 4). In that argument comedy, or Wilde's comedy—the text fudges the distinction (p. 79)—was stigmatized as a kind of inherently inauthentic genre, a social form deliberately hiding

[43] Brooks, *Well-Wrought Urn*, 17–18.

from the high moral absolutes of tragedy. Comedy, they stated, was a genre of 'moral relativism'. In reintroducing those distinctions into the discussion of *1 Henry IV*, however, the conceptual framework is badly strained, perhaps beyond repair. Implicit in the original distinction was a depreciation of comedy as inherently inferior to tragedy, precisely because of comedy's supposed limitation to the merely fashionable and contingent. In transferring that discussion to the case of Shakespeare, an attempt is made to mitigate the implied censuring of *1 Henry IV* by granting the comic a potential for its own kind of excellence: the play is said to give us 'one of the wisest and fullest commentaries on human action *possible to the comic mode* . . .' (p. 386, emphasis mine). The very extravagance of the language here ('wisest', 'fullest'), however, under-mines the earlier claim, which had seemed clear and stable in the context of Wilde, of comedy's inherent inferiority. But the muddle is left unresolved. We are simply told to insert the first theory into the new context without any other modification.

I suggest the following hypothesis to explain the anomaly. The anthology begins with a clear dualism between a social, comic world seen as contingent and inauthentic and a transcendant realm of essence and authenticity, which, when put in contact with the inauthentic social world, creates the tragic and heroic. This schema has a number of advantages for the New Critics. First, of course, it preserves a clear and stable moral vision of, as they put it, 'absolutes'. Meaning and value are posited as accessible if remote and in a transcendant realm; this is of course a view perfectly compatible with several versions of the Christian tradition, and we know that this was no small concern of the original New Critics—notably for Brooks, an Anglican.

But the schema also seems to offer a space for modernity. The social world has its own, if inferior sphere of autonomy where Modernist 'relativism' is free to reign. Here there are no dogmatic absolutes, but a play of non-antagonistic tensions and petty quarrels, all of which are in principle capable of being resolved through Anglican latitudinarianism and urbane compromise.

Now in terms of political theory, this amounts to a marked retreat from radical activism. The social realm is deprived of the level of ethical dignity that creates high principles. Or rather, it becomes assumed that any such application of transcendent principles to society would bring about a foreordained tragic, if heroic, outcome. The choices are bleak: glorious and isolated defeat vs. an acceptance of the contingencies of the world as such and a playing of the world's game with full knowledge of its inauthenticity—the tainted solution of Wilde, as the authors see it.[44]

In the discussion of *1 Henry IV*, however, another possibility begins to emerge, one that the authors are drawn into without apparently realizing that it has transformed the terms of their original distinctions. The rejection of Falstaff, discussed, as I noted above, only very late in the commentary, introduces into the comic world the kind of antagonistic clash of values that cannot be accommodated by common sense and compromise. The social realm, even while remaining contingent and inauthentic, is no longer purely 'comic' in the sense of genial and without basic antagonisms. What makes it so, as they see, is the necessity of action in the world, of choice. The world of complex comedy is moved a step closer to the dignified and transcendental tragic realm. But it remains contingent and relativistic because no clear solutions to the dilemmas seem possible: no matter which way Hal chooses, he loses something; he cannot simultaneously embody all the implied values of the play. But how could such a basically tragic, or at least, bitterly ironic situation, remain comic?

One solution, and one quite popular with many in their generation, would be to read the situation in the light of a kind of existential absurdity, inflected comically in a kind of defiant Nietzschean joy. But such a solution has already been rejected as a 'relativism' unworthy of Shakespeare. Instead, through the essentially Hegelian strategy I defined above, Brooks and Heilman smuggle God back into the supposedly abandoned social world—precisely by defining the space of the play as art instead of the social. If the necessity of choosing spoils the comedy as they define it, then the solution is to refuse to choose: 'If the prince must choose between two courses of action', they write in the climactic final paragraph, '—and of course, he must choose—we as readers are not forced to choose' (p. 387).

A dualism is thereby reinstated, but through different categories. If we follow Fredric Jameson's practice of creating a Greimas *combinatoire* in an attempt to get at a repressed, 'political unconscious', an unrealized possibility inherent in the categories of thought adopted, we will see something interesting:

---

[44] This is also the structure of the unhappy choice between a failed if glorious Old South and a realistic but inauthentic capitalist New South that the Fugitives had faced. There, too, the 'solution' was a move to a symbolic, aesthetic realm.

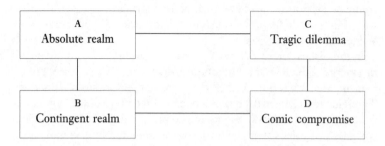

The combinations formed by the two horizontal axes—tragedy involving an absolute realm, comedy involving a contingent realm—are of course the two posited definitions of these genres given in the early discussion of Wilde. But what of the two possible diagonal axes—the possibilities of a tragedy of contingency or of a comedy of absolutes? These combinations would, of course, completely transform the initial definitions, but each is a possible solution to the anomalies presented by the 'complex comedy' of *1 Henry IV*: its perceived 'seriousness' and its unhappy choices could be reinscribed in terms of some sort of worldly tragedy of contingency, or it could be reconceptualized into a high synthesis of the comic and absolute values. As it turns out, neither of these possibilities is explicitly mentioned in the text. The initial definitions are allowed to stand without any kind of overt modification. But as we observe the logical torturing that the theory of the comic undergoes as it is applied to the case of the Henry IV play, we can certainly observe places in the text where the hypothetical diagonal axes can be glimpsed.

Contingent tragedy, that is, a kind of degraded, relativistic tragedy due to the clash of contingent interests of no absolute moral importance, appears to be the fate of Hal and Falstaff in the world of choice to which they are condemned. This is also the bleak realm to which those who actually attempt to transform the social world through its own contingent, relativist values—the Marxists and perhaps now, it is silently thought, those foolish, failed Agrarians—are condemned.

The second diagonal axis—the combination of absolutes and comedy—is, I would argue, precisely the possibility inherent in the thought-categories in use here that is repressed. It is essentially the instance of the Agrarian (or any other social) Utopia, a world conceived as a harmonious realm of genial compromise and concord at the same time embodying the eternal principles and verities which, as they appear in the actual text, can have only a tragic existence. The impossibility of even thinking this position in the *combinatoire* is accomplished, of course, by the logic of the initial identification of absolute values and tragedy, with all the rigidity and lack of applicability to Shakespeare's text that went along with it.

The solution that we saw at work in the text came about, I would argue, only by discarding the logic of the original oppositions between an absolute tragic and a contingent comic. The bleak choices implied there were outflanked by a new distinction between the social and the literary—outflanked that is, if our interest is now radically restricted to the purely literary. The social world is left trapped in the quagmires caused by the necessity of choice. The literary world is constituted, precisely, as that realm where we do not have to choose, the world of 'complex comedy' and 'irony' in which we can see both Hal and Falstaff as full and complex beings with their unique version of the good (and the bad) which we can distinguish and value, even if we can conceive of no way to avoid an unhappy outcome for each.

The secret of this last strategy is, as I have argued, a version of Hegel's Absolute Knowledge, the attempt to adopt the standpoint of God toward the characters, resolving all the unresolvable contradictions in an act of faith. And with this happy option available—the transformation of the world as a social text, resistant to desire, into a literary text, entirely malleable and pliable to libidinal transformation and interpretation—the original framework of authentic tragedy/inauthentic comedy is transformed. The case of tragedy—that heroic attempt to confront the world with its corruption, seems, as compared to this new comic irony, more and more remote, and abstract and theoretical. In fact, as tragedy is implicitly reinflected in brief remarks in the commentary on *1 Henry IV*, it comes to seem distant, austere, and inhuman: 'Comedy, after all, does not treat the lives of saints or heroes: it does not attempt to portray the absolute commitment to ultimate issues—the total commitment which transcends, tragically and heroically, the everyday world that we know' (pp. 386–7). Again tragedy's presence, as in the anthology as a whole, is deferred, for some more 'ultimate' occasion—which never comes. We are inserted instead into a valorized comic vision that depends for its efficacy on the very aestheticist move—the separation of art and society—which the New Critics strenuously opposed on a theoretical level as missing the relevance of literature to the contemporary world.

Apparently, this was too much to tell the students; perhaps it was too

much to admit to themselves. The original framework, with its advo-
cacy of strong principles in religion, urbane relativism in politics, is
allowed to stand, despite the dismantling those distinctions underwent
in the discussion of Hal and Falstaff.

The British Connection

Brooks and Heilman's analysis, while it manifests repressions and
feints, assumptions and smugglings that I would argue are typical of
New Criticism as a whole, is obviously a single document that cannot
be construed as a complete embodiment of the critical movement it
stands for here. In trying to trace the contours of New Criticism's
complex location in the history of Shakespeare criticism, one is conscious of the aptness of Foucault's term 'genealogy' as a trope well
suited to the idiosyncracies, breaks, accidents, and oddnesses of the
transmission of ideas in the processes of cultural history. While I have
here tried to emphasize the importance of the Fugitive-Agrarians in
the constitution and then institutionalization of New Criticism in
American universities, it is of course important to understand the
influence of a series of British family connections in this process as
well. I will therefore conclude the discussion of the New Critics and
Shakespeare with a look at the family resemblances of American and
British Modernist critics; then attempt to situate this unique Anglo-
American construct in a broader history of modern Western culture;
and finally, examine in this context, and that of the general dynamic of
insurgency finding its accommodation outlined above, a number of the
roads taken and not taken in subsequent literary criticism.

A central transatlantic connection was supplied by that Anglo-
American Modernist *par excellence*, T. S. Eliot, who was clearly a
source of authority and inspiration in the constitution of all the major
schools of Shakespeare criticism for the forty-year period between
1930 and 1970. We have seen Eliot's indirect but seminal influence on
the innovations in criticism developed by G. Wilson Knight; a more
direct influence will be apparent in the historical criticism of E. M. W.
Tillyard to be discussed in the next chapter. And Eliot has emerged
once more in the present chapter as a major source for Ransom and
American New Criticism in general. As was true of the earlier critics,
the influence had little to do with Eliot's published remarks on
Shakespeare. Eliot seems always to have had his greatest influence
from the margins of his own essays: 'Hamlet and His Problems' is

remembered, not for its short-lived attempt to denigrate Shakespeare's play, but for its definition of the 'objective correlative'; and Eliot's greatest impact on Shakespeare studies came, I would argue, from the brief and undeveloped remarks on the dissociation of sensibility in 'The Metaphysical Poets' rather than any of several direct pronouncements on Shakespeare. We have seen how those remarks were behind the New Critical version of literary history promulgated by Cleanth Brooks and how they informed the emphasis on problematic unity, with its derivative concepts of tension and irony, that was the special hallmark of the American New Criticism's spatial analyses.

Of the other acknowledged New Critical British father-figure, I. A. Richards, less has emerged in the present study. Tillyard, we will see, acknowledged Richards as the single progenitor of a broadly construed 'analytic criticism', and Ransom devoted virtually a third of *The New Critics* to a discussion of his pioneering methods. But—apart from his seminal insistence on close analysis of literary texts, of course—perhaps Richards's most important contribution to the development of American New Criticism in Shakespeare was his encouragement in the early Twenties of his student William Empson. Shakespeare was a central figure in Empson's ground-breaking *Seven Types of Ambiguity* and its two important sequels *Some Versions of Pastoral* and *The Structure of Complex Words*. Without Empson's provocative demonstrations of 'ambiguity' at work in central literary works, American New Criticism would surely have taken a different shape. In fact, in the British context, it is difficult to find clear continuity between Empson and critics of a younger generation. *Scrutiny*, as will be shown below, went in its own direction, while, of course, figures like Knight and Tillyard lacked Empson's orientation to the resistance of the fine detail in their haste to build their larger unifying structures. But in the American New Critics, in their close readings and emphasis on tension and irony, one can find a clear continuity from Empson.[45] They certainly were ardent admirers of Empson. Ransom wrote, for example, of *Seven Types of Ambiguity*, 'I believe it is the most imaginative account of

[45] In the light of the analysis of Brooks and Heilman's critical practice, I want to take issue with the claim by Terry Eagleton that Empson's 'ambiguity' is 'open-ended' while the New Critics' performances were always resolvable into a 'closed' unity. I would state in contrast that the appeal to 'closed unity', which is certainly a feature of New Critical practice—particularly Brooks's—has to be read suspiciously as I have done above and should be seen as a rhetorical and ideological gesture not necessarily inherent in the techniques employed. Empson is, as Eagleton says, virtually never guilty of such rhetoric. But of course Empson rarely tried to go beyond situating himself as a gadfly to established criticism; his 'open-endedness' was in a sense as much of an accommodation

reading ever printed, and Empson the closest and most resourceful reader that poetry has yet publicly had'. Ransom's praise of Richards is in comparison much more qualified.[46]

Working out of much the same theoretical fathers and with much the same values was of course the *Scrutiny* group headed by F. R. Leavis. And we are fortunate in having, in Francis Mulhern's *The Moment of 'Scrutiny'*, a thorough and nuanced history of a journal which, thirty-five years after its demise, still seems to haunt much of Britain's literary Left.[47] The parallels between Leavis's group as described by Mulhern and the New Critics are striking, all the more so when the Fugitive-Agrarian roots of the American New Critics are understood, as they have not always been, especially in Britain.[48] The central value shared by both the Leavisites and the American New Critics is a deep distrust of contemporary industrial society as a product of modernization. Both groups looked back to a past agrarian 'organic society' as a model of a more humanly adequate and richer mode of existence. Both groups, too, influenced by Eliot's theory of the dissociation of sensibility, looked to the Age of Shakespeare and Donne as a privileged moment of the organic society at its ripest point producing its greatest language. Both saw in the Modernist literary movement a body of work which could contain the lost vision and values of the organic society in an industrial and degraded age. And

to established practices as a challenge to it, since it reflected a strategy of taking aim only at carefully chosen targets in the Establishment rather than attempting a frontal assault on it. But given the—as I see it—illusory quality of New Critical 'unity', the difference between Empson and the Americans is much less clear-cut than Eagleton has it—see *Literary Theory: An Introduction* (Minneapolis: University of Minnesota Press, 1983), 51–3.

[46] Ransom, *The New Criticism*, 102. The love-affair was not without its problems, of course. Cleanth Brooks criticized Empson in a number of reviews—praising him for many points as well, of course. But the thrust of the criticism is suggested by Brooks's accusation that Empson is 'an incorrigible amateur'. For this phrase and a survey of Brooks on Empson, see Wellek, *History of Criticism*, vi. 205–6.

[47] The very existence of a study like Mulhern's is probably the best indication of the continuing interest of the British Left in Leavis. On Leavis's influence on (and lack of appreciation for) the classic work of the late Raymond Williams, see Terry Eagleton, 'Resources for a Journey of Hope: The Significance of Raymond Williams', *New Left Review*, 168 (March/April 1988), 3–11. Significantly Leavis is one of the few critics to get a chapter to himself in Eagleton's *The Function of Criticism: From 'The Spectator' to Post-Structuralism* (London: Verso, 1984), 69–84.

[48] This is particularly noticeable in the introductory essay by David Robey, 'Anglo-American New Criticism', in *Modern Literary Theory: A Comparative Introduction*, ed. Ann Jefferson and David Robey (London: Batsford, 1986), 73–91. By comparison, Eagleton's recent brief treatments are much better informed—see *Literary Theory*, 46–53 and *Function of Criticism*, 85–92.

both developed techniques of 'close reading' unprecedented in critical history and bringing to the elucidation of literary texts a new discipline, precision, and standard of rigour that makes the work of even the greatest of pre-twentieth-century commentators seem amateurish in comparison.

At moments each recognized the affinities with the other group's work. Ransom's *Kenyon Review* published in 1946 a review by Eric Bentley of L. C. Knight's *Explorations*, in which Bentley praised *Scrutiny* as 'one of the best literary journals of today'. 'There is more "new criticism" in them', Bentley continued, 'than in all the other works of the "new school" put together.' The British group, he said, had not just mapped out terrain to be conquered but had 'actually occupied the territory and issued new maps'.[49]

Quick to relish the foreign appreciation, Leavis duly noted the 'handsome bouquet' which Bentley's remarks constituted for him and returned some compliments concerning *Kenyon Review*—as well as defence against the few critical points Bentley had made in passing.[50]

The two groups, however, had adopted contrasting approaches in relating to established academic institutions, and the contrast was perhaps most pointed at the very moment of mutual recognition in the late Forties and early Fifties. Ransom and his followers, as I noted, chose a strategy of accommodation that was, in spite of the predicted opposition of positivist scholars, remarkably successful in recasting English studies in America. Leavis, facing what was arguably a more closed, less flexible opposition, displaying a personality that all observers agreed was petulant and defensive, and evincing a militant purposiveness and loyalty to his inciting values and strategy that only Tate among the Fugitive-Agrarians shared, saw himself and *Scrutiny* as embattled and under siege at the very moment of New Criticism's initial triumphs in America.[51] The last issue of *Scrutiny*, containing a 'Valediction' by Leavis accusing his enemies of engaging in an organized conspiracy to suppress references to himself and his journal

---

[49] Eric Bentley, 'This is the New Criticism', *Kenyon Review*, 8 (Autumn 1946), 673. This review was a prelude to Bentley's anthology of essays from *Scrutiny*, *The Importance of Scrutiny* (1948), which was the first introduction of the journal to the American public.

[50] F. R. Leavis, ' "The Kenyon Review" and "Scrutiny" ', *Scrutiny*, 14 (Dec. 1946), 134–6.

[51] This is not to say that Leavis was not involved in a similar kind of 'professionalization' to that of his American counterparts, as Eagleton delineates in his treatment in *The Function of Criticism* (p. 81), but that Leavis's relation to the academic Establishment was more antagonistic than was that of the American New Critics except Tate.

in other publications, appeared in 1953 as American New Criticism
was consolidating its victory.

Ultimately Leavis and followers achieved a deep and wisespread
influence in the British academy and outside of it—if nothing quite so
sweeping and *institutionalized* as the hegemony of American New
Criticism. Mulhern attempted to describe *Scrutiny*'s legacy in this way:

A quarter-century has passed since Leavis's 'parting salute'. In that time,
Scrutiny has grown in prominence, and become an ineffaceable image in the
memory of the national culture. Its nineteen volumes have been reprinted by
one of the most venerable publishing houses in the land, and given still wider
currency in a two-volume anthology published soon afterwards. It has been
extensively discussed, by champions and critics alike, and obsessively referred
to, on a thousand academic and journalistic occasions. For all but a year of that
quarter-century, its chief editor persevered in the campaigns that he had
initiated in the early thirties, attracting widespread partisanship and, on at least
one notorious occasion [the debate with C. P. Snow on 'two cultures'] inciting
England's intellectuals to polemical acts of rare extremism.... It is as if
Scrutiny's career was not simply an episode, an 'origin' to which certain
phenomena can retrospectively be ascribed, but, as Walter Benjamin might
have said, an *Ursprung*, an irruption never 'ended', into a cultural order
perpetually vulnerable to its impact.

So, the moment of *Scrutiny* persists . . .[52]

Thus the highly critical remarks on New Criticism published in
Scrutiny's last years should be placed in this specific context and not be
allowed to obscure the remarkable cultural parallel formed by the two
autonomous groupings. The real value of the later *Scrutiny* critique of
its American cousins lies in its zeroing-in on the effects which the
accommodation with academia was already having on the American
school. In a 1952 *Scrutiny* review of several works of American criticism, Robin Mayhead took Reuben Brower's New Critical *The Fields of
Light* to task for being too preoccupied with literary technique to the
detriment of the moral and critical aspects of modern literature.[53] And
while these remarks were made in the context of a generally positive
review of Brower's pioneering effort to apply New Critical precepts to
the novel, Mayhead was much more censuring in his remarks on
Cleanth Brooks's *Modern Poetry and the Tradition*. He faulted Brooks
for, as he saw it, breaking little new ground in his proposals for a new
literary history and accused Brooks of a 'radical superficiality' in a

[52] Francis Mulhern, *The Moment of 'Scrutiny'* (London: New Left, 1979), 305–6.
[53] Robin Mayhead, 'American Criticism', *Scrutiny*, 19 (Oct. 1952), 65–75.

number of generalizations and interpretations that he felt were unsupported. Philip Rahv, who had opposed a number of Ransom's suppositions, was praised in contrast to Brooks for his social-minded, anti-formalist, and anti-theoretical practices.

Mayhead's remarks, I would argue, are extremely perceptive in grasping the direction New Criticism was being pushed along through the pressures of professionalization in the academy, but his remarks on Brooks, particularly, seem coloured by a sectarian insistence on the letter of Leavisite literary history (Brooks is faulted for not understanding, as Leavis had claimed, that Pope should be seen as in the Metaphysical 'line'; and in general the pioneering nature of Brooks's work in an American context, rather than that of the *Scrutiny* coterie at Cambridge, is misunderstood). Put in a larger perspective than that provided by the immediate post-war years, however, the deep resemblances between Leavis's group and Ransom's are striking—and important confirmations of the impact of the Modernist aesthetic paradigm, particularly as mediated by Eliot, on the formation of critical practice in both Britain and America.

New Criticism's Road Not Taken

The American New Critics, I believe, should certainly be situated with the *Scrutiny* group in the same European-wide reaction against positivism that Mulhern defined as the larger intellectual context for the British grouping. What Mulhern wrote of Leavis could certainly, with some minor changes in terminology, be applied to the writings of Ransom, Tate, Brooks, and their followers:

In its strict circumscription of positivist reason, *Scrutiny* echoed a theme that was stated in countless variations, from Freud's scientifically-inspired exploration of the unconscious to Bergson's irrationalist celebration of intuition and the *élan vital*. The Leavisian epistemological themes of 'recognition' and 'inwardness', of cultural knowledge as 'recreation', as the identity of knower and known, belong to that tradition of *Verstehen* (sympathetic understanding) whose representatives include the Germans Dilthey and Rickert, the Italian Croce—and, in another very different variant, Max Weber.[54]

Mulhern went on to add the social-science theorists Mosca, Pareto, Durkheim, and Moller to his list.[55] What he omits of course—perhaps

[54] *Moment of 'Scrutiny'*, 307.
[55] Ibid., p. 308.

it seemed too obvious — was the gigantic international and anti-positivist movement that was Modernism.

The peculiar doctrines of the objectification of the text which
became so prominent in Wimsatt's late New Critical formulations, but
which can be found in embryo in earlier writings, call for qualifications
of these Continental affiliations and speak of a strong Anglo-American
empirical strain that differentiates New Criticism from, for example,
German hermeneutic theory. But the anti-positivism which New Criticism shares with these doctrines is certainly among its strongest, most
thematized characteristics. Allen Tate in particular could be militant
and caustic in this regard. On one occasion he predicted that the
positivist approach to literature would unwittingly deprive students of
their critical faculties and help usher in a nightmarish American consumerist version of Nazi censorship. In such a society, he continued,
'. . . we were to be conditioned for the realization of a *bourgeois* paradise
of gadgets and of consumption, not of the fruits of the earth, but of
commodities.' And even if America averts a total catastrophe like
Germany's, Tate felt a consumerist ' "democracy" of appetites, drives,
and stimulus-and-response has already affected us'.[56]

These themes suggest an affiliation of New Criticism with a strain of
anti-positivism which, I believe, has never been linked with the New
Critics previously but which is an especially important connection to
grasp in the present era of the debunking and denunciation of the
entire New Critical enterprise. There is a limited but striking convergence of interests and ideas between the American New Critics and
the Frankfurt School, who could play, as I argued in the Introduction,
an important role in consolidating the critical gains of the post-New
Critical (but still anti-positivist) present. It is in fact probably these
affinities which account for the relatively modest impact that Frankfurt
themes have had in Anglo-American literary studies, as opposed to a
much greater influence in sociology and communications theory.
Many of the Frankfurt aesthetic themes seemed too close to the ideas
of the New Critical father-figures being repressed to be taken in their
own, ultimately very different context.

One way into the convergence is a look at the brief relationship
which Adorno had with Ransom's *Kenyon Review* in the late Forties.
Adorno had participated during the war years in a Los Angeles forum

---

[56] Allen Tate, 'The Present Function of Criticism', in his *Collected Essays* (Denver,
Colo.: Swallow, 1959), 5–6. See also the essays in the same collection 'The Man of
Letters in the Modern World' and 'Miss Emily and the Bibliographers'.

on art and religion in modern life, where he, perhaps despairing of being able to bridge the considerable gap between his own philosophical assumptions and those of his audience, gave his intervention into the discussion in the form of a series of numbered theses. The talk somehow came to Ransom's attention, and he was impressed enough to print it in his journal and write a response to it. Adorno subsequently contributed a review to *Kenyon*, but he left America in 1949 to return to Germany, and the collaboration never developed further. Nevertheless the brief passing of these two ships revealed fascinating similarities in approaches to art theory between the two men, whose political affiliations and interests were otherwise so opposite.

In his essay, Adorno insisted, against what he saw as a pervasive tendency at the conference and in some contemporary art theory, on a firm separation between religion and art as distinct, historically separated practices; furthermore, he argued, art's historically constituted autonomy had been a distinct liberation threatened now from a number of directions.[57] In trying to define his peculiar notion of art's autonomy and to ward off the accusation of 'attempting to revise good old aestheticism, the idea of *l'art pour l'art* which has now been pronounced dead so many times' ('Nothing of this sort is my aim', he insisted), Adorno gave one of his clearest and most accessible explanations of the notion of the art-work as a monad which I mentioned in the Introduction—the idea that it is in the formal aspects of art that its relation to the social is expressed and mediated.

While Adorno cautiously described himself as a music theorist, Ransom was able to recognize that Adorno was for 'collectivism in politics', but, he goes on (correctly) to assure his readers, '. . . not . . . fanatically'. Clearly Ransom found Adorno's intervention extremely stimulating—he reprinted the essay of reply in the collection *Beating the Bushes*—and he found much with which to agree. The separation between art and religion, which he had insisted upon in his own way, for his own distinct reasons, for many years, seemed to him very happily formulated in Adorno's theses:

His social ideal has no room in it for religion yet provides a special asylum for art. But art is curiously close to religion in his very original and engaging description of it, as a concrete monad representing the universal concretion itself; that is to say, as a construction from which the experient receives cosmic or ontological vision. . . . It is not attached to the practical life which falls under

[57] T. W. Adorno, 'Theses upon Art and Religion Today', *Kenyon Review*, 7 (Autumn 1945), 676–82.

the overall survey of the political economy. It is free, and Mr. Adorno awards to it an *imperium in imperio*. That is a handsome concession which many collectivists have not made.[58]

Adorno would certainly not own every jot and tittle of this paraphrase: 'epistemological', rather than 'cosmic or ontological' would come nearer to his own conceptions, and Ransom assumed a hostility to religion which is not quite accurate either. But both theorists had found in art a possible weapon against the levelling and sterilizing processes of capitalist modernization, and both believed fiercely in the need to preserve art's autonomy, not in order to escape from social reality but in order to preserve the alternatives to it contained within the forms of art.

In addition, for both the Frankfurt School and for New Criticism, art constituted a kind of knowledge—richer, fuller, value-laden, and multiply perspected—that served as an essential critical foil to the abstracting and value-free conceptualizations of positivism in all its forms. Significantly, the very term 'positivism' was a bugbear for both groupings, and for similar reasons: it epitomized for both groups the scientistic homogenization of life and theory that was anathema to each, caught up as they were in their different ways in the anti-positivist crusades of international Modernism. Strikingly too, both were outraged by the consumerist superficialities of post-war American culture. How unlike the received idea of New Criticism, which became in its academic home a set of procedures for grinding out abstract readings of texts, isolated from any socially critical significance, are the pages of Ransom's *Kenyon Review* in the late Forties!

Ultimately, of course, the moment of dialogue between Ransom and Adorno became a curiosity, a lone signpost of a road not taken in American criticism. Rather than developing the potential for cultural and social criticism it clearly contained, academic New Criticism, as both *Scrutiny* and Ransom himself saw clearly, become reduced to its own techniques, becoming a professional discipline with writings addressed only to other professionals, writings which remained unread and whose real social purposes could only be understood in terms of credentialing in a scramble for jobs, tenure, and fame. The result, in Edward Said's perceptive observation, has been a complete denial of the 'materiality' of the literary text, its existence as 'a cultural object

---

[58] John Crowe Ransom, 'Art and the Human Economy' (1945); repr. in his *Beating the Bushes: Selected Essays 1941–1970* (New York: New Directions, 1972), 129.

sought after, fought over, possessed, rejected, achieved in time'.[59] Instead, as Said wrote, both the literary and the critical texts exist in academic New Criticism in a fantastic abstracted timelessness 'working alone within itself'.[60] And this is, as Said points out, a condition which has continued well into the post-New Critical period, as we shall see in Chapter 5.

But the triumph of New Criticism, even in this compromised form, by no means simply erased the positivist literary methods it had been designed to replace. The triumph did mean that positivism would have to find an accommodation with Modernism to survive in the now transformed academic ethos brought about by New Criticism.

In Shakespeare studies, such a transformation of the older positivism was the accomplishment of E. M. W. Tillyard's historical criticism, which managed an accommodation with Modernism all the more potent because disguised.

[59] Edward W. Said, 'Roads Taken and Not Taken in Contemporary Criticism', *Contemporary Literature*, 17 (1976), 339.

[60] Ibid., p. 337.

4

Professionalism, Nationalism, Modernism
The Case of E. M. W. Tillyard

The Context of Tillyard's Innovations

As John Crowe Ransom was undergoing the change of mind and heart that would find such widespread support in American academia, as F. R. Leavis was winning friends and making enemies with equal ardour at Cambridge—as these two related organizers of the New Critical revolution were at the height of their powers, one of the original designers of the Cambridge English curriculum, E. M. W. Tillyard, was having second thoughts on the direction being taken by the new discipline of English studies. Tillyard, whose account of the formation of English at Cambridge I will consider further below, found Leavis in particular a figure who had gone too far and produced a new dogmatism, which in turn he held responsible for a new generation of students who he believed were 'less ready to think for themselves, more burdened by liberty, and more desirous of being told what they ought to believe'.[1] These were words that could just as easily, perhaps more justly, be said of the implied student audience of Tillyard's own writings on the histories. That Tillyard's ideas were presented to students as revealed truth for more than a generation, regardless of his own intentions, is quite undeniable.

In any case, Tillyard's angry words suggest an alienation from the direction that Cambridge New Criticism had taken from Empson to Leavis.[2] Out of this disillusion with the Cambridge version of New Criticism would come two related books, *Shakespeare's History Plays* and *The Elizabethan World Picture* (they were originally designed to be one book, but Tillyard separated out *The Elizabethan World Picture*

---

[1] E. M. W. Tillyard, *The Muse Unchained: An Intimate Account of the Revolution in English Studies at Cambridge* (London: Bowes and Bowes, 1958), 77.

[2] The alienation from Empson was expressed in the following remarks: 'Anyone quick to distinguish the rotten from the ripe and to sniff the taint of incipient corruption might now have guessed that an impulse had attained its maximum strength and that henceforward a decline or coarsening might be expected' (*Muse Unchained*, 130), he wrote of Empson's *Seven Types of Ambiguity*.

because of its length), which must surely be ranked as among the most influential works of Shakespearian criticism in the twentieth century. In the Fifties and Sixties these two works of Tillyard became the models of and sources for the only major methodological challenge to New Critical hegemony in academic Shakespeare studies, the leading works within what Renaissance scholars referred to as 'historical criticism'. One critic of the Seventies summarized Tillyard's influence this way: '. . . for an entire generation of scholars without effective exception, Tillyard's conclusions were accepted.'[3] Part of Tillyard's powerful influence resulted from the strategic social importance of those institutions where his work prevailed. Graham Holderness, for example, reports that Tillyardian concepts have dominated the assumptions of British O and A level examinations, and thus been disseminated in Britain at a mass level for decades.[4] In the United States Tillyard's works have been a pedagogical staple over the same period, and Tillyardian views have permeated the apparatus of the textbook editions of Shakespeare and, massively, into scholarly literature on the subject. The influence of any one writer is notoriously difficult to measure, of course, and many critics have refused to take their Tillyard straight, playing off the Tillyardian theme of 'order' in the *Henriad* against a perceived and equally positive 'life' or 'comic' theme embodied by Falstaff, then using some New Critical concept of tension, irony, or balanced opposition to contain the revealed contradictions.[5] In such readings it is impossible to decide whether the New Critical formal categories predominate over the (modified) Tillyardian content, or whether, as Holderness plausibly argues, the New Critical oppositions and nuances are simply a displacement and transference of an implicitly hegemonic Tillyardian valuation of order in the public sphere.[6] But there is also a sufficiently large body of criticism based on Tillyardian themes and methods to document a very considerable influence beyond his contribution to various attempted syntheses in the Fifties and Sixties.

Ironically few books of such influence in a given literary field are

[3] Edward Pechter, 'Falsifying Men's Hopes: The Ending of "1 Henry IV"', *Modern Language Quarterly*, 41 (Sept. 1980), 211–30.

[4] Graham Holderness, *Shakespeare's History* (New York: St. Martin's Press, 1985), 198.

[5] See, for example, the syntheses proposed by Harold Goddard, *The Meaning of Shakespeare* (Chicago, Ill.: University of Chicago Press, 1951), 161–214, and Leonard Unger, *The Man in the Name: Essays on the Experience of Poetry* (Minneapolis: University of Minnesota Press, 1956), 3–17.

[6] Holderness, *Shakespeare's History*, 198.

now in such disfavour among that field's specialists as are Tillyard's works at present among Renaissance scholars. Tillyard's works have in the last twenty years suffered a reversal of fortune in influence more meteoric and startling than their original climb to pre-eminent influence, and they have become the target of a major revisionist effort that in one sense can be seen as ushering in the era of the Postmodern Shakespeare to be discussed in the concluding chapter. In any case the rise and fall of Tillyard constitutes major evidence for one of the basic premisses of this study: that literary criticism, far from being what it appears, a disinterested inquiry into the meaning and value of an accepted canon of masterworks, is instead a complexly overdetermined discourse shaped by politics, aesthetics, and institutional discipline. It is these multiple 'interests' underneath the surface of critical discourse that can account for the shifts of trends, methods and schools of thought, often accompanied by violent rhetoric and personal vituperation. The case of Tillyard is an excellent example of these multiple influences at work.

Because of the centrality of Tillyard's work in the Shakespeare studies of the period 1940–70, the period when many of today's active Shakespeare scholars were trained, and because the rapid rise and fall of his reputation is so palpable an instance of the hidden political dimension of literary studies at work, several contemporary critics have undertaken analyses of Tillyard with which I share many values, perceptions, and methods.[7] But because most recent critiques of Tillyard have been British,[8] they have to a large extent ignored Tillyard's considerable influence and importance in American Shakespeare studies. In an American context, as I shall argue below, the British

---

[7] Recent influential critiques of Tillyard have been made by Jonathan Dollimore, 'Introduction: Shakespeare, Cultural Materialism and the New Historicism', in *Political Shakespeare: New Essays in Cultural Materialism*, ed. Jonathan Dollimore and Alan Sinfield (Ithaca, NY: Cornell University Press, 1985), 6, and Dollimore and Sinfield, 'History and Ideology', in *Alternative Shakespeares*, ed. John Drakakis (New York: Methuen, 1985), 206–8. See also Holderness, discussed in what follows. American critiques of Tillyard, with different inflections, were popular in the Seventies—see n. 8 below.

[8] There have also been important American critiques of Tillyard, which will be discussed below. Many of Holderness's themes, for example, were first sounded, albeit without the development Holderness gave them, by Robert Ornstein's 1972 broad attack on the historical criticism epitomized by Tillyard, *A Kingdom for a Stage: The Achievement of Shakespeare's History Plays* (Cambridge, Mass.: Harvard University Press, 1972), 1–32. Like the more recent Britons, Ornstein noted in particular a thinly disguised celebration of the idea and tradition of the British monarchy, of the supreme importance of national unity, and of the need for order against the rabble.

critique's emphasis on the nationalist, politically quietistic uses to which Tillyard was put in his heyday has much less applicability, and his relation to Modernist aesthetics is in turn of much more importance. In what follows I focus largely on Tillyard's impact in America in an attempt to redress this imbalance and present a view of Tillyard's rise and fall that partially endorses but also critiques the British analyses offered to date. I argue that while Tillyard's criticism certainly contributed to the structures of domination of British war-time and post-war society (as several critics have stressed), it also, like any other cultural document, presented multivalent possibilities and functions which ultimately must be taken into account not only in the American but also in the British context.

In one sense, Tillyard's effort was a holding action against the Modernist encroachments into academia I have been describing, a reversion to the positivist literary history which had never really had a chance to develop at Cambridge, though it was ensconced elsewhere. The enthusiastic reception of Tillyard's work in America was in important part a grateful reaction from practitioners of the older paradigm towards a work that promised to make their own efforts relevant again. Thus Tillyard's work on the histories can be read as an attempt to re-function the nineteenth-century 'historical values' which G. Wilson Knight and the New Critics had frontally attacked. The re-functioning was such, however, that it led to an accommodation with Modernism, which 'seeped through' Tillyard's surface historicism. The result was an enormously successful synthesis that collapsed with unexpected rapidity with the overturning of the Modernist paradigm which it had mediated into a new critical synthesis—and a fascinating case-study of the functioning of professional literary criticism as a social institution in modern capitalism.

Contemporary Critiques of Tillyard

The most fully developed critique of Tillyard to date is Graham Holderness's *Shakespeare's History*, a work to which I have already out of necessity referred. Holderness's is an ambitious attempt to treat both Elizabethan historiography and twentieth-century literary criticism, using both to present readings of the plays and criticisms of contemporary film productions of the works in question—it might have benefited, in fact, from greater focus. Here I can only address the section dealing with twentieth-century Shakespeare criticism, particularly, of course, that on Tillyard. Holderness's work is, I believe, representative of both the vices and virtues of much of recent British Marxism. It is perhaps less influenced by Foucault and post-structuralism in general than the related works which I will briefly discuss in Chapter 5, but it has recognizable affinities to the work of the *New Left Review* group. In particular there is a pronounced indebtedness to Mulhern's *The Moment of 'Scrutiny'* to which I alluded in the previous chapter. In fact, from my point of view, the major theoretical problem in Holderness's book lies in its uncritical reliance on Mulhern's critique of traditional culture—a critique which in turn Mulhern developed from what I take to be a flattening, unnuanced reading of Raymond Williams. Since my reading of Tillyard is sufficiently different from Holderness's, despite many shared assumptions and values, and since the differences are rooted, I feel, in our differing interpretations of Raymond Williams's now classic account of the dialectical interplay of the concepts of 'culture' and 'society', a brief digression on these theoretical basics is in order.

Both Mulhern and Holderness seem to have difficulty in keeping in play the rich and contradictory analysis of 'culture' which Williams bequeathed to the British Left some thirty years ago. Williams's classic *Culture and Society* (1958) was a deeply felt and personal, yet text-based and rigorous attempt at a mediation between Leavis and Marx, written with only local and limited direct reference to either and with a constant attention to the working-class culture into which Williams himself had been born. By triangulating these three, shall we say 'points of view', Williams attempted to take Leavis without his élitism and idealism, 'Thirties Marxism' without its doctrinaire systematizing and reductionism, and working-class culture, in its clearly subordinated position to an official culture which necessarily contained much that the working class could not do without. From this new position, Williams narrated a materialist account of the shifting meaning of a series of what he called 'key words'—*industry, democracy, class, art,* and, most important of all, *culture*. Like Leavis, Williams saw that the line of English criticism from Burke and Coleridge to his contemporaries Eliot, I. A. Richards, Orwell, and Leavis himself, had centred around developing a notion of 'culture' that, however conservatively inflected, was oppositional to 'the bourgeois idea of society',[9] that is, 'an idea of

---

[9] Raymond Williams, *Culture and Society: 1780–1950* (London: Chatto & Windus, 1958; repr. New York: Harper Torchbooks, 1966), 328.

society as a neutral area within which each individual is free to pursue his own development and his own advantage as a natural right' (p. 325). Rooted as it was in a common language and in daily give and take between the social classes, 'culture' could not be rigidly divided into 'bourgeois' and 'proletarian' branches, as many contemporary Marxists assumed. Thus Williams, in *Culture and Society*, separated himself from the group he called 'the Marxists' and instead followed his own theoretical programme of great originality and insight.

Nearly twenty years later, when he came to write the volume on literary theory for the Oxford paperback series Marxist Introductions of which he was one of the editors, Williams presented himself as an engaged Marxist. Truly, however, it was not Williams who had changed, but contemporary perceptions of what it meant to be 'Marxist'. New generations of Leftists had rejected the orthodox pretensions of a unitary Marxism–Leninism that in holding state power proved itself deeply ideological and authoritarian. Williams himself described his excitement at contact with developments in Western Marxism in the Sixties in the work of Sartre, Goldmann, and Althusser and his discovery of such formally repressed unorthodox theorists as the Frankfurt School and Antonio Gramsci.[10]

Williams's praise of Gramsci is particularly significant, and the short, dense chapter on Gramsci's key concept of 'hegemony' in Williams's *Marxism and Literature* confirms the deep affinity between Gramsci and Williams's own early work: both theorists insisted that traditional culture could not be reduced to some class affectation and that it had both conformist and oppositional potential.

To return from this brief digression to the accounts of Tillyard and Tillyard's Cambridge by Holderness and Mulhern, then, I might put my basic objection to their overall analysis this way: each writer loses track of the autonomy of culture and tends to view it too simply as monolithically engaged in reinforcing and maintaining capitalist social relations.

Both Holderness and Mulhern focus attention on the Cambridge line that begins with Matthew Arnold, goes to the Newbolt Report, and climaxes with the *Scrutiny* polemics of F. R. Leavis and associates.[11] The role played by 'culture' is reduced essentially to simple

[10] Raymond Williams, *Marxism and Literature* (Oxford: Oxford University Press, 1977), 4.
[11] Holderness, *Shakespeare's History*, 150–3 and Francis Mulhern, *The Moment of 'Scrutiny'* (London: New Left, 1979), *passim*.

repression as an ideology disseminated through the educational apparatus, inculcating values of nationalism, social hierarchy, and political quietism in bringing about a stable bourgeois hegemony in twentieth-century England. While of course this analysis gets at an important part of the truth, it erases much that was central to Williams's painstaking working-out of the paradoxical oppositional role that culture also played.[12]

A Gramscian reading of the Matthew Arnold–Newbolt–Leavis–Tillyard tradition in the spirit of Raymond Williams would bring out, I believe, the relative autonomy of that tradition and its social agents from the major coercive aspects of capitalist domination and emphasize the double-edged potential of intellectuals and culture in the formation of hegemony and counter-hegemonies. Gramsci's ruminations on the role of traditional humanistic culture and training are also worth consideration. While Gramsci thought that all human activity had an intellectual dimension and that the modern age required a new stratum of intellectuals trained in technical and industrial activity for true working-class emancipation,[13] he by no means thought that traditional humanist culture was simply a class-based affectation, even though it had been reserved for the children of the upper classes. Instead, he argued, a 'general, humanistic, formative culture' allowed these classes to 'lead' more specialized intellectuals and would be needed as the basis of national education in an egalitarian society of self-management. That is, for Gramsci, traditional culture, deprived of its hermetic separation from the technical and scientific, was to play a decisive role in the formation of potentially autonomous, power-sharing agents in a post-revolutionary society — and in the struggle leading up to such an outcome.

Of course, all of these Gramscian assertions are open to challenge and qualification. I bring them up here not because they are flawless — supplementation by Foucault's insights into power/knowledge would be welcome, in my view, for example — but because of the provocative nature of these themes in the context of recent critiques of Tillyard and the broad educational tradition which he represents. In many

---

[12] This widely shared analysis, incisive and perfectly adequate in certain contexts, can be traced back, as Francis Mulhern noted, to an aside made by Perry Anderson in a 1968 *New Left Review* article. See Perry Anderson, 'Components of the National Culture', *New Left Review*, 50 (May–June 1968), 3–57, especially the section on literary criticism, pp. 50–6.

[13] Antonio Gramsci, *Selections from the Prison Notebooks of Antonio Gramsci*, ed. and trans. Quintin Hoare and G. N. Smith (New York: International, 1971), 9.

ways, I believe, Tillyard's partial turn *away* from the cultural tradition is what makes him most problematic. Let me turn, however, to the strength rather than the weakness of Holderness on Tillyard.

At the centre of Holderness's analysis of Tillyard is what I take to be an important and significant insight into the social and political uses of literary criticism: he argues that Tillyard's *Shakespeare's History Plays* cannot be fully understood without grasping its origins in the culture and politics of war-time Britain. Like two other works of similar inspiration—G. Wilson Knight's explicitly patriotic *The Olive and the Sword* and Olivier's production of *Henry V*, Tillyard's work was embedded in ideologies of national unity, the muting of social conflict, and the celebration of a kind of jingoism. What distinguished Tillyard's work from the other two and doubtlessly contributed to Tillyard's far longer-lasting influence was, Holderness astutely argues, precisely the absence of any topical rhetoric of 'relevance' to the war-time crisis.[14] Nevertheless, Tillyard's reading of the *Henry IV* plays as enacting the triumph of the value of order over the social chaos represented by Falstaff is in retrospect clearly a product of the overriding need for national unity of the war years. Tillyard himself seemed to recognize the connection in an aside that is otherwise undeveloped:

The school of criticism that furnished [Falstaff] with a tender heart and condemned the Prince for brutality in turning him away was deluded. Its delusions will probably be accounted for, in the later years, through the facts of history. The sense of security created in nineteenth-century England by the predominance of the British navy induced men to rate that very security too cheaply and to exalt the instinct of rebellion above its legitimate station. They forgot the threat of disorder which was ever present with the Elizabethans. Schooled by recent events we should have no difficulty now in taking Falstaff as the Elizabethans took him.[15]

The passage, as Holderness notes, is the unique locus in either of Tillyard's works on the histories where the overwhelming 'outside' events of the war years break through; in addition, note Tillyard's confidence that these events, rather than creating the meaning he imputes to the rejection of Falstaff, in fact only fortuitously aid in revealing the authentic, historically authorized truth—a position, of course, quite in line with the suppositions of the positivist historical criticism which Tillyard is developing. From my perspective, however,

[14] Holderness, *Shakespeare's History*, 192.
[15] E. M. W. Tillyard, *Shakespeare's History Plays* (1944; repr. New York: Macmillan, 1946), 291.

it is a particularly revelatory aside testifying to otherwise repressed conditions of the production of Tillyard's text.

More than forty years later, Tillyard's confidence that, through simple advances in scholarship, he was now in possession of the truth of Shakespeare's text, cannot, of course be sustained. In the first place, as we shall see below, H. A. Kelly has demonstrated that Tillyard's use of Hall's *Chronicles of the Union of the Two Noble and Illustré Famelies of Lancastre and Yorke* (1540) as the key to understanding the (as they seem to us) multiple Shakespearian perspectives and unresolved clashes of vision and rhetoric in the overthrow of Richard II and the rise of Henry IV amounted to an unjustifiably selective use of available evidence from Elizabethan historical writings that did scant justice to the complexities either of Tudor historiography or of Shakespeare's texts.[16]

Moreover the notion that Shakespeare's texts are amenable to some single, univocal interpretation of the sort advanced by Tillyard and his contemporaries is now rightly seen as a reversion to positivist professionalism. From our perspective the question is clearly not whether Tillyard was 'right'; in his own terms, clearly he was not. Rather our problem is to understand why such a selective and reductive reading of the plays was so powerfully influential. The diagnosis of contemporary British Marxist-influenced criticism gets at an important part of the case for the British context: Tillyard clearly was so influential because his reading contributed a mythologically powerful component of the then current cultural hegemony in war-time and post-war Britain. This interpretation is perfectly consistent with a plainly evident if little discussed coupling of Shakespeare and British nationalism that goes back centuries. Anyone who has read in the literature of eighteenth-century Shakespeare criticism with an open eye can scarcely be surprised at a connection between the praise of Shakespeare and the nationalistic celebration of his native land, for the apotheosis of Shakespeare as the great national poet that took place in that period was a decidedly nationalistic and anti-French affair.[17]

---

[16] H. A. Kelly, *Divine Providence in the England of Shakespeare's Histories* (Cambridge, Mass.: Harvard University Press, 1970). Holderness, too, emphasizes the importance of Kelly's study (*Shakespeare's History*, 19–23).

[17] See for example Thomas Purney, 'Shakespeare and Francophilia' and Mark Akenside, 'Shakespeare Attacks Francophilia' for instances of anti-French bardolatry in the eighteenth century in *Shakespeare: The Critical Heritage*, ed. Brian Vickers, 6 vols. (London: Routledge & Kegan Paul, 1974), ii. 316–21 and iii. 359–62. The titles cited are not from the eighteenth-century but were supplied by Vickers.

However Tillyard was influential not only in his homeland but conspicuously and decidedly in the burgeoning post-war Shakespeare industry of the United States. This successful transplanting of influence to a different soil, where the specifically patriotic overtones of Shakespeare's works have never been so important, suggests other dimensions to Tillyard's influence not captured in Holderness's and the others' analyses. By shifting attention to Tillyard's influence in North America in the post-war era, we will find it necessary to expand the analysis beyond the directly political and nationalistic factors rightly stressed by Holderness for war-time Britain. I will suggest two modifications in approach. The first analyses the role played by positivist professionalism in Tillyard's work, a dimension not sufficiently recognized in the British critiques. Second I will argue that Modernist aesthetics, as a relatively autonomous social force with its own complex and ambivalent relation to hegemony, played a more important role in Tillyard's enormous influence than it has been credited with to this point.

Theoretically speaking, this will mean a shift from the not fully satisfactory political-ideological framework of recent British Marxism to a Gramscian conception of hegemony that takes into account the Foucaultian and Frankfurt themes I raised in the Introduction: the political effects of institutions and their discourses and the relative autonomy of art in modern capitalism. This analysis in turn will serve as a preparation for the final section of this chapter, which assesses some strengths and weaknesses of the developing attempt to construct an anti-Tillyard counter-hegemony in contemporary Shakespeare criticism, a discussion which will set the stage for an examination of the various contemporary trends in Chapter 5.

Tillyard's Self-Understanding

Interestingly enough, Tillyard has provided his own account of that crucial episode in the genesis of modern English studies, the formation of the English curriculum at Cambridge after World War I, an event of which he, along with I. A. Richards and M. D. Forbes, was a principal architect. While this work, *The Muse Unchained*, can certainly be made to fit into the largely negative account of the social function of English studies I have been describing (see Mulhern, for instance), my own reading suggests a different approach. The most important point to note is that modern British education did not spring fully armed out of the forehead of Matthew Arnold; and English studies, identified as perhaps the key link in post-war Establishment culture in Britain by Anderson and many others, was at its birth an insurgent cultural force fighting for its existence against powerful enemies in an already fully formed bourgeois hegemony. And while the new discipline was ultimately brought into the national hegemony and served socially regressive (as well as 'progressive') functions, its complex social dynamics deserves study and the avoidance of reductionist formulas. Tillyard gives an account of himself as, in those early days after the war at Cambridge, a kind of World-War-I-era angry young man: 'We were "progressives," . . . young men in a hurry', he wrote (p. 77). He had great hopes that the new English curriculum might make a substantial contribution to ending English insularity, but he never doubted that the main role of the curriculum was to supplant the classics in preparing men for business and the professions (p. 59). From our current perspective, he is probably best described as a moderate among the insurgent culturalists.

From the beginning in Tillyard's account, the problem of the new English curriculum is posed in terms of finding the right balance between satisfying the professional disciplinary requirements of constituting an adequate knowledge/power and of fulfilling an Arnoldian cultural mission which he takes for granted. In his view, the enemies of the unformed discipline at post-war Cambridge were two apparent opposites: philology, well established at Cambridge by the turn of the century as an early professional practice and a force in the newly established Cambridge English programme, and the journalistic practices—what Tillyard called the method of 'praise and gossip'— practised by his ally in the fight against philology, Sir Arthur Quiller-Couch (p. 87). For Tillyard, however, both approaches trivialized what he considered at the heart of the educational potential of English literature—its aesthetic and intellectual content. The problem was that, at the point at which English was becoming a major part of the modern university curriculum, literary culture had already. been institutionalized in these two separate forms: academia and journalism, neither of which proved able to form the basis of a viable curriculum, the first not 'cultural' enough in those early days, the second lacking professional rigour. We can read in Tillyard's discussion yet another variation of the culture and society conflict defined by Williams ('professionalism' being primarily the outcome of the bureaucratic phase of capitalist society, as I argued in Chapter 1). To anticipate my argument for a moment, one reason for Tillyard's enormous influence was that his works embodied a kind of Elizabethan Compromise between these two contending forces: Tillyard managed to fuse aspects of the cultural tradition emphasized by Holderness and Mulhern with a modernizing and positivist ideology of professionalism that Holderness and Mulhern underestimate.[18] I have emphasized here how, well before the Newbolt Report, the first attempts to 'modernize' literary studies followed the model of the natural sciences through such endeavours as textual 'disintegration', philology, and, in America, approaches like E. E. Stoll's dramatic history. Put in that context, the case of Tillyard represents a moment in which the positivist tradition, on the side of 'society', answers 'culture' back: Tillyard's work is nothing if not an attempt to insert the values and practices of American academic professionalism into the 'culture'-dominated enclaves of Cambridge and among its New Critical followers.

To be sure, the Tillyardian synthesis was not meant to jettison the educational, culturing role of literary studies. Rather Tillyard apparently hoped that by following the lead of Basil Willey's studies in 'the borderline of thought and literature', of Lovejoy's *Great Chain of Being*, or of Theodore Spencer's *Shakespeare and the Nature of Man* — all recognizable sources for the methodology of his own works on the histories — he could retain the educational and aesthetic values that were for him the core of what was right about Cambridge English while providing an intellectually viable alternative to Leavis — and to the arid 'Oxford habit of promoting editions of texts' (p. 129). But to

---

[18] I am thinking primarily of Holderness's account of the 'organic society' motif in Leavis and Tillyard as simply reactionary (*Shakespeare's History*, 150–9). Mulhern is better on grasping the interplay between the forces of society and culture in the formation of English studies after World War I (*Moment of 'Scrutiny'*, 3–41), but even so his emphasis constantly stresses the philistine and 'clubby' aspects of traditional culture while maintaining a symptomatic silence on the immensely negative potential of instrumental-administrative reason — note, for example, Mulhern's treatment of the scientism and professionalism of I. A. Richards (pp. 25–8); the impression conveyed is that traditional culture was the main component of bourgeois hegemony in the Britain of the early twentieth century, while administrative-technical reason was, on the whole, a welcome corrective to the flabby thinking of the traditionalists. If, as I believe, such an analysis amounts to substituting the dynamics of University life for those of society as a whole, gravely underestimating the role of instrumental reason in producing modernized society, and underestimating the critical and progressive function that can be played by 'culture' within the larger society (because it creates a 'space' from which a critical stance and practice toward society can be developed, as well as harbouring less liberatory potentials), then the dangers of a purely negative critique of culture developing its own form of philistinism should be clear.

contain the insurgent direction in which Leavis was taking 'culture', it would be necessary, Tillyard implicitly recognized, to become more 'professional'. What should be obvious from a reading of Tillyard— particularly *The Muse Unchained*, which Mulhern used, but Holderness did not—is the extent to which he is reacting *against* Richards's and Leavis's attempts (G. Wilson Knight is nowhere to be found as an influence among the Cambridge group) to make Shakespeare part of a resurgent, Modernist culture.[19] This reaction is most apparent in the pages of the longer and more specific of the two related works, *Shakespeare's History Plays*, and I propose to examine the influence of older professional practices from positivist literary history in that work before considering the covert Modernist component of Tillyard's synthesis, most easily apparent in *The Elizabethan World Picture*. All in all, Tillyard emerges from this analysis as a consummate English moderate who had remarkable success in what was a nearly impossible balancing act.

Tillyard's Positivist Professionalism

Tillyard made no secret of his debt to American professional scholarship. In the Preface to *The Elizabethan World Picture*, he acknowledged the influence of 'recent American work on Renaissance thought' and noted a general parallel with Theodore Spencer's work. In the acknowledgements of *Shakespeare's History Plays*, Tillyard again referred to Spencer and credited Lily B. Campbell as another source of his method. Lovejoy's methodology of the history of ideas was another obvious American predecessor whose influence Tillyard indicated retrospectively in *The Muse Unchained*.

Now in some sense, Tillyard's work went on to supersede that of many of his predecessors for good reason; none of them had really tackled the problem of 'Shakespeare's historical background' with Tillyard's combination of generalization and conciseness.[20] The nearest rival in this regard, Spencer's *Shakespeare and the Nature of*

---

[19] Holderness, however, does censure Tillyard's works as having 'systematically denied the relevance of modern thought to a historical understanding of Shakespeare's time' (*Shakespeare's History*, 17) and he groups Tillyard with L. C. Knights and J. Dover Wilson as promulgating 'authoritarian' readings of the histories (p. 19). From my perspective, both of these charges are accurate, with the qualifications implied in the section below on Tillyard's covert Modernism.

[20] In addition to Lily Campbell's *Shakespeare's 'Histories': Mirrors of Elizabethan Policy* (1947) and Spencer's work cited above, other American historical critics working before Tillyard were Hardin Craig, John W. Draper, and O. J. Campbell.

Man, was simply far less useful to subsequent scholars than were Tillyard's works with their broad notions of 'world picture' and 'Tudor myth', both of which could be accepted by a critic without his or her necessarily buying completely into Tillyard's reading of particular works. And, as I will argue below, none of them managed to combine their nineteenth-century methodologies with Modernist aesthetic values in quite the fashion which Tillyard managed.

However, despite the unique features which would help lead to Tillyard's pre-eminence, much of his method was decidedly familiar. In essence, *Shakespeare's History Plays* is that most familiar of positivist literary-critical forms, a study of sources: Tillyard's main argument might be summarized as a claim that Holinshed is much less central to the overall conception of the two historical tetralogies than was Hall's *Chronicle*. The first, and more influential half of the book leads its readers through a rapid survey of Elizabethan historiography set in the context of the doctrines of order and hierarchy which Tillyard had described in *The Elizabethan World Picture*. We read of medieval historians, Polydore Virgil, Thomas More, Spencer, Sidney, and Warner in chapters 2 and 3 while chapter 4 engages in an even more familiar essay in literary history on the English Chronicle Play. Part II, 'Shakespeare', presents readings of eight histories informed by the source study but engaged also in dialogues with such now forgotten literary historians and generalist critics as C. L. Kingsford, Peter Alexander, J. S. Smart, and Mark van Doren.

What raised Tillyard's study above the level of ordinary 'source-hunting', however, was the attempt to synthesize the sources with a general cultural pattern that appeared, in a phrase Engels once used in a flight of hubristic fancy, to explain almost everything. Tillyard provided the intelligible framework on which a generation of scholars could hang the results of their more particular labours. Needless to say, it was a framework marked with the features of the time and the institutions in which it was produced. Tillyard's two masterworks were written within the war-time nationalist preoccupations of Churchill's England, the Modernist values and categories of British New Criticism, and as an alternative—a positivist and retrogressive one—to the Leavisite version of Modernist criticism which he found so distasteful. Let me begin with the ways in which Tillyard can be said to be reviving an essentially nineteenth-century critical methodology.

G. Wilson Knight had, in the introduction to *The Wheel of Fire*, provided a comprehensive list of the categories of the kind of literary positivism which he took as the Other to be contained and condemned. At the centre of the list was Aristotelian cause-and-effect structured as a chronological sequence in a narrative plot, a 'temporal' mode of construing the text which was the very opposite of the 'spatial' hermeneutic Knight himself advocated. Related to this temporal hermeneutic were the methods of source study, which Knight criticized as based in a specious causal logic; critical attempts to define authorial intentionality, held to impose an alien structure of rationality on the products of non-rational imagination; and character study, which Knight felt was almost invariably tinged with notions of intentionality and moralism which confused art with life.[21] Although Knight does not state it, these are clearly categories related to the great tradition of late nineteenth-century realism, an aesthetic paradigm which coexisted with late Romanticism and early Modernism and, indeed, continues to attract practitioners to the present age. And they are the 'historical values' which Quinones claimed had originated in the Renaissance and were overthrown by Modernism's revolt against teleological history.

These are also the chief categories around which Tillyard's *Shakespeare's History Plays* is organized. The central claim of Tillyard's work is to have discovered what he calls the 'pattern' of history which informs the grand march of the two major historical tetralogies: 'a universally held and still comprehensible scheme of history: a scheme fundamentally religious, by which events evolve under a law of justice and under the ruling of God's Providence, and of which Elizabeth's England was the acknowledged outcome' (pp. 320–1). It is a series of causes and effects unfolding in time and constituting a teleological history which stages the eventual triumph of order over disorder.

The pattern, which Tillyard and later critics labelled the 'Tudor Myth', was formed by the following causal narrative, found in its purest form, Tillyard believed, in Hall (and 'Shakespeare's was nearly the same' as Hall's, Tillyard tells us on p. 61), and confused and botched in Holinshed: Richard II is wrongfully overthrown by the usurper Henry IV—although Richard himself had helped create the conditions of his own overthrow and deserved some punishment; Henry IV compounds his wrong by ordering Richard's murder, but because he humbles himself, God postpones his punishment until the reign of his grandson, Henry VI; Henry V, in the meantime, is a

glorious king whose successful reign is a sign of God's ultimate bene-
volent purposes; but the punishment of Henry IV's crimes comes to
fruition in the Yorkist overthrow of the Lancastrian dynasty, with the
malevolent reign of Richard III seen as a temporary triumph of evil
finally overcome when Providence leads Henry Tudor to marry the
Yorkist heir, uniting the two dynasties in the person of Henry VIII and
his daughter, Elizabeth (pp. 59–61).

Tillyard emphasized the causal construction of this schema:
'Shakespeare', he wrote, 'was more interested in the chain of cause
and effect than in the ideas that history repeats itself . . .' (p. 155), but
'behind all the unfolding of civil war there is the great lesson (implied
always and rarely stated) that the present time must take warning from
the past and utterly renounce all civil dissension' (p. 155). In short,
behind the apparent clashes of rhetoric and ideology can be discerned
an (oddly unthematized) moral and political lesson of the need for
order and authority. And because Shakespeare's great theme is but
haphazardly enunciated in the Shakespearian texts themselves, it is
necessary to go outside the text, into the Anglican homily *Against
Disobedience and wilful Rebellion* (p. 65) and, above all, into Edward
Hall's *Chronicles of the Union of the Two Noble and Illustré Famelies of
Lancaster and York* to supplement a Shakespearian text which
everywhere else is celebrated for its organic unity and wholeness (for
example pp. 176, 236); there is no escape from the 'sources' which
Knight had denounced as inessential and false to a true appreciation of
the Shakespearian imagination, just as morality, cause and effect, and
character (see, for example, the celebration of Prince Hal as a figure of
'large powers, Olympian loftiness, and high sophistication . . .',
pp. 269–82) are all necessary categories of analysis for a proper reading of the histories. Tillyard's *Shakespeare's History Plays* is, in that
sense, a pointed rejection of spatial hermeneutics and a celebration of
an older hermeneutics of realist narrative techniques.

Something needs to be established, however, concerning those
readings of the two historical tetralogies which form the second half of
the work. They are nuanced and often sensitive accounts of the plays
with a good deal of attention devoted to questions of aesthetic quality.
Tillyard's major claim concerning the *Henry VI* plays, for example, is to
have demonstrated Shakespeare's 'masterly inclusiveness that raises to
greatness a series of plays which in the execution are sometimes
immature and ineffective' (p. 150). *2 Henry VI* is praised in particular
as 'a fine piece of construction' to be 'enjoyed' as such (p. 176), while *3*

Henry VI is said to be something of an aesthetic let-down (p. 190). *Richard II* must be understood as non-realistic and symbolic in order to be appreciated as a fine work, if a lesser one than the great masterpiece of *1* and *2 Henry IV* (p. 244). Finally, *Henry V* is seen as a frank failure (p. 306). There is no sense, as there often was, say, in the works of E. E. Stoll, that Shakespeare was an unsophisticated and one-dimensional dramatist.

Nevertheless Tillyard's critical suppositions remain positivist and pre-New Critical in an important sense: his aim is to provide a settled and unitary reading of the plays, with ambiguities resolved and cruxes decided—however nuanced and complex the actual discussions leading to such decisions are. Tillyard thus vindicates the professional academicians whose programme had been established in the age of positivism: he produces the body of knowledge and methodology without which Shakespeare can only be misunderstood. Far more than Leavis or Knight, Tillyard supposes that only a professional training and formation in the historical culture of Shakespeare's era can equip us to understand the Great National Poet. Through Tillyard, the old-fashioned English professor, who had taken such hard knocks of late from the likes of Knight, the Leavises, and Tate and who had been sent back to school by Ransom and Brooks, came back into his own with only modest retooling needed. And this vindication of the early values and methods of the profession is the first secret of Tillyard's extraordinary success.

But if Tillyard's work on the histories is in some sense a clear reversion to an older, pre-Modernist critical paradigm, just as clearly it is a reversion that is not a complete reduplication. Rather than situating his audience *within* the teleololgical history he finds in Hall and Shakespeare, as the classic German 'philosophical critics' had done, he presents such a historical 'pattern' as part of a vanished past that can only be recovered through a professional reproduction of the text. His book is so necessary, Tillyard keeps telling us, precisely because *we* are now so different in our historical suppositions. As democrats, we need to be constantly reminded that Shakespeare is a monarchist; we are secular, but Shakespeare is religious and a believer in Providence; and, most symptomatically, we are no longer believers in 'progressive' Whig history, while Shakespeare, Tillyard asserts, assumes a religious and providential version of what our Victorian forebears took for granted. This last point is established in an extraordinary passage that is worth reproduction:

We can gauge that importance [of the pervasiveness of the Tudor Myth] by thinking of another great pattern of English history, which might be called the Whig pattern and which probably began to take shape after 1688. It is only its simpler and cruder versions that can justly be compared with the Tudor pattern of Hall and Davies of Hereford: I mean those found in the children's history books of the Victorian age and now popularly referred to as '1066 and all that'. Those versions anthologized and interpreted history with an assured prejudice against which the ordinary person had no defence, and had an incalculable influence on men's minds. The Tudor pattern had the same kind of power but with the important differences that it was not instilled by systematic educational means and that it did not spread nearly so wide. It was in fact the possession not of the average school-boy but of the more thoughtful portion of educated Elizabethan society. In that restricted portion it must have been a dominant idea. (pp. 63–4)

Note the metaphorical link between Elizabethan providential historiography and the secularized version of the Victorian generations. This casual linkage, in the light of the decisive consensus now in place *against* Tillyard's views of Elizabethan historiography (and which I will discuss shortly), is more than suggestive of the true origins of that pervasive 'pattern' which Tillyard projected on to the Elizabethan past. Tillyard has saved positivist history by mythologizing it and placing it in a vanished Golden, if unenlightened age. While his suppositions of univocal meaning to be validated through source work is essentially positivist, his own implicit theory of history is not; and while he clearly finds the historical 'pattern' he imputes to Hall and Shakespeare compelling and attractive, it would not be accurate to say he claims for it any validity except as a recovery of the lost past. His own notion of history is thus not very different from that of Leavis and Brooks, based as it is like theirs in the Modernist speculations of T. S. Eliot concerning a lost Elizabethan golden age of organic society and unified sensibility—and, Tillyard would now add, of a sense of historical meaning and purposefulness lost to us moderns. But before further exploring this hidden Modernist dimension of an apparently positivist theoretical framework, let me specify the links I am positing between Tillyard's Tudor myth and a defunct nineteenth-century historiography.

Tillyard had, in *Shakespeare's History Plays*, reproduced as an inherent vision of Shakespeare's histories a version of the great teleological historical pattern that dominated much of nineteenth-century thought—the pattern, for example, codified by Hegel's celebrated and notorious diagnosis of Napoleon as an embodiment of

Reason marching through history leading to the glorious denouement of the Prussian constitutional monarchy; of the positivist vision of a progressive accumulation of scientific knowledge completing Enlightenment and ushering in a new golden age; of the triumph of Democracy and Liberty as the West spread its enlightened institutions into the backward regions of the planet; of the popular version of Darwin according to which Nature reached its *telos* in the culminating production of Man; of those parts of Marx and Engels, canonized by both Second and Third Internationals, in which the inevitable outcome of the contradictions of capitalism is a proletarian revolution which produces the complete emancipation of the human race.[22] In short, Tillyard's Elizabethan pattern was, as H. A. Kelly shrewdly observed, 'an ex post facto Platonic Form, made up of many fragments that were never fitted together into a mental pattern until they felt the force of [Tillyard's] own synthesizing energy'.[23] But the source was not only Tillyard's synthesizing energy; he was in fact borrowing a form from the larger culture and reading it back into Shakespeare.

Thanks to H. A. Kelly's scholarly labours, we are now in a position to appreciate how much Tillyard imposed in his reconstruction of the grand 'pattern' in Shakespeare's history. Far too few readers took Tillyard at his word when he asserted, 'I do not pretend to be deeply read in the English chronicles, nor have I studied the sources of Shakespeare's Histories with the minute care of a man editing the separate plays' (p. 319). Kelly's impressive 1970 study *Divine Providence in the England of Shakespeare's Histories* is an understated but devastating complete reworking of the ground Tillyard had ploughed, and by the time Kelly has finished, little indeed remains of Tillyard's unified Elizabethan historical 'pattern'. The decisive move Kelly makes is to include in his analysis a body of material which Tillyard simply ignored—the fifteenth-century chronicles of the Wars of the Roses which had supplied the sixteenth-century historians studied by Tillyard with their 'raw' narrative material. According to Kelly the fifteenth-century writers are easily divisible into clear political camps: Lancastrian, anti-Lancastrian, and then Yorkist, according to which claim to the throne the writer is championing. It then becomes possible for Kelly to follow how these differently inflected narrative strands

---

[22] See Hayden White, *Metahistory: The Historical Imagination in Nineteenth-Century Europe* (Baltimore, Md.: Johns Hopkins University Press, 1973) for a definitive and nuanced account of many of these narrative strands.

[23] Kelly, *Divine Providence*, 298.

become incorporated into the ideologically complex narratives of the sixteenth century, most of which show few signs of the 'unitary' Tudor myth which Tillyard claimed to characterize several of them. In addition, Kelly takes a close look at the specifics of the pattern which Tillyard tried to define as the informing schema of the histories and asks a simple, fundamental, but, I believe, unanswerable and embarrassing question: why should Shakespeare be assumed to accept a 'concept of divine wrath extending for generations over a whole people for a crime committed in the remote past', a concept which 'presupposes the kind of avenging God completely foreign to the piety of the historiographers of medieval and Renaissance England' (p. 300). Shakespeare's great accomplishment in the histories, Kelly concludes, was to 'unsynthesize the syntheses of his contemporaries and to unmoralize their moralizations' (p. 304). Now Kelly is perhaps too trusting of the 'objective' basis of *his* own scholarship for his own good, but as a corrective to Tillyard, his accomplishment is great indeed. What he undoes in Tillyard is precisely the kind of Victorian moralizing that Modernist criticism had banished but which Tillyard, for his own inscrutable reasons, needed to reproduce, distanced and projected, as part of the lost legacy of a glorious English past.

Tillyard's Modernism

If there is a double message in Tillyard's treatment of history in *Shakespeare's History Plays*, if he appears to invoke against contemporary Modernist spatialization the necessity of taking into account the historical values, but then assigns the most important of those values, the sense of purpose or of teleology, into a vanished golden age, there are other muted Modernist connections in his masterworks, connections which were, I believe, important reasons for Tillyard's meteoric rise and fall. For Tillyard's work is a complex synthesis in which both Modernist and anti-Modernist impulses are brought into an uneasy fusion.

We might clarify the situation and the relation of Tillyard to his more uncompromisingly Modernist Cambridge colleagues with an analogy to the Tudor Reformation. Tillyard's criticism can be seen as representing a peculiar balancing-point, a kind of *via media* between the opposing trends of positivist professionalism and the older cultural tradition. To pursue the analogy, we might consider Leavis's *Scrutiny* to represent a kind of insurgent Puritan Protestantism within the forces of culture, while the older philological and technical approaches represented the old creed, which Tillyard, for all his latitudinarianism, could no longer countenance—but parts of which he attempted to incorporate. In the historical method which he borrowed from American developers, Tillyard saw a professional alternative to philology, and hence the possibility of a cultural Elizabethan Compromise that, indeed, formed the basis for a new hegemony for a generation, as had its historical original. His historical *method* satisfied the need for disciplinary content by providing a body of knowledge other than skill in explication of texts, but it avoided the 'aridity' of, say, Stoll's theatrical history or of classical philology, by virtue of an aesthetic dimension that derived from Tillyard's affiliation with the cultural tradition. It was this latter quality in particular, I believe, that gave *The Elizabethan World Picture* its enormous influence, even beyond the obvious appeals of its professionalism and its pedagogical utility, particularly in America, where, as I have noted, the specifically nationalistic quality of Tillyard's works on the histories was not influential. In a paradoxical way—given the overt historicist and even antiquarian veneer of Tillyard's writing—this aesthetic dimension, if not the totality of his critical methodology, is essentially Modernist. Tillyard's concepts of 'Tudor Myth' and of 'Elizabethan World Picture' owe much of their force and much of their easy and quick acceptance in the post-World War II era to the anti-Romantic revolution in taste and aesthetic criteria associated with the Modernism of T. S. Eliot.

Tillyard's Modernist affinities can be glimpsed partially in his heavy reliance on notions of 'organic unity' throughout the discussion of the plays in *Shakespeare's History Plays* (pp. 147, 162, 176, 236, and 254); like Knight, he rejects the disintegrators out of hand, assuming as a matter of course that Shakespeare was the sole author of the *Henry VI* plays (pp. 131, 161). In addition, Tillyard supplies evidence for a Modernist connection in *The Muse Unchained*. Eliot, Joyce, and Lawrence figure prominently in his discussion of English studies at Cambridge, and Eliot is singled out for special emphasis as a critic whose *Sacred Wood* was nothing short of 'explosive' in its impact. In that work Eliot taught a generation to be suspicious of the high value on individual 'originality' that the commonplaces of post-Romantic criticism had assumed. Instead, he argued in an immensely influential essay, what counted was not individual uniqueness, but the poet's relation to an entire literary Tradition (the capital letter is called for here):

One of the facts that might come to light in this process is our tendency to insist, when we praise a poet, upon those aspects of his work in which he least resembles anyone else. In these aspects or parts of his work we pretend to find what is individual, what is the peculiar essence of the man. We dwell with satisfaction upon the poet's difference from his predecessors, especially his immediate predecessors; we endeavour to find something that can be isolated in order to be enjoyed. Whereas if we approach a poet without this prejudice we shall often find that not only the best, but the most individual parts of his work may be those in which the dead poets, his ancestors, assert their immortality most vigorously.[24]

To be sure, Eliot's Tradition is not the same thing as Tillyard's Elizabethan World Picture. Eliot seems to have in mind a cultural continuum defined by a kind of pantheon from Homer to the present. But Eliot prepares his readers for a Tillyardian reading of Shakespeare by decisively shifting attention away from the idea of the poet as an individual genius to the idea of an impersonal poet whose mind is a 'medium' (p. 53) for 'something which is more valuable' (pp. 52–3) than the poet's merely subjective personality. In effect the poet 'surrenders' to the 'mind of Europe' and the 'mind of his own country' (p. 51). With such ideas widely disseminated, Tillyard's notion of Shakespeare's relation to Elizabethan thought is easily accepted and felt to be aesthetically as well as intellectually correct. Tillyard's connection to Eliot becomes clear when he writes a passage like the following:

It is easy, and up to a point true, to think of Shakespeare as transforming by his genius the material of Holinshed and the dramatic type of the Chronicle into something uniquely his own. But to leave one's thought at that is a large error; for what Shakespeare transformed was so much more than Holinshed and the Chronicle Play. . . . Shakespeare's Histories are more like his own Comedies and Tragedies than like others' Histories, and they do not so much try out and discard a provincial mode as present one of his versions on the whole contemporary pattern of culture.[25]

While Tillyard has not given over the idea of Shakespearian originality, he has qualified that originality heavily and made of his author a spokesman for Tudor orthodoxy, a move that is made much easier after Eliot's writings.

Why give this cultural conservatism the name of Modernist? The

---

[24] 'Tradition and the Individual Talent', *The Sacred Wood: Essays on Poetry and Criticism* (1920; repr. New York: Barnes, 1964), 48.

[25] Tillyard, *Shakespeare's History Plays*, 11.

truth is that a longing for the older, 'organic' civilizations of the pre-capitalist past, often accompanied by right-wing politics, was a widespread characteristic of Anglo-American Modernism, involving such figures as the Fugitive-Agrarian poets and critics, D. H. Lawrence, Ezra Pound, and many more. Again, Raymond Williams's classic study *Culture and Society* provides a welcome delineation of the paradoxes of the situation for British society and culture. Suffice it to say here that the aesthetic sensibility we call Modernism arose as part of larger social, economic, and cultural developments, in many ways in reaction to the hegemony of instrumental reason in post-Enlightenment Western society. Modernism was no political monolith; it gave rise to reactionaries and revolutionaries (with often little in between these two political poles). That is, there was an international Modernist aesthetic paradigm on which various ideologies were inscribed. Eliot (and a number of Anglo-Americans), through the inscription of a nostalgic, reactionary ideology, produced a conservative strain of Modernism that saw capitalist civilization as empty, bureaucratic, and soulless, as compared to the (mythologized) pre-industrial epoch, and which consequently admired the 'organic' civilizations of the past or of contemporary 'primitives'. This tendency in Modernism celebrated a defunct past somehow recreated through art and literature in the present.[26] I mentioned in Chapter 2 Eliot's role in the rediscovery and canonization of Donne and the Metaphysical tradition, which Eliot had made synonymous with a lost 'unification of sensibility' in his celebrated essay on the Metaphysical Poets. This was the essay Tillyard cited in *The Muse Unchained* as particularly influential in the Cambridge ethos that had formed his own literary sensibility. With this influence in mind, Tillyard's *Elizabethan World Picture* takes its place as another of the Modernist celebrations of the lost Golden Age of the Elizabethan and Jacobean periods. Tillyard's descriptions of the cultural unity and totality of the Elizabethan epoch connect directly with the notion of unified sensibility and should be seen as an elaboration and development of Eliot's Modernist myth-making. And of course, Tillyard's little book is not without its own aesthetic charms: *The Elizabethan World Picture* may have been written without artistic pretence, but the vision of totality which it disseminated can be—and has been—read and contemplated as an artefact of intricate aesthetic value, both in itself and as a schema 'read into' the great European

[26] See Mulhern for a differently inflected account of these themes, *Moment of 'Scrutiny'*, 268–90.

masterworks of the Middle Age and Renaissance, with Shakespeare's works as perhaps the major example.

Of course I would not wish to deny that Tillyard's notion of the World Picture articulates with some adequacy a prevailing part of the hegemonic culture of Elizabethan England. Tillyard's model has some historical adequacy, although it is surely one-sided and fails to take note of counter-hegemonic tendencies as they are manifest both in historical documents and in Shakespeare's plays. To put it bluntly, in a formulation a number of critics have anticipated, Tillyard mistook a ruling-class ideology—Tudor propaganda, if you will—which sought to impose on a tradition-minded and resistant island kingdom a new authoritarian monarchy—for the 'organic' philosophy of a unitary culture. Tillyard certainly recognizes that the 'world picture' was the property of the aristocracy rather than the popular classes[27] and recognizes the political usefulness to the rulers of such beliefs,[28] but he never moves from these observations to any theory of legitimation or ideology, such as have his successors, the new historicists. There is, doubtless, a definite level of historical adequacy to Tillyard's reconstructions, however mis-theorized. But even granting this level, I would argue that the force of the appeal of his works was largely aesthetic. The Elizabethan World Picture, with its multiply interconnected and corresponding orders, its unification of man, nature, and God, and of the cosmic, the political, and the psychological, is described by Tillyard in both works I am discussing with barely repressed delight and admiration—in a spirit quite faithful to his earlier insistence on the aesthetic and humanist mission of English studies and equally faithful to his testimony to the impact of Modernism on English at Cambridge. Tillyard's taste for the mental gymnastics of complexly corresponding planes had been anticipated in one of the founding documents of Modernist aesthetics, Baudelaire's celebrated lyric 'Correspondances'. Now Baudelaire had as his probable source for his use of the term the strange writings of one of the most influential crackpots in literary history, Emanuel Swedenborg,[29] while of

---

[27] Tillyard, *Shakespeare's History Plays*, 243.

[28] Ibid., p. 66.

[29] This brief characterization will have to substitute for a more detailed but hopelessly tangential discussion of the ideas and sources of what many commentators have seen as a basic document of Symbolist aesthetics. See, for example, J. Pommier, *La Mystique de Baudelaire* (Paris: Les Belles Lettres, 1932), 17–23 and Lloyd James Austin, *L'Univers poétique de Baudelaire: Symbolisme et Symbolique* (Paris: Mercure de France, 1956).

course Tillyard worked from Elizabethan documents. But the apparent coincidence of interest between the Paris bohemian and the Cambridge don is symptomatic of a deeper affinity: a sharing of Modernism's preoccupation with an absent world of meaning, beauty, and presence. Is it not clear that in Tillyard's detailed descriptions of the Elizabethan World Picture can be discerned a libidinal investment similar in kind to that celebrated by Baudelaire?

It is this aesthetic dimension which is lacking in the ground-breaking discussion of the theme of 'lost hierarchies, lost wholes' in Mulhern[30] and which helps explain the faintly unsatisfying feeling one gets after reading what is, as far as it goes, a quite lucid analysis.

The factors involved in the production of Tillyard's critical texts, then, connect outward to social dynamics to a far greater extent than those texts—or most of their first generation of readers—explicitly admitted. As the late product of a cultural insurgency that overthrew the old central role of the classics and philology in British university education, as an attempted solution to the problem of founding an adequate knowledge/power for a newly institutionalized profession, as an expression of a Modernist longing for an always absent wholeness and meaningfulness, as a conservative expression of the patriotic ideology of wartime—Tillyard's work was a remarkable synthesis of conflicting impulses and tendencies that, for a time, was the centre that held for a generation of Shakespeare scholars, and its influence can by no means be considered simple and univocal. Using this analysis, I would now like briefly to survey some of the tendencies of the emerging reaction against Tillyard. We will see a complex situation in which the Tillyardian compromise survives a considerable assault in the Fifties and Sixties only to succumb unexpectedly to what amounts to a paradigm crisis and then shift in literary studies beginning about 1970. And in the conclusion to this chapter, I will address some problems inherent in this attempted cultural insurgency before moving to a consideration of contemporary Shakespeare studies in the final chapter.

The Reaction to Tillyard: Towards Counter-Hegemony?

If Tillyard's work was a kind of cultural Anglicanism offered as an alternative to Leavisite Puritanism and if it achieved a pre-eminent status among a generation of Shakespeare scholars seldom seen for

[30] Mulhern, *Moment of 'Scrutiny'*, 268–90.

any single work of scholarship, it never achieved *universal* acceptance. For example, as I noted in the previous chapter, the more radical and aggressively Modernist approach to Shakespeare developed in *Scrutiny* persisted and developed after the war and found American analogues and (limited) allies in the New Criticism. Even during the war years, Tillyard's historical approach had not gone unchallenged. Leonard Dean, in a critique of the American historical critic Theodore Spencer which is clearly relevant to Tillyard's work as well, argued that Shakespeare's art could not simply be assimilated to the commonplace thought of the Elizabethan Age without great danger of reduction, while in a 1944 review in *Scrutiny* L. C. Knights had similiar reservations about Spencer's work and explicitly linked Spencer and Tillyard—although Knights praised Tillyard's work as 'useful' in addition to expressing considerable reservations about its potential for producing reductive readings of Shakespeare.[31]

Views in harmony with these critiques gained new prominence immediately after the war when Una Ellis-Fermor[32] and Derek Traversi,[33] writing separately, and Cleanth Brooks and Robert Heilman, writing together in the analysis I discussed in Chapter 3, all produced remarkably similar readings of *1* and *2 Henry IV* rejecting Tillyard's claim that Hal was Shakespeare's version of an ideal king. Ellis-Fermor and Traversi in particular argued that there was something intrinsically corrosive to the inner spirit in all political and public activities; and the famous crux at the end of Part 2 concerning the rejection of Falstaff enacted Shakespeare's understanding that Hal's political success—which we are dramatically led to applaud—carries with it a deterioration in the new king's humanity which no rationalization can disguise.[34]

[31] Leonard F. Dean, 'Shakespeare's Treatment of Conventional Ideas', *Sewanee Review*, 52 (Summer 1944), 414–23 and L. C. Knights, 'Shakespeare and the Elizabethan Climate', *Scrutiny*, 12 (Spring 1944), 146–52.

[32] Una Ellis-Fermor, *The Frontiers of Drama* (1945; repr. New York: Methuen, 1964), 34–55.

[33] Derek Traversi 'Henry IV—Part I' and 'Henry IV—Part II', *Scrutiny*, 15 (Winter 1947 and Spring 1948), 24–35 and 117–27.

[34] John Danby, *Shakespeare's Doctrine of Nature: A Study of 'King Lear'* ((London: Faber, 1949), 82–97), should also be mentioned as an influential, New Critically premissed and implicitly anti-Tillyard work; and, as I noted previously, a number of critics (for example, Harold Goddard, *The Meaning of Shakespeare* (Chicago, Ill.: University of Chicago Press, 1951), 161–214, and Samuel Hemingway, 'On Behalf of That Falstaff', *Shakespeare Quarterly*, 3 (October 1952), 307–11) attempted to 'synthesize' Tillyard's reading with other interpretations. One index of Tillyard's influence, by the way, is the circumspect tone of many of his critics in this period, even in *Scrutiny*, where

In spite of these counter-positions, however, Tillyard was defended by numerous influential critics in his long 'march through the institutions' via examinations, textbooks, and academic scholarship. One sign of influence in unexpected places was the spirited defence of Tillyard offered in the name of Marxism by the American Marxist Shakespearian Paul Siegel as late as 1986[35] and, in a similar vein, though earlier, the use of a basically Tillyardian framework by both critics in a debate over *1 Henry IV* between an admitted liberal and a self-described Marxist in a (none too illuminating) *College English* debate.[36] Marshall McLuhan, too, can be counted among the champions of Tillyardian interpretations of the *Henriad* after the War.[37]

Thus in the Fifties and Sixties Tillyard's was the major critical force challenging the hegemony within Shakespeare studies—if I may depart from the properly Gramscian sense of the term—of New Criticism. Observers differed over which critical school should be seen as 'leading'. In one well-known research guide, the author states baldly that 'Whether one agrees or disagrees with it, Tillyard's [book] has become the traditional interpretation of the history plays.'[38] But a second standard reference opined that, 'Despite its endorsement by scholars, historical criticism [in Shakespeare studies] has been less

L. C. Knights habitually tempered his criticism with a certain praise, a characteristic approach that Knights repeated in other discussions of Shakespeare and politics in the Fifties and Sixties—see, for example, *Poetry, Politics and the English Tradition* (London: Chatto, 1954), 30–1 n. 12 and *William Shakespeare: The Histories* (London: Longmans Green, 1962), 15–16. We should notice too that these new readings are based also in a change in formal aesthetic notions: the recognition of clashing discourses and the resulting conceptual and aesthetic tensions certainly have a formal dimension. The breakdown of an aesthetic of organic unity, basic to the New Critical revolution, is displayed, too, in a shift in the terms of discussion of the ancient question of whether the two Henry IV plays are autonomous or form a single unit. I will return to this symptomatic shift in the next chapter.

[35] See Paul N. Siegel, *Shakespeare's English and Roman History Plays: A Marxist Approach* (Rutherford, NJ: Farleigh Dickinson University Press, 1986). See also his 'Tillyard Lives—Historicism and Shakespeare's History Plays', *Clio*, 9 (1980), 5–23. The article retrospectively indicates Tillyard's influence on Siegel's 1957 *Shakespearean Tragedy and the Elizabethan Compromise* (New York: New York University Press, 1957).

[36] William B. Stone, 'Literature and Class Ideology: *Henry IV, Part One*', *College English*, 33 (May 1972), 891–900; and Richard M. Eastmen, 'Political Views in *Henry IV, Part 1*: A Demonstration of Liberal Humanism', *College English*, 33 (May 1972), 901–7.

[37] Marshall McLuhan, ' "Henry IV", a Mirror for Magistrates', *University of Toronto Quarterly*, 17 (Jan. 1948), 152–60.

[38] David Bergeron, *Shakespeare: A Study and Research Guide* (London: Macmillan, 1975); quoted in Holderness, *Shakespeare's History*, 192.

influential than its chief rival inside and outside the academy—the so-called new criticism.'[39]

In retrospect, however, a certain complicity between historical criticism and New Criticism is evident. I speak of complicity not to imply guilt but to indicate a certain relationship between ideas in which an apparent antagonism conceals unarticulated assumptions which work together to help form an age's mental structures.

In this case, the 'complicity' duplicates that well-known relation between the categories of the public and the private which are arguably structural in capitalist society: the argument between the historicists and the New Critics was really over which side of the public/private antinomy to stress and give priority to. Tillyard saw clearly enough that Falstaff had his charms, but he thought that civic virtue required his repression. The New Critics saw and rarely denied the need for the public virtues highlighted in the transformation of Hal to Henry V; they simply regretted the toll that such necessity exacted on private virtues. Basically, both approaches work from within the same category system. Writing in 1959, for example, L. C. Knights opined, 'What we have in *Henry IV* therefore is a realistic portrayal of the ways of the world and an insistent questioning of the values by which its great men live—with a consequent ironic contrast between public profession and actuality.'[40] In effect Knights grants Tillyard's account of the play's politics: that a 'good' king *must* be this way is agreed by both; they differ over how political exigency affects the 'inner man'. That this dilemma is historically specific and ideological is noticed by neither.

Around 1970 however—doubtless under the impact of the Vietnam era and the student insurgency which marked the late Sixties and early Seventies in both American and British universities—a fundamental change begins to occur: a paradigm crisis, usually the preliminary stage of a paradigm shift, can be observed to begin. One of the earliest harbingers of the new paradigm was an essay written in 1966 (but published posthumously in 1969) by Sigurd Burckhardt, who was writing on the same campus and within much the same ethos as Herbert Marcuse. Rather than implicitly granting Tillyard's view that the political theory behind Shakespeare's dramatic vision in the *Henriad* was essentially a providential Tudor myth, Burckhardt took on

---

[39] 'Historical Criticism', *The Reader's Encyclopedia of Shakespeare*, eds. O. J. Campbell and E. G. Quin (New York: Crowell, 1966).

[40] L. C. Knights, *Some Shakespearean Themes* (Palo Alto, Calif.: Stanford University Press, 1960), 40.

Tillyard's central Tudor myth theory frontally, arguing that there was no unified, totalistic 'Elizabethan World Picture' which united Tudor and Shakespearian conceptions in some grand scheme. Instead, Burckhardt argued, 'Shakespeare ... discovered that the ... golden unity of the Elizabethan world picture was in truth a lethal mixture of two mutually inconsistent and severally inadequate models of succession ...'.[41] In this insistence on clash and disparity which cannot be reduced to unity, we have perhaps the first sounding of a truly Postmodernist Shakespearian criticism; unfortunately Burckhardt took his own life before his achievement could be recognized.

In 1968, out of Cambridge, Wilbur Sanders developed the critique of Tillyard's use of Tudor commonplaces in interpreting Shakespeare, displaying a more polemical edge in his critique than his predecessors in that vein, Traversi and Knights, had shown.[42] Times were changing.

In 1970 H. A. Kelly published his own frontal assault on Tillyard's thesis of a providential history as the dramatic framework of the *Henriad*, adding extensive documentation to Burckhardt's insight that Elizabethan culture must have been more divided and contentious than Tillyard's widely disseminated account had allowed. And in 1972 Robert Ornstein, drawing on New Critical methodology to be sure, echoed Leonard Dean's 1944 scepticism over whether Shakespeare's texts could be assumed simply to mirror an age's commonplace assumptions. But he added to this argument a reading of Hall's *Chronicle*, a major source for Tillyard's argument, and thus took on Tillyard on his own ground.

By 1975 the critical consensus was so broken and open to new influences that *PMLA*, that bellwether of what 'the profession' considers 'excellent' at a given moment, printed Roy Battenhouse's sophistical *tour de force* on Falstaff, a study reminiscent of the inspired Shandean mental gymnastics of Maurice Morgann's eighteenth-century demonstration that 'Falstaff is no coward'—itself a product of changing critical paradigms at the end of the neo-classical era. Battenhouse, well known for his development of a 'Christianizing' version of historical criticism in Shakespeare studies, argued with an apparently straight face that behind Falstaff's antics can be intuited an 'inner intent [of] a charitable almsgiving of brotherly self-humiliation and

[41] Sigurd Burckhardt, *Shakespearian Meanings* (Princeton, NJ: Princeton University Press, 1968), 83–6.
[42] Wilbur Sanders, *The Dramatist and the Received Idea: Studies in the Plays of Marlowe and Shakespeare* (Cambridge: Cambridge University Press, 1968), 73 and 361, n. 3.

fatherly truth-telling'.[43] Outraged letters appeared in a subsequent issue,[44] but the editors were not moved. By 1980 Gordon Ross Smith could unleash what is arguably the most polemical of the several anti-Tillyard tracts,[45] and Edward Pechter, in an article cited at the beginning of this chapter, could pronounce Tillyard critically deceased.

If the demolition is complete, what can we learn of the practice of literary criticism from this tale? One outcome has been a new awareness of the social role and function of literary criticism as an institution within modern culture related in complex ways to political, social, and aesthetic trends, the connection to which has often been suppressed in the recent past. In the next chapter I will briefly discuss several of the new critical trends articulating these insights, which, of course, I am here attempting to expand and develop. In Britain Jonathan Dollimore, Alan Sinfield, and Graham Holderness and in America what has been called a new literary historicism (best exemplified by Stephen Greenblatt's *Renaissance Self-Fashioning* and subsequent essays by Greenblatt and others inspired by that work) can be understood as growing directly out of the reaction to Tillyard.[46] Along with the development of feminism and of deconstruction, the critique of Tillyard in fact turns into a full-fledged paradigm shift around 1980, after about a decade of 'crisis'.

But if we can certainly speak of a paradigm shift in progress in the Eighties, are we equally justified in speaking of a counter-hegemonic criticism under construction? As we shall see in the next chapter, each of the new trends has been marked by a culturally and politically insurgent spirit, perhaps more explicit in the British than the American works; but recognizable in all of them is a continuity with the radical culture of the Vietnam-war era, in which Tillyard's hegemony came to an end. The current movement takes its inspiration from the Vietnam war-era values of anti-authoritarianism, anti-imperialism, and suspicion of nationalism and patriotism. A wholly unpredictable—and to

[43] Roy Battenhouse, 'Falstaff as Parodist and Perhaps Holy Fool', *PMLA* 90 (Jan. 1975), 32–52.

[44] *PMLA* 90 (Oct. 1975), 919–20.

[45] Gordon Ross Smith, 'A Rabble of Princes: Considerations Touching Shakespeare's Political Orthodoxy in the Second Tetralogy', *Journal of the History of Ideas*, 41 (1980), 29–48.

[46] Recent anti-Tillyard trends in American new historicism are well summarized in Jonathan Goldberg, 'The Politics of Renaissance Literature: A Review Essay', *English Literary History*, 49 (1982), 514–42 and in the introduction to Alan Sinfield, 'Power and Ideology: An Outline Theory and Sidney's Arcadia', *English Literary History*, 52 (1985), 259–77.

my mind welcome resurgence of Marxism, under the influence of Foucault, Derrida, and the other well-known figures of the French intellectual Left, has become a feature of Anglo-American literary culture for the first time since the end of World War II, paradoxically in the age of Reagan and Thatcher, which of course, has otherwise been marked by the retreat and confusion of the Left across a broad front of political and cultural institutions. It is this paradox of a critical insurgency coming to prominence within academia during an era of Anglo-American political reaction that poses particular and rarely confronted problems for the new critical movements. For it is remarkable that with very few exceptions—feminist, ethnic, and gay studies being essentially separate developments from the one I am addressing here—there has been no external social movement outside the ranks of college professors to which the insurgency relates. Even the formerly obligatory references to the working class within Marxist rhetoric have all but disappeared (for understandable and intellectually honest reasons, to be sure). Instead the new movements have developed through a direct appeal to the professorate itself and become institutionalized as legitimate and desirable 'fields', methods, or approaches within literary studies. Since in the present study I have assumed the relevance of a Gramscian theory that recognized that meaningful cultural insurgency would necessarily work through the established institutions of a society if it would be effective, I do not raise these points in order to profess scandalization or innocent shock. It is quite possible that the political effects of this development are yet to come, just as Leavis's social impact, or so it seems to me, was delayed until the revolt of the liberal arts students in the Sixties. But at the present, bourgeois hegemony in America and in Britain would appear to be undamaged by the assault, and one is forced to ponder the depressing possibility that in the Eighties Walter Benjamin's sardonic observation that the Left wastes its energies in seeking to politicize art while the Right gains power in aestheticizing politics became once more applicable.

In the context of the absence of mass political insurgency, in fact, the attempt to politicize literary criticism, while it rests on sound analysis and reasoning and an admirable willingness to expose the untenable assumptions of the previous generations of academic literary criticism, is itself hard put to ground itself socially.[47] The danger is that

[47] Edward W. Said has been exemplary in voicing similar concerns in recent years. See for example his 'Opponents, Audiences, Constituencies, and Community', *Critical Inquiry*, 9 (Sept. 1982), 1–26.

the radical politics will themselves become simply a posture, a debating position from within the interminable flux of discourse-formation within the academy. Politics would then become basically a performance without external social significance—a species of Utopian drama grounded more in hope than in *The German Ideology*'s 'real material conditions'.

While in many ways the new criticisms of the Eighties represent a fundamental departure for academic Shakespeare studies, it is also true that the currents I have been tracing in this study—the often opposed, but at times complicit forces of culture and aesthetics on the one hand and professionalization on the other—continue to work in shaping discourse about Shakespeare. The question is, to what extent have new critical discoveries changed the terms of the interaction, and to what extent are we seeing a simple variation on an all too familiar pattern?

5

Toward the Postmodern Shakespeare
Contemporary Critical Trends

Intimations of Change

In her introduction to the important 1985 critical anthology *Shakespeare and the Question of Theory*, Patricia Parker speaks of the 'theoretical ferment' of recent years as having finally penetrated into the field of Shakespeare studies. 'Larger theoretical developments', she writes, 'have had their echo in what is now amounting to a wholesale reconsideration of the Shakespearian corpus—from the controversy over what constitutes an authoritative "text" for plays which exist in so many versions, to the perception of a kinship between Derridean wordplay or Bakhtinian heteroglossia and Shakespeare's own inveterate punning, from the exploration by feminist critics of the differing roles of women in Shakespeare to the reopening of historical and ideological questions in ways other than a simple return to the static conservatism of Tillyard's long-influential *Elizabethan World Picture*.'[1]

As Parker herself implies, the advent of such a collection (along with its slightly earlier cousins *The Political Shakespeare* and *Alternative Shakespeares*) at so late a date as 1985 (long since 'Derrida, Foucault and the others first burst upon the consciousness of English-speaking readers almost a generation ago', she writes) attests to the remarkable resistance within the field of Shakespeare studies to outside influences which had long since become familiar in other areas of literary study. Clearly factors such as the large numbers of Renaissance and Shakespeare scholars and the system of specializations and periodization worked to insulate Shakespeare criticism from larger outside developments—for a time. The barriers having now been surmounted, however, the new tendencies are asserting themselves with great rapidity, and have 'changed the face of Shakespeare studies', accord-

---

[1] Introduction, *Shakespeare and the Question of Theory*, ed. Patricia Parker and Geoffrey Hartman (New York: Methuen, 1985), p. vii.

ing to E. A. J. Honigmann, 'more suddenly than ever before'.[2] Contemporary opinion tends to distinguish three different recent strands: feminism, deconstruction proper, and the new historicism. All of these, I believe, can be seen as interrelated—not only to each other, but also to an emerging Postmodernist aesthetic paradigm, one of whose marks is its unusually close connection to critical theory. And each of the three, as we will see, grapples in its own way with the problems inherent in the limitations of a now almost completely professionalized writing situation for Shakespeare criticism.

As I argued in Chapter 2, the shift from Modernism to Postmodernism has involved an element of violent suppression of continuity—a suppression partially indicated by the very valuing of breaks, discontinuity, and heterogeneity in several versions of contemporary theory itself. The resulting situation is a complex one, involving not only clear conceptual differences and reversals but also hidden continuities from a now devalued Modernist past. The strategy of this concluding chapter, accordingly, will involve a look at the depletion and then dismantling of the dominating Modernist critical paradigms which have been the subject of this book, after which the now emerging alternative paradigms will be examined, not so much in their own terms, but in the context of the breaks and continuities they display in relation to a recent past of instrumentalized Modernism.

The Situation in the Sixties

By about 1960, as I have indicated, Shakespeare studies were dominated by two competing but increasingly complicit critical paradigms: a historical critical methodology descended from nineteenth-century positivism but, under Tillyard's influence, also containing elements of Modernism; and a New Critical methodology more openly Modernist in its affiliations than historicism but with its earlier critical edges blunted and rendered harmless in favour of abstract and purely formalist textual choreography.

After the initial flush of each had worn away, neither of these methodologies proved capable of mounting a significant challenge to the instrumentalizing dynamics of a professionalism which each also, in its own way, both accommodated and challenged—even though

---

[2] E. A. J. Honigmann, 'The New Shakespeare?', *The New York Review of Books*, 35, No. 5 (31 Mar. 1988), 32.

academic criticism was thoroughly transformed in many other ways as a result of the rise of these new critical paradigms.

Much the same could be said of two critical trends that rose up in the Sixties as part of the developing 'crisis' of critical methodologies: Northrop Frye's 'myth criticism' and continental structuralism. Each of these tendencies, as Fekete argued in *The Critical Twilight*, was a clear reaction against New Criticism in the direction of scientism and further professionalization; each argued that the study of literature demanded its own science based on the insight that literature could only be properly understood in its own terms, as an autonomous language-like structure whose connections to social reality were superficial and misleading. Frye's impact on Shakespeare studies was large, helping to transform discussion of the comedies from the embarrassment of relative neglect to something like centre-stage for a time, but in retrospect it seems clear that Frye's innovations were assimilated to the late, highly professionalized New Critical paradigm, ultimately proving to be much less revolutionary than the polemical rhetoric of *An Anatomy of Criticism* suggested.

The structuralist revival of the Sixties and Seventies, which had a strong vogue in much of academic literary studies, had much less direct impact on Shakespeare studies. If there were several structuralist or semiotic studies of Shakespeare,[3] the field as a whole proved remarkably resistant to this French import. Shakespeare criticism in the Fifties and Sixties remained generally insulated from larger developments and tended toward a homogenized synthesis of New Critical sensitivities to ambiguities with the historical lore of post-Tillyard historical criticism. There was perhaps a reaction against the earlier New Critical image-pattern studies and a turn toward interpreting Shakespeare as drama more than as poetry. But this hardly amounted to a major paradigm shift, and the result was a competent, informed body of work marked by timidity of spirit and a serene indifference to any larger social currents. Predictably, it was read by few outside the field since its real purpose was to serve as a professional credential among a largely self-selected coterie. Given this

---

[3] See, for example, Terence Hawkes, *Shakespeare's Talking Animals: Language and Drama in Society* (London: Edward Arnold, 1973); A. Johnson, *Readings of 'Antony and Cleopatra' and 'King Lear'* (Pisa: ETS, 1979); K. Elam, *The Semiotics of Theater and Drama* (New York: Methuen, 1980) and *Shakespeare's Universe of Discourse: Language Games in the Comedies* (Cambridge: Cambridge University Press, 1984). There are several other examples in Italian; see Drakakis, *Alternative Shakespeares* (New York: Methuen, 1985), 231 n. 1 for a fuller listing.

professionalization, there was virtually no pretence of operating within a sphere of public discourse, a sphere which in any case had been transformed in fundamental ways by the new electronic media.

As the Sixties progressed, an unforeseen problem in the academicization of both historical criticism and New Criticism began to emerge: repetition. In the case of the New Criticism of *1* and *2 Henry IV*, if I may continue the survey begun in the previous chapter, the number of attempts simply to reassert the 'balances' and complex irony of the play is astounding. Many of these take the form of 'syntheses' of earlier criticism; the majority, quite unselfconsciously, simply present a 'reading' of the play through familiar New Critical topics that were already present in Brooks and Heilman and justify themselves through the peculiar and unique set of nuances and qualities of tension and irony that they 'discover'.[4] At times they bow in the direction of older positivist notions of making 'an original contribution

[4] A list of such essentially repetitive New Critically-influenced readings of the *Henry IV* plays in the post-war period, in alphabetical order by author, would include: Paul J. Aldus, 'Analogical Probability in Shakespeare's Plays', *Shakespeare Quarterly*, 6 (Autumn 1955), 397–414; Herschel Baker, Introduction to *Henry IV, Parts 1 and 2*, ed. G. Blakemore Evans (*The Riverside Shakespeare*; Boston: Houghton Mifflin, 1974), 842–6; Edward I. Berry, 'The Rejection Scene in *2 Henry IV*', *Studies in English Literature 1500–1900*, 17 (Spring 1977), 201–18; Astere E. Claeyssens, '*Henry IV, Part I*', in *Lectures on Four of Shakespeare's History Plays* (Pittsburgh: Carnegie Institute of Technology, 1953), 19–34; Robert J. Fehrenbach, 'The Characterization of the King in *1 Henry IV*', *Shakespeare Quarterly*, 30 (Winter 1979), 42–50; Michael Goldman, 'Falstaff Asleep', in *Shakespeare and the Energies of Drama* (Princeton, NJ: Princeton University Press, 1972), 45–57; G. R. Hibbard, '*Henry IV* and *Hamlet*', *Shakespeare Survey*, 30 (1977), 1–12; Norman Holland, Introduction to *Henry IV, Part Two*, in *The Complete Signet Classic Shakespeare*, ed. Sylvan Barnet (New York: Harcourt, 1972), 678–85; L. C. Knights, 'Shakespeare's Politics: With Some Reflections on the Nature of Tradition', *Proceedings of the British Academy* (London: Oxford University Press, 1957), 115–32; Anthony La Branche, ' "If Thou Wert Sensible of Courtesy": Private and Public Virtue in *Henry IV, Part One*', *Shakespeare Quarterly*, 17 (Autumn 1966), 371–82; Eric La Guardia, 'Ceremony and History: The Problem of Symbol from *Richard II* to *Henry V*', *Pacific Coast Studies in Shakespeare*, ed. W. F. McNeir and T. Greenfield (Eugene: University of Oregon Books, 1966), 68–88; Honor Matthews, 'The Character of the Usurper', in *Character and Symbol in Shakespeare's Plays* (Cambridge: Cambridge University Press, 1962), 44–67; Richard L. McGuire, 'The Play-within-the-Play in *1 Henry IV*', *Shakespeare Quarterly*, 18 (Winter 1967), 47–52; A. P. Rossiter, 'Ambivalence: The Dialectic of the Histories', in his *Angels with Horns and Other Shakespeare Lectures*, ed. Graham Storey (London: Longmans Green, 1961), 40–64; Benjamin T. Spencer, 'The Statis of *Henry IV, Part II*', *Tennessee Studies in Literature*, 6 (1961), 61–9; Walker Saxon, 'Mime and Heraldry in *Henry IV, Part I*', *English*, 11 (Autumn 1956), 91–6; Gordon W. Zeeveld, ' "Food for Powder"—"Food for Worms" ', *Shakespeare Quarterly*, 3 (July 1952), 249–53. I draw on my editorial work in *Shakespearean Criticism*, Vol. I, for this list; brief annotations on each of these articles may be found there, pp. 444–50. Lest my characterizations of these critical writings seem harsh, let me state clearly that such repetition is a characteristic of the 'normal science' that Kuhn described as taking place

to knowledge', but one's impression in reading them now is, on the whole, of their lack of self-consciousness, as if the readings they present were spontaneous, unspoiled by knowledge of the previous criticism—a state of innocence that was quite probably genuine in those heady days of rapid expansion of the educational apparatus, journals, and the professorate.

Similarly, historical critics, in somewhat smaller numbers, sought out previously undiscovered aspects of Elizabethan culture to buttress the prevailing 'picture' of an orderly, authority-loving, hierarchical society—with diminishing returns.[5] Of course, there were often genuine elements of novelty in these studies, which used different materials than Tillyard's, such as emblem books, Pauline theology, and the like, to support his basic picture of the era. But the unwitting repetition began to suggest just how quickly the widespread adoption of both New Critical and Tillyardian reading techniques would exhaust the field of the accepted literary canon. The methods certainly encouraged a plurality of 'interpretations', but a plurality was not an infinity, and, for the case of New Criticism, the number of ways to describe the tensions, ambiguities, and ironies of any work was, at a practical level in any case, decidedly limited. The professionalized

in the absence of crisis or shift, and that nuances which made each article seem more or less original at its time of publication tend to disappear after a paradigm shift of the sort that has recently taken place in Shakespeare studies.

[5] Examples of readings of the *Henry IV* plays in the post-war period that, from the distance of today, seem essentially footnotes to Tillyard's account (not including those mentioned in the text) are, again in alphabetical order: V. J. Emmett, Jr., '*1 Henry IV*: Structure, Platonic Psycholology, and Politics', *Midwest Quarterly*, 19 (Summer 1978), 355–69; Sherman H. Hawking, 'Virtue and Kingship in Shakespeare's *Henry IV*', *English Literary Renaissance*, 5 (Autumn 1975), 313–43; Robert G. Hunter, 'Shakespeare's Comic Sense as it Strikes us Today: Falstaff and the Protestant Ethic', in *Shakespeare: Pattern Excelling Nature*, ed. David Bevington and J. L. Halio (Newark: University of Delaware Press, 1978), 125–32; William B. Hunter, Jr., 'Falstaff', *South Atlantic Quarterly*, 50 (January 1951), 86–95; Lawrence L. Levin, 'Hotspur, Falstaff, and the Emblem of Wrath in *1 Henry IV*', *Shakespeare Studies*, 10 (1977), 43–65; Harry Morris, 'Prince Hal: Apostle to the Gentiles', *Clio*, 7 (Winter 1978), 227–45; D. J. Palmer, 'Casting off the Old Man: History and St. Paul in *Henry IV*', *Critical Quarterly*, 12 (Autumn 1970), 265–83; Robert B. Pierce, *Shakespeare's History Plays: The Family and the State* (Columbus: Ohio State University Press, 1973), 171–217; M. M. Reese, *The Cease of Majesty: A Study of Shakespeare's History Plays* (London: Edward Arnold, 1961); Irving Ribner, *English History Plays in the Age of Shakespeare*, rev. edn. (London: Methuen, 1965), 151–93; Paul N. Siegel, 'Shakespeare and the Neo-Chivalric Cult of Honor', in his *Shakespeare in His Time and Ours* (Notre Dame, Ind.: University of Notre Dame Press, 1964), 122–62. I draw again on my work in *Shakespearean Criticism*, Vol. I, where annotations on these articles may be consulted, pp. 444–50.

New Critical paradigm, restricting itself to formal discussions of the autonomous operations of texts creating plurisignification, was rapidly approaching depletion in the Sixties, while the historical critics were exhausting their own limited veins of material as well.

Beneath the apparent stasis, however, it is possible to discern a kind of movement, particularly in the New Critical paradigm. One of the truly 'formalist' lines of approach to the *Henry IV* plays in this period — the small body of essays discussing the centuries-old question of the 'unity' or lack of it of the two plays — can serve to reveal a movement beneath the surface calm in this period. Adorno's dictum that the formal elements of any art can upon analysis be revealed as carrying traces of the social moment which produced it seems to be at work here. One is struck by the unanimity of the turn in favour of the position that the two Henry IV plays must be seen as distinct and autonomous. Just a few years earlier, the concurrence of J. Dover Wilson and Tillyard for the opposite view had seemed definitive, but the tide turned very quickly. We have seen how central to New Critical practice the assumption of the unity of the work was in Brooks and Heilman's hands. It was in effect the means of bringing meaning and coherence to the shattered fragments of modernity, a place-holder for the Absolute. But the unity they posited was never an 'easy' one; it bristled with contradictions, tensions, and ironies that had to be struggled with and contained — the more the better in some ways, even if this stretched the plausibility of the final, containing act of unification to — often past — the breaking-point.

In post-war discussion of the question of unity of *1* and *2 Henry IV*, we can trace a similar, almost palpable straining and then breaking of the posited unity of the two plays. A change was developing in the horizons of aesthetic perception, and no one was quite aware of its significance.

The two basic positions of the debate — that the two plays are continuous, forming a single unit of analysis, or, alternatively, that they should be seen as separate and autonomous works — had been defined as early as the eighteenth century. The clergyman and literary amateur John Upton wrote in 1748 with complete assurance that Parts 1 and 2 are as separate from each other as Sophocles' Oedipus plays.[6] But he was answered seventeen years later in the authoritative tones of Samuel Johnson: 'Mr. Upton thinks these two plays improperly called

---

[6] Excerpted in Harris, *Shakespearean Criticism* (Detroit, Mich.: Gale, 1984), i. 289. Upton's work was entitled *Critical Observations on Shakespeare*.

The First and Second Parts of Henry the Fourth. . . . These two plays will appear to every reader, who shall peruse them without ambition of critical discoveries, to be so connected that the second is merely a sequel to the first; to be two only because they are too long to be one'.[7]

The Romantic paradigm, with its emphasis on organic unity, tended on the whole to support Johnson. Schlegel went so far as to speak of the ten Shakespearian histories constituting a single work, 'an historical heroic poem in the dramatic form',[8] and this agglomerating tendency, along with the concept of artistic organic form which gave it birth, tended to migrate into the Modernist era, whether in the habit of unifying *Richard II* and *Henry V* with the *Henry IV* plays as the 'second tetralogy' or the *Henriad*, or in amalgamating only the latter two in the mode of Dover Wilson and Tillyard.

Modernizing American academic critics of the early part of the century, with their positivist suspicion of all things Romantic, including organic unity, were much more likely to argue for the autonomy of the two plays.[9] But when in the Forties two such redoubtable authorities as J. Dover Wilson and Tillyard[10] each argued in influential places that the two *Henry IV* plays should be considered a single, ten-act play, it seemed that unification had swept the field. It is therefore more remarkable that within another decade the tide shifted against unity. In 1948 M. A. Shaaber cautiously but firmly dissented from the two Britons on textual and historical grounds.[11] And Clifford Leech, in part of a New-Critical-influenced questioning of the suppositions of Tillyard's historical approach, argued more boldly in 1953 that Part 2 belongs in its themes and atmosphere more with such plays as *Troilus and Cressida* and *Measure for Measure* than with Part 1.[12] Leech justified

---

[7] *The Yale Edition of the Works of Samuel Johnson*, ed. Arthur Sherbo (New Haven: Yale University Press, 1968), vii. 49; excerpted in Harris, *Shakespearean Criticism*, i. 291.

[8] Schlegel, *Lectures on Dramatic Art and Literature*, ed. A. J. W. Morrison, trans. John Black, 2nd edn. (London: Bell, 1892), 414; excerpted in Harris, *Shakespearean Criticism*, i. 309.

[9] See Harry T. Baker, 'The Problem of "II Henry IV" ', *English Journal*, 15 (April 1926), 289–98, excerpted in Harris, *Shakespearean Criticism*, i. 347–8; and Robert Adger Law, 'Structural Unity in the Two Parts of "Henry the Fourth" ', *Studies in Philology*, 24 (April 1927), 223–42, excerpted in Harris, *Shakespearean Criticism*, i. 348–51.

[10] Introduction, *The First Part of the History of Henry IV* by William Shakespeare, ed. John Dover Wilson (Cambridge: Cambridge University Press, 1946), pp. ix–x; E. M. W. Tillyard, *Shakespeare's History Plays* (1944; repr. New York: Macmillan, 1946), 264.

[11] M. A. Shaaber, 'The Unity of "Henry IV" ', in *Joseph Quincy Adams: Memorial Studies* (Washington, DC: Folger Shakespeare Library, 1948), 217–27, excerpted in Harris, *Shakespearean Criticism*, i. 387–9.

[12] Clifford Leech, 'The Unity of "2 Henry IV" ', *Shakespeare Survey*, 6 (1953), 16–24.

his disunifying position in terms of a positive argument *for* the unity of Part 2 in its own terms, picking up the well-wrought urn of unity with one hand just after apparently knocking it to the ground with the other. The culmination of this tendency was L. C. Knights's work in two essays of *Some Shakespearean Themes* which I alluded to in the previous chapter (Chapter 4, n. 40), readings which separated the two plays in the name of the autonomous organic unity of each and made the kind of large revisionary claims for the importance of Part 2 that gave *Scrutiny* such interest (pp. 26–64). Thereafter, with the exception of critics like Alvin Kernan, who discussed the tetralogy in terms of a heuristic and thematic (rather than aesthetic) unity,[13] it becomes difficult to find critics in the Johnson–Wilson–Tillyard mould on the question of unity.

The surprising unanimity in the turn toward viewing the two *Henry IV* plays as autonomous rather than 'unified' is suggestive of a larger paradigmatic trend away from the valorization of organic unity that was Modernism's heritage from Romanticism. But the tendency in *Henry IV* criticism was, as I have indicated, ambivalent: it dismissed one version of 'unity' in the name of a second, if less inclusive unity, and thereafter the question largely faded from critical discussion.

We can take up the narrative of evolution from within the Modernist critical paradigms, however, if we turn to a different play, one whose anomalies and problematics have made it virtually a 'blank screen' on which could be projected the disparate critical methodologies of the history of Shakespeare criticism: *Timon of Athens*.

Unity and Timon of Athens

The reasons for *Timon*'s unique position in the history of Shakespeare studies have been well documented. The anomalies begin with its inclusion in the First Folio itself. The play was placed between *Romeo and Juliet* and *Julius Caesar* in the gap that had been created by the withdrawal of *Troilus and Cressida* from the Folio. But *Timon* occupied fewer pages than had *Troilus*, and later scholars have been able to deduce the last-minute substitution of plays from several bibliographical oddities created by the change.

In addition to this suggestion of some hesitation by the Folio compilers to include the play in their canonical collection, editors since

[13] Alvin Kernan, 'The Henriad: Shakespeare's Major History Plays', *The Yale Review*, 59 (October 1969), 3–32.

Samuel Johnson have agreed that the Folio text—the only surviving textual source for the play—is unusually problematic at several levels, from inconsistencies in the naming of the characters to suspected missing scenes and garbled passages.[14] Johnson posited the tampering of the player-editors to explain certain of the play's obscurities.[15] The Victorian modernizers seized on the play as a prime example of the need for positivistic textual criticism. Indeed *Timon* was the first play of Shakespeare's to be 'disintegrated': the English scholar Charles Knight, in his edition of the play published in 1843, argued that the anomalies of *Timon* could only be understood if two authors rather than one were posited and that Shakespeare had partially rewritten an earlier play, leaving his project incomplete. Thus, the argument went, the Folio's text was an amalgamation of scenes and passages by two different hands, one Shakespeare's, the other an unknown earlier poet.

But Knight's was only the first of several mutually contradictory disintegrationist theories for *Timon*, based on the same suggestive but slender evidence. As I mentioned in Chapter 1, there have been at least five proposed 'second authors', and all the logically possible variations on the question of whether Shakespeare was first or second author, collaborator, or sole author of a rough or advanced draft have been argued.[16]

Despite the long-standing suspicions concerning the play's textual integrity, a distinguished line of critics, from the eighteenth century through the twentieth, has found much to praise in *Timon*. The first full-scale analyses were undertaken in nineteenth-century Germany, in the monumental surveys of Ulrici and Gervinus. But their pioneering attempts to show *Timon* as embodying organic unity were largely ignored in the English-speaking world,[17] where biographical efforts to

[14] For this account and much of what follows, I draw on my work on the section on *Timon* in Harris, *Shakespearean Criticism*, i. 451–536. Additional valuable sources are Francelia Butler, *The Strange Critical Fortunes of Shakespeare's 'Timon of Athens'* (Ames: Iowa State University Press, 1966) and John Ruszkiewicz, *Timon of Athens: An Annotated Bibliography* (New York: Garland, 1986). The latter source includes a succinct but bibliographically detailed account of the authorship controversy, including some recent arguments for dual authorship (pp. xx–xxii).

[15] Johnson, viii. 707; excerpted in Harris, *Shakespearean Criticism*, i. 454–55.

[16] See n. 42, Chapter 1. See also Ruszkiewicz, *Timon of Athens Bibliography*, pp. xx–xxi. Incidentally, one of Fleay's first presentations to the New Shakspere Society was 'On the Authorship of "Timon of Athens" ', *Transactions of the New Shakspere Society* (1874), 130–51; Fleay thought Shakespeare was the second author and that Cyril Tourneur was responsible for the text he was revising.

[17] However, in a revealing aside, G. Wilson Knight confessed that his boyhood 'hobby' was reading Gervinus—see *Neglected Powers: Essays on Nineteenth and Twentieth*

read in the play symptoms of some Shakespearian dark night of the soul predominated at the turn of the century.

Fittingly, a new chapter in *Timon* criticism was inaugurated by the Modernist 'spatial' hermeneutics of G. Wilson Knight. Near the end of *The Wheel of Fire*, Knight included a chapter on *Timon* which ranked it with the greatest of Shakespeare's works. Knight defined a 'spatial' (i.e. organic) unity of imagery and theme that for him was so transcendentally evident that the authorship and biographical questions which had dominated the previous generation's discussions did not arise. Through the power of his Modernist version of organic unity, the play came alive for Knight as a titanic masterpiece.

Subsequent critics working within the Modernist paradigms pioneered by Knight have generally hesitated to accord to *Timon* the masterpiece status insisted upon—over and over—by Knight. Una Ellis-Fermor spoke for many when she denied to *Timon* the status of achieved art-work without which organic unity was a meaningless category, while she also retained a post-disintegration faith in Shakespeare's single authorship of the play. Her solution was to argue that the play was not only unfinished but that the resulting text constituted an artistic failure in that its design was 'not wholly comprehended and subdued by imagination'.[18] But the case of *Timon* was in reality a scandal within the realm of academic discourse; it was a text that seemed to defy any paradigmatic consensus-formation and made a mockery of surviving positivist notions of literary studies as a discipline with a progressive accumulation of knowledge.

In the post-war era the favoured way out of this impasse has been to attempt to specify the genre of *Timon*. Through such a strategy, the 'formalist' elements of the New Critical paradigm could be mobilized and organic unity 'saved' by defining it in terms of some new—for *Timon* at any rate—generic form that was held capable of containing the tensions, ambiguities, and dissonances of the text. At the same time, the search for *Timon*'s genre could also make use of the historicist archive of specialized knowledge of Renaissance, classical, and medieval literary forms and/or an array of Renaissance ideologies and commonplace thoughts *à la* Tillyard. No wonder then, that the *Timon* criticism of the Modernist epoch is dominated (in a quantitative sense)

Century Literature (New York: Barnes and Nobles, 1971), 9. Knight's celebrated if controversial encomium to *Timon*, to be discussed below, shows decided indebtedness to Gervinus's account.

[18] Una Ellis-Fermor, ' "Timon of Athens": An Unfinished Play', *The Review of English Studies*, 18 (July 1942), 270–83.

by attempts to define the genre of the play. Such an approach safely contained the play's resistances to the dominant critical paradigms while allowing critics to synthesize both historical and New Criticism, having it both ways. In fact even Knight's seminal Modernist reading of the play made a gesture in this direction with a claim that *Timon* was 'a parable, or allegory', but the context makes it clear that Knight used these generic terms to underlie his view that the play was not to be read as a realist drama.[19]

At a later date, however, O. J. Campbell construed Knight's claim as one of genre classification and countered with his own argument that *Timon* was instead a 'tragic-satire'.[20] In 1946 A. S. Collins argued that *Timon* was Shakespeare's version of a morality play, a diagnosis seconded later by David Bergeron.[21] Willard Farnham grouped *Timon* with *Macbeth*, *Antony and Cleopatra*, and *Coriolanus* as a 'late tragedy',[22] while Clifford Leech varied that theme by seeing the play as transitional between the tragedies and the romances.[23] Robert C. Elliott classed the play in 1960 among the meta-satires ('the satirist satirized') studied in his monograph.[24] By 1964 the French critic Bernard Paulin focused on the generic controversy as a major question in the literature on *Timon*, arguing that only the traditional classification of 'tragedy' did the play justice.[25] Thereafter, as the academy expanded, contributions to the generic debate proliferated. A representative list would include: Anne Lancanshire ('secularized, anti-traditional morality play' like Marlowe's *Faustus*), E. A. J. Honigmann (genre indeterminate), Northrop Frye ('*idiotes* comedy'), M. C. Bradbrook ('anti-shew' or tragical pageant), Maurice Charney ('dramatic fable' similar to morality plays), Francis Fergusson (elements of 'classical comedy'), John Holloway (a stripped-down tragedy), G. K. Hunter (late tragedy),

---

[19] G. Wilson Knight, *The Wheel of Fire: Interpretation of Shakespeare's Tragedy* (1930; repr. Cleveland, Ohio: Meridian, 1964), 220.

[20] O. J. Campbell, *Shakespeare's Satires* (New York: Oxford University Press, 1943), 168–97.

[21] A. S. Collins, ' "Timon of Athens": A Reconsideration', *The Review of English Studies*, 22 (Oct. 1946), 96–108 and David Bergeron, '*Timon of Athens* and Morality Drama', *CLA Journal*, 10 (March 1967), 181–8.

[22] Willard Farnham, *Shakespeare's Tragic Frontier: The World of His Final Tragedies* (Berkeley: University of California Press, 1950), 39–78.

[23] Clifford Leech, '*Timon* and After', in his *Shakespeare's Tragedies and Other Studies in Seventeenth-Century Drama* (London: Chatto and Windus, 1950), 113–36.

[24] Robert C. Elliott, *The Power of Satire: Magic, Ritual, Art* (Princeton, NJ: Princeton University Press, 1960), 141–67.

[25] Bernard Paulin, 'La Mort de "Timon d'Athens" ', *Études anglaises*, 17 (Jan.–Mar. 1964), 1–8; excerpted and trans. in Harris, *Shakespearean Criticism*, i. 509–11.

Alvin Kernan (Renaissance satire), F. W. Brownlow ('metaphysical tragedy'), D. A. Traversi ('mature tragedy'), William W. E. Slights ('*genera mixta*' of satire, masque, anti-masque, and tragedy), and Rolf Soellner ('pessimistic tragedy').[26]

While a focus on genre provided an almost irresistible application of the available paradigms to a recalcitrant text for the reasons discussed above, the resulting plethora of mutually exclusive answers to the same question could only in the long run cast doubt on the efficacy of the paradigms in use. Either the profession would have to abandon any pretensions to 'reproducibility' of results and opt for some form of institutionalized but radical pluralism (the favourite solution in rhetoric, but essentially a mask over the continuing workings of the very non-pluralistic processes of disciplinary power in hiring, tenure, promotion, and publication)—or it would need to find a way to out-flank these difficulties and re-establish the norms of professionalism through new critical paradigms. Sometime around 1970, doubtless, as I suggested earlier, under the influence of the cultural and political ferment of the Vietnam era, but also because of the depletion and impasses of existing critical paradigms, we can observe a number of attempts in both these directions as the literary profession diagnosed itself as in 'crisis'.

In *Timon* criticism the beginnings of a paradigm shift can be observed in four innovative interventions: by Cyrus Hoy (1972), Richard Fly (1973), Susan Handelman (1979), and Lesley Brill

---

[26] See Anne Lancanshire, ' "Timon of Athens": Shakespeare's "Dr. Faustus" ', *Shakespeare Quarterly*, 21 (Winter 1970), 35–44; E. A. J. Hongimann, ' "Timon of Athens" ', *Shakespeare Quarterly*, 12 (Winter 1961), 3–20; Northrop Frye, *A Natural Perspective: The Development of Shakespearean Comedy and Romance* (New York: Columbia University Press, 1965), 72–117; M. C. Bradbrook, *The Tragic Pageant of 'Timon of Athens*', (Cambridge: Cambridge University Press, 1966); Maurice Charney, Introduction to *Timon of Athens*, *The Complete Signet Classic Shakespeare* (New York: Harcourt, 1972); Francis Fergusson, *Shakespeare: The Pattern in the Carpet* (New York: Delacorte Press, 1970), 258–63; John Holloway, *The Story of the Night: Studies in Shakespeare's Major Tragedies* (Lincoln: University of Nebraska Press, 1961), 121–34; G. K. Hunter, 'The Last Tragic Heroes', *Later Shakespeare*, ed. J. R. Brown and B. Harris (London: Edward Arnold, 1966), 11–28; Alvin Kernan, *The Cankered Muse: Satire of the English Renaissance* (New Haven, Conn.: Yale University Press, 1959), 192–246; F. W. Brownlow, *Two Shakespearean Sequences: 'Henry VI' to 'Richard II' and 'Pericles' to 'Timon of Athens'* (Pittsburgh, Pa.: University of Pittsburgh Press, 1977), 216–34; D. A. Traversi, *An Approach to Shakespeare*, 3rd edn. (Garden City, NY: Doubleday, 1968), 474–90; William W. E. Slights, ' "Genera mixta" and "Timon of Athens" ', *Studies in Philology*, 74 (January 1977), 36–62; and Rolf Soellner, *Timon of Athens: Shakespeare's Pessimistic Tragedy* (Columbus: Ohio State University Press, 1979).

(1979). All of these writers, in their own ways, foreshadow the emerging paradigms of the Postmodernist era.

Taking the New Critical paradigm to—or past—its breaking-point, Richard Fly in 1973 announced the end of organic unity as an aesthetic criterion for evaluating *Timon*: 'In its stark refusal to fuse its disparate parts into an organic whole', he wrote, '*Timon of Athens* achieves, at best, a magnificence of a disturbingly uneven and disjunctive nature.'[27] Prefiguring themes of an American deconstruction in its infancy (though of course with many traces of no longer fashionable rhetoric as well), Fly argued that *Timon* simultaneously confronted us with two undecidable perspectives, with the result that the play ends situated in an abyss, which it thematizes. Here Fly has made explicit that condition of 'moral relativism', of order-defying disparities in Shakespeare, which Brooks and Heilman attempted with so much skill and complexity to exorcize and obfuscate. And in so doing, the abandonment of a concept of organic unity was, I would argue, pivotal, indeed, paradigm-breaking.

Six years later Lesley Brill also saw that the scandal of *Timon*'s critical history had implications for the profession's critical methodology: 'The diversity of responses to *Timon* . . . must derive from its polysemous construction rather than from the whimsey of contentious teachers of English', he wrote.[28] It now becomes the task of professional criticism not to attempt to define a plausible single reading of the play (to play the game of pluralism) but rather to analyse the text to account for the phenomenon of the previous 'pluralism'. '. . . all reasonable interpretations [of *Timon*] are set forth in a plenty that is finally as undiscriminating as paucity', he writes. And later:

> By presenting all interpretations of its action, *Timon* prevents us from wholly advocating any one. It excludes only exclusivity and fixes the ambiguity of life unambiguously. It claims for the lies of art and for feigning artists a special honesty. It traps its readers, like its characters, into thinking that they have discovered the truth about a false world. It is an ocean; it is very like a camel, a weasel, a whale; it fairly strives to appear foul, rots to grow ripe. It is nothing, and it is all things.[29]

In effect Brill is making the case for literary theory: instead of compounding the number of disparate readings of the various canonical

---

[27] Richard Fly, 'The Ending of "Timon of Athens": A Reconsideration', *Criticism*, 15 (Summer 1973), 242.

[28] Lesley Brill, 'Truth and "Timon of Athens"', *Modern Language Quarterly*, 40 (March 1979), 20.

[29] Ibid., p. 36.

texts, he argues, the profession should attempt to define the conditions which have led to the scandal of institutionalized non-consensus.

Writing within what was a relatively marginalized school of Freudian criticism in 1974, Susan Handelman broke new ground in *Timon* criticism in a reading that was in many ways typical of more new things to come, specifically the various hermeneutics of suspicion deployed in the service of feminism. Handelman broke with the empiricist strain of prevailing Anglo-American critical practice by focusing her analysis of *Timon* around an *absence* within the text which she then diagnosed through a feminist-inflected Freudianism. Noting that 'In *Timon* there is neither good art nor good women', and seeing this absence as the key to the mood of rage of the play, Handelman argued that the drastic reversals—in particular that of Timon from philanthropist to mis-anthrope—are all built around his inability to accept sexual difference. We will see that later feminist Shakespearians did not follow in this specific direction, but in Handelman's reading of *Timon* can be seen the feminist values and the willingness to experiment with previously marginalized critical discourses that will later emerge more prominently.

And in a 1973 offering by Cyrus Hoy (who was later to thematize and theorize the profession's methodological crisis in *The Critical Circle*), we see an analysis of *Timon* in what are recognizably the terms of the new historicism of a decade later. Hoy's method can properly be called historicist because he attempts to ground his reading of the play within the matrix of Renaissance discourses and ideologies; unlike Tillyard, however, and like the new historicists to come, the history he sees is one of social tensions and defiance of authority, rather than Tillyard's stable Elizabethan World Picture and Tudor Myth:

The imaginative vision that produced Shakespeare's Jacobean tragedies was conditioned by that crisis of the Renaissance—that counter-Renaissance, as it is sometimes termed, brought on by those innovations in science and religion, political and moral philosophy that are associated with the names of Copernicus and Luther, Machiavelli and Montaigne. The effects of these have often been described. They issue in the recognition that truth is not absolute and completely objective but relative, that morality has a double standard (one for rulers, the other for the ruled), that the intellect is of no avail in scrutinizing the wisdom of God, that the earth is not the centre of the universe.[30]

---

[30] Cyrus Hoy, 'Jacobean Tragedy and the Mannerist Style', *Shakespeare Survey*, 26 (1973), 49.

Hoy goes on to break with the positivism of the old historicism, too, by seeing the play as open-ended rather than univocal in a sense discoverable through historical research, although this notion is more implied than developed. But in many ways his analysis is suggestive of the directions that would be taken in later years by, for instance, Jonathan Dollimore in his influential *Radical Tragedy*.

Let me make it clear that neither Hoy nor any of the other critics I have been discussing has individually invented a new paradigm, nor are the parallels of their work with later developments indicative of some mysterious *telos* at work in the *Zeitgeist*. Rather, each of them should be seen as exploring the limits and contradictions of the older paradigms within which each works in ways suggestive of components of things to come. We are witnessing in the realm of literary criticism the process that Kuhn described long ago as the crisis that proceeds the paradigm shift, a crisis that often sets the terms for the emerging paradigm(s). All four critics I have discussed are displaying the influence of an aesthetic sensibility no longer quite the same as the Modernism that influenced Knight, Tillyard, and the classical New Critics. But they have not yet announced the break with the old that seems to begin in Shakespeare studies just after 1980.

Postmodernist Aesthetics

Are we justified in linking the breakdown of the old Modernist-influenced critical paradigms and the rise of new ones with an emerging Postmodernist aesthetic paradigm? Are not these developments wholly explainable in terms of the autonomous processes taking place within the institution of academic literary criticism independent of any events in a larger, more diffuse aesthetic sphere?

The short answer to these questions is two-fold: institutional and disciplinary processes are certainly at work in affecting the changes noted, as are social and political currents, mediated through lived experience and ideology. But after taking these into account, it should be clear that now, as in the past, one of the most difficult to define and yet most potent influences on our perception of cultural monuments like Shakespeare is the influence of contemporary artistic and literary practice. These changes in aesthetic forms and perceptions, it seems clear to me, are as always interactive with the global social and economic processes around them. There is no better starting-point in attempting to define the quality of that interaction than the much discussed essay of Fredric Jameson, 'Postmodernism, or The Cultural Logic of Late Capitalism'.[31]

Jameson's ground-breaking (but uneven) essay attempts to define the aesthetic qualities of the Postmodern and link them in turn to changes at a global, systemic level. He then traces the process of mediation through which such global changes become manifest in daily life. In many ways Jameson's is the most successful effort to do for the post-World War II period what Walter Benjamin had done for Baudelaire's Paris: map the new sense of space and time created by the impact of television, suburbanization, expressways, and shopping malls, just as Benjamin brought attention to the impact of the new shopping arcades and urban crowds of *belle époque* Paris.

The connection which Jameson posits between the new global forms of multinational capitalism and daily life and art strike me as perfectly consistent with Adorno's and Benjamin's theoretical model and should not be read as some reversion to a discredited base-superstructure Marxism—a charge Jameson left himself open to by his use of the dated language of clear-cut 'stages' of capitalism.[32]

The weakness in Jameson's argument, from my point of view, lies rather in some of the details of his scheme of changing perceptions of time and space. Jameson sees the Postmodern as involving a de-emphasis of the temporal and historical and a concomitant spatialization. As I argued in Chapter 2, however, such spatialization was already well underway in the High Modernism of the Twenties, and the Modernist spatialization of the nineteenth-century 'historical values' was one of its defining motifs. The difference between the Modernist and Postmodernist spatializations, it seems to me, is that Modernist space is 'centred' and unified as in a G. Wilson Knight reading of Shakespeare, whereas Postmodern space is decentred and disjunc-tured, characterized, as Jameson indicated, 'by the loss of our ability to position ourselves within this space and cognitively map it'.[33]

The question of Postmodernism has been, to say the least, con-troversial, and while I find myself advocating certain modifications in

[31] Fredric Jameson, 'Postmodernism, or The Cultural Logic of Late Capitalism', *New Left Review*, 146 (July–Aug. 1984), 53–92. For varied and wide-ranging discussion of Jameson's views on Postmodernism, see *Postmodernism/Jameson/Critique*, ed. Douglas Kellner (Washington, DC: Maisonneuve, 1989).

[32] For a still relevant critique of the notion of 'stages', see, as Anders Stephanson has pointed out in a different connection, Marcuse's *Soviet Marxism: A Critical Analysis* (New York: Columbia University Press, 1958).

[33] Quoted in Anders Stephanson, 'Regarding Postmodernism—A Conversation with Fredric Jameson', *Social Text*, 17 (Fall 1987), 33.

the terms of the contemporary debate on the subject, my main focus will be to trace an emerging Postmodernist Shakespeare criticism. Much of the debate about Postmodernism has centred on its relation to Modernism proper. Here I will assume, as I suggested in Chapter 2, a condition of fluid boundaries between what is properly Modernist, what Postmodernist.

There is clearly a large measure of continuity. At a certain level of abstraction the *basic* social place and role of art and its related disciplines in capitalist society have been remarkably stable since the completion of the Enlightenment and the rise of Romanticism. Art has remained grounded within the commodity sphere of the capitalist market and continued its double role of both criticizing and offering a socially harmless escape from that society.[34] In fact, as a number of critics have observed, the paradigm shifts constituting Modernism and now Postmodernism can be understood in part in terms of a desire to break out of the socially affirmative role that domesticated Romanticism and then Modernism had assumed in their respective late stages—and given that desire, a repression of continuities with the past would be expected. In recent Shakespearian criticism there are certainly such repressed continuities to be found, as I will demonstrate shortly.

Even given this fluidity, however, there remain fundamental changes in how we create and perceive cultural artefacts that justify the term Postmodernism. Here, in connection with recent changes in Shakespeare studies, I want to isolate two such characteristics of the Postmodern, one developed by Jameson, the second by Andreas Huyssen and Craig Owens in separate studies, that I believe confirm my

---

[34] Almost every phrase in these assertions has been disputed in the complex contemporary debate on Postmodernism. Peter Bürger in particular has suggested that Adorno's views on the autonomy of art should be understood as themselves historical, rooted in the Modernist era and increasingly in need of modification in the postmodern present—see *Theory of the Avant-Garde*, trans. Michael Shaw (Minneapolis: University of Minneapolis Press, 1984)—a position that seems just enough for Adorno's best-known work, but in need of qualification given the prefigurations of what could be called Postmodernism in Adorno's posthumous *Aesthetic Theory*. The essays collected in Jonathan Arac (ed.), *Postmodernism and Politics* (Minneapolis: University of Minnesota Press, 1986) present a valuable array of discussions of the intersections of the Postmodern, contemporary versions of Marxism (including the Frankfurt School), and French post-structuralism. And yet if the proper level of abstraction is grasped, the commodification and relative autonomy of art can be seen as structural constants undergoing continual development and modification, particularly in the periods of paradigm shift like the present. The lessening distinction between popular culture and high art, to take one key issue, reveals a critical dimension in popular culture which Adorno was blind to as well as showing that Modernism's artistic autonomy had complicit and ideological dimensions.

assertion that we are now witnessing the emergence of a Postmodernist Shakespeare through the development of critical paradigms which incorporate aspects of contemporary Postmodernist aesthetics — just as previous generations had created the Modernist Shakespeare through a similar, partly conscious, partly unconscious assimilation of the aesthetic present.

The relevant characteristics are the abandonment of organic unity as an aesthetic value and practice and the overthrow of a series of formerly privileged hierarchical oppositions through a Postmodernist anti-hierarchical impulse (as, for example in the collapse of the High Modernist distinction between 'art' and 'popular culture' or in the championing of the various Others of Western rationality like women and Third World peoples). I want first to establish the centrality of these notions to contemporary theorists of the Postmodern before moving to consider how they enter into the constitution of the main emerging critical tendencies in today's Shakespeare studies.

Jameson's analysis of the Postmodern conceptualizes the loss of unity I am positing in terms of a 'fragmentation' and decentring of subjectivity, drawing on well-known themes from Derrida and Foucault, but linking them explicitly with such artistic practices as:

the poetry of John Ashbery, for instance, but also the much simpler talk poetry that came out of the reaction against complex, ironic, academic modernist poetry in the '60s; the reaction against modern architecture and in particular against the monumental buildings of the International Style, the pop buildings and decorated sheds celebrated by Robert Venturi in his manifesto, *Learning from Las Vegas*; Andy Warhol and Pop art, but also the more recent Photorealism; in music, the moment of John Cage but also the later synthesis of classical and 'popular' styles found in composers like Philip Glass and Terry Riley, and also punk and new-wave rock, with such groups as the Clash, the Talking Heads and the Gang of Four; in film, everything that comes out of Goddard — contemporary vanguard film and video — but also a whole new style of commercial or fiction films, which has its equivalent in contemporary novels as well, where the works of William Burroughs, Thomas Pynchon and Ishmael Reed on the one hand, and the French new novel on the other, are also to be numbered among the varieties of what can be called postmodernism.[35]

In trying to find the commonalities of this eclectic collection, Jameson

[35] Jameson, 'Postmodernism and Consumer Society', in *The Anti-Aesthetic: Essays on Postmodern Culture*, ed. Hal Foster (Port Townsend, Wash.: Bay Press, 1983), 111. This is an early version of Jameson's 'Postmodernism, or the Cultural Logic of Late Capitalism', which I have already cited.

focused on a common reaction against various high Modernisms and defined a common thematization of fragmentation and the decentring of the subject as having replaced an older Modernist thematics of alienation.[36] At the level of form, these same changes are also manifest, as Jameson goes on to argue at a later point: 'The former work of art, in other words, has now turned out to be a text, whose reading proceeds by differentiation rather than by unification'.[37] We will see exactly such a movement taking place in the emerging paradigms of Postmodernist Shakespeare studies and thereby constituting perhaps the single most decisive break with the Modernist Shakespeare of the recent past.[38]

The second important component of the emerging Postmodernist aesthetic paradigm is its anti-hierarchical impulse and practice, an impulse theorized briefly in Jameson but more fully in the essays of Andreas Huyssen, particularly in the stimulating 'Mass Culture as Woman: Modernism's Other'.[39] The particular critical methodology practised by Huyssen there, to be sure, has been influenced by Derrida's models of deconstruction. The method involves identifying a binary opposition in which one of the two terms is privileged, held to be the master of the second (denigrated and subordinated) element of the pair. But as Derrida showed, the priority of the first is bogus: it can be shown to have been always already implicated with and in the second, which, rather than being derivative, secondary, or subordinate, turns out to be always already part of the first—as in Derrida's celebrated deconstruction of the ancient opposition between writing and speech. Huyssen, working with concepts from Adorno and Benjamin, attempts to rethink their central notion of art in its relation to popular culture through a deconstruction of the binary opposition formed by the two. He then studies that deconstruction in terms of a common nineteenth-century coding in which the popular was seen as

---

[36] Jameson, 'Postmodernism, or Cultural Logic', 63.

[37] Ibid., p. 75.

[38] Jameson is not alone in linking the end of the aesthetics of organic unity with Postmodernism. Bürger also made the same point in his provocative discussion of the avant-garde, and like Jameson sees Benjamin's theory of allegory as providing a starting point for an alternative aesthetics (Bürger, *Theory of Avant-Garde*, 68–82). Similarly, François Lyotard, *The Postmodern Condition: A Report on Knowledge*, trans. Geoff Bennington and Brian Massumi (Minneapolis: University of Minnesota Press, 1984), speaks of the need to resist the 'nostalgia of the whole and the one' (p. 81). I will return briefly to Lyotard in n. 40 below.

[39] Huyssen, *After the Great Divide: Modernism, Mass Culture, Postmodernism* (Bloomington: Indiana University Press, 1986), 44–62.

female, the artistic as male. He sees a clear homology between these two related pairs in terms of an untenable and oppressive subordination of one over the other in '[t]he traditional dichotomy, in which mass culture appears as monolithic, engulfing, totalitarian, and on the side of regression and the feminine ("Totalitarianism appeals to the desire to return to the womb," said T. S. Eliot) and modernism appears as progressive, dynamic, and indicative of male superiority in culture . . .' (p. 58). In contrast, according to Huyssen, the Postmodern undoes both of these oppositions:

One of the few widely agreed upon features of postmodernism is its attempt to negotiate forms of high art with certain forms and genres of mass culture and the culture of everyday life. I suspect that it is probably no coincidence that such merger attempts occurred more or less simultaneously with the emergence of feminism and women as major forces in the arts, and with the concomitant reevaluation of formerly devalued forms and genres of cultural expression (e.g. the decorative arts, autobiographic texts, letters, etc.). (p. 59)

Drawing on Jameson and Lyotard's widely discussed *The Postmodern Condition*,[40] Craig Owens made a similar argument linking feminism and the Postmodern in a discussion of several works of contemporary visual arts. Interestingly, Owens stresses the centrality of the end of the era of Western colonialism to the formation of the Postmodern, seeing women, the peoples of the so-called Third World, and nature itself as Others constituted by Western civilization in its four-hundred-year period of world domination—Others which are now 'in revolt' against Western domination and hierarchy in a movement which becomes mediated into the new Postmodernist aesthetics.[41] These aspects of Postmodernism are both readily apparent in the emerging practice of

---

[40] The specific thesis of Lyotard's often stimulating *The Postmodern Condition*—to the effect that the postmodern is the condition of having seen through all the *grands récits* of received tradition—was shrewdly analysed by Fredric Jameson as part of the general reaction in the French intelligentsia against 'various Marxist and Communist traditions in France, whose prime target on the philosophical level is the Hegel/Lukács concept of "totality" (often overhastily assimilated to Stalinism or even to the Leninist party on the political level)' (Foreword to Lyotard, p. x). Its relevance to the non-French intellectual world is therefore indirect, and its description of the Postmodern seems to me essentially at one with the revolt against the 'historical values' in favour of spatialization of early Modernism.

[41] Craig Owens, 'The Discourse of Others: Feminists and Postmodernism', in Foster, *Anti-Aesthetic*, 57–82.

new historicists and feminists in contemporary Shakespeare studies, as we shall see.

Postmodernism at Work in Shakespeare Studies

The impact of these shifts in aesthetic form on Shakespeare studies can be seen at a number of levels and in a variety of competing critical paradigms. In the context of the discussion of the various forms of the Modernist Shakespeare of the previous chapters, the impact in particular of the end of the assumption of the art-work's organic unity should be understood as decisive in bringing about a basic change in how we read Shakespeare. We have already seen several instances of the crucial place held by the concept of organic unity in Modernist-influenced critics. In this regard the Modernists were good Romantics, following Schlegel and Coleridge, who had made of Shakespeare the major example of the concept of organic unity they developed in opposition to neo-classicism.

Without such a notion G. Wilson Knight could never have developed his 'spatial' hermeneutics, with its positing of interconnected, ultimately unified imagery. Tillyard's Elizabethan World Picture, too, another Modernist spatial construct, owed much of its power to an underlying notion of organic unity which provided the connections among the various levels and correspondences of the cultural unity he projected on to the Elizabethan era. And we have seen how the positing of organic unity, virtually as an act of faith and place-holder for the Absolute, was a central component of New Critical readings of complex texts. I have described how in the Seventies, as these Modernist critical paradigms underwent a crisis of depletion and historical irrelevancy, the notion of unity as an aesthetic value could be observed as in transition, even under attack. Finally, new paradigms arose, based on different, Postmodernist notions of space and its structure, calling into question not only organic unity but all sorts of previously stable hierarchies and privileges.

I have spoken, too, of hidden continuities persisting in the paradigm shift of our time. Chief among these is certainly the continued domination of literary criticism by professional academics, and we have seen what a powerful and corrosive force professional practice was in the taming and domestication of that element of social and political critique which could be found in Modernism and its allied critical paradigms. I want to conclude here, then, with a brief survey of the new emerging Postmodern paradigms in Shakespeare studies (they are of course active in other literary fields) with particular attention to the prospects each shows at this early stage of being able to resist or blunt the processes of instrumentalization inherent in professionalism.

Deconstruction

With its tactics of decentring apparently unified texts and of deconstructing received hierarchies of all sorts, deconstruction's relation to the Postmodern aesthetics I outlined above is readily apparent. Of course, several other 'sources' must be taken into account to do justice to the theoretical revolution which deconstruction has helped to make. For example, 'theory' had already taken hold in the leading centres of American English studies—first through Frye, then phenomenology and structuralism—when deconstruction burst on to the scene in the alien guise of Derrida's hermetic texts, then in the more recognizable but still scandalous forms of the 'Yale School' deconstruction of Paul de Man, Geoffrey Hartman, J. Hillis Miller, and Harold Bloom. And the relation between the French and American deconstructive practices and contexts is a complex one which has of late found lucid commentators.[42] Here I can only touch on a small portion of the relevant issues.

While recognizing that its abandonment of organic unity and its adoption of a technical philosophical vocabulary are profoundly different from earlier New Critical practices, we can also recognize a strong continuity between American deconstruction, particularly, and New Criticism, reproducing almost exactly the ambiguous relation of Modernism to Postmodernism—and for obvious reasons. It is clear that any resemblances between New Criticism and Derrida are fortuitous ones, for the French literary establishment proved singularly impervious to this Anglo-American construct, and Derrida is no exception. But the Yale critics were operating in an American context virtually defined by New Critical suppositions, and their version of

---

[42] See particularly the collected essays, especially the Introduction by Wallace Martin, of *The Yale Critics: Deconstruction in America*, ed. Jonathan Arac, Wald Godzich, and Wallace Martin (Minneapolis: University of Minnesota Press, 1983); Art Berman, *From the New Criticism to Deconstruction: The Reception of Structuralism and Post-Structuralism* (Urbana: University of Illinois Press, 1988); and Howard Felperin, *Beyond Deconstruction: The Uses and Abuses of Literary Theory* (1985; repr. Oxford: Oxford University Press, 1987). As will become clear, my own position on deconstruction emerges largely through a dialogue with Felperin.

deconstruction necessarily took New Criticism as a father-figure to be slain and replaced, perhaps simply reproduced in new guise.[43] Certainly when Paul de Man said of his own methodology, in that dry authoritarian tone that so rankled Frank Lentricchia, 'The whole of literature would respond in similar fashion ... there is absolutely no reason why analyses of the kind here suggested for Proust would not be applicable, with proper modifications of technique, to Milton or to Dante or to Hölderlin. This will in fact be the task of literary criticism in the coming years',[44] he was envisioning a new 'Criticism, Inc.' in the tradition of the strategizing John Crowe Ransom—a set of professional tasks for a new generation to replace the now completely filled in agenda of Ransom's New Criticism. But there is no apparent rationale, no larger social context of the sort we have seen the ex-Fugitive-Agrarians preoccupied with, in this new generational homework assignment so casually made.[45] In that sense, deconstruction would seem the emptiest of professional methodologies.

But nothing about deconstruction is simple or one-dimensional, and this apparently pointless gesturing in the abyss has numerous other potentialities. The recent revelations of de Man's collaborationist phase in Nazi-occupied Belgium, for example, have suggested to more than one observer that the ascetic emptiness of his criticism is to be taken as penitential and reparational. And Felperin himself concluded that of all the contemporary critical approaches, only textual deconstruction had shown itself capable of preserving the aesthetic and literary qualities of poetic language, and this capability tips the scales for him in what is otherwise a kind of stand-off between textualizing and contextualizing post-structuralist reading strategies.

Certainly deconstruction, in both French and American versions, is as anti-positivist as one could desire: it marks the end, for the time being at least, of the trend since Northrop Frye to create a 'science' of literary studies analogous to physics or biology. In all its versions it announces the impossibility of positive knowledge of any sort, and with its *jouissance* in the play of *différence* can be taken as a kind of celebration of subjectivity against objectivity—explicitly in the practice of

---

[43] See William E. Cain, *The Crisis in Criticism: Theory, Literature and Reform in English Studies* (Baltimore, Md.: Johns Hopkins University Press, 1984).

[44] Paul de Man, *Allegories of Reading: Figural Language in Rousseau, Nietzsche, Rilke, and Proust* (New Haven, Conn.: Yale University Press, 1979), 16–17.

[45] Cf. Felperin, *Beyond Deconstruction*, 140.

Geoffrey Hartman, according to the dedication of his *Saving the Text*, 'For the Subject'.[46] And although Derrida's emphasis and context is quite different,[47] even he, with his playful close readings replete with their breath-taking leaps, associations, and word-play, makes a clear anti-positivist assertion of the subjective—albeit, of a subjectivity without a subject.

Thus it is possible to see textual deconstruction as a vehicle for a Postmodernist cultural tradition which would supersede a depleted Modernism but continue to resist under new conditions the sterilizing effects of bureaucratic capitalism which we have seen at work since the late nineteenth century. Certainly deconstruction seems well suited to subvert the usual methods of classification and instrumentalization which have been among the favoured tactics of academic positivism. It is well suited, too, to re-function received literary texts into Post-modern (anti-)aesthetic spaces, renewing cultural resources that have recently threatened to pale and languish. This aesthetic potentiality of deconstruction, I take it, is the major point of Howard Felperin's eloquent and cogent argument in *Beyond Deconstruction*. The textual practice in particular of Derrida and the late Barthes offers suggestive examples of this potentiality.

It is already clear, however, that textual deconstruction is open to the very same processes of professionalization that neutralized the socially critical components of an earlier New Criticism. Stripped down to its own techniques, deconstruction offers one more opportunity to go

---

[46] Here it is important to distinguish between American and French deconstructionists, as Art Berman has argued: the American critics, and Hartman and Bloom in particular, have inflected deconstruction as a celebration of the freedom of the subject seemingly much more continuous with a previous phase of phenomenology than has Derrida for whom, in Berman's words, 'the self is constituted by language, beyond which there is nothing to know' (*From New Criticism to Deconstruction*, 5). Deconstruction is, of course, not only post-structuralist, but post-phenomenological as well, and in the case of Derrida, with his preoccupation with Heidegger, Nietzsche, and Husserl, much more centrally post-phenomenological than post-structuralist. As such deconstruction has mounted a sustained critique of the notions of a unitary Self and of a privileged subjectivity that had long gone unquestioned in Anglo-American literary studies, and in that sense, particularly if Derrida is construed as the major instance, is as 'anti-subjectivist' as it is 'anti-objectivist'. Certainly the traditional Arnoldian account of the literary tradition as a set of timeless truths illuminating an eternal human nature has no place in deconstructive practice, and to the extent that American New Criticism was based on those Arnoldian premisses, deconstruction announces the end of New Criticism as readily as it does positivistic literary history.

[47] See Art Berman, *From New Criticism to Deconstruction, passim*.

through the canon in yet another series of 'close readings'[48] continuing the 'criticism of credentialing' that earlier brought Renaissance studies to the crisis of irrelevancy in which the field was mired in the Sixties and Seventies. I am far from the first critic to note that such a process already seems well begun in the pages of the professional journals. And the early attempts at deconstructive readings of Shakespeare which I will briefly examine here, for example, are not reassuring in this vein even when they are cogent and intelligent, as several are.

How important is deconstruction in today's Shakespeare studies? Deconstruction's impact is maddeningly difficult to define: on the one hand, there is a pervasive influence operating at levels like the new textual criticism and new editions of the works, new theatrical productions, and a marked redefining of disciplinary strictures in the production of criticism. Indeed it might plausibly be argued that deconstruction has been the major conduit into Renaissance studies of the Postmodern sensibility.

But because Derrida has directed his primary attention to philosophical texts and issues, and because the Yale deconstructors had begun their careers as specialists in the nineteenth century who had early been concerned with reversing New Criticism's valorization of the Renaissance over Romanticism, deconstructive close readings of Shakespeare are among the most prominent texts of neither deconstruction in general nor of contemporary Shakespeare criticism. More typically in Shakespeare studies, deconstructive tactics have been combined with historicizing strategies and inflected by way of Foucault in the works of new historicism and cultural materialism to be examined below—and, of course, though through a different kind of historicizing, in the book you are reading. Examples of 'pure' close reading—what Felperin has called 'textual' post-structuralism rather than 'contextual' post-structuralism *à la* the new historicism—have been fewer than might be supposed.

One prominent collection of such textual deconstruction is Section I, 'Language, Rhetoric, Deconstruction', of the critical anthology *Shakespeare and the Question of Theory* (co-edited by Patricia Parker and Geoffrey Hartman), comprised of four examples of language-oriented

---

[48] Felperin sees this tendency, which he calls deconstruction becoming an 'empty technology of the text' (*Beyond Deconstruction*, 141) as precisely the problem to overcome in developing it into a critical practice which could function as a late twentieth-century 'defence of poetry' (p. 115).

'textual' rather than 'contextual' deconstructive approaches. What is notable of all four of these examples— in addition to the intellectual liveliness of them all—is their tentativeness, their self-presentation as 'demonstration models', examples of how the methodology might work, rather than matured critical practice with a sense of its own accomplishment. Felperin demonstrates some basic tenets of deconstructive practice leading to a redefinition of literary language, Freund sketches and calls for an elaborated Bloomian literary history of the Renaissance using *Troilus and Cressida* as her instance of the anxiety of influence in Shakespeare, and Parker calls for renewed, post-structuralist-inflected interest in Renaissance rhetoric in her deft reading of a crux in *Othello*. Even Geoffrey Hartman, who of all these critics is least suited to assume a beginner's stance in regard to deconstructive criticism, writes a subtle but slight demonstration that 'language' must be seen to be prior to 'character' in Shakespearian drama, concluding with the familiar observation that 'There is no "present": no absolute gift, or moment of pure being' (p. 51). Is there a sense operating that in Shakespeare studies only such deconstructive 'beginnings' are appropriate, even in 1985? This is not to say, however, that these beginnings are not intellectually rewarding in many ways.

The opening article, Howard Felperin's '"Tongue-tied our queen?": The Deconstruction of Presence in *The Winter's Tale*', (pp. 3–18), is a textbook demonstration of how to see a Shakespearian text deconstructing itself from within. Felperin finds a Derridean play of interpretive uncertainty to be a theme of the play itself, through the groundlessness of what, in the world of the play, represents the divine confirmation of Hermione's innocence—the oracle from Apollo. Shakespeare, Felperin writes, chose to leave the god's presentation of the oracle as an off-stage action, denying us the kind of stage presence of similar theophanies he had created in *Pericles* and *Cymbeline*. The result is that, if we examine the issue closely, there is no confirmation of the oracle's authority—we are plunged into a deconstructive abyss of interpretive undecidability in the absence of any confirming divine authority: the play itself thematizes its own textuality, its own enactment of the deconstructive *mise-en-abyme*: 'Once cut off from the presence of their divine speaker, with his univocality of meaning and intent, Apollo's words enter the realm of the human, the fallible, the ambiguous, in sum, the interpretable, where they can be contradicted or dismissed, for all we know, with impunity. . . . By separating Apollo's words from their sacred and authenticating voice, Shakespeare adumbrates a larger problem of interpretation, one that bedevils the world of the play from the outset' (p. 8). And that problem, it devolves, is nothing less than 'linguistic indeterminacy' (p. 8), 'a fall into a condition of multivocality or equivocation, a new helplessness to avoid finding a certain duplicity in what is said, meanings that may or may not have been intended' (p. 10).

As Felperin goes on to argue, true to his deconstructive premisses, *The Winter's Tale* in this interpretation simply enunciates a quality that is true of *any* text whatsoever—and hence becomes a new condition for critical practice, always already present in Shakespeare. The article ends with an assertion that poetic language is characterized by precisely this making explicit the groundlessness of ordinary language.

Taken at face value, the article seems to be precisely the kind of 'demonstration model' essay I spoke of above: it is a kind of deconstructive primer, demonstrated out of Shakespeare rather than out of Plato or Rousseau, apparently meant to initiate those specialists who had not worked through the 'primary' deconstructive documents.

Put in the context of Felperin's contemporaneous *Beyond Deconstruction*, however, the article is at once more precise and much wider in its implications. In that book Felperin had diagnosed contemporary critical practice as mired in positivism and scientism, and he championed deconstruction as both rigorous and aesthetic, the only hope in the modern academy for preserving art and literature against the encroachments of imperializing science. With its theoretical rigour, deconstruction can always be called on to deconstruct and hence fend off any of the contextualizing or historicizing claims which other contemporary critical methods might make against it; but it also, he argues, preserves the aesthetic in its close attention to, and celebration of, language as such.

The desire at work in my reading of the anthologized article to supplement it with something less simply performative and more theoretical probably stems from the way its very brevity and rigour seem to impede Felperin from achieving the aesthetic bravura which he demonstrated in several passages of his book, complementing the article's silence on this theme. In comparison, the chapter on Shakespeare's sonnets, and in particular the brief remarks on *The Winter's Tale* (pp. 195–7), in *Beyond Deconstruction* not only make claims for this quality but demonstrate them in a quite dazzling critical practice.[49]

Felperin, who had published in 1972 a very different reading of *The Winter's Tale*,[50] is more conscious than many another revisionist critic of the determining role of the aesthetic present on one's reading of the art-works of the past: '... it is not the text but our perception of the text that has radically altered', he writes in his later essay in *Shakespeare and the Question of Theory* (pp. 14–15).

But the basically uneasy relationship between such clearly Post-modern critical procedures and texts from a decidedly different cultural context which they would illuminate emerges — where else? — in a footnote: 'The astute reader will have recognized a certain resonance between my reading of *The Winter's Tale* and Jacques Der-rida's critique of western logocentricity' (p. 18, n. 9), Felperin writes coyly. And he goes on to quote a Derridean passage on the play of sign-substitution and deferral that comes into view when the transcen-dental signified is bracketed, invoking the abyss of indeterminacy which his own reading had demonstrated as a Shakespearian thematic in the play. And yet, in the ambiguous tone (ironic? sardonic? impatient with an editor's comment?) of his phrases 'astute reader' and 'certain resonance', we can discern a hesitation as to where to 'place' the deconstructive enterprise: in 'Shakespeare', in 'the text', in the critic, or in Postmodernist discourse?[51]

The answer provided in *Beyond Deconstruction* is Felperin's rendition of de Man's coinage, the 'foreknowledge' of the text: '[t]he text is only accessible, only exists through interpretation, and must thus always already hold the potential insight that enables recognition of the blind-ness of any of its constructions' (p. 119). Furthermore, the text, as a space constituted by the play of difference and deferral, always already surpasses its various social and historical contexts, which then, in this argument, become something less than crucial to our reading. Fur-

---

[49] Another version of Felperin's discussion of the sonnets is included in the recent anthology *Shakespeare and Deconstruction*, ed. G. Douglas Atkins and David M. Bergeron (New York: Peter Lang, 1988).

[50] Howard Felperin, *Shakespearean Romance* (Princeton, NJ: Princeton University Press, 1972), 211–45.

[51] Compare with this the similar uneasiness in Freund's carefully composed for-mulas: 'In the climate of contemporary critical discourse, however, it is becoming possible to show how the Shakespearean self-reflexive forays of wit match, remarkably, the wit of the deconstructionist enterprise' (Parker and Hartman, *Shakespeare and the Question of Theory*, 22). Here more than in Felperin, perhaps, the critic has lost touch with the Derridean theories which make the 'match' something less than 'remarkable'.

thermore, the most interesting literary texts, like Shakespeare's sonnets, or like *The Winter's Tale*, are self-constituting aesthetic spaces
afloat in the abyss whose self-constituting properties, always already
there, we can now see in the wake of post-structuralism (pp. 181–2)—
not to mention, I might add, Mallarmé and Wallace Stevens.

Such suppositions are powerfully enabling for a project to recoup
Shakespeare and the other major authors in an anti-aesthetic Postmodernist age in which the older interpretations have begun to lose
their power. They make a clear claim for the necessity of reading the
past from within the *Jetztzeit*, of resisting the temptations of the siren
of unmediated access to the past.

At the same time, however, it is difficult to see how they avoid the
charge of dissolving the otherness of the past into the present—or at
least of wishing away this issue through the basic hypostatization contained in the doctrine of textual foreknowledge. Agency—the activity
of concrete humans reading and interpreting in concrete social space-
times—is occluded with a vengeance, just as surely as in the Althusserian and early Foucault texts which Felperin had (rightly in my view)
objected to for this very fault. This deconstructed Shakespearian text
is located in that fantastic, abstracted space–time of which Said has
spoken so eloquently, that apparent nowhere and nowhen that is actually the terrain of twentieth-century professionalized academic literary-critical discourses in contention for professional power. The
continuity between this kind of deconstruction and earlier New Criticism, pointed out by Lentricchia, Said, Cain, and a host of others,
should be only too apparent. In all these cases, the text is represented
as existing in an ahistorical space in which language seems to perform
its magic independently of any communities of interpreters—even
while interpretation itself, in the case of the deconstructive critics, is
affirmed abstractly. Both critical procedures seemed haunted by a
ghost in their machinery—references to Shakespearian intentionality
crop up repeatedly, against the grain of their anti-*auteur* critical
presuppositions.[52]

[52] Intentionality in New Criticism is discussed in Chapter 3 above. In Felperin's
essay, the ghost of intentionality can be detected in such phrases as '. . . and Shakespeare
makes even more explicit and unequivocal the already clear pronouncement of his
source' (p. 6) and '*The Winter's Tale*, with a self-understanding extraordinary even for
Shakespeare, dramatizes not only the precariousness of its own linguistic enterprise but
the unhappy consequences of our positive incapability of accepting such precariousness
as the condition of fiction' (p. 15). The first quotation presents an intentionality later
seen as subverted by the textuality of the play, but the second asserts a self-conscious
thematization of textuality by a presciently deconstructionist Shakespeare.

In this connection, it is remarkable that in the supposedly ground-breaking criticism of *Shakespeare and the Question of Theory*, the hold of the New Critical tradition of an article's undertaking a 'reading' of a single text is virtually unshakeable. Here, too, the influence of professional requirements and the New Critical tradition is all too apparent. In fact it may make better sense to classify such criticism as Postmodernist New Criticism to underline the continuity and get at the most important of the differences between the newer method and its antecedent. The method is still New Critical in its habits of close reading of a single text spatially arrayed in timeless abstraction; but it is Postmodernist in its abandonment of a fiction of a unified, centred space in which all tensions are absorbed and overcome.

Given the protean potentialities of deconstructive criticism, however, it would be inappropriate to take the writers of *Shakespeare and the Question of Theory*, however prestigious its provenance, as the only representative deconstructive critics of Shakespeare. A number of critics have in the past suggested a meaningful dichotomy between an apparently apolitical deconstruction, best exemplified by the Yale critics, which has been content to demonstrate repetitively the un-decidability of textual meanings, and a politically engaged, left-wing deconstruction, developed by such figures as Gayatri Spivak and Michael Ryan, which has argued that the method only comes into its own as the concrete deconstruction *of* the ideological supports of power and privilege and recognizing in the method an inherent materialist bias and impetus to ideology-critique. In principle such a practice would take us out of the abstracted timelessness I have just been describing and return us to a dialectical play between past and present in reading.

The recent collection *Shakespeare and Deconstruction*, cited above, would seem to locate itself somewhere between these two poles. Gary Waller's essay makes a cogent case for the position that deconstruction can combine with historicism to preserve a sense of both past *and* present in our readings of texts,[53] while Atkins stresses that deconstruction *can* make a difference and has political implications — albeit ones that 'will likely appear to some as more conservative than other efforts that attempt to go through and beyond deconstruction in order to address social and political questions' (p. 3). Felperin repeats much of his concern with the self-constituting and reflexive text from

[53] Gary Waller, 'Decentering the Bard: The Dissemination of the Shakespearean Text', *Shakespeare and Deconstruction*, 21–45.

Beyond Deconstruction, preserving thus the aesthetic power of the method to re-function classic texts as Postmodern art-works—a direction pursued by a number of the other contributors in their own ways. In short, it is a stimulating, multidimensional collection that can be seen as an attempt to reopen one of the untaken roads in recent Shakespeare studies, that of 'textualizing' deconstructive close readings—a moment largely bypassed by the development of the new historicism.

There are also now several examples of more explicitly activist left-wing deconstruction in Shakespeare studies,[54] with the most interesting and provocative of them, I believe, Terry Eagleton's *William Shakespeare*.

This is not to suggest that Eagleton's book is exemplary or definitive; indeed, the book is seriously undertheorized, a 'demonstration' performance that leaves its readers with numerous unanswered questions. But it is both sophisticated and suggestive of numerous ramifications for future criticism.

Eagleton, too, seems to be uneasy with the problem of *where* to situate the deconstruction—but he covers the uneasiness, in a very Freudian way, with a joke: 'Though conclusive evidence is hard to come by, it is difficult to read Shakespeare without feeling that he was almost certainly familiar with the writings of Hegel, Marx, Nietzsche, Wittgenstein and Derrida. Perhaps this is simply to say that though there are many ways in which we have thankfully left this conservative patriarch behind, there are other ways in which we have yet to catch up with him.'[55] This is charming and disarming, and one feels like an unhip curmudgeon in considering the matter more precisely. One reader, Gary Taylor, has suggested that the tongue-in-cheek quality of passages like the above is the clue to the book's brevity, which, Taylor says, is to be taken as part of a strategy of parodying academic dis-

[54] Christopher Norris, for example, shows us alternatives to the reading-of-a-single-text approach to deconstructive criticism in 'Post-structuralist Shakespeare', his contribution to the British anthology *Alternative Shakespeares*, ed. John Drakakis (London: Methuen, 1985), 47–66. Norris draws attention to the commonalities in the apparently polar approaches to Shakespeare taken by Samuel Johnson and F. R. Leavis, concluding that *no* single reading of a play can do more than 'add another chapter in the case-book of endlessly dissenting views' on Shakespeare, revealing not some impossible "essence" of Shakespeare, but the story of their own devising' (p. 66). The following essay by Malcolm Evans, 'Deconstructing Shakespeare's Comedies', shows a witty appreciation of the domestication of deconstruction into a 'souped-up, mildly hallucinogenic formalism' (p. 77). See also Evans's book, *Signifying Nothing: Truth's True Contents in Shakespeare's Text* (Brighton: Harvester, 1986).

[55] Terry Eagleton, *William Shakespeare* (Oxford: Basil Blackwell, 1986), pp. ix–x.

course.[56] But if this is so, it must be said that Eagleton in his recent works is in danger of making that strategy go threadbare, and most readers will wish for much more theoretical situating than Eagleton delivers here, even after appreciating the scandalous humour.

Comparison with the deconstructive strategies of *Shakespeare and the Question of Theory* can provide one way into Eagleton's strategy. In comparison with Felperin, to start there, there is little notice given to the topic of the undecidability of the text in Eagleton's book; instead we are given a series of determinate thumbscale readings of eighteen or so plays, each with a definite, even univocal, interpretation of the play in question. The provocative opening statement of the book (reproduced on the dust jacket), which names the witches in *Macbeth* as 'the heroines of the piece', the site of the 'positive value of *Macbeth*', is clearly meant as a scandalous signal that what follows is a reading, to use the title of an earlier collection of Eagleton essays, 'against the grain' of received academic opinion. There is no attempt to engage a community of other academic readers of the play; rather Eagleton simply 'reads' through his own cultivated sensibility as a representative of a left-political, post-Leavis, post-Althusserian discourse-community. This is the self-parodying 'unprejudiced reader' invoked in his introduction: 'To any unprejudiced reader—which would seem to exclude Shakespeare himself, his contemporary audiences and almost all literary critics—it is surely clear that positive value in *Macbeth* lies with the three witches' (pp. 1–2).

In thus developing a politicized deconstructive textual criticism based on a Left discourse-community, Eagleton is flaunting some basic premises of professionalism and is thereby taking a different direction from much of the British post-Althusserian literary left, which has opted instead largely for historicizing, contextualizing strategies (I will briefly discuss these 'cultural materialists' in the next section). Admirable as this is in many ways, it is a gesture undercut by the very institutions of impeccable professional correctness and prestige from which Eagleton's discourse emanates (Oxford University, Basil Blackwell Publishers) and by the unspoken theoretical sophistication of his apparatus, constitutive of advanced professional credentials.

The anti-professionalist gesturing, however, which at one level is quite palpable, exacts its own costs. It leads Eagleton to forgo a Der-

[56] Gary Taylor, *Reinventing Shakespeare: A Cultural History 1642–1986* (New York: Weidenfeld & Nicolson, 1989), 295–7.

ridean engagement in the processes of metalanguage, and he all but
ignores the aesthetic qualities of the works. And by ignoring the critical
history of the texts in question, he can sound irritatingly opinionated,
as pre-New Critically arrogant as E. E. Stoll. Such a case is the brief
discussion of *Othello*, in which it is not hard to detect the ghost of
F. R. Leavis's critique of that play. For Eagleton like Leavis, the title
character is notable mainly for his obtuseness and the hollowness of
his language ('too literal and gullible . . . and at the same time too
wildly fanciful' (p. 66) is how Eagleton puts it). Similarly, *Hamlet* is in
danger of being reduced to a deconstructionist conceit: the character
Hamlet 'is pure deferral and diffusion, a hollow void which offers
nothing determinate to be known' (p. 72). And in *Timon* Eagleton sees
no reason to doubt that there is a clear moral judgement condemnatory
of the title character's 'grotesque generosity', where other recent
critics have seen only disjuncture, fragmentation, and undecidableness.

In short, Eagleton gives us a deconstruction which performs *a*
determinate reading which is constantly engaged ethically and politically, but dependent on a series of categories and values simply taken
for granted, never spelled out to the readership—but certainly
debatable, to say the least. At his best, as for example in a brilliant
discussion of the self-contradictions of love and desire in the comedies
(pp. 18–21), Eagleton will be relished by many who do not share his
politics.

On the other hand, this unabashed use of his own sensibility and
community puts Eagleton in plenty of company, good and otherwise,
including the most celebrated of Shakespeare critics. Certainly
Dryden, Johnson, Coleridge, Eliot, and all the figures examined in this
work never hesitated to use the texts to enunciate their own—and their
communities'—sense of meaning, value, and propriety; indeed, a
cogent argument could be made that of the many 'uses' of literary
criticism, this one is the most valuable and coherent, and one of the
great losses of the professionalization of criticism has been the
weakening of this function.[57]

Rather than create a theoretical context for his readings, however—

----

[57] As noted in Chapter 1, Eagleton's *The Function of Criticism* presents a version of the
story of the professionalization of literary criticism, and in his conclusion he calls for a
paradoxical return to criticism's 'traditional role' of criticizing the state and social
institutions. But as he points out, only by engaging in rigorous investigations of the
processes of symbol-formation can we fulfill the traditional critical function.

one can certainly be construed from several of his recent works[58] —
Eagleton chooses instead to plunge in and show us his method at work.
He proceeds by identifying—or constituting—in the given text a theme
displaying the deconstructive properties of deferral, non-identity, and
resistance to hierarchy. Shakespeare thus emerges as something of a
deconstructionist *avant la lettre* here as well as in the other deconstructive practices examined. Such an effect is inherent in the premises
concerning the nature of language which Derrida and his followers
have developed, since language is held to be deconstructive—always
already deconstructed—in its very nature. But here a sense of what will
seem to many an illegitimate 'reading into' the text, above and beyond
the 'foreknowledge' effect defined by de Man and discussed by
Felperin, is heightened by the clear 'presence' of the political interest I
described above. Perhaps all one should say is that different audiences
will be delighted or infuriated that Eagleton's book is as much about—
perhaps more about—the late twentieth-century encounter between
Marxism and deconstruction than it is about its purported subject,
William Shakespeare.

This feat of 'using' Shakespeare implicitly to address twentieth-
century problematics is achieved by the deft selection of the themes to
be studied at work in the plays. The initial and most returned to
thematic is an opposition between body and language, which Eagleton
casually introduces us to in meditations on *Macbeth* and *Richard II*. But
as the play of meanings of that opposition unfolds across several of the
plays, its intertextuality with some of the central binary concepts of
Western Marxism becomes clear: with, for example, Hegel's bondage/
freedom, Marx's materialism/idealism, Heidegger's and Sartre's in-
itself/for-itself, Saussure's signified/signifier, Lacan's desire/law,

---

[58] See the Preface, *Against the Grain: Essays 1975–1985* (London: Verso, 1986) for
Eagleton's own account of his turn away from the Althusserianism of his early *Criticism
and Ideology* (London: New Left Books, 1976) to a more recent attempt to use Walter
Benjamin to 'diversify Marxist theory with ... openings toward feminism and some
aspects of post-structuralism' (p. 6), including an opening to deconstruction and to
'pleasure and playfulness which could not be grimly deferred until theory had done its
work' (p. 6). The turning-point would thus seem to be charted in his *Walter Benjamin:
Or, Towards a Revolutionary Criticism* (London: Verso, 1981). Presumably, then, *William
Shakespeare* is an example of the kind of playful, politically inflected, partially
deconstructive criticism called for in Eagleton's recent theory, its undisguised reading of
the past through the lenses of the present a Benjaminesque 'blasting' from history of a
layered constellation made possible by reflection on the present's constituting relation to
the past. It is, nevertheless, also marked by all the contingencies of Eagleton's political
allegiances, including an unalloyed admiration of Lenin and Trotsky—see *Walter
Benjamin*, 174–9.

Lévi-Strauss's nature/culture, Derrida's presence/absence—and even Eliot's and Leavis's feeling/thought.

The central theoretical problem of the book is enunciated, coyly and playfully, as a problematic of *Richard II*:

How real is the signifier is a question which *Richard II* constantly poses. Language is something less than reality, but also its very inner form; and it is difficult to distinguish this 'proper' intertwining of signs and things ... from that 'improper' commingling of the two which springs from the imperial interventions of the autonomous sign, shaping reality to its self-indulgent whims. ... Fiction seems inherent in reality; politics works by rhetoric and mythology, power is histrionic, and ... society itself is a dramatic artefact, demanding a certain suspension of disbelief on the part of its members. (pp. 12–13)

Just as this is doubtless an excellent thematization of recurrent motifs in Shakespeare, it is just as surely a posing of what is perhaps the central problem of a would-be deconstructive Marxism: in the wake of Derrida and company, how 'real', indeed, is the signifier for materialism? How can we do justice to the always already mingled nature of language and materiality in human experience without falling into either crude idealisms or materialisms. Not surprisingly Eagleton does not solve this problem—neither for that matter did Shakespeare, as he says somewhat petulantly in the book's conclusion, and a testimony to the power of the writing is that we momentarily assent to this claim of Shakespearian prescience and failure.

Of interest in charting how far Eagleton has come from his early Althusserian phase is the new prominence given to Marx's discussion of the 'fetishism of commodities' from *Capital*, which Althusser had danced around, fearing it to be a remnant of undigested Hegelianism in the 'mature' Marx. In the light of deconstruction, however, it now appears as the central instance where Marx deconstructs the opposition between materiality and language/culture/ideology. Marx theorized a 'fantastic', imaginary social belief (that commodities are the source of their own—for Marx social—value), which, however, even though it is imaginary still constitutes a 'material' network of social relations (the capitalist economy). In some of the most interesting passages of the book, Eagleton explores the analogy of this reified commodity-system with other reified systems, as in the problematics of the general and the particular in law, of uniqueness and sameness in love and desire, and of *langue* and *parole* in language itself:

... all these systems involve exchange and equivalence, which is in itself a stabilizing factor; but because they are necessarily indifferent as systems to particular objects or uses, they tend to breed an anarchic state of affairs in which everything blurs indiscriminately into everything else, and the system appears to be engaging in transactions for its own sake. There is, in other words, something in the very structures of stability themselves which offers to subvert them.... (p. 57)

In short, Eagleton seems less interested in the textuality of Shakespeare's works than he is in opportunistically using those works as the occasion to examine the 'social text' constituted by those reified systems of the symbolic order in which we are condemned to live—the economy, the law, sexuality, and language. In thus making of the Shakespearian texts 'another Nature', he implicitly returns to the oldest topic of praise in the history of Shakespeare commentary— perhaps the cultural tradition had never let go of that extravagant *topos*. More important, he makes a maddeningly understated, but suggestive, highly synthesizing contribution to the problematics of Postmodern Marxism—without ever telling us so.

In *William Shakespeare* Eagleton demonstrates the political relevance of non-historicist deconstruction, showing its potential of escaping from the strictures of Lentricchia and so many others that it is con- demned to political quietism and professionalism. It is not so clear, however, whether the substitution of a Left speech community as the source of many of the critical categories for that of academic pro- fessionals (who are actually implicitly addressed too), or the tactics of determinate readings 'against the grain', which ignore those of other discourse communities also laying claim to the right to interpret Shakespeare, can stand up against the charge that they are as arbitrary and even as authoritarian as those discourses which are the clear but unannounced Other of this effort. Speaking from a similarly over- determined site (as who is not?), I can only pose the question without pretending to answer it univocally.

The New Historicism and Cultural Materialism

If, as I have argued, the end of organic unity as a formal aesthetic property and the subversion of binary hierarchies are the two key components of the Postmodernist critical revolution, it is clear that both of these features were thematized and defined most influentially in deconstructive critical practice, in particular that of Derrida. But the

Postmodern and the post-structuralist are not simply to be conflated, and there are several examples of 'home-grown' Postmodernisms developed autonomously from French post-structuralism. Since, in American Shakespeare studies, the impact of properly structuralist methodologies was decidedly limited, we could only expect the mediation of the Postmodern to take forms less tied to the assimilation of Saussure and Genette than has been the case in France. Ironically, American deconstruction, with its clear Oedipal relation to New Criticism despite its invocation of Derrida, is a key case in point. And the same thing is true, in its essentials, of much of the new historicism. British cultural materialism constitutes a related but separate case, which I shall discuss shortly.

Of course if American deconstructionists have invoked the name of Derrida, American new historicists and British cultural materialists have named Foucault as a theoretical model, perhaps with more justice than their colleagues. And the differences which Said defined between the two post-structuralisms of Derrida and Foucault—that the former's method moves us *into* the text, but the latter's moves us *in* and *out* of it[59]—are important differences too for distinguishing deconstruction and new historicism in Shakespeare studies. For when Foucault moves us out of a text, it is into the archive of roughly contemporaneous writings, and then into the historically specific institutions which produced them. A similar difference is clearly perceivable between the characteristic 'timelessness' of American deconstruction and the persistent attempts of the new historicism to place on centre-stage the question of historical difference. But while the analogy to Derrida and Foucault is meaningful, it should not be taken as exhaustive: many of the concrete differences between the two trends in contemporary Shakespeare studies stem from the disparate parentage of the two: deconstruction's descent from New Criticism, and, as we will see, the new historicism's links with New Criticism's old nemesis, positivist historical criticism.

In addition, many of the similarities between deconstruction and the new historicism derive from their common influence by Postmodernism, with all its entangled relations to post-structuralism. With their new sensitivity to the plight of the colonialized New World and African populations during the early European expansion of the Renaissance, and with their employment of Lacanian and Foucaultian notions of a

---

[59] Edward W. Said, 'The Problem of Textuality', *Critical Inquiry*, 4 (Summer 1978), 674–714.

decentred self (and their literary corollary, the decentred text), both the new historicism and cultural materialism are clearly, too, involved in Postmodern aesthetics as previously defined.

At the current moment, the new historicism has become something of a phenomenon, attracting widespread attention well beyond the usual circles of Renaissance specialists—of, for example, the editors of *The New York Review of Books*, a journal which has not in recent years manifested much interest in either newer trends in literary theory or in Shakespeare studies.[60]

This quick success of the movement has even prompted Jean Howard, certainly a friend of the newer criticism within Renaissance studies,[61] to ask in print whether new historicism may ultimately be seen as a 'backlash phenomenon: a flight from theory or simply a program for producing more "new readings" suited to the twenty-five-page article and the sixty-minute class'.[62] Edward Pechter, on the other hand, has even stronger misgivings, but they centre on what he believes to be new historicism's 'Marxist' endorsement of the idea that the 'will to power' is at the centre of life[63] (one had thought the phrase and the notion to be Nietzsche's). Such disparate diagnoses—fear on the one hand that an apparently insurgent methodology will prove a strategy of containment, fear on the other that an intellectually powerful method will subvert the Arnoldian mission of literary studies—bespeak a criticism on the brink of becoming a major cultural force. Rather than attempt to adjudicate between either of the two fearful prognostications I have just cited—both of which have plenty of precedent in earlier twentieth-century criticism—I wish instead to situate the new historicism in the context of the present study.[64] In addition,

[60] I refer to the respectful if sceptical review by the well-known Shakespearian E. A. J. Honigmann of Greenblatt's recent books *Shakespearean Negotiations: The Circulation of Social Energy in Renaissance England*. See 'The New Shakespeare?', cited above, n. 2.

[61] See her eloquent 'Scholarship, Theories, and More New Readings: Shakespeare for the 1990s', *Shakespeare Study Today*, ed. Georgianna Ziegler (New York: AMS, 1986), 127–51.

[62] Jean Howard, 'The New Historicism in Renaissance Studies', *English Literary Renaissance*, 16 (Winter 1986), 19.

[63] Edward Pechter, 'The New Historicism and Its Discontents: Politicizing Renaissance Drama', *PMLA* 102 (May 1987), 292–303.

[64] There are now several accounts of the new historicism within Renaissance studies to which the interested reader can refer for fuller bibliographical information than I supply here. See Jonathan Goldberg, 'The Politics of Renaissance Literature: A Review Essay', *English Literary History*, 49 (1982), 514–42; Jean Howard, 'The New Historicism in Renaissance Studies', cited above; Edward Pechter, 'The New Historicism and Its Discontents: Politicizing Renaissance Drama', cited above. Without the bibliographical

the American new historicism has clear links to (as well as differences with) what is coming to be called British cultural materialism. Because the two have at times been conflated in other treatments of the movement, I will bring out some important national distinctions in what follows.

The American effort can be traced back to the work in the Seventies by Stephen Orgel attempting to define a concrete social and political dimension to the court masque,[65] an effort arising out of the historical-New Critical synthesis of the late Seventies. But a turning-point is definitely marked with the appearance of Stephen Greenblatt's *Renaissance Self-Fashioning: From More to Shakespeare* in 1980. Greenblatt's work broke the long, unspoken taboo within Renaissance studies of interrogating the relation between the canonical masterpieces of Renaissance literature with the horrifying colonialist policies pursued by all the major European powers of the era, including Elizabethan and Jacobean England. And he undertook his inquiry by means of a sophisticated notion of the subject partially borrowed from Lacan combined with a sensitivity to the epistemological pervasiveness of culture learned equally from Foucault and the American anthropologist Clifford Geertz. The result was a provocative, multidimensional redirecting of the English literary Renaissance into a relation with a cultural matrix of power, repression, and subjection. The flavour of this effort is perhaps best conveyed in some sardonic remarks Greenblatt makes on C. S. Lewis's claim over a generation ago that Wyatt's court poetry should be seen as 'material for social occasions'. Lewis had put it this way: 'The whole scene comes before us. . . . We are having a little music after supper. In that atmosphere all the confessional or autobiographical tone of the songs falls away.'[66] Greenblatt then comments: 'But is this really what it meant to write from within the court? Entertainments in the court of Henry VIII must have been like small talk with Stalin' (pp. 136– 7).

---

detail of the above, but an excellent introduction to the new historicism, is Terence Hawkes, 'Lear's Maps: A General Survey', *Deutsche Shakespeare Gesellschaft West Jahrbuch* (1989), 134–47. Of great interest, too, is a recent anthology of critical essays discussing the new historicism from several points of view, *The New Historicism*, ed. Aran Veeser (New York: Routledge, 1989).

[65] Stephen Orgel, *The Illusion of Power: Political Theater in the English Renaissance* (Berkeley: University of California Press, 1975).

[66] *English Literature in the Sixteenth Century, excluding Drama* (Oxford: Clarendon, 1954), 230; quoted in Stephen Greenblatt, *Renaissance Self-Fashioning: From More to Shakespeare* (Chicago, Ill.: University of Chicago Press, 1980), 136.

In Greenblatt's re-placement of Lewis's after-dinner banter to a *realpolitik* world of imprisonments and executions can be intuited an entire paradigm shift. The Elizabethan world is no longer the idealized golden age, the long-sought-after organic society of both Tillyard and Leavis. It is instead a world more like our own—this of course is not coincidental—where there are not only illusions of freedom and work-ings of power but also, as Jean Howard has written, 'one can see acted out a clash of paradigms and ideologies, a playfulness with signifying systems, a self-reflexivity, and a self-consciousness about the tenuous solidity of human identity which resonate with some of the dominant elements of postmodern culture'.[67] The new historicism, like deconstruction, is a product of the Postmodernist epoch. But it is a critical practice in which the Postmodernist anti-hierarchical impulse is given much greater play than has been the case to date among the American deconstructors. In particular the political dimensions of such critiques are brought to the fore as Greenblatt focuses attention on the marginalization and dehumanizing of suppressed Others, both in literary texts (the cases of Marlowe's *Jew of Malta* and Shakespeare's *Othello*) and in history, as he and his colleagues admirably acquaint literary scholarship with such non-Tillyardian topics as the use of European diseases as a weapon against native Americans in the settle-ment of the New World.

The relationship between such critical innovations and the historical present is at times evident to Greenblatt himself, who, for example, alluded to such an enabling conjunction in the Introduction to *Renais-sance Self-Fashioning*: '. . . if cultural poetics [a term later superseded by "new historicism"] is conscious of its status as interpretation, this consciousness must extend to an acceptance of the impossibility of fully reconstructing and reentering the culture of the sixteenth cen-tury, of leaving behind one's own situation: it is everywhere evident in this book that the questions I ask of my material and indeed the very nature of this material are shaped by the questions I ask of myself' (p. 5).

And yet in the chapters of the book, chapters each of which, Greenblatt asserts, is 'intended to stand alone as an exploration whose contours are shaped by our grasp of the specific situation of the author or text' (p. 8), consciousness of the present is allowed to dissolve into a familiar historical reconstruction which appears to recover the truth of

---

[67] Howard, 'New Historicism', 16–17.

the past unproblematically.[68] In this, of course, the new historicism is very much at one with its older forebears, positivist and Tillyardian historicism, each of which also occasionally intuited how the present helped shape the lenses through which the past was being viewed, but which ordinarily understood their task as simply bracketing the present in order to reach an objective past.[69] One crucial difference is that, according to the evidence of the Introduction, Greenblatt fully realizes the problematics of that procedure. His attempt to work within that problematic is certainly powerfully original and a welcome opening of the windows in the closed space of previous academic historicism. But it is still unclear whether the new historicism can fully escape the positivist practices of the old. My suspicion is that the rules of professionalism are at work in producing the quietistic relation to the present that is evident in most of the American new historicists' works: it is easier to take on the old historicists on their own ground, to confront them with historical 'facts' that the old framework is simply unable to accommodate, and thus win an easy victory. The danger, of course, is that such victories will be like the ones produced by the original New Critics' accommodations with the structures of professionalism during that earlier paradigm shift, when everything changed, and yet nothing changed.

In Britain, the situation, and the problems, are somewhat different. There, the analogous theoretical construct, sometimes also called new historicism, but more often 'cultural materialism' (by way of tribute to the late Raymond Williams, who coined the term to describe his own approach), refers to a group of critics led by Jonathan Dollimore and Alan Sinfield who have been explicitly 'Marxist'; and however shifting this signifier has become, it has been studiously avoided by their American counterparts. Otherwise, however, there are quite notable convergences of values and methods, including a common valuing of Foucault, between these family relations. Dollimore's *Radical Tragedy* was perhaps the first sustained sounding of the themes of the British version of new historicism, and the recent anthology *Political*

---

[68] A similar criticism is made by both Howard, in 'The New Historicism in Renaissance Studies' and Pechter, in 'The New Historicism and Its Discontents'.

[69] Jonathan Goldberg has been on the whole an exception in this regard, as a simple reproduction of the title of one of his most provocative works should indicate: *Voice Terminal Echo: Postmodernism and English Renaissance Texts* (New York: Methuen, 1986). Goldberg's work is one of the places where deconstruction and the new historicism meet; he therefore escapes the perhaps too easy classifications of my discussion of contemporary Shakespeare criticism.

Shakespeare: New Essays in Cultural Materialism is the best representative of the trend; indicative of the cross-fertilization in process between the two national groupings, it should be noted, are the inclusion in that volume of essays by Americans Greenblatt and Leonard Tennenhouse.

British cultural materialism has roots in an activist British Left that give it different qualities, different strengths and weaknesses, from the much more academically oriented American new historicism. As I noted, quotations and references to Marx are much more in evidence in the British writings, and there are many more references to contemporary culture and politics than one typically finds among the Americans. These British critics can take advantage of networks of activist faculty, connected through such journals as *Red Letters* or the much better known *New Left Review*. Could one expect to find in an American work a passage on Shakespeare like the following from one of the more provocative products of the milieu I am describing?

In particular the sign of the literary greatness of Shakespeare has played a major part in remaking the late feudal world in the image of the bourgeois settlement that grew up inside it, and eventually brought it down.... Shakespeare's texts, their universality, their 'broad humanism'—even their beauty—have served, in the hands of left and right, to secure in an alien history a value and a point of reference by which the other can be identified as the same, and thus tamed, explained, and even appreciated. ... what is at issue is not that Shakespeare's corpus has been reproduced in order to be reshaped to present needs. ... Nor is it necessary to deny that there are features in the Shakespearian text which lend themselves particularly well to the uses that have been found for them: this probably accounts for their 'greatness' in so far as the literary tradition has been able to celebrate what is, unknown to itself, a narcissistic self-confirmation, 'recognizing' in Shakespeare's transitional and contradictory *œuvre* those elements which are truly its own. It is simply that another history must be written if our account of that corporeal past is not to be merely a case of recapitulating in the pre-revolutionary texts the themes and structures which it was precisely the task of the revolution to establish, by *destroying* the polity whose complex index the Shakespearean discourse was.[70]

In what follows Barker never quite argues for lessening an evaluation of Shakespeare's 'greatness'—a term which his quotation marks indi-

---

[70] Francis Barker, *The Tremulous Private Body: Essays on Subjection* (London: Methuen, 1984), 14–15.

cate must at least be placed under suspicion—but he does wish to redefine its terms and to question the conventional critique of the late
Jacobeans as sensationalistic and decadent, thereby advocating a shift
of emphasis in literary history that would make Shakespeare less
singular. But it should be noticed how more attuned his account is to
the processes of historical periodization and its relation to the ruling
hegemony of the contemporary world—and then to canon-formation
and curriculum-designing—in short, to the social function of literature
in the present—than are virtually any of the American new historians'.
There is a sense of passion and commitment quite different from, say,
Greenblatt's personal but unpolitical accents.

This is not to say, however, that Barker and the other British
cultural materialists are without their own weaknesses, many of which
are intimately connected with what I take to be strengths. The connections to a political Left bring with them, along with passion and commitment, occasional suggestions of the familiar Left vices of
dogmatism and sectarianism. For example, one could gather from
reading Barker and Dollimore's *Radical Tragedy* that humanist English
professors' valorization of subjectivity and 'great works' has been the
main support of the capitalist social order for decades. In effect, as I
argued briefly in the previous chapter, British post-Althusserian
Marxism has yet to assimilate fully the impact of what I here have
called modernization on literary studies and has consequently produced a distorted and one-sided critique of traditional culture, seen only
as a reactionary force in academia and in society. As a result, the
autonomy of culture from politics, which is granted in theory, is too
often forgotten in practice, and a Manichean class-struggle is projected on to disputes which can ill support such political moralization.
At times, reading Barker, one fears having somehow re-entered the
discourse of *International Literature* in the Thirties—or even the *Pooh
Perplex*'s parody of that style—as, for example, in a randomly chosen
passage like the following:

The bourgeoisie, forgetting its revolutionary past as quickly as was decently
possible (and, in England at least, before the classes beneath could learn
anything of significance from it) soon constructs its own discursivity within
which it is next to impossible to think the proposition that the represented—
historical reality itself—is a thing produced. ... It remains a pressing contemporary task to continue Brecht's work and in transvaluating the reception
of the pre-naturalist Jacobean theatre to mobilize it as a critical weapon against
the very naturalism that stifled it ... (p. 21)

The drumbeat of this prose, with its talk of pressing tasks and critical weapons against such dastardly forces as theatrical naturalism, is something that North American letters are blessed to be without. And I note in passing that the Marx–Foucault synthesis implied in Barker's book is a much more problematic enterprise, given Foucault's often stated aversion to orthodox Marxism, than Barker ever indicates.

Dollimore's 1984 work *Radical Tragedy*, a work to which Barker is evidently indebted, is grounded quite consciously in this post-Althusserian Marxist discourse which I briefly described in the Introduction as a stream now drawing closer to broader post-structuralisms of several sorts. Like Greenblatt's *Renaissance Self-Fashioning*, it displays an indebtedness to Foucault and Lacan (and unlike Greenblatt, to Althusser), but where Greenblatt can pass easily into references to the young Marx, Habermas, American anthropology, and a host of other eclectic sources, Dollimore steers a much tighter path by means of a narrower group of approved, post-structuralist-sanctioned theorists which could never include the three I mentioned above—all of whom, for different reasons, having been seen by Althusserians as tainted with 'essentialist' or 'humanist' thinking. The result is a book which strikes many readers as itself tainted with a theological quest for doctrinal purity even while it engages issues of central importance to contemporary theory with insight and intelligence. We might look, for example, at an important passage where Dollimore attempts to face up to the vexed problem of the 'fit' between his new analysis of the Renaissance and so many themes of contemporary Postmodernist theory:

It might be thought that to use the writing of Marx, Brecht, Foucault and others to elucidate early seventeenth-century England, far from restoring a correct historical context for its drama, is itself an unhistorical procedure. Certainly the obvious differences between that period and a more recent materialist tradition should not be minimised. Nevertheless the one has its roots in the other. Brecht develops his dramatic theory in relation to the theatre of the earlier period, and there are real similarities between Althusser's theory of ideology and Montaigne's account of custom. . . . Additionally Perry Anderson has pointed out that much of Althusser's Marxism was drawn directly from Spinoza (1632–97). . . . For the purposes of the present argument the most significant figures . . . are [Galileo and Machiavelli]; Galileo because the decentring of man in Jacobean tragedy was contemporaneous with, and influenced by, the revolution whereby 'man' and 'his' planet were displaced both from the real and the metaphysical centre of the universe:

Machiavelli, because, as Gramsci has argued, he was a pioneer of the 'philosophy of praxis', the most important formulation of which, says Gramsci, is Marxism.[71]

Notice in this formulation the ghost of positivist historicism, as in Tillyard's claim that the British experience of an invasion threat allows us to see clearly what was always there, but for our Whig blinders: Falstaff's perfidy. Here, and throughout the book, Dollimore argues that an anti-humanist, decentred philosophy was already in place in the seventeenth century and now swims into our view since we have removed our post-Enlightenment, humanist blinders. There is a new canon formation at work here, a new list of approved 'greats' who had the good fortune to foreshadow Marx and Foucault. Of course, this is a procedure very much against the grain of the last-mentioned theorist, who had mounted so eloquent a protest over the kind of anti-genealogical search for origins and continuities undertaken here by Dollimore. It is a procedure of the sort objected to by Fredric Jameson when he took exception to a post-structuralist tendency to 'absolutize any historical category of idealism and to thematize any form of error or false consciousness as a transhistorical category'.[72] Of course present theoretical developments *do* indeed cause the past to appear differently, and I have no quarrel with the broad enterprise, pioneered by Dollimore among others, of 're-writing the Renaissance' accordingly. But the treatment of new post-structuralist and Postmodernist categories as in some sense 'objective'—which seems to me an implication of Dollimore's argument above—repeats an illusion shared by both older 'scientific' Marxism and positivist historicism.

Dollimore is far more effective when, as in the Introduction to *Political Shakespeare*, he interrogates the totalizing tendency of Greenblatt, borrowed from the 'structuralist' Foucault, to conceptualize the workings of power as a web so tight that there is no escape from it. In his insistence on demystifying this monolithic view of power and showing the ways in which resistance to power can form in spite of strategies of containment,[73] Dollimore makes use of a suppler Foucault and also displays the continuing influence of Raymond Wil-

---

[71] Jonathan Dollimore, *Radical Tragedy: Religion, Ideology and Power in the Drama of Shakespeare and His Contemporaries* (Brighton: Harvester, 1984), 154–5.

[72] Fredric Jameson, *Political Unconscious: Narrative as a Socially Symbolic Act* (Ithaca, NY: Cornell University Press, 1981), 59 n. 36.

[73] *Political Shakespeare: New Essays in Cultural Materialism*, ed. Jonathan Dollimore and Alan Sinfield (Ithaca, NY: Cornell University Press, 1985), 11–12.

liams's original contributions to the British Left as still potent—and needed more than ever.

At the beginning of this discussion of the new historicism and cultural materialism, I indicated that the apparently divergent fears of Howard and Pechter—that the new methodology might prove an attack on 'theory' or, alternatively, that it might destroy the Arnoldian mission of humanizing capitalist society—both had a familiar ring. Equally, however, both fears are real and undismissible. They derive directly from the material condition of English studies as an institution in modernized societies, and the ultimate position of the new historicism will clearly depend on how it adapts to those conditions.

There are certainly enough openings to an earlier positivism and enough continuity with the older historicism to envision Howard's fears coming true. Greenblatt and Dollimore could be used, like Tillyard, to supply a new set of themes and ideas for 'readings' of works that continue the pluralist game of the criticism of credentialing. Similarly, the totalizing tendencies of Greenblatt's theory[74] and the doctrinaire residues of the Althusserian phase of British post-Althusserian Marxism suggest a potential for turning the new historicism into an ideological practice for a socially isolated and élitist professorate content to explain the powerlessness of everyone else as a bitter (non) acknowledgement of their/our own impotence.

Against these powerful tendencies are the values of liberation and critique, the grasp of the interconnections of the past and present, and the consciousness of the complicities of much of English studies in imperialism and patriarchialism. The depletion of the Modernist 'cultural' mission is now apparent virtually everywhere, but it may prove possible to re-function culture in the new conditions of Postmodernism and to confront the situation of a radical professorate in a politically quiescent society without succumbing to either élitism or despair. Some valuable suggestions for such a positive eventuality can be glimpsed, I believe, in certain aspects of contemporary Shakespearian feminism.

Feminist Criticism

Of the three Postmodernist-influenced critical practices under discussion here, that which can conveniently be labelled 'feminist' has the

[74] In the opening chapter of his most recent book Greenblatt has criticized his earlier views of Shakespeare's England as a 'totalizing society' as too monolithic, implying a

greatest claim to autonomy from the others, but, as we shall see, it has sufficient affinities to more than justify the claim of a connection to Postmodernism. Unlike the other two, it has clear links to a large and significant mass movement beyond academia, and its intervention within Shakespeare studies was a direct outcome of the influence of that movement. Its grounding in a social 'interest' (the emancipation of women) is overt, again in direct contradistinction to deconstruction and to American new historicism if not British cultural materialism, and it is much less theoretically unitary, making use of a variety of pre-existing and emerging critical paradigms inflected to suit the interest being served. Despite such theoretical disparateness, however, feminist Shakespearians form a distinct interacting discourse community.[75]

The influence of a feminist mass movement on Shakespeare studies is easy to document, thanks to the publication of the feminist critical anthology *The Woman's Part* in 1980. In the Introduction the editors explain how in 1976 the convening of a Special Session of Feminist Criticism of Shakespeare at the annual MLA convention showed widespread, spontaneous interest in a feminist intervention in Shakespeare studies and at least two other projects to that end already underway.[76] The editors report approximately 100 submissions to their announced critical anthology,[77] and their acknowledgement of previous feminist theorists—de Beauvoir, Firestone, Greer, Mitchell, Rowbotham, Dinnerstein—is drawn directly from the larger American women's movement of the Seventies.

The Woman's Part was by no means the sole pioneer of Shakespearian feminism; the editors, in a conscious attempt to found what they called a 'tradition', list a number of past works with feminist connections, and they acknowledge in particular the then recent work of Phyllis Rackin (p. x) and Juliet Dusinberre (pp. 7–8). But the book was a milestone and is still revelatory of some of the unique and shared characteristics of Shakespearian feminism.

'structural unity and stability of command belied by much of what I actually knew about the exercise of authority and force in the period'—see *Shakespearean Negotiations: The Circulation of Social Energy in Renaissance England* (Berkeley: University of California Press, 1988), 1–20.

[75] For fuller bibliographical detail on feminist Shakespearian criticism, see Peter Erickson, 'Feminist Criticism of Shakespeare', in *The Study of Women: History, Religion, Literature and the Arts*, ed. Helen Tierney (Westport Conn.: Greenwood, forthcoming).

[76] One of these resulted in two special issues of the journal *Women's Studies* on feminist Shakespeare criticism—see Vol. 9, nos. 1–2 (1981–2).

[77] Preface, *The Woman's Part: Feminist Criticism of Shakespeare*, ed. Carolyn Lenz, Gayle Greene, and Carol Neely (Urbana: University of Illinois Press, 1980).

The editors are explicit, for example, in noting the opportunistic but selective borrowing from existing critical paradigms. This 1980 anthology expresses a 'substantial debt to New Criticism'. The debt is qualified, it is true—and I will return shortly to this point—with the proviso that such use is for a purpose 'other than, larger than, the discovery of unity in the text'. There is also a clear debt to historical criticism and psychoanalysis, reader-response theory, Marxism, structuralism, and, in one case, to what will come to be called deconstruction. The index lists seven references to Freud, one to Marx, but no mention of either Foucault or Derrida.

Operating just underneath a deliberately cultivated 'pragmatic and provisional' eclecticism, however, can be discerned tactics which are recognizably Postmodernist in the two senses I defined above. There is in the first place a deliberate suspension of the search for the 'organic unity' of the work, particularly that New Critical unity formed through the unification (and therefore subordination) of dramatic conflict and ambiguity. Second, this feminist discourse obviously is founded in one of the central anti-hierarchical impulses of the present period, the interrogation of the long historical subordination of female to male with all its attendant subordinations. Only through the suspension of unity and the disabling of female textual subordination is it possible for the 'woman's part' to emerge from the Shakespearian text from the safely contained contours of previous traditional readings.

Let me cite as an example one particular essay that has aged well in the years since the publication of the work, Madelon Gohlke's ' "I wooed thee with my sword": Shakespeare's Tragic Paradigms'.[78]

Influenced by Gayatri Spivak's Marxist-feminist inflection of deconstruction, Gohlke follows a strategy of analysing certain metaphors in the play in order to arrive at an understanding of 'unconsciously held cultural beliefs' particularly as they determine the play's thinking about the roles of men and women. She discovers clearly patriarchal ideology at work in such passages as Hamlet's verbal denigration of Ophelia and his fantasy of Gertrude's betrayal. 'Interwoven into the patriarchal structure of Shakespeare's tragedies', she writes, 'is an equally important matriarchal vision' (p. 159), and she is able to demonstrate with the new tools of deconstruction the impossibility of subordinating one 'vision' to the other.

---

[78] Madelon Gohlke, ' "I wooed thee with my sword": Shakespeare's Tragic Paradigms', in *Woman's Part*, 150–70.

More clearly here than anywhere else in the book, we see a convergence between a version of New Criticism committed to disowning unity, but committed to the ambiguity of the text, and more properly Derridean procedures of close reading. Later deconstructors might take exception to various aspects of this original discourse, but there are clear parallels—and a common influence from Postmodernist aesthetics.

A case in point is Coppélia Khan, who makes use of Melanie Klein's feminist-inflected psychoanalysis, which is unrelated to post-structuralism. But her strategy of suspending previously assumed hierarchies (centrally, male heroic violence/female submissive pacifism) allows her to read *Romeo and Juliet* as a play representing the 'tragic self-destruction of patriarchal society'[79] and displays its own anti-hierarchical connections to the Postmodern.

While feminist criticism shares with deconstruction and the new historicism a common indebtedness to Postmodernism, it displays a very different relationship from the other two to professionalism. This in fact is the characteristic that gives feminist criticism much of its interest, as I will stress below. Coming as it did in the wake of Kate Millet's widely publicized *Sexual Politics*, much of the earlier feminist criticism attempted to answer the scandalously unprofessional question, was Shakespeare a feminist or a male chauvinist? Of course, professionalized critical paradigms were brought to bear in the attempts to answer such inquiries. In fact, two feminist studies employing historicist methods tended to set the terms for this debate. In the earlier of the two, Juliet Dusinberre staked out the ground for Shakespeare as a feminist, arguing in detail that a kind of feminism was implied in Puritan ideas on marriage reform and the Puritan attack on medieval notions of chastity; Shakespeare's idealized female characters, Dusinberre argued, embodied the influence of such new ideas.[80]

She was answered by Lisa Jardine in 1983 in terms broadly condemnatory of much contemporary feminist criticism. Jardine argued in contrast that Elizabethan and Jacobean Puritanism, as well as aristocratic humanism, had only very limited effects on women's social condition, actually serving to place women in a double-bind of con-

---

[79] 'Coming of Age in Verona', in *Woman's Part*, 171–93.

[80] Juliet Dusinberre, *Shakespeare and the Nature of Women* (London: Macmillan, 1975). Dusinberre emphasizes that she sees Puritanism as a broad movement within the Church of England that attempted to place greater emphasis on Calvinist Protestantism. The sectarianism and hostility to the theatre which we associate with the Puritanism of a later day were not prominent in the movement which she defines.

flicting 'duties'. Read in this particular context, she argues, Shakespeare's plays are implicated in the same double-binds.[81]

A third position within this controversy—an outright condemnation of Shakespeare's 'patriarchialism'—has been far rarer than might be supposed.[82] Much more influential has been the anti-hierarchical 'opening-up' of the text to feminist perspectives pioneered in Dusinberre (through historicism) and *The Woman's Part* writers (through a modified New Criticism and feminist psychoanalysis).

Because of this willingness to make flexible and opportunist use of critical methodologies which are now decidedly of an older paradigm, Kahn and others of these comparatively early feminists have been taken to task in the Eighties as post-structuralism has sought to impose its own narratives and categories on critical history. Linda Bamber, author of *Comic Women, Tragic Men*, has had the dubious distinction of being attacked in this regard from both sides of the Atlantic in two of the most prominent anthologies of new critical methods. She came under the fire of Jonathan Goldberg in *Shakespeare and the Question of Theory* and Kathleen McLuskie in *The Political Shakespeare* as 'reductive' (McLuskie, p. 89) and given to 'rigidity' and 'blindness' (Goldberg, p. 117). It will be necessary, then, to pause briefly over Bamber's work in order to get concretely at the causes of the rhetorical polemics.

In her 1983 *Comic Women, Tragic Men* Bamber took as her context Dusinberre and Kahn, wishing to define herself in opposition to, as she saw it, their attempts to interpret Shakespeare as if his work directly supported and developed feminist ideas (p. 1). At the same time, she believed, the Shakespearian texts could not simply be

---

[81] *Still Harping on Daughters: Women and Drama in the Age of Shakespeare* (Totowa, NJ: Barnes and Nobles, 1983).

[82] Jonathan Goldberg, in his 'Shakespearean Inscriptions: The Voicings of Power', in Parker and Hartman, *Shakespeare and the Question of Theory*, 116–37), feared that such a position ('Shakespeare ... inevitably expressing the positions of a patriarchal culture', p. 117) was becoming 'the forefront of a new approach to Shakespeare', and he feels it is a straitjacket ill-suited to Shakespeare's complex texts. But the major example of this trend that he cites, Linda Bamber's *Comic Women, Tragic Men: A Study of Gender and Genre in Shakespeare* (Stanford, Calif.: Stanford University Press, 1982), actually situates itself as a reaction to Kate Millet's style of indictment as well as to Dusinberre's claims for Shakespearian feminism (p. 1). Shakespeare cannot be assimilated to feminism, she writes—but he is still 'a hero for feminists not because he shares the feminist perspective but because in every genre but history he associates the feminine with whatever is outside himself he takes most seriously' (pp. 5–6). There is plenty here for Goldberg to argue with—and I will return to the interesting confrontation between these two. My point is, however, that Bamber doesn't assimilate Shakespeare to patriarchy any more than to feminism.

assimilated to the ideologies of patriarchy either. Her solution is to attempt to distinguish between a 'masculine' point of view in Shakespeare (that sees woman as Other) and outright 'sexual chauvinism' which she believes not to characterize Shakespeare's texts. The theoretical underpinning of this attempt is developed from her inflection of Simone de Beauvoir's celebrated discussion of woman as Other in *The Second Sex*, by way of Bamber's extended meditation on, and reaction to, Leslie Fiedler's use of the concept of otherness in *The Stranger in Shakespeare*. The result is a theoretical framework which is a kind of one-take *combinatoire*: the Self in Shakespeare is always masculine, the Other Feminine; but the comedies are built around the female Other, the tragedies around a masculine Self. After an opening chapter which established this framework, the book explores it in five additional chapters of readings of several plays.

Now when McLuskie excoriates Bamber for her being reductive or Jonathan Goldberg complains of her rigidity and blindness, it is not difficult to see their point. Bamber's analyses are devoid of the notion of 'textuality', of the complex chains of signification which such basic dichotomies as those she explores inevitably generate as they unfold. She had not been influenced by the criticism which defined such insights, and so her assertions seem too simple and unnuanced.

On the other hand, if we place Bamber within *her* proper critical paradigm and take a broader, more material view of all of the critical texts and their social situations, we will see ways in which rather than being in direct conflict (in one sense they certainly are), this kind of feminism and post-structuralism are simply disparate but related Postmodernist paradigms bespeaking different social 'places', different enabling assumptions, and representing different reactions to the changing situations of Shakespeare studies in an emerging Postmodernist age.

Bamber's book clearly speaks out of the 'moment' of *The Woman's Place*;[83] it derives from largely Anglo-American critical paradigms at a moment when the long hegemonic anti-theoretical biases of empiricism were only just giving way to a growing perception of a need for

---

[83] This point needs qualification, however. Bamber's book has been criticized for a relative isolation from the work of other feminist critics, even though in a broader sense it derives from many of the same political and critical sources. The relative isolation is described succinctly by Lynda E. Boose, Review of *Comic Women, Tragic Men, Modern Philology*, 82, no. 1 (Aug. 1984), 91–5).

'theory'. And had not one of the first of the theoretical imports, Lévi-Strauss's structuralism, authorized the practice of *bricolage*, the taking to hand of whatever theoretical materials one was in possession of and building with them? Such theoretical structures as were built in this process would seem rigid and reductionist only if they were taken as permanent dwellings for literary critics to inhabit. Their builders, in contrast, understood them differently—as temporary structures enabling critics to make certain discoveries which could then be abandoned as one moved on to other areas. In the words of the preface to *The Woman's Part*, the theory is always 'pragmatic and provisional' (p. 3); the *interest* underneath the theory, the will to emancipation, would supply the more permanent habitation for an emerging paradigm of (pragmatic) American feminists.

Clearly, then, an attitude toward theory emerges here quite distinct from, say, Goldberg's or McLuskie's. There is a deliberate cultivation of pluralism. A single, shared theory has been avoided, through whatever combinations of serendipity and planning. Unity has been supplied by a social practice rather than a theory. But because deconstruction and the new historicism exist, precisely, as theoretical constructs without a clear social base outside the academy,[84] they tend to overestimate the social power of theory as such.

At least three recent productions of Shakespearian feminism have addressed the issue of an apparent conflict between feminism and its new historicist critics. Each of them does so by attempting to define the material conditions under which the competing discourses have been produced, a direction I obviously find promising. In a closely reasoned analysis of the competing claims of American new historicists and feminists in Shakespeare studies, Peter Erickson attempts to define the social and ideological differences of the two critical trends. He finds the origins of the labels used by each group to be symptomatic of the differences between them: 'The term "feminist" comes from a political movement outside academic research . . .' he writes. ' "New historicism", the phrase coined by Stephen Greenblatt to describe the methods he himself pioneered . . . has a proprietary appearance whether intended or not. Both labels present problems.'[85]

Feminism, with its extra-academic affiliations, is looser, more

---

[84] In the case of British cultural materialism's links to the Left, the same problem is just deferred one more step. The question then becomes the problem of the Marxist Left's social base.

[85] Peter Erickson, 'Rewriting the Renaissance, Rewriting Ourselves', *Shakespeare Quarterly*, 38 (Autumn 1987), 330.

decentralist, less clearly defined; the new historicism, by contrast, if not without pluralism and disputation, is tighter and better defined— more 'centred' around certain authoritative founding texts like Greenblatt's.[86] Shrewdly, I believe, Erickson goes on to identify the most enabling critical 'blindspot' of the new historicism in its refusal to address its own political situation in the present:

... a primary reason for the tension between new historicism and feminist criticism lies not only in their disagreement about the relative importance of gender, but also in their conflicting attitudes toward the present. In general, where new historicism regards the present as an influence to be neutralized, or escaped, feminist criticism views the present—including the lives we are living or able to imagine now—as a vital resource and a source of strength.[87]

Erickson goes on to make several important qualifications to these observations. The feminist present should not be used to collapse the historical differences which the new historicists rightly insist on, and he finds in the work of Louis Montrose a partial exception to his strictures. But the main point, I believe, that feminist criticism has been much more open to the reality of the impact of the present on our readings of the past than has the new historicism, is well taken[88] and crucially important.

Similarly Lynda E. Boose has recently surveyed the state of debate on the family in Shakespeare studies and focused attention on the feminist-new historicist confrontation,[89] arguing that the failure of American new historicism to pursue questions of gender systems and the family—'new historicism's progressive reassertion of the priority of the public and political over the private and domestic'[90]—constitutes an ideological blindspot connected to its critique of the Shakespearian feminists. Quite accurately, I believe, Boose pinpoints the investment of much new historicism in power-oriented professional discourses that feminists have been much more aware of and in opposition to— though they have of course not solved all the problems inherent in

[86] Ibid., pp. 330–1.

[87] Ibid., p. 335.

[88] Erickson cites Jean Howard's 'The New Historicism in Renaissance Studies' and Margaret W. Ferguson's Introduction to *Rewriting the Renaissance* as having made similar comments on the new historicism (*Rewriting the Renaissance: The Discourses of Sexual Difference in Early Modern Europe*, ed. Margaret W. Ferguson, Maureen Quilligan, and Nancy J. Vickers (Chicago, Ill.: University of Chicago Press, 1986), xv–xxxi).

[89] Lynda E. Boose, 'The Family in Shakespeare Studies; or—Studies in the Family of Shakespeareans; or—The Politics of Politics', *Renaissance Quarterly*, 40 (Winter 1987), 707–42.

[90] Ibid., p. 738.

attempting both to make use of and refashion the social position of professionals:

> Existing within a discipline that increasingly valorizes theory and scorns the idea of literary criticism as a pluralistic community of interpretive acts, feminist literary criticism—which is frequently defined as something more like an 'approach' than a coherent and definable 'theory'—repeatedly goes at buffets with itself over this issue. There are those who see defining an adequately theorized position as both essential for survival and a mark of maturity within the discipline. There are others, however, who view 'theory' as aridly male and see the most fundamental definition of feminist criticism as radically inseparable from pluralistic interpretation and resistance to self-theorizing. In all these internal debates, what liberal American feminism has seemed most uneasy about is the totalizing tendency of theory—the impulse that necessitates contestation and turns the literary profession into a shoot 'em out at the You're-Not-O.K. Corral. . . . But that American feminist criticism has remained reluctant to embrace the dialectical model of a perpetually competitive struggle for power and dominance is not only a resistance that is thoroughly consistent with the gendering process of socialization. It is equally a political assertion of difference meant to affirm those particular behaviors that culture has marked out as 'female'.[91]

Boose also speaks of on-going changes within the Shakespearian feminist community, involving a greater attention to historical specificity and welcoming the potential contributions which the new historicism could make to the feminist project[92]—a potential, however, which she finds still unfulfilled.

The most recent of these three 'defences' of feminism, by Carol Neely, is most explicit in addressing the charge, often heard from poststructuralist-influenced critics, that Shakespearian feminism has been 'essentialist', that is, invested in notions of unchanging human and gender natures. Neely argues instead that there is convergence between the approaches to gender taken by feminism and post-structuralism in a shared assumption that 'gender roles are culturally and textually constructed'.[93] She goes on to define a series of differences with the newer methods as well, affirming the usefulness of a notion of 'femaleness' which is 'part biological, part psychical, part experiential, part cultural and that is not utterly inscribed by and in thrall to patriarchal ideology and that makes possible female discourse, a

---

[91] Ibid., pp. 718–19.
[92] Ibid., pp. 726, 730.
[93] Carol Thomas Neely, 'Constructing the Subject: Feminist Practice and the New Renaissance Discourses', *English Literary Renaissance*, 18 (Winter 1988), 7.

women's literary history, a feminist critique which can do more than lament its own inevitable co-optation or suppression'.[94] If these assertions by Neely, a co-editor of *The Woman's Part*, can be taken as representative of American Shakespearian feminism as it has developed since 1976, then the charge of 'essentialism' seems at best partial and at worst misleading. And in her objections to the more totalizing and monolithic tendencies of the new historicism, there is a distinct similarity to concerns voiced by several American and British new historicists.

From my point of view, a cross-fertilization and mutual influence among all three of the recent trends I am discussing would be the most welcome development, and signs of such a development are most apparent within the field of feminist theory. The 1989 annual meeting of the Shakespeare Association of America included a seminar on 'Materialist-Feminist Criticism of Shakespeare' in which the eighteen participants attempted to work out theoretically and practically a new version of feminism more influenced by Marxism, the new historicism, and deconstruction[95] than was the case with what participants began to call the 'older' Shakespearian feminism. But there need be no great wall between the older and newer feminisms. If the older feminism in Shakespeare studies had been theoretically marked by the contingencies of its moment of birth with investments in critical methodologies which are ageing fast, its practitioners are also changing and developing[96] — and it has allowed us to glimpse possibilities which seemed to elude the other two Postmodernist critical discourses I have examined here: the possibilities of a self-conscious confrontation by literary professionals with the forms and enabling assumptions of their power/knowledge. Feminism can make one of its greatest contribu-

---

[94] Ibid., p. 7.

[95] Here, too, there was no unanimity, but several contributors attempted to define the complex interactions of class and gender within specific plays. Frequently cited as a theoretical source for the newer feminism was the anthology *Feminist Criticism and Social Change: Sex, Class, and Race in Literature and Culture*, ed. Judith Newton and Deborah Rosenfelt (New York: Methuen, 1985), especially 'Introduction: Toward a Materialist-Feminist Criticism' by the editors. Of relevance also is the experience of American socialist-feminist theory from the Seventies—see Barbara Ehrenreich, 'Life Without Father: Reconsidering Socialist-Feminist Theory', *Socialist Review*, 14, no. 1 (Jan.–Feb. 1984), 48–57.

[96] Coppélia Kahn, a contributor to *The Woman's Part*, for example, writes: 'Feminist criticism is moving so fast now that the critical premises of many of its modes are subjected daily to fresh interrogations'—see Review of *Broken Nuptials in Shakespeare's Plays* by Carol Thomas Neely, *Shakespeare Quarterly*, 38 (Autumn 1987), 371. And see Neely's 'Constructing the Subject', cited above, n. 93.

tions by continuing to insist on speaking to larger social needs outside the profession and by continuing to develop alternative, less power-centred modes of professional interaction as the profession begins at last to become aware of the sea of professionalism in which it is swimming.

Prospects for the Postmodern Shakespeare

The methods of critique I have employed throughout this study have necessarily been negative, attempting to capture the movement of cultural development and confront it with its ideological blindspots and omissions. Here I want to step back from that approach momentarily, or rather extend the negative critique forward to a positive moment. I want to speak of the directions I wish, in a frankly Utopian mode, Shakespeare studies could proceed along if it is to confront and overcome the tensions I have uncovered as impelling its recent history.

In the first place, I hope Shakespearians can join in the tentative efforts now underway everywhere to rethink and refashion 'culture' for a Postmodern era. So much of the excitement of the older Shakespearian criticism of our century—the great interventions of Knight, of Leavis and *Scrutiny*, of Tillyard, and of the American New Critics—derived from their passionate commitment to renew the cultural tradition that they saw as one of the bulwarks against an otherwise value-destroying modernization. In our era, their efforts are manifestly depleted and inadequate, made obsolete by the vast social and cultural changes which of course their conserving efforts could not halt.

In our day, 'culture' needs to be seen to include the products of the electronic revolution and the collapse of the old distinction between high art and the popular; it needs to be decentred, opened up to the voices of the marginalized and repressed majority who have been excluded and denigrated even in the greatest and most indispensable works of our heritage. But the work of the agents of culture that Raymond Williams and Gramsci, Benjamin and Adorno, identified as crucial for a liberatory outcome of the capitalist phase of human history must be reinvented for a new age and new audiences. Already, there is no reason to doubt—on the contrary, there is every reason to suppose—that Shakespeare's works will continue to find new interpretations and new audiences in Postmodern culture. We have only now begun to move in this direction.

For most Shakespearians, there is no escaping the confines of a profession which is now, for better and for worse, the main repository of the older cultural traditions which it continually undermines. The underlying forms of this profession—derived from its basis in power and bureaucracy—have proved more resistant to critique and transforming practice than has its sometimes nemesis, the cultural tradition. If we can speak of a beginning in process for a Postmodern re-functioning of culture, we are really still searching for effective strategies to resist the corrosive, normalizing powers of an almost invisible process in which so many of us are caught up, without giving up the Utopian, critical dimension of professionalism, which has produced so much of value along with dross. And if there is no transformation of the basic social structures that have created today's professionalized literary criticism through wishful thinking or nostalgic longing for an idealized past,[97] there is certainly an opportunity in the present climate of change to re-examine and rethink such basic components of the literary profession as specialization through periods, the role of critical writing as credential and as social contribution, and the relation of literature to other aspects of culture.

If Shakespeare studies could proceed with the kind of self-critical, imaginative, and unthreatened transformation of this sort, then the Postmodern Shakespeare, in complex archaeological relations with its previous history, would then become the most widely experienced and most widely influential Shakespeare of all.

---

[97] The idealization of the past and a naïve view that we could simply return to it are the great weaknesses of the recent report from the National Endowment for the Humanities by its chairman, Lynne V. Cheney, *Humanities in America: A Report to the President, the Congress, and the American People* (Washington, DC: National Endowment for the Humanities, Sept. 1988). Nevertheless, Cheney used the work of Gerald Graff and others in writing the report, and the critique of what she terms 'overspecialization' as corrosive to the social mission of the humanities is often on-target. Ironically, from my point of view, Cheney goes on to attack as a twin evil the emergence of 'politicizing' tendencies in literary study, tendencies which I believe have the greatest potential for making the humanities socially relevant again.

Bibliography

ACKERMAN, JAMES S., 'The Demise of the Avant-Garde: Notes on the Sociology of Recent American Art', *Comparative Studies in Society and History*, 11 (Oct. 1969), 371–84.

ADORNO, THEODOR, *Aesthetic Theory*, ed. Gretel Adorno and Rold Tiedmann, trans. C. Lenhardt (Boston: Routledge, 1984).

—— 'Theses upon Art and Religion Today', *Kenyon Review*, 7 (Autumn 1945), 676–82.

ALTHUSSER, LOUIS, *For Marx*, trans. Ben Brewster (London: New Left Books, 1977).

—— 'Ideology and Ideological State Apparatuses (Notes towards an Investigation)', in his *Lenin and Philosophy and Other Essays*, (New York: Monthly Review Press, 1971), 127–86.

ANDERSON, PERRY, 'Components of the National Culture', *New Left Review*, 50 (May–June 1968), 3–57.

APPLEBEE, ARTHUR N., *Tradition and Reform in the Teaching of English: A History* (Urbana, Ill.: National Council of Teachers of English, 1974).

ARAC, JONATHAN (ed.), *Postmodernism and Politics* (Minneapolis: University of Minnesota Press, 1986).

ATKINS, G. DOUGLAS, and BERGERON, DAVID M. (eds.), *Shakespeare and Deconstruction* (New York: Peter Lang, 1988).

BAMBER, LINDA, *Comic Women, Tragic Men: A Study of Gender and Genre in Shakespeare* (Stanford, Calif.: Stanford University Press, 1982).

BARKER, FRANCIS, *The Tremulous Private Body: Essays on Subjection* (London: Methuen, 1984).

BATSLEER, JANET *et al.* (eds.), *Rewriting English: Cultural Politics of Gender and Class* (London: Methuen, 1985).

BATTENHOUSE, ROY, 'Falstaff as Parodist and Perhaps Holy Fool, *PMLA* 90 (January 1975), 32–52.

BENJAMIN, WALTER, *Illuminations*, ed. Hannah Arendt, trans. Harry Zohn (New York: Schocken, 1969).

BENTLEY, ERIC, 'This is the New Criticism', *Kenyon Review*, 8 (Autumn 1946), 672–4.

BERGERON, DAVID, *Shakespeare: A Study and Research Guide* (London: Macmillan, 1975).

BERMAN, ART, *From the New Criticism to Deconstruction: The Reception of Structuralism and Post-Structuralism* (Urbana: University of Illinois Press, 1988).

BERMAN, MARSHALL, *All That Is Solid Melts into Air: The Experience of Modernity* (New York: Simon and Schuster, 1982).

BLOOM, HAROLD, *The Anxiety of Influence: A Theory of Poetry* (New York: Oxford University Press, 1973).

— 'The Central Man: Emerson, Whitman, Wallace Stevens', *Massachusetts Review*, 7 (Winter 1966), 23–42.

— 'The Internalization of Quest-Romance', in *Romanticism and Consciousness: Essays in Criticism*, ed. Harold Bloom (New York: Norton, 1970), 3–24.

BOOSE, LYNDA E., 'The Family in Shakespeare Studies; or—Studies in the Family of Shakespearians; or—The Politics of Politics', *Renaissance Quarterly*, 40 (Winter 1987), 707–42.

— Review of *Comic Women, Tragic Men: Gender and Genre in Shakespeare*, *Modern Philology*, 82, No. 1 (August 1984), 91–5.

BOVÉ, PAUL, *Intellectuals in Power: A Genealogy of Critical Humanism* (New York: Columbia University Press, 1986).

BRADBURY, MALCOLM, and McFARLANE, JAMES (eds.), *Modernism* (New York: Penguin, 1976).

BRADLEY, A. C., 'The Rejection of Falstaff' (1902); repr. in his *Oxford Lectures on Poetry* (London: Macmillan, 1959), 247–78.

BRAVERMAN, HARRY, *Labor and Monopoly Capital: The Degradation of Work in the Twentieth Century* (New York: Monthly Review Press, 1974).

BRISTOL, MICHAEL, *Shakespeare's America, America's Shakespeare* (London: Routledge, 1989).

BROOKS, CLEANTH, *The Well-Wrought Urn* (New York: Harcourt, 1947).

— and HEILMAN, ROBERT B., *Understanding Drama* (New York: Holt, 1945).

BURCKHARDT, SIGURD, *Shakespearean Meanings* (Princeton, NJ: Princeton University Press, 1968).

BÜRGER, PETER, *Theory of the Avant-Garde*, trans. Michael Shaw (Minneapolis: University of Minneapolis Press, 1984).

BUTLER, FRANCELIA, *The Strange Critical Fortunes of Shakespeare's 'Timon of Athens'* (Ames: Iowa State University Press, 1966).

CAIN, WILLIAM, E., *The Crisis in Criticism: Theory, Literature and Reform in English Studies* (Baltimore, Md.: Johns Hopkins University Press, 1984).

CAMPBELL, LILY, *Shakespeare's 'Histories': Mirrors of Elizabethan Policy* (San Marino, Calif.: Huntington Library, 1947).

CAMPBELL, O. J., and QUIN, E. G. (eds.), *The Reader's Encyclopedia of Shakespeare* (New York: Crowell, 1966).

CARR, E. H., *Socialism in One Country (1924–26)*, vol. 1 (1958; repr. Harmondsworth: Penguin, 1970).

CHAMBERS, E. K., *Shakespeare: A Survey* (London: Sidgewick & Jackson, 1925).

CHENEY, LYNNE V., *Humanities in America: A Report to the President, the Congress, and the American People* (Washington, DC: National Endowment for the Humanities, September 1988).

CLEMEN, WOLFGANG, *The Development of Shakespeare's Imagery* (London: Methuen, 1951).

COLERIDGE, S. T., *Shakespearean Criticism*, extracted in *English Romantic Writers*, ed. David Perkins (New York: Harcourt, 1967), 496–502.

COWAN, LOUISE, *The Fugitive Group: A Literary History* (Baton Rouge: Louisiana State University Press, 1959).

— *The Southern Critics: An Introduction to the Criticism of John Crowe Ransom, Allen Tate, Donald Davidson, Robert Penn Warren, Cleanth Brooks, and Andrew Lytle* (Dallas, Tex.: University of Dallas Press, 1972).

DANBY, JOHN, *Shakespeare's Doctrine of Nature: A Study of 'King Lear'* (London: Faber, 1949).

DE GRAZIA, MARGRETA, 'The Essential Shakespeare and the Material Book', *Textual Practice*, 2, No. 1 (Spring 1988), 69–87.

— *Shakespeare Verbatim: The Reproduction of Authenticity and the 1790 Apparatus* (Oxford: Oxford University Press, 1991).

DE MAN, PAUL, *Allegories of Reading: Figural Language in Rousseau, Nietzsche, Rilke, and Proust* (New Haven, Conn.: Yale University Press, 1979).

DEAN, LEONARD F., 'Shakespeare's Treatment of Conventional Ideas', *Sewanee Review*, 52 (Summer 1944), 414–23.

DEWS, PETER, 'Adorno, Post-Structuralism and the Critique of Identity', *New Left Review*, 157 (May/June 1986), 28–44.

— *Logics of Disintegration: Post-Structuralist Thought and the Claims of Critical Theory* (London: Verso, 1987).

DOLLIMORE, JONATHAN, 'Introduction: Shakespeare, Cultural Materialism and the New Historicism', in Dollimore and Sinfield, *Political Shakespeare*, 2–17.

— *Radical Tragedy: Religion, Ideology and Power in the Drama of Shakespeare and His Contemporaries* (Sussex: Harvester, 1984).

— and SINFIELD, ALAN, 'History and Ideology', in Drakakis, *Alternative Shakespeares*, 206–27.

— (eds.), *Political Shakespeare: New Essays in Cultural Materialism.* (Ithaca, NY: Cornell University Press, 1985).

DRAKAKIS, JOHN (ed.), *Alternative Shakespeares* (New York: Methuen, 1985).

DREYFUS, HUBERT, and RABINOW, PAUL, *Michel Foucault: Beyond Structuralism and Hermeneutics*, 2nd edn. (Chicago, Ill.: University of Chicago Press, 1983).

DUSINBERRE, JULIET, *Shakespeare and the Nature of Women* (London: Macmillan, 1975).

EAGLETON, TERRY, *The Function of Criticism: From 'The Spectator' to Post-Structuralism* (London: Verso, 1984).

— *Literary Theory: An Introduction* (Minneapolis: University of Minnesota Press, 1983).

— *Walter Benjamin: Or, Towards a Revolutionary Criticism* (London: Verso, 1981).

— *William Shakespeare* (Oxford: Basil Blackwell, 1986).

EASTMAN, ARTHUR M., *A Short History of Shakespearean Criticism* (New York: Random, 1968).

EASTMEN, RICHARD M., 'Political Views in *Henry IV, Part I*: A Demonstration of Liberal Humanism', *College English*, 33 (May 1972), 901–7.

EHRENREICH, JOHN, and EHRENREICH, BARBARA, 'The Professional-Managerial Class', in *Between Capital and Labor*, ed. Pat Walker (Boston, Mass.: South End, 1979), 5–45.

ELIOT, T. S., *The Sacred Wood* (1920; repr. New York: Barnes, 1964).

— Introduction to G. Wilson Knight, *The Wheel of Fire*.

— *Selected Essays* (New York: Harcourt, 1964).

— 'Shakespearean Criticism: I. From Dryden to Coleridge', in *A Companion to Shakespeare Studies*, ed. Harley Granville-Barker and G. B. Harrison (1934; repr. Cambridge: Cambridge University Press, 1949).

ELLIS-FERMOR, UNA, *The Frontiers of Drama* (1945; repr. New York: Methuen, 1964).

— ' "Timon of Athens": An Unfinished Play', *Review of English Studies*, 18 (July 1942), 270–83.

ERICKSON, PETER, 'Rewriting the Renaissance, Rewriting Ourselves', *Shakespeare Quarterly*, 38 (Autumn 1987), 327–37.

FEKETE, JOHN, *The Critical Twilight: Explorations in the Ideology of Anglo-American Literary Theory from Eliot to McLuhan* (London: Routledge, 1977).

FELPERIN, HOWARD, *Beyond Deconstruction: The Uses and Abuses of Literary Theory* (1985; repr. Oxford: Oxford University Press, 1987).

— *Shakespearean Romance* (Princeton, NJ: Princeton University Press, 1972).

FINEMAN, DANIEL A., Biographical Introduction to Maurice Morgann, *Shakespearean Criticism*, ed. Daniel A. Fineman (Oxford: Clarendon, 1972), 3–36.

FLEAY, FREDERICK GARD, 'On the Authorship of "Timon of Athens", *Transactions of the New Shakspere Society*, 1st ser. 1 (1874), 130–51.

— *Shakespeare Manual* (1876; repr. New York: AMS Press, 1970).

FOSTER, HAL (ed.), *The Anti-Aesthetic: Essays on Postmodern Culture* (Port Townsend, Wash.: Bay, 1983).

FOUCAULT, MICHEL, *The Archaeology of Knowledge*, trans. A. M. Sheridan Smith (New York: Pantheon, 1972).

— *The Order of Things: An Archaeology of the Human Sciences* (New York: Vintage, 1973).

FRANK, JOSEPH, 'Spatial Form in Modern Literature', in *Criticism: The Foundations of Modern Literary Judgment*, rev. edn., ed Mark Schorer, Josephine Miles, and Gordon McKenzie (New York: Harcourt, 1958), 379–92. Originally published in the *Sewanee Review*, 53 (Spring, Summer, and Autumn 1945), 221–40, 433–56, 643–53.

— 'Spatial Form: Thirty Years After', in Smitten and Daghistany, *Spatial Form in Narrative*, 202–43.

—— *The Widening Gyre: Crisis and Mastery in Modern Literature* (New Brunswick, NJ: Rutgers University Press, 1963).

Frankfurt Institute for Social Research, 'Ideology', in *Aspects of Sociology*, trans. John Viertel (Boston, Mass.: Beacon, 1973), 182–205.

FRIEDRICH, HUGO, *The Structure of Modern Poetry from the Mid-Nineteenth to the Mid-Twentieth Century*, trans. Joachim Neugroschel (Evanston, Ill.: Northwestern University Press, 1974).

FURNIVALL, FREDERICK JAMES, 'The New Shakspere Society: The Founder's Prospectus Revised', in the supplement to *Transactions of the New Shakspere Society*, 1st ser. 1, (1874).

GERVINUS, G. C., *Shakespeare Commentaries*, trans. F. E. Bunnett, rev. edn. (London: Smith, Elder, 1877).

GOLDBERG, JONATHAN, 'The Politics of Renaissance Literature: A Review Essay', *English Literary History*, 49 (1982), 514–42.

—— 'Shakespearian Inscriptions: The Voicings of Power', in Parker and Hartman, *Shakespeare and the Question of Theory*, 116–37.

GOULDNER, ALVIN W., *The Two Marxisms: Contradictions and Anomalies in the Development of Theory* (New York: Seabury, 1980).

GRAFF, GERALD, *Professing Literature: An Institutional History* (Chicago, Ill.: University of Chicago Press, 1987).

GRAMSCI, ANTONIO, *Selections from the Prison Notebooks of Antonio Gramsci*, ed. and trans. Quintin Hoare and G. N. Smith (New York: International, 1971).

GREENBLATT, STEPHEN, *Renaissance Self-Fashioning: From More to Shakespeare* (Chicago, Ill.: University of Chicago Press, 1980).

—— *Shakespearean Negotiations: The Circulation of Social Energy in Renaissance England* (Berkeley: University of California Press, 1988).

GREG, W. W., *The Shakespeare First Folio: Its Bibliographical and Textual History* (Oxford: Clarendon, 1955).

GRIFFITHS, L. M., *Evenings with Shakspere: A Handbook to the Study of His Works* (Bristol: Arrowsmith, 1889).

GUILLÉN, CLAUDIO, 'On the Forms of Literary Change', in *Proceedings of the 8th Congress of the International Comparative Literature Association*, vol. I: *Three Epoch-Making Literary Changes: Renaissance—Enlightenment—Early Twentieth Century*, ed. Béla Köpeczi and György Vajda (Stuttgart: Bieber, 1980), 43–60.

GUTTING, GARY (ed.), *Paradigms and Revolutions: Appraisals and Applications of Thomas Kuhn's Philosophy of Science* (Notre Dame, Ind.: University of Notre Dame Press, 1980).

HABERMAS, JÜRGEN, 'The Entwinement of Myth and Enlightenment', *New German Critique*, 26 (Summer 1982), 13–30.

—— 'Modernity—An Incomplete Project', in Foster, *The Anti-Aesthetic*, 3–15.

—— *The Philosophical Discourse of Modernity: Twelve Lectures*, trans. Frederick Lawrence (Cambridge, Mass.: MIT Press, 1987).

— 'Taking Aim at the Heart of the Present', *University Publishing*, 13 (Summer 1984), 5–6.

— *Towards a Rational Society: Student Protest, Science, and Politics*, trans. Jeremy Shapiro (Boston, Mass.: Beacon, 1970).

HALLIDAY, F. E., *Shakespeare and His Critics* (London: Duckworth, 1949).

HARRIS, LAURIE (ed.), *Shakespearean Criticism*, vol. 1 (Detroit, Mich.: Gale, 1984).

HAWKES, TERENCE, 'Lear's Maps: A General Survey', *Deutsche Shakespeare Gesellschaft West Jahrbuch* (1989), 134–47.

— *That Shakespeherian Rag: Essays on a Critical Process* (New York: Methuen, 1986).

HEGEL, G. W. F., *The Phenomenology of Mind*, trans. J. B. Baillie (New York: Harper, 1967).

HELD, DAVID, *Introduction to Critical Theory: Horkheimer to Habermas* (Berkeley: University of California Press, 1980).

HOHENDAHL, PETER U., 'The Dialectic of Enlightenment Revisited: Habermas' Critique of the Frankfurt School', *New German Critique*, 35 (Spring/Summer 1985), 3–26.

— 'Habermas' Philosophical Discourse of Modernity', *Telos*, 69 (Fall 1986), 49–65.

HOLDERNESS, GRAHAM, *Shakespeare's History* (New York: St Martin's Press, 1985).

HONIGMANN, E. A. J., 'The New Shakespeare?', *The New York Review of Books*, 35, no. 5 (31 Mar. 1988), 32–3.

HORKHEIMER, MAX, and ADORNO, THEODOR, *Dialectic of Enlightenment*, trans. John Cummings (New York: Seabury, 1977).

HOWARD, JEAN E., 'The New Historicism in Renaissance Studies', *English Literary Renaissance*, 16 (Winter 1986), 13–43.

— 'Scholarship, Theories, and More New Readings: Shakespeare for the 1990s', in *Shakespeare Study Today*, ed. Georgianna Ziegler (New York: AMS, 1986), 127–51.

— and O'CONNOR, MARION F. (eds.), *Shakespeare Reproduced: The Text in History and Ideology* (New York: Methuen, 1987).

HUYSSEN, ANDREAS, *After the Great Divide: Modernism, Mass Culture, Postmodernism* (Bloomington: Indiana University Press, 1986).

ISAACS, J., 'Shakespearean Scholarship', in *A Companion to Shakespeare Studies*, ed. Harley Granville-Barker and G. B. Harrison (1934; repr. Cambridge: Cambridge University Press, 1949), 305–24.

JACKSON, T. A., 'Letters and Documents: Marx and Shakespeare', *International Literature*, 2 (Feb. 1936), 75–97.

JACOBY, RUSSELL, *Social Amnesia: A Critique of Conformist Psychology from Adler to Laing* (Boston, Mass.: Beacon, 1975).

JAMESON, FREDRIC, *Marxism and Form: Twentieth Century Dialectical Theories of*

Literature (Princeton, NJ: Princeton University Press, 1971).

—— *The Political Unconscious: Narrative as a Socially Symbolic Act* (Ithaca, NY: Cornell University Press, 1981).

—— 'Postmodernism and Consumer Society', in *The Anti-Aesthetic: Essays on Postmodern Culture*, ed. Hal Foster (Port Townsend, Wash.: Bay Press, 1983), 111–25.

—— 'Postmodernism, or The Cultural Logic of Late Capitalism', *New Left Review*, 146 (July–Aug. 1984), 53–92.

JARDINE, LISA, *Still Harping on Daughters: Women and Drama in the Age of Shakespeare* (Totowa, NJ: Barnes and Nobles, 1983).

JAY, MARTIN, *The Dialectical Imagination: A History of the Frankfurt School and the Institute of Social Research, 1923–1950* (Boston, Mass.: Little, 1973).

JONES, G. P., 'Visions and Revisions: Recent Shakespeare Publications', *University of Toronto Quarterly*, 52 (Fall 1982), 106–14.

KAHN, COPPÉLIA, Review of Carol Thomas Neely, *Broken Nuptials in Shakespeare's Plays*, *Shakespeare Quarterly*, 38 (Autumn 1987), 368–71.

KELLY, H. A., *Divine Providence in the England of Shakespeare's Histories* (Cambridge, Mass.: Harvard University Press, 1970).

KERMODE, FRANK, *Romantic Image* (London: Routledge, 1957).

KNIGHT, G. WILSON, *Gold-Dust: With Other Poetry* (London: Routledge, 1968).

—— *The Imperial Theme: Further Interpretations of Shakespeare's Tragedies* (New York: Barnes and Noble, 1931).

—— *Neglected Powers: Essays on Nineteenth and Twentieth Century Literature* (New York: Barnes and Noble, 1971).

—— *Shakespearean Dimensions* (Towata, NJ: Barnes and Noble, 1984).

—— *The Wheel of Fire: Interpretation of Shakespeare's Tragedy* (1930; repr. Cleveland, Ohio: Meridian, 1964).

KNIGHTS, L. C., *Poetry, Politics and the English Tradition* (London: Chatto, 1954).

—— 'Shakespeare and the Elizabethan Climate', *Scrutiny*, 12 (Spring 1944), 146–52.

—— *Some Shakespearean Themes* (Palo Alto, Calif.: Stanford University Press, 1960).

—— *William Shakespeare: The Histories* (London: Longmans Green, 1962).

KUHN, T. S., 'Comment', *Comparative Studies in Society and History*, 11 (Oct. 1969), 426–30.

—— 'Postscript—1969', in his *The Structure of Scientific Revolutions*, 2nd edn. (Chicago, Ill.: University of Chicago Press, 1970), 174–210.

—— *The Structure of Scientific Revolutions* (Chicago, Ill.: University of Chicago Press, 1962).

LAKE, DAVID J., *The Canon of Thomas Middleton's Plays: Internal Evidence for the Major Problems of Authorship* (Cambridge: Cambridge University Press, 1975).

LARSON, MAGALI, *The Rise of Professionalism: A Sociological Analysis* (Berkeley, Calif.: University of California Press, 1977).

LEAVIS, F. R., ' "The Kenyon Review" and "Scrutiny" ', *Scrutiny*, 14 (Dec. 1946), 134–6.

LEE, SIDNEY (ed.), *The Dictionary of National Biography*, Supplement, Jan. 1901–Dec. 1911 (London: Oxford University Press, 1912).

LENTRICCHIA, FRANK, *After the New Criticism* (Chicago, Ill.: University of Chicago Press, 1980).

LENZ, CAROLYN, GREENE, GAYLE, and NEELY, CAROL (eds.), *The Woman's Part: Feminist Criticism of Shakespeare* (Urbana: University of Illinois Press, 1980).

LEVIN, HARRY, *Shakespeare and the Revolution of the Times: Perspectives and Commentaries* (New York: Oxford University Press, 1976).

LEVINE, LAWRENCE W., *Highbrow/Lowbrow: The Emergence of Cultural Hierarchy in America* (Cambridge, Mass.: Harvard University Press, 1988).

LUKÁCS, GEORG, *The Theory of the Novel*, trans. Anna Bostock (Cambridge, Mass.: MIT Press, 1971).

LYOTARD, FRANÇOIS, *The Postmodern Condition: A Report on Knowledge*, trans. Geoff Bennington and Brian Massumi (Minneapolis: University of Minnesota Press, 1984).

McLUHAN, MARSHALL, ' "Henry IV", a Mirror for Magistrates', *University of Toronto Quarterly*, 17 (Jan. 1948), 152–60.

MARDER, LOUIS, *His Exits and His Entrances: The Story of Shakespeare's Reputation* (Philadelphia, Pa.: Lippincott, 1963).

MARX, KARL, *The Eighteenth Brumaire of Louis Bonaparte* (New York: International, 1963).

— and ENGELS, FREDERICK, *The Manifesto of the Communist Party*, in Karl Marx, *Political Writings*, vol. i: *The Revolutions of 1848*, ed. David Fernbach (New York: Vintage, 1974).

MAYHEAD, ROBIN, 'American Criticism', *Scrutiny*, 19 (Oct. 1952), 65–75.

MULHERN, FRANCIS, *The Moment of 'Scrutiny'* (London: New Left, 1979).

NECHKINA, M., 'Shakespeare in Karl Marx's "Capital" ', *International Literature*, 3 (March 1935), 75–81.

NEELY, CAROL THOMAS, 'Constructing the Subject: Feminist Practice and the New Renaissance Discourses', *English Literary Renaissance*, 18 (Winter 1988), 5–18.

ORNSTEIN, ROBERT, *A Kingdom for a Stage: The Achievement of Shakespeare's History Plays* (Cambridge, Mass.: Harvard University Press, 1972).

OWENS, CRAIG, 'The Discourse of Others: Feminists and Postmodernism', in Foster, *The Anti-Aesthetic*, 57–82.

PARKER, PATRICIA, and HARTMAN, GEOFFREY (eds.), *Shakespeare and the Question of Theory* (New York: Methuen, 1985).

PECHTER, EDWARD, 'Falsifying Men's Hopes: The Ending of " 1 Henry IV" ', *Modern Language Quarterly*, 41 (Sept. 1980), 211–30.

—— 'The New Historicism and Its Discontents: Politicizing Renaissance Drama', *PMLA* 102 (May 1987), 292–303.

POLLARD, A. W., *The Foundations of Shakespeare's Text* (London: Oxford University Press, 1923).

POSTER, MARK, *Foucault, Marxism, and History: Mode of Production versus Mode of Information* (Cambridge: Polity, 1984).

PUSHKIN, A. S., 'Notes on Shylock, Angelo, and Falstaff', trans. Albert Siegel, *The Shakespeare Association Bulletin*, 16 (Jan. 1941), 120–1.

QUINONES, RICARDO J., *Mapping Literary Modernism: Time and Development* (Princeton, NJ: University of Princeton Press, 1985).

—— *The Renaissance Discovery of Time* (Cambridge, Mass.: Harvard University Press, 1972).

RABINOW, PAUL, Introduction, *The Foucault Reader*, ed. Paul Rabinow (New York: Pantheon, 1984).

RANSOM, JOHN CROWE, 'Art and the Human Economy', in his *Beating the Bushes: Selected Essays, 1941–1970* (New York: New Directions, 1972), 128–35. Originally published in *Kenyon Review*, 7 (Autumn 1945), 683–8.

—— *The New Criticism* (Norfolk, Conn.: New Directions, 1941).

—— 'Poets and Flatworms', *Kenyon Review*, 14 (Winter 1949), 159–60.

—— 'A Strategy for English Studies', *Southern Review*, 6 (1940–1), 226–35.

—— *The World's Body* (1938; repr. New York: Scribner, 1964).

RAULET, GERARD, 'Structuralism and Post-Structuralism: An Interview with Michel Foucault', trans. Jeremy Harding, *Telos*, 55 (Spring 1983), 195–211.

ROBERTSON, J. M., *The Genuine in Shakespeare: A Conspectus* (London: Routledge, 1930).

—— *The Shakespeare Canon* (London: Routledge, 1922).

ROBEY, DAVID, 'Anglo-American New Criticism', in *Modern Literary Theory: A Comparative Introduction*, ed. Ann Jefferson and David Robey (London: Batsford, 1986) 73–91.

RUSZKIEWICZ, JOHN, *'Timon of Athens': An Annotated Bibliography* (New York: Garland, 1986).

RYAN, MICHAEL, *Marxism and Deconstruction: A Critical Articulation* (Baltimore, Md.: Johns Hopkins University Press, 1982).

RYAN, STEVEN, 'The Importance of Thomas S. Kuhn's Scientific Paradigm Theory to Literary Criticism', *The Midwest Quarterly*, 19 (Winter 1978), 151–9.

SAID, EDWARD, 'Opponents, Audiences, Constituencies, and Community', *Critical Inquiry*, 9 (Sept. 1982), 1–26.

—— 'The Problem of Textuality', *Critical Inquiry*, 4 (Summer 1978), 674–714.

—— 'Roads Taken and Not Taken in Contemporary Criticism', *Contemporary Literature*, 17 (1976), 327–48.

SALE, ROBERT, 'G. Wilson Knight', *Modern Language Quarterly*, 29 (Mar. 1968), 77–83.

256 *Bibliography*

SANDERS, WILBUR, *The Dramatist and the Received Idea: Studies in the Plays of Marlowe and Shakespeare* (Cambridge: Cambridge University Press, 1968).

SHAKESPEARE, WILLIAM, *The Riverside Shakespeare*, G. Blakemore Evans *et al.* (Boston, Mass.: Houghton Mifflin, 1974).

SIEGEL, PAUL N., *Shakespeare's English and Roman History Plays: A Marxist Approach* (Rutherford, NJ: Farleigh Dickinson University Press, 1986).

—— 'Tillyard Lives—Historicism and Shakespeare's History Plays', *Clio*, 9 (1980), 5–23.

SINFIELD, ALAN, 'Power and Ideology: An Outline Theory and Sidney's *Arcadia*', *English Literary History*, 52 (1985), 259–77.

SMITH, GORDON ROSS, 'A Rabble of Princes: Considerations Touching Shakespeare's Political Orthodoxy in the Second Tetralogy', *Journal of the History of Ideas* (1980), 29–48.

SMITTEN, JEFFREY R., and DAGHISTANY, ANN (eds.), *Spatial Form in Narrative* (Ithaca, NY: Cornell University Press, 1981).

SPANOS, WILLIAM, 'The Apollonian Investment of Modern Humanist Education: The Examples of Matthew Arnold, Irving Babbitt, and I. A. Richards', *Cultural Critique*, 1 and 2 (Fall 1985 and Winter 1985–6), 7–72, 105–34.

SPURGEON, CAROLINE, *Shakespeare's Imagery: And What It Tells Us.* (Cambridge: Cambridge University Press, 1935).

STAVISKY, ARON Y., *Shakespeare and the Victorians: Roots of Modern Criticism* (Norman: University of Oklahoma Press, 1969).

STEPHANSON, ANDERS, 'Regarding Postmodernism—A Conversation with Fredric Jameson', *Social Text*, 17 (Fall 1987), 29–54.

STOLL, E. E., *From Shakespeare to Joyce: Authors and Critics; Literature and Life* (New York: Ungar, 1944).

—— 'Falstaff', *Modern Philology*, 12 (Oct. 1914), 65–108.

—— *Shakespeare and Other Masters* (1940; repr. New York: Russell, 1962).

—— *Shakespeare Studies: Historical and Comparative in Method* (New York: Stechert, 1942).

STONE, WILLIAM B., 'Literature and Class Ideology: *Henry IV, Part One*', *College English*, 33 (May 1972), 891–900.

SWINBURNE, ALGERNON CHARLES, *A Study of Shakespeare* (1909; repr. New York: AMS, 1965).

TATE, ALLEN, *Collected Essays* (Denver, Colo.: Alan Swallow, 1959).

TAYLOR, GARY, *Reinventing Shakespeare: A Cultural History 1642–1986* (New York: Weidenfeld & Nicolson, 1989).

TILLYARD, E. M. W., *The Elizabethan World Picture* (1943; repr. New York: Vintage, n.d.).

—— *The Muse Unchained: An Intimate Account of the Revolution in English Studies at Cambridge* (London: Bowes and Bowes, 1958).

—— *Shakespeare's History Plays* (1944; repr. New York: Macmillan, 1946).

TRAVERSI, DEREK, 'Henry IV—Part I' and 'Henry IV—Part II', *Scrutiny*, 15

(Winter 1947 and Spring 1948), 24–35 and 117–27.

TYLER, THOMAS, 'Shakspere Idolatry', *Transactions of the New Shakspere Society*, 1st ser. 12, Pt. 2 (1887–92), 191–212.

VAN RENSSELAER WESTFALL, ALFRED, *American Shakespearean Criticism: 1607–1865* (New York: Wilson, 1939).

VISWANATHAN, S., *The Shakespeare Play as Poem: A Critical Tradition in Perspective* (Cambridge: Cambridge University Press, 1980).

WELLEK, RENÉ, *A History of Criticism, 1750–1950*, 6 vols. (New Haven, Conn.: Yale University Press, 1955–86).

WELLMER, ALLBRECHT, 'Truth, Semblance, Reconciliation: Adorno's Aesthetic Redemption of Modernity', trans. Maeve Cooke, *Telos*, 62 (Winter 1984–5), 89–115.

WELLS, SUSAN, *Dialectics of Representation* (Baltimore, Md.: Johns Hopkins University Press, 1985).

WIDDOWSON, PETER (ed.), *Re-Reading English* (London: Methuen, 1982).

WILLIAMS, RAYMOND, *Culture and Society, 1780–1950* (1958; repr. New York: Harper, 1966).

—— *Key Words: A Vocabulary of Culture and Society*, rev. edn. (New York: Oxford University Press, 1983).

—— *Marxism and Literature* (Oxford: Oxford University Press, 1977).

WILSON, J. DOVER, *The Fortunes of Falstaff* (Cambridge, Cambridge University Press, 1943).

WILSON, FRANK P., *Shakespeare and the New Bibliography*, ed. Helen Gardner (Oxford: Clarendon, 1970).

Index